the Gospel
and Globalization

Exploring the Religious Roots
of a Globalized World

December 2009

To Henk,

With gratitude for your generosity.

Mik

Edited by

Michael W. Goheen
Erin G. Glanville

Regent College Publishing · Geneva Society
Vancouver, B.C., Canada

THE GOSPEL AND GLOBALIZATION: EXPLORING THE RELIGIOUS ROOTS OF A GLOBALIZED WORLD

Published 2009 by REGENT COLLEGE PUBLISHING
5800 University Boulevard / Vancouver, British Columbia
V6T 2E4 / Canada / www.regentpublishing.com

with
GENEVA SOCIETY
www.genevasociety.org

Cover image by Ben Goheen
Typeset by Dan Postma

Library and Archives Canada Cataloguing in Publication

The Gospel and globalization : exploring the religious roots of a globalized world / edited by Michael W. Goheen and Erin G. Glanville.

Includes bibliographical references.
ISBN 978-1-57383-440-7

1. Globalization—Religious aspects—Christianity. 2. Globalization—Religious aspects—Islam. 3. Capitalism—Religious aspects—Christianity. 4. Capitalism—Religious aspects—Islam. 5. Globalization—Moral and ethical aspects. 6. Globalization—Economic aspects. 7. Christian ethics. 8. World politics. I. Goheen, Michael W., 1955- II. Glanville, Erin G., 1980-

BL65.G55G68 2009   201'.7   C2009-902767-4

For Phoebe Shalom,
because the future is secure

Table of Contents

Preface

This book gathers together a number of essays that seek to uncover the foundational beliefs shaping globalization from the standpoint of the Christian gospel. As editors our interest in globalization does not originate from an expertise in the social sciences—economics, politics, international relations or the other disciplines in which globalization is a hot topic. Rather our concern with the issue comes because we see globalization as one of the most powerful *religious*[1] forces in our world today. Mike's area of expertise is worldview and mission studies; Erin's is cultural studies. It is out of our investments in these disciplines that we are concerned to analyse globalization in terms of its dangers but also its opportunities for Christian communities to bear witness to the good news that Jesus Christ is Lord of history and that God is working in history to bring about his kingdom of *shalom*.

Robert Webber believes that "the most pressing spiritual issue of our time" is the question 'who gets to narrate the world?'[2] Recognising that the Christian church at times has misused power to narrate the history of the world in directions that benefits itself, we humbly offer that the Bible, which reveals the mighty acts of God, climactically in Jesus Christ, and in and through the church is the true story of the world. Other powerful stories at work in our global world include the Islamic story of world history and the supposedly secular story of Western globalization. In a masterful concluding chapter of his book *Bible and Mission* Richard Bauckham describes the missionary encounter between the Bible, on the one hand, and globalization and consumerism, on the other, as the primary battle facing the church today. Both stories offer a metanarrative of history by which Bauckham means "an attempt to tell a single story about the whole of human history in order to attribute a single and integrated meaning to the whole".[3] As the church inhabits the biblical story it will find moments of consonance with but, also and necessarily, come into some conflict with the forces of globalization. The Enlightenment worldview-story, which has shaped the West for several centuries, is now one of the most powerful forces in our global world, and it carries with it both positive and negative potential. For Christians who want to be

8

faithful in their calling to engage their culture and times with the gospel it is essential that they understand the foundational and religious dynamics of the metanarrative of globalization. Only then can the church embody and struggle for the *shalom* of the kingdom that will surely come for the whole globe at the end of history.

The Hebrew word *shalom*, often translated 'peace', is a word used by the Hebrew prophets to describe the world as it was meant to be. It is a life of justice and harmony in which humans and all of creation prosper. All human relationships—relationships with God, with each other, and with the non-human creation—are made right and become a flourishing, interrelated whole. Human rebellion at the beginning of human history shattered the harmony of God's good creation, but the Bible tells the story of God's work to restore that *shalom*. The church has been invited to participate in this story both to *embody* that coming peace and justice and to be an instrument of it. Since the story of Western globalization is powerful and offers potentials for fuller *shalom* but at the same time is responsible for destroying that *shalom*, the church must understand those dynamics to participate faithfully in its mission.

The essays gathered in this book come from two primary sources. Some of them were given as LambLight lectures[4] that are offered each year on Trinity Western University's campus. The LambLight lectures are lectures given by significant visiting scholars who treat a contemporary topic in a popular, relevant and informative way. A good number of these essays began their life as a LambLight lecture. Others were contributed in response to an invitation of the editors to enrich and widen the analyses offered by these lectures. As editors we are thankful for the overwhelmingly positive response we received from each of these authors to our request for an essay that would treat globalization from the standpoint of its underlying beliefs, and for the superb quality of the contributions.

We would like to thank a number of people. Our life-partners, Marnie Goheen and Mark Glanville, were very encouraging throughout the process. The Geneva Board which oversees the chair that Mike occupies, and Pieter and Fran Vanderpol who fund that chair made this book possible by their support in a number of ways. Brittany Groen and Dan Postma offered their gifts in editing and typesetting respectively while Ben Goheen designed the cover for the book. Bill Reimer and Rob Clements from Regent Press, and Robin Parry from Paternoster, were helpful along the way in bringing this book to birth. Erin would also like to thank her colleagues at McMaster University, who inhabit a variety of stories and whose perspectives have given her broader insights into the undercurrents of globalization.

Our prayer is that this book would equip the church to be more faithful to the gospel as it lives in the midst of the powerful forces of globalization. If it succeeds in this it will be worth the many hours of work that has brought this book to light.

Michael W. Goheen, Burnaby, B.C., Canada
Erin G. Glanville, Sydney, NSW, Australia

NOTES

[1] The way we are using the word "religious" will become clear in the later essays. Perhaps the first paragraphs of Egbert Schuurman's essay in this book offers a brief synopsis.

[2] Robert Webber, *Who Gets to Narrate the World? Contending for the Christian Story in an Age of Rivals* (Downers Grove, IN: Intervarsity Press, 2008), 11.

[3] Richard Bauckham, *Bible and Mission: Christian Witness in a Postmodern World* (Grand Rapids, MI: Baker Books, 2003), 87.

[4] The name "LambLight" comes from Revelation 21:23-24 where the author describes the New Jerusalem: "The city does not need the sun or the moon to shine on it, for the glory of God gives it light, and the Lamb is its lamp. The nations will walk by its light, and the kings of the earth will bring their splendour into it".

Introduction

by Michael W. Goheen and Erin G. Glanville

A critical question for Christians to ask if they want to live faithfully in the world is, 'What time is it?' Where are we at in our culture's story? What are the most powerful dynamics and forces that are shaping our world today? Perhaps three words begin to answer these questions—at least for those of us living in the West: globalization, postmodernity, and consumerism. These three words are all closely related and are variously interpreted. Yet they point to very real culturally and globally formative powers today. This book gathers together essays by leading and emerging Christian academics that probe the complex phenomenon of globalization from different angles.

Numerous volumes have appeared on this subject since the middle of the 1990s which indicates that globalization has become one of the key terms used in an attempt to understand the spirit of our times. Robert Schreiter suggests that "globalization, for better or for worse, is the single most adequate way of describing the context in which we work today".[1] Perhaps Renato Ruggiero, first director-general of the World Trade Organization, is correct in his assessment of the significance of globalization when he says that it is a reality "which overwhelms all others".[2] If Christians want to live faithfully in this time, being instruments of the *shalom* and justice of the kingdom of God, they must take time to gain insight into this significant phenomenon. The proliferation of literature on this topic and the diverse ways in which globalization is understood make it necessary to place these essays in a broad interpretative framework.

The Gospel as Starting Point

Every analysis of globalization depends on certain clues as decisive for seeking understanding. The authors of this book share a common commitment to the good news announced by Jesus Christ as *the* clue for understanding our world. We recognise that many in our secular world will find this odd and dismiss a religious approach to the various processes of globalization as archaic or even dangerous. However, if what Jesus announced two millennia ago is true—and his claims can, of course, be rejected on the basis of another, more decisive clue—then we have no option other than to start with this message as the clue to seeing the world aright.

Jesus makes the astounding announcement that God is acting decisively and climactically in him for the renewal of all of human life and of the whole creation. This proclamation comes as part of a long story narrated in the Old Testament. It is a story of God who brings into existence the whole creation, who governs universal history and rules all nations, and who is guiding the history of all nations to its climactic goal. It is a story of his patient acts in history to restore the creation from the evil and misery that comes from human rebellion. It is, in the language of 19th century historiography, universal history, or in the more recent language of postmodernity, a metanarrative, if by these terms we mean something like a true story about the meaning of the world and history as a whole.

Jesus claims that in him this story has found its centre and its meaning. God's promised restoration, the *telos* of universal history is being made known and accomplished in his person and work. In his life he demonstrates God's saving power as he launches an all-out attack on evil in its many forms—pain, sickness, death, demon-possession, immorality, loveless self-righteousness, special class privilege, broken relationships, oppression, hunger, poverty, and death. In his death the climactic battle takes place: here God gains a victory over the evil that enslaves his creation. God's accomplishment of restoration at the cross settles the course of cosmic history. The resurrection inaugurates the age to come when God will renew the entire cosmos and the whole of human life in all nations. Jesus promises that he will one day complete his work when he returns. Until then Jesus commissions his followers to continue his work as they embody and announce the presence of God's liberating rule.

If this message is true, then its significance bursts beyond that private sphere called 'religion', something we value for our worship and personal ethics. Rather than being an entertaining religious tale it becomes a 'secular announcement' or 'public truth' for all people in all times.[3] It is concerned with the whole human situation and not only some area called 'religion'. The message of Christ is a claim that offers a comprehensive understanding of the world and of history. Jesus' invitation to repent and believe is nothing less than a summons to believe his remarkable claims and to inhabit the world of the biblical narrative as the true story of the world. It is an appeal to take the person and work of Jesus Christ as *the fundamental clue* for the interpretation of the rest of the world—from interpreting the responsibility we have to other human beings to the decisions we make regarding foreign policies and national economic policies. The authors who have written for this volume have embraced that call, and the good news of Jesus Christ is the clue they have followed in an attempt to understand the confusing events of our time, including the dynamics of globalization.

In starting with the gospel for our interpretation of the world, including our interpretation of the realities of globalization, questions centred in three themes are important starting points: First, how is this dynamic of globalization rooted in God's intent and design for creation and for history? Is the historical unfolding of culture across territorial boundaries in the processes of globalization part of God's original plan for creation? The second theme centres on the presence of sin in creation: how has globalization been corrupted by human rebellion? How has cultural development across territorial boundaries been twisted by idolatry—perhaps of a technological or economic type? And the third theme keys on the hope we have in the promised final restoration that is already present: are the processes of globalization as they exist today open to healing and renewal? To establish a framework for globalization from the standpoint of the gospel would mean approaching the topic with those kinds of questions.

But, of course, we cannot remain at a general 'theological' level.[4] We must be able to connect these basic affirmations to a plausible understanding of contemporary globalization that accounts for the various realities of our global world and that engages the diverse theories of globalization. We need to seek a biblically-directed account of historical development that discerns God's original creational purpose for the unfolding of various cultural institutions and societal forms. Globalization can be understood as the continuing development of cultures in such a way that they cross territorial boundaries and connect various peoples into an interrelated whole. In this increasing interrelation and fluidity we realise with Simon Gikandi the bind we are caught in as we attempt to evaluate globalization: "It is precisely because of the starkness of [the] division [between developed and underdeveloped sectors in the world] that the discourse of globalization seems to be perpetually caught between two competing narratives, one of celebration, and the other of crisis."[5] Globalization could be the source of mutual enrichment for the common good, taking place through increasing global interdependence. However, the beneficial potential of global interconnectedness has more often not been realised. Poverty and environmental damage seem to follow in the wake of the global market. And so we must probe the question of what is hindering the common good. What are the powers and structures that thwart the favourable possibilities of enriching global interdependence? Rather than finding ourselves always stuck in the ruts of celebration and crisis, the authors in this volume wish to move in the direction of "globalization for the good".[6] That is, we wish to explore what healing paths are open to us today. In a global world racked with growing poverty, environmental destruction, an assault on indigenous cultures, displaced peoples, the diminishment of human flourishing through technological tyranny and excessive consumption, rampant militarism, fundamentalist religious approaches that fuel conflict, and reductionistic visions of art, literature, and education, can we stimulate our imaginations with visions of healing ways to live?

Religion—A Missing Piece in Globalization Studies

In the exploding literature on this topic, authors use the word 'globalization' in a variety of ways. Perhaps the most common approach is to reduce globalization to *economics*. Globalization then refers to a coalescence of political, technological, and economic factors that are now producing a global market. This global market is made possible by relaxed trade barriers, developments in information and communication technology, the ease of air travel, the development of multinational and transnational corporations and, perhaps especially, global financial capital. It is the spread of global capitalism around the world.

Rebecca Todd Peters offers a typology of four competing theories that she believes currently dominate globalization discourse.[7] The first she terms "neoliberal", a theory that refers to an integrated global economy which promotes economic growth and increased trade, and is best facilitated by free markets and economic competition. The second she labels "social development", an approach indebted to John Keynes that is critical of the invisible hand of the market in the first theory and so supports governmental intervention. Yet this second group is as equally committed as the first is to the economic opportunities of capitalism that will produce global economic development and growth. These first two theories are basically uncritical of the global spread of capitalism and the emergence of a global market. The other two theories that she describes bring strong criticisms to the table: they are resistance movements against the devastating results of a global economy, such as environmental destruction, growing poverty, unjust and oppressive business practices, the displacement of peoples, cultural imperialism, and more. The third theory, which Peters calls "localization" or "earthist", is primarily concerned with earth justice. It is concerned with creating *shalom* amongst people, the land on which they live, and the creatures with which they live. Ecological and environmental justices are the uppermost concerns. The fourth theory, labelled "neocolonial" or "postcolonial", addresses the powers of globalization that are destroying life for the dispossessed and marginalised peoples of the world. This approach is more concerned with discovering the political power necessary to challenge current dynamics in globalization.

Todd's typology is helpful for mapping out many of the voices analysing globalization today. Yet, it primarily focuses on globalization as an economic dynamic. The fact that the preponderance of literature on globalization points to the global spread of capitalistic economic processes alerts us to two very important observations about globalization. In the first place, the bloc of Western capitalist nations—led especially by the United States—is a powerful, perhaps the most powerful player in the global process. Of course, they are not the only players; Islam and China, for example, are major forces. Nevertheless, to understand globalization will require an analysis of the cultural forces of Western culture. Second, the economic sphere has come to play an exaggerated role in Western culture. The economic vision of Enlightenment thinkers like Adam Smith has come to full-flower in Western culture in the 20th century and is now a major force in globalization. Both of these observations will be important for the purposes of this book.

Many other scholars have sought to expand our understanding of globalization beyond the economic sphere. In their book *Global Transformations*, David Held and his co-authors open up the multi-dimensional nature of globalization as they successively treat political globalization, military globalization, trade globalization, financial globalization, business globalization, global migration, cultural globalization, and environmental globalization.[8] Jan Aart Scholte treats a number of core forces of globalization including rationalist knowledge, capitalist production, automated technology, and bureaucratic governance.[9] Schreiter sees globalization as marked by the interconnection of four features: advances in communications technologies, the dominance of neoliberal capitalism, a new but developing alignment in the political order, and dramatic sociocultural changes arising from the changes in communications, economics and politics.[10]

Studies of this more inclusive variety bring us to two further conclusions: First, globalization is a multi-faceted and interlocking phenomenon that involves more than economics. These studies are steps beyond treating it only as an economic phenomenon: if globalization involves cultural development and interdependence beyond territorial boundaries, then globalization will involve all the various areas of human communal life including social, political, economic, cultural, technological, judicial, aesthetic, and ethical. And these areas of life do not stand beside each other as independent entities but each sphere coheres with all others, contributing to and receiving their meaning from the total structure. How they cohere and relate to each other, of course, remains an open question. Second, if economics has acquired inflated significance, then this will have social and cultural implications. Education, the arts, and social relationships, for example, will be shaped by the globalization process as it is led by economics.

Nevertheless, what is missing from almost all of the available literature on globalization is a detailed analysis of the powerful role of religion. In globalization literature there is, according to Max Stackhouse, a "substantive deficit" by the "studied exclusion" of religion. This is simply "intellectually mistaken" since the "architecture of every civilization is grounded, more than any other factor, in religious commitments that point to a source of normative meaning beyond the political, economic, and cultural structures themselves". When scholarly analysis of globalization "dogmatically excludes" the formative, integrative, and directing power of religion "such scholarship simply does not see major aspects of the world it seeks to study".[11] Stackhouse summarises: "The neglect of religion as an ordering, uniting and dividing factor in a number of influential interpretations of globalization is a major cause of misunderstanding and a studied blindness regarding what is going on in the world."[12]

There is something absurd in the fact that at a time when religions are playing such a major role in global affairs, both for good and for bad, their role goes unrecognised by secular scholarship. Further, since Christianity has played such a dominant role in shaping the West and setting into motion various dynamics that shape globalization today, ignoring the Christian roots and continuing influence of Christianity is to fundamentally misunderstand globalization. Peter Berger warns that those "who neglect religion (as a cause) in their analysis of contemporary affairs do so at great peril".[13] Yet such is the prejudice and blindness of secular Western scholarship today on the topic of globalization.

This leads Stackhouse to undertake the monumental effort of exposing these deficiencies. In four edited volumes, he has collected the essays of numerous authors in order to demonstrate the powerfully formative role of religion in globalization today. In the series' final volume he articulates his own public theology in which he attempts to recover the resources of the Christian faith for a more just and equitable globalized world. Certainly these volumes have begun to correct the puzzling absence of religious forces in discussions of globalization.

The Religious Core of Western Culture

Stackhouse correctly believes that religious faith "shapes the public ethos of civilizations".[14] He defines faith "as confidence in a comprehensive worldview . . . that is accepted as binding because it is held to be, in itself, basically true and just . . ." This religious faith or worldview "provides a framework for interpreting the realities of life in the world, it guides the basic beliefs and behaviors of persons and it empowers believers to seek to transform the world in accordance with a normative ethic of what should be".[15] When a "religion becomes widely shared, it shapes an ethos that gives identity to a particular culture and tends to promote a social ethic that fosters distinctive public institutions. It molds civilizations".[16] Religious faith may be theistic but it also may be humanistic and naturalistic like the Buddhist religion or the secular-humanist ideology of Marxism.[17]

This religious faith is not one more aspect of human culture alongside of others; it is a formative and unifying power underlying the various social, political, cultural, economic, technological, and ethical dynamics of a culture. As John Hutchison says, "religion is not one aspect or department of life beside the others, as modern secular thought likes to believe; it consists rather in the orientation of all human life to the absolute".[18] Thus to miss the role of religion in globalization is a major omission! With this understanding of religion Stackhouse is in company with a number of cultural theologians,[19] worldview scholars,[20] and missiologists[21] who see religion as *the* formative core and directing centre of society, a view shared by most, if not all, the authors of articles in this book.

Attempts to analyse the religious powers shaping our global world require sensitivity to extreme complexities indeed. Perhaps it was easier a century ago when various civilisations were formed primarily by a particular religious vision that held sway for the communal life of vast swaths of people. And much of that remains.[22] Whether or not this is the case, the present globalizing and pluralistic moment features ongoing encounters and interactions among many incommensurable religious forces. Identifying the most powerful of these religious forces is helpful for understanding the dynamic of religion in globalization.

Alongside the Christian story that we have laid out above, two of the most potent religious forces in globalization today are Islam and the religious commitments shaping mainstream Western culture. Both of these religious visions are variously explored by authors in this volume, albeit with the majority of attention given to the Western religious ethos. It is precisely at this point that most authors in this volume will differ from the valuable work of Stackhouse. He believes that sociocultural forces originating in the West most often identified with globalization "were formed in societies fundamentally stamped by Christian theological ethics". He continues that if "we do not understand this, we will not understand whence globalization came, what is driving it, how it works, and what it would take to alter, reform, redirect, or channel it".[23] Thus, his project is to identify and recover the Christian roots of globalization in his public theology as resources to shape globalization in a more just way.

It is indeed true that the West and thus its formative role in globalization have been deeply shaped by the Christian interpretation of history. Moreover it is also the case that recovering that story will offer important resources to shape globalization in a more equitable way. The problem is that there is *another* significant and long term religious formative power at work in the West. In fact, we would argue, it is the more powerful. Michael Polanyi's memorable metaphor offers a vivid picture of this religious power. He believes that the emergence of modern Western culture is the explosive combination of the flame of the Christian gospel with the oxygen of Greek rationalistic humanism.[24] We might say—to switch the two elements in Polanyi's graphic image—that modernity is the result of an explosion of the flame of humanism, igniting in the oxygen of the gospel. And to the degree that the oxygen of the Christian tradition has been burned away in the secularising process of the West, it is the power of humanism that is shaping the West today, and thus that is one of the most dynamic powers in globalization.

In his review of the Stackhouse series, Jonathan Chaplin presses the same issue. While Stackhouse identifies Christianity as the driving religion of the West and globalization, Chaplin notes that

> . . . the volumes do not confront with sufficient robustness the question of whether the modern West has been equally, if not more, influenced by the *religion of secular humanism* and its offshoots in Enlightenment rationalism, liberalism (and capitalism . . .). Many would argue that this has been the most powerful of the 'dominions' governing the modern world. And they would reply to Stackhouse's assertion about Christianity by insisting that it is a late-form of secular humanism that is driving the processes of globalization.[25]

Noting that the third volume on the 'dominions' treat classical religions, like tribal religions, Confucianism, Hinduism, Buddhism, and Islam, Chaplin queries further " . . . why is there no dedicated chapter in the third volume on the massive civilizational power of this secular religion of modernity? This is a significant lacuna, especially since a main indictment of the West by many non-Western religious believers is precisely the oppressive consequences of secular modernity on their own cultures."[26]

The secular humanism of the early 21st century has taken a liberal, capitalistic form in which economics plays a dominant, globalizing role. Indeed, one might speak of the *totalitarian* influence of economics in the Western story. During the medieval period, the authority of the church took a totalitarian place and often violated the role of the state, family, education, and other dimensions of society. In the communist system the state took a totalitarian stance and frequently encroached on the rightful place of other areas of human life. In a similar way, today economic dynamics are distorting various aspects of cultural and social life in the process of globalization. Thus one will expect, not only to see the distorting effects of economic idolatry on the various spheres of life in the processes of globalization, but also reactions both from within and from without against the deformity it produces.

If this is true it will be important to observe the distortions secular humanism has undergone in its current capitalistic form as one of the powerful dynamics at work in globalizing processes today. Our commitment to placing economic concerns into mutual relationship with other aspects of human life is one of the primary concerns—although not the only one—that will appear in the pages of this volume.

A Christian approach to thinking through globalization may not simply come from either the celebration or the crisis camps. Christians live as part of their culture and of this global world as prophetic voices, as *critical participants*. The church does not stand outside of their globalizing world, but stands within it as cultural players, seeking to shape it in a more just and sustainable way. The prophets of the Old Testament not only denounced the idolatry of Israel and the nations they also shaped a new imagination for how one might live faithfully in a world dominated by idolatry.

The critical participant finds it necessary to distinguish between dynamics of globalization which may be liberating and enriching and ones that may be oppressive and unjust. Goudzwaard distinguishes between at least "two different types of globalization".

> The bad, sacrificial type orients all cultures and the whole of this world to the necessity of an unconditional obedience to the rules of a rapidly expanding tunnel economy in which future ends always prevail over present life and work situations, and where the common belief is that "There is No Alternative" (TINA). The other type of globalization could be called the healing type. It is oriented to the design (*oikonomion*) of a coming Sovereign, who as Good Shepherd is asking all of us for a greater inclusion of the weak in our economies, for preventive care of creation, and for a deep respect for the richness of other cultures, things that are in the long run only possible (TATA, "There Are a Thousand Alternatives") on the basis of a saturation of the rich.

The essays in this volume are not only concerned to critique the present distortions of globalization that arise from economic idolatry but also to stimulate an alternative, more hopeful, imagination for what a globalization shaped by good stewardship, justice, and equity might

look like. While some essays will lean further in the direction of prophetic critique, others will tend toward shaping a liberated imagination.

Book Chapters

Richard Bauckham examines the Bible's global perspective with
an eye to its relevance for our contemporary context. He argues that
the Bible tells a story of globalization in which God intends to rec-
oncile all nations extending his redemptive blessings to the ends of
the earth. However, next to this narrative of global blessing, there is
a counter-narrative of global domination and exploitation in which
unity is sought through subjugation of peoples by powerful rulers and
empires. Both of these narratives shed light on the processes of globalization in our time and on our call to live faithfully to the gospel.

Jonathan Chaplin interacts with the important "God and Globalization" series edited by Max Stackhouse, offering a rich and nuanced
critical analysis. While deeply appreciative of Stackhouse's direction,
he raises significant questions especially about the meaning of religion and the role of liberal humanism in globalization. Chaplin further
develops a theory of globalization in which he formulates a biblically-
guided, creation-based account of its historical development, and elu-
cidates the norms by which globalization should be governed.

Michael Goheen traces the historical development of the religious
faith of Western humanism noting especially the rise of economic
idolatry. He observes that globalization is an extension of this story
into a global arena, and shows how the religious commitments of
modernity have excluded third world nations from the benefits of the
global market and have contributed to increasing poverty and debt.

Craig Bartholomew understands globalization to be primarily a
modern phenomenon led by economic forces and driven by consumerism. He examines postmodernity as another contender for the spirit of
the present, which offers a convincing critique of modernity, but concludes that globalization is the dominant religious force of our time.
It is the triumph of economic and consumerist modernity on a global
scale. He closes with concrete suggestions about how Christians might
live out their faith in this context.

Bob Goudzwaard is concerned with the relationship between globalization and the science of economics. He notes that, while social
scientists critique globalization as an intentional project, economists
simply accept it as a given process, and analyse it in terms of objective
facts and data. Yet globalization is not a neutral and inevitable process.
It is the deliberate, global spread of the modern Western worldview.
The beliefs of this worldview underlie both globalization as a process
and also as economic reflection on that process. He calls for a deeper

and broader examination of the economic analysis of globalization—
one that recognises and embraces God's norms for economic life.

Paul Spencer Williams sees globalization as primarily economic
in nature. Economics is what drives the political and cultural aspects
of globalization. He analyses two religious forces driving contemporary capitalism—utilitarian individualism and economic growth.
He believes that capitalism is self-destructive if it continues without
political intervention and regulation. Williams turns to the biblical notion of Jubilee as a corrective and asks how Christians should live in
a global world.

Brian Walsh enters the discussion of globalization with a critical
review of Naomi Klein's influential *The Shock Doctrine*. He appreci-
ates her disturbing and devastating critique of neo-liberalism yet he
uncovers the Keynesian economic vision that shapes Klein's critique
and solution. Walsh believes this story to be far too thin to offer answers to our global problems. Alternatively, he offers the far more
radical biblical story as an answer to the oppressive powers of globalization. This is a story of liberation, especially seen in the practices of
Jubilee and Sabbath, accomplished by Jesus at the cross. Followers of
Jesus who live in this story will embody and pursue the vision of an
economy of care—care for people and creation.

Peter Heslam strikes a strong, hopeful chord as he pursues the
question of how business can contribute to a healthier globalization.
He unfolds the role of business in terms of its moral and environmental
agency, suggesting business *can* play a transforming role. This transformative paradigm takes account of the powerful creational place of
business in the world, and of the biblical story of creation, fall, and
redemption, while avoiding the extremes that cast business into either
a demonic or a messianic role.

John Hiemstra offers the story of Canada's oil sands development
as a concrete example of the structures and processes of economic
globalization. He demonstrates how both the media and scholarly
analyses of this phenomenon remain deeply committed to the faith
that underlies economic globalization and therefore are unable to offer a substantial critique. He then identifies the spiritual impetus of
globalization as the Enlightenment's faith in economic progress which
enables him to offer a deeper and broader analysis of globalization and
its problems.

Egbert Schuurman elaborates the Islamic critique of Western
technology—a critique that is in part responsible for the growing tension between the Islamic and Western worlds. He believes the Islamic
critique ultimately stands against the humanist faith of the Enlightenment that is driving the spread of technology in and beyond the
West through the process of globalization. Interestingly, Schuurman
suggests the Islamic critique has much in common with a Christian

22

critique. He concludes by asking what it might look like if the spiritual impetus of technology was faith in God who establishes norms for flourishing, exhibits a stewardly love for his creation, and displays a deep concern for justice for all peoples.

Jim Skillen examines the clash of two global powers—Islam and the United States—in light of the various religious stories that shape their cultures. While Islam is considered a religion, it finds expression in various political and legal institutions. The United States, on the other hand, is considered a political entity, but it is driven by a deeply religious story which furnishes its identity and purpose. Skillen examines the way each power envisions the end of history and how those beliefs shape their roles in a globalized world. He finishes with a series of questions, posing various possibilities for global interaction between these two visions of history, and then, challenges Christians to engage the world self-critically while accepting neither civic religion nor false ideologies.

Bob Goudzwaard investigates the relationship between globalization, global warming, and the modern worldview. Globalization is a powerful and rapid dynamic of economic growth through technological development that now envelopes the world. It is the fruition of the modern Western worldview with its roots in Europe now extending its reach to the whole globe. Commitment to this uncontrolled and fast-paced economic growth is leading directly to numerous economic and environmental problems, including global warming. Goudzwaard invites Northern churches to assess our economic-driven cultures through the eyes of the South Asian churches. This will provide a reality check to imbalanced and unbridled economic growth by calling us to remember that we in the West already have enough.

Robert Joustra takes on the challenging task of providing a Christian analysis of religious fundamentalism in globalization. Tracing the political history of the terms 'religion' and 'fundamentalism', he argues that both terms in Western conceptions are dependent on the roots of Enlightenment liberalism and so are limited in their ability to help us understand recent clashes between Islamic nations and the West. Instead, Joustra sees the contemporary conflicts as a post-secular call to revitalise our understanding of the place of religion in the world.

Erin Glanville invites us into a question. In a world of jet-setting Western tourists—a world made small by air travel, discretionary income, and struggling third world economies—what should a Christian's posture be? She presents two postcolonial responses to globalization (anti-colonialism and diasporism) as useful for uncovering one root of present global inequalities, that of colonial history. Building on postcolonial insights, Glanville then turns to stories of refugees, the disenfranchised diaspora in our contemporary global order, to discover a uniquely Christian response to global inequality. She calls readers to listen carefully to the voices of displaced and refugee-ed peoples, to bear witness to their stories, and to live as created beings in the world—a small and interrelated place, as God made it.

David Koyzis addresses the debate, argued vigorously on opposing sides, over whether the processes of globalization are leading to one homogenised world unified by Western culture or to a clash between various civilizations. He concludes that it is not clear which trend is more evident but that perhaps the solution is to see that both sides have correctly grasped, albeit from different angles, the same interconnected phenomena which we now called globalization. He concludes with a challenge to Christians to unmask the religious roots that are shaping the various ideologies at work in globalization.

Calvin Seerveld asks how art can enrich urban life in a global world. He examines the nature of cities and the meaning of 'glocal', a concept he believes orients us in a normative way in a globalized world. Glocal is a committed vision that is globally aware but acts locally in the place one calls home. He shows how art can foster this kind of glocal vision with a number of examples from Chicago and Toronto.

Susan VanZanten examines narrative exchanges in published world literature in a global context. Resisting major literary theories that reduce literature to economic commodities, to aesthetic expressions, or to products of power systems, she advocates for Christian literary theorists to acknowledge the complex interactions of all these facets of creation. Her article ends with a challenge to Christians to read global literature for the purpose of making neighbours rather than for the purpose of distinguishing ourselves from others.

Harro Van Brummelen analyses the way globalization is shaping education today. He envisions students educated to be global citizens who are not individual consumers but are rather part of a community of disciples. This can only happen if schools resist the globalizing trend of education driven by the idol of economic growth and instead seek to pursue an education for discipleship that aims at global *shalom*.

Rod Thompson reinvents our understanding of play. He rejects the consumerist mentality of the privileged who, in a greedy and carelessly self-centred way, view the world as their playground. In its place, he advocates for purposeful play that has room for moments of silence, lament, and the mundane. Thompson's narrative is woven together with Athalia Bond's story that exemplifies this struggle. He concludes that Christians must play by the rules of grace, love, and hope. The world is our playground because God has made it so, and therefore understanding his rhythm for our lives will keep us from reaching the pits of depression and boredom that characterise much of consumerist cultures.

24

NOTES

Robert Schreiter, "Major Currents of Our Times: What They Mean for Preaching the Gospel", in *Catholic News Service*, 31, 11 (16 August 2001). It can be found online: http://www.dominicains.ca/providence/english/documents/schreiter.htm (accessed 7 May 2009).

[2] Renato Ruggiero, "Ruggiero calls for trading system to be kept in line with globalization process", World Trade Organization Press Release, 22 February 1996; http://www.wto.org/english/news_e/pres96_e/pr043_e.htm (accessed 4 March 2009).

[3] The language of 'secular announcement' and 'public truth' is that of Lesslie Newbigin who used these terms to make clear the universal validity of the announcement of the gospel. Cf. *The Finality of Christ* (London: SCM Press, Ltd., 1969), 48; *Truth to Tell: The Gospel as Public Truth* (Grand Rapids, MI: Eerdmans, 1991).

[4] Cf. Chaplin's essay elsewhere in this book.

[5] Simon Gikandi. "Postcoloniality and Globalization", *South Atlantic Quarterly* 100.3 (2001), 629.

[6] Cf. Peter Heslam (ed.), *Globalization and the Good* (Grand Rapids, MI: Eerdmans, 2004).

[7] Rebecca Todd Peters, *In Search of the Good Life: The Ethics of Globalization* (New York: The Continuum International Publishing Group Inc., 2004); "The Future of Globalization: Seeking Pathways of Transformation", *Journal of the Society of Christian Ethics*, 24, 1 (2004), 105-133. See Max Stackhouse's critique of Todd Peters which he believes is simplistic because she misses religion as a causative factor. (*God and Globalization. Volume 4: Globalization and Grace* [New York: The Continuum International Publishing Group Inc., 2007], 37).

[8] David Held, Anthony McGrew, David Goldblatt, and Jonathan Perraton, *Global Transformations: Politics, Economics and Culture* (Stanford, CA: Stanford University Press, 1999).

[9] Jan Aart Scholte, *Globalization: A Critical Introduction* (New York: St. Martin's Press, 2000).

[10] Schreiter, "Major Currents of Our Times".

[11] Max Stackhouse with Diane B. Obenchain (eds.), *God and Globalization. Volume 3: Christ and the Dominions of Civilization* (Harrisburg, PA: Trinity Press International, 2002), 10-11.

[12] Max Stackhouse, *Volume 4: Globalization and Grace*, 57.

[13] Peter Berger, *The Desecularization of the World* (Grand Rapids, MI: Eerdmans, 2000), 18.

[14] Stackhouse, *Volume 4: Globalization and Grace*, 7.

[15] Ibid.

[16] Ibid, 8.

[17] Ibid, 7-8.

[18] John A. Hutchison, *Faith, Reason, and Existence* (New York: Oxford University Press, 1956), 210.

[19] Paul Tillich, *Systematic Theology* III (Chicago: University of Chicago, 1963), 100-113; *Theology of Culture* (New York: Oxford University Press, 1959), 1-9; Emil Brunner, *Christianity and Civilization. Second Part: Specific Problems* (New

York: Charles Scribner and Sons, 1948), 129-133; Langdon Gilkey, *Society and the Sacred* (New York: The Crossroads Publishing Co., 1981). Cf. Brian J. Walsh, Langdon Gilkey: *Theologian for a Culture in Decline* (Lanham, MD: University Press of America, 1991), 71-126.

[20] Brian J. Walsh and J. Richard Middleton, *The Transforming Vision: Shaping a Christian Worldview* (Downers Grove, IL: InterVarsity Press, 1984), 15-39; Brian J. Walsh, *Subversive Christianity: Imaging God in a Dangerous Time* (Bristol, UK: The Regius Press, 1992), 13-50; Michael W. Goheen and Craig G. Bartholomew, *Living at the Crossroads: An Introduction to Christian Worldview* (Grand Rapids, MI: Baker, 2008), 67-71; James W. Sire, *Naming the Elephant: Worldview as a Concept* (Downers Grove, IL: InterVarsity Press, 2004), 122-133; David Naugle, *Worldview: The History of a Concept* (Grand Rapids, MI: Eerdmans, 2002), 267-274; James Olthius, "On Worldviews", *Christian Scholar's Review*, XIV, 2 (1985), 153-164; Henry R. Van Til, *The Calvinistic Concept of Culture* (Grand Rapids, MI: Baker Book House, 1959), 37-45.

[21] J. H. Bavinck, *The Impact of Christianity on the Non-Christian World* (Grand Rapids, MI: Eerdmans, 1948), 45-62; *An Introduction to the Science of Missions* (Philadelphia, PA: Presbyterian and Reformed Publishing Co., 1960), 169-190; cf. Paul J. Visser, *Heart for the Gospel, Heart for the World: The Life and Thought of a Reformed Pioneer Missiologist Johan Herman Bavinck [1895-1964]* (Eugene, OR: Wipf and Stock Publishers, 2003), 136-183, 282-293; Harvie M. Conn, "Conversion and Culture", in John R. W. Stott and Robert Coote (eds.), *Down to Earth: Studies in Christianity and Culture* (Grand Rapids, MI: Eerdmans, 1980), 147-172; Lesslie Newbigin, *Foolishness to the Greeks: The Gospel and Western Culture* (Grand Rapids, MI: Eerdmans, 1986), 1-20; cf. Michael W. Goheen, *"As the Father Has Sent Me, I am Sending You": J. E. Lesslie Newbigin's Missionary Ecclesiology* (Zoetermeer, NL: Boekencentrum, 2000), 341-344.

[22] Cf. Samuel Huntington, *The Clash of Civilizations and the Remaking of World Order* (New York: Simon and Schuster, 1996).

[23] Stackhouse and Obenchain, *Volume 3: Christ and the Dominions of Civilization*, 12.

[24] Michael Polanyi, *Personal Knowledge: Toward a Post-Critical Philosophy* (Chicago: University of Chicago Press, 1958), 265-266.

[25] Jonathan Chaplin, Review essay on Max Stackhouse et al, *God and Globalization*, Vols. 1, 2, 3 (Trinity Press International, 2000-2002), *Political Theology* 5, 4 (October 2004), 499-500. A revised, longer version of this article including a review of volume four is included in this book entitled "God, Globalization, and Grace: An Exercise in Public Theology". He echoes this criticism there as well.

[26] Chaplin, "Review", 500.

The Bible and Globalization

by Richard Bauckham

It is debated whether globalization is a new phenomenon of the late twentieth century or goes much further back in history. Of course, this depends on definitions and on which aspects of contemporary globalization are stressed. But it may well be doubted whether the term can usefully be applied to anything in the biblical world of two millennia and more ago. Of course, people in that biblical world had no idea how much larger the inhabited world was than the world they knew. But they already thought globally about the world as far as it was known to extend. Moreover, they spoke about God and the world he created and will redeem in terms that contain, in principle, the whole of this world, whatever the extent of that may actually be found to be. It makes sense to speak of the Bible's global perspective, and the attempt to enter and to understand that perspective may prove relevant to our contemporary context too.

The Supra-Global God

The Bible has a global[1] perspective because its God is supra-global, God over all the world. As transcendent beyond the world, this God can be the one source of all things and the goal in which the world will find its unity in the end. This God is the world's Creator, Sustainer, Ruler, Carer, Lover, Saviour and Judge. Not that God is concerned only with generalities; he observes the death of a sparrow. He works his global purpose through and for the sake of all his particular creatures, human and others. Nor does his transcendence mean remoteness from the world; in Jesus, the incarnate Son of God, God goes to the lengths of solidarity with all his human creatures, and in the Spirit God is deeply and pervasively present throughout his creation. Truly to know this God is inconsistent with every kind of narrow self-interested parochialism or nationalism; rather it lifts the worshipper of God out of a perspective centred on self or a restricted group and into an orientation in love towards all that God loves. Finally, and rather crucially for our purposes, this God is the unique God who tolerates no rivals. Every human attempt to elevate something within the world to godlike status is destructive because the world has been made to find its unifying focus only in the God who made it.

The Bible's perspective is global because it is God-centred. One way to enter this perspective at the right point is to echo some of the language of the Psalms:

> For you, O LORD, are most high over all the earth;
> you are exalted far above all gods (97:9).
> God is king over the nations;
> God sits on his holy throne (47:8).
> The LORD is good to all,
> and his compassion is over all he has made (145:9).
> He will judge the world with righteousness,
> and the peoples with his truth (96:13).
> Make a joyful noise to the LORD, all the earth;
> break forth into joyous song and sing praises (98:4).

Racial Unity and Cultural Diversity (Genesis 10)

For a biblical presentation of global humanity, we must go to the 'primeval history' of Genesis 1-11, which serves, within the biblical canon, to sketch the nature of the world within which the rest of the biblical narrative takes place. After the Flood, there is something like a new beginning for creation. In God's covenant with Noah's family and with all other living creatures, God declares his commitment to his creation and sets terms for them to live within it (Genesis 9:1-17). Already we see that the whole of the biblical history that follows has a universal context and relevance, even if this universal horizon may often recede from view behind the more immediate subject matter.

The 'global' scene is set more concretely in chapter 10, a "genealogical map of the world"[2] as the world was known to ancient Israel. Here are all the peoples of the known world, all descended from Noah. From our perspective it is a limited world, but from ancient Israel's perspective it pushes the boundaries of the human race. It stretches from Spain in the west (Tarshish) to Iran in the east (Elam), from the Russian steppes in the north (Ashkenaz) to Ethiopia in the south (Cush). Within those limits it gives a remarkably detailed and comprehensive catalogue of peoples and places. While many of them are familiar from the histories and prophecies of the Old Testament, some occur only rarely or never outside this catalogue, and some are unidentifiable to modern scholars. Nations are included in this inventory not merely for the sake of their historical relationships with Israel, but in a serious and knowledgeable attempt to represent the diversity of nations and places that compose the whole human world. It is a world so far oblivious of Israel, so much so that Canaan is allotted to the Canaanites without comment (10:19). But it is the human world as God's creation, the result of the Creator's intention that humans should fill the earth (Genesis 1:28; 9:7).

While the world of Genesis 10 is concretely limited by the geographical horizon of Israel at some particular historical period, there is also a sense in which it is designed to transcend that limitation. The number of descendants of Shem, Ham and Japheth listed is precisely seventy.[3] This is a significant number. It must be related to the more common symbolism of the number seven in the Bible, and probably suggests completeness. The number seven in the Bible regularly indicates completeness, but it can also designate a limited number that is intended to stand, representatively, for all. Similarly, we could see the seventy nations of Genesis 10 as a representative list, its seventy quite specific actual nations standing for all nations on earth. It would, of course, be absurd to expect Genesis to name nations or places utterly unknown in Israel's world—Japan or New Zealand or even Britain— but the universal horizon projected by Genesis 10 and the rest of the canonical writings that presuppose it encompasses representatively all other inhabited parts of the world.

When Paul told the Athenian intellectuals that "from one (ancestor)" God "made all nations to inhabit the whole earth" (Acts 17:26), he certainly had Genesis 10 in mind. This chapter, with its derivation of every people from one of the three sons of Noah, clearly presents the human race as what we would now call a single species and the nations as having a fundamental natural kinship with each other. There is no reference to biological differences between them.

On the other hand, there is considerable emphasis on what we would call cultural diversity. The chapter has a refrain, repeated after the list of descendants of each of the sons of Noah and then, with reference to the whole genealogy, at the end:

> These are the descendants of Japheth[4] in their lands, with their own languages,[5] by their families, in their nations (10:5b).

> These are the descendants of Ham, by their families, their languages, their lands, and their nations (10:20).

> These are the descendants of Shem, by their families, their languages, their lands, and their nations (10:31).

> These are the families of Noah's sons, according to their genealogies, in their nations, and from these

the nations spread abroad on the earth after the flood (10:32).

Each nation has its own land, its own language, and its own inter-generational continuity (families or clans). Together these determine what we would call its distinct cultural identity. Moreover, Ellen van Wolde, picking up detailed features of the way the nations and their lands are depicted, finds a socio-cultural classification in the division of humanity into the descendants of the three sons of Noah:

> The descendants of Japheth are the inhabitants of the coastal regions and the islands. . . . These are population groups which not only live in the west but also belong to the seafaring nations. Whereas in the case of the descendants of Japheth above all the inhabitants of the islands or the coast are named, with Ham we have the great cultivated lands from Egypt to Mesopotamia. This is also why Nimrod is described at such length: he is presented as the founder of a kingdom. He builds . . . the great cities of the then known world. . . . [T]he other descendants of Ham, like Egypt and Canaan, are also sedentary groups which live in a vast area, in villages or cities. . . . The descendants of Shem similarly appear in another light. . . . No cities or villages are mentioned in connection with the descendants of Shem, but only nomadic settlements or tents. . . . As well as being a geographical and ethnographical division, Genesis 10 is thus a sociographic description of the social groups:
>
> *Shem is the father of all the children of Eber: the nomads.*
> *Ham is the father of all the inhabitants of kingdoms and*
> *cities: those who are sedentary.*
> *Japheth is the father of all the dwellers of the coasts and*
> *islands: the seafarers.*[6]

The more carefully we study it, the more sophisticated this cata-logue of the nations appears. What van Wolde's examination displays is the economic distinction between peoples who are primarily seafarers or agrarian farmers or nomads, along with the fact that these different economic bases account for a variety of forms of social life.

Genesis 10's refrain with its four elements of nations, lands, lan-guages and clans is significantly echoed elsewhere in Scripture, though not in precisely this form. Two occurrences in the book of Daniel are in-structive for the way the biblical narrative works with a global horizon. In Daniel 4:1, king Nebuchadnezzar addresses "all peoples, nations, and languages that live throughout the earth". This is a conventionally hyberbolic reference to all his subjects,[7] since, although the Babylonian empire came far short of encompassing even the whole of the world known to the peoples of the Middle East at that time, it was the largest that had existed up to that time and is treated in Daniel as the first of the succession of world empires that dominated the Middle East from the sixth century BCE onwards. From Nebuchadnezzar down to the Roman emperors and beyond, the rulers of such empires typically claimed the whole world as theirs. (Similarly, it used to be said of the British Empire that the sun never set on it.) But in Daniel 7:13, when the figure like a human being ("one like a son of man") comes to the judgement seat of God, there is given to him "dominion and glory and kingship, that all peoples, nations, and languages should serve him". This is God's global kingdom removed from the nations to be given to the figure the New Testament identifies as Jesus Christ.

The book of Revelation also imitates the fourfold formula of Genesis 10, and uses it seven times, varying the terms and their order (as Genesis 10 itself does) such that no one occurrence is the same as any of the others:

> every tribe[8] and language and people and nation (Revelation 5:9)
> all nations and tribes and peoples and languages (7:9)
> many peoples and nations and languages and kings (10:11)
> peoples and tribes and languages and nations (11:9)
> every tribe and people and language and nation (13:7)
> every nation and tribe and language and people (14:6)
> peoples and multitudes and nations and languages (17:15).

This is an instance of the many types of universalistic language used in Revelation. The universality is enhanced by the repetition of the fourfold phrase (four is the number of the earth, with its four directions and four corners) seven times (seven is the number of completeness). The formula is used both of the church, the people of God redeemed from all nations (5:9; 7:9), and of the inhabitants of the world to whom the Gospel is proclaimed (14:6), over whom the beast rules (13:7) and whom Babylon the harlot exploits (17:15). The global perspective of the primeval history (Genesis 10), following creation, returns in Revelation as the global perspective of the end-time history, prior to new creation.

The fourfold formula may indicate an awareness, on the part of the biblical authors, of the fluidity of human groupings and their canons of self-identity, which depend on kinship, language, geography, history and other factors in varying proportions. There are no neatly divided or permanently stable 'nations' in the real world. A sense of this complexity is conveyed by reference not simply to "all the nations" (itself a common biblical phrase), but to "peoples and tribes and languages and nations".

United in Challenging God (Genesis 11:1-9)

The enigmatic story of the building of the Tower of Babel envisages the last moment at which humanity was entirely at one. But they seek to secure this unity by overstepping the limits of the created condition. The tower that reaches for heaven expresses their aspiration for godlike power and status. The 'name' they wish to make for themselves challenges the God whose name is uniquely exalted above all creation. Their sin essentially repeats the primal sin of Adam and Eve who sought to be like God. As the last episode of the primeval history of Genesis 1-11, the story warns that the unity of the human race, which has its source in God, can be authentically sought and found only in the worship of God, not in the arrogant pretension to be God. There is also, in God's words "this is only the beginning of what they will do" (Genesis 11:6), a hint that more and worse along the same lines can be expected as human history unfolds.

God takes action to "confuse their language" and "to scatter them abroad over the face of all the earth" (11:7, 9). It looks like judgement, but, like many divine judgements, it is also a blessing in disguise. After all, it fulfils the command of God to humanity to fill the earth (Genesis 1:28) and it results in the situation portrayed, to all appearances quite positively, in Genesis 10. The action God takes enforces the created limits of humanity that make for humanity's good. The multiplicity of places in which humans live and the multiplicity of languages they speak, with all the diversity of human culture that these things entail, are the means for humanity to develop the multiform riches of human achievements of all kinds. Rather than the hubristic uniformity of the construction of the Tower, the geographical and cultural diversity of human history is how God prefers people to live. This does not mean that humans are supposed to forget or to renounce their original unity. It means that that unity should be expressed not in suppression of diversity but in fulfilment of it. It means that humans must seek the kind of unity that is appropriate to finite creatures, rather than reaching for the status that is appropriate only to God.

That the linguistic diversity resulting from Babel is fundamentally a human good can be confirmed from the story of the coming of the Spirit at Pentecost in Acts 2. This event has often been seen as a reversal of the judgement at Babel, because, miraculously, everyone in the crowd hears the apostles "in the native language of each" (Acts 2:5). What is certainly reversed is the barrier to communication that languages create, but it is noteworthy that the barrier is not transcended by enabling everyone in the crowd to understand the one language in which the apostles speak. In fact, the apostles had only to speak in two languages, Greek and Aramaic, for virtually all these Jews gathered from throughout the *diaspora* to understand them. Greek and Aramaic were the *linguae francae* of the world, very much like English today. The miracle actually subverts that ordinary human means of breaking through the barriers of diversity. Instead, it affirms the native languages of all the people present.

Symbolically, at Pentecost, the nations scattered from Babel are gathered again, this time to the place where God comes down to them unequivocally in blessing, not in judgement. They find a new form of international community, one that is constituted not by its aspiration to divinity but by its worship of the only God of all the world.

After Babel

The primeval history leaves us with humanity, in all its diversity, populating the whole world. Although this situation is a blessing to humanity, it is far from the goal of God's purpose for his human creatures. The deep-rooted, sinful aspiration to divinity, expressed at Babel just as much as in Eden, still exists. The aspiration has been impeded by God's action at Babel, but not removed. It continues to spoil human life and infects all the achievements of the nations.

How God deals with this, how God heals human evil and brings humanity to the kind of fulfilment he always intended, is, of course, the story the rest of the Bible tells. It starts, remarkably, with Abraham and Sarah, just two people. From the global panorama of Genesis 10, the story narrows to become the very particular story of one human couple. But this particular story also begins with God's promise to Abraham, which will be repeated frequently in Genesis:

> I will make of you a great nation, and I will bless you, and make your name great, so that you will be a blessing. I will bless those who bless you, and the one who curses you I will curse, and in you all the families of the earth shall be blessed (Genesis 12:2-3).[9]

In the first place, this promise announces a new reality in the world of the nations: Abraham's descendants, Israel, a people that does not appear in Genesis 10, uniquely the people that God, starting with Abraham, is going to create for himself. But the goal of God's selection of Abraham from all the nations is wider than Israel. It is the blessing of all the families of the earth. (Note that the term "families" is used in

Genesis 10:5, 20, 31.) The reason God creates a new nation in the midst of all the nations detailed in Genesis 10, is so that, thereby, he may bless all those nations.

The Bible's story from Abraham onwards is therefore a story of globalization. God's blessing on Abraham himself is to be extended to all the nations and to the ends of the earth. God starts with the particular in order to bless all. Later he will once again start with one particular human, Jesus, a descendant of Abraham, a member of God's people Israel, the one who lived, died, and rose to new life on behalf of all others. In the gospel, taken to the ends of the earth by the church, Jesus is 'globalized'. The good news that he has achieved God's purpose for the world reaches all the nations and invites them into the living unity that Jesus himself forms with all who believe in him.

But as well as this story of globalization, the Bible's central story, the Bible knows also a counter-narrative. If the former is a narrative of global blessing and salvation, the latter is a narrative of global domination and exploitation. Both narratives begin after Babel, but whereas the first seeks the unity of the human race in the worship of God, the latter seeks it, like the builders of the Tower, in the arrogant aspiration to be God. The goal of the counter narrative is the same as that of the builders of the Tower, but because it begins after Babel, in the world of humanity scattered and divergent, it proceeds not through common consent and conspiracy but through domination. The counter-narrative tells how time after time powerful rulers and nations reach for world domination. They aspire to divinity by subjecting the others. They climb the ziggurat of power in order to rule the world, as God does, from the heavens. Although many empires figure in the counter-narrative, it is telling that the paradigm of them all is Babylon. (Babel and Babylon are the same word in Hebrew.) In Babylon the Great, world metropolis and mistress of the world, as the Book of Revelation depicts her, we finally see the culmination of what the builders of the Tower merely began (Genesis 11:6).

Nebuchadnezzar the World Ruler (Daniel 4)

In the book of Daniel, King Nebuchadnezzar II, the most famous king of ancient Babylon, serves as a paradigm case of rulers who aspire to godlike, global empire. We have already noticed how he speaks of his subjects as "all peoples, nations, and languages that live throughout the earth" (Daniel 4:1), with allusion to the world as Genesis 10 depicts it. Chapter 4 of Daniel tells a tale that in a strangely powerful and haunting way (haunting perhaps especially for those who know William Blake's picture of Nebuchadnezzar in his bovine state) conveys one of the most persistent biblical messages about power. Here, as elsewhere in Scripture, we learn that God alone is sovereign over all; that God humbles the arrogant and exalts the lowly; that human power, with its penchant for *hubris*, is easily corrupted into tyranny; that only those may rightly rule who, renouncing any aspiration to divine power and recognising their essential creaturely solidarity with those they rule, neither exalt themselves to rival God nor assume superiority over those they rule; that they alone can be trusted to exercise their power for the good of the powerless.

In Nebuchadnezzar's dream he sees a tree (4:10-15) that stands in the centre of the earth, reaches the sky, and overshadows the whole earth. This is the mythical world tree that appears also in Ezekiel (31; cf. 17:22-23) and the parables of Jesus (Matthew 13:31-32; Mark 4:31-32), always as a symbol of global power. In Nebuchadnezzar's dream it may well, at first sight, seem an unambiguously positive image of Nebuchadnezzar's beneficent world empire. It corresponds to Nebuchadnezzar's depiction of himself as "prosperous" (Daniel 4:4: *ra'anan*),[10] a word that almost always elsewhere refers to trees as "verdant" or "flourishing", sometimes metaphorically to people whose prosperity is like the flourishing of a tree. This usage can be very positive (e.g. Psalm 92:12-13). The tree in Nebuchadnezzar's dream, because it is so flourishing, provides food for all living creatures, shade and shelter for animals and birds (Daniel 4:12). No doubt this is Nebuchadnezzar's rule as he himself imagines it. In that case, the brutally emphatic command to fell the tree (4:14) comes as a rude shock.

However, a second look at the image of the tree suggests that its flourishing has a more ominous aspect. Tall trees, reaching up to heaven, can symbolise the arrogance of the powerful (Isaiah 2:12-13; 10:33-34; Ezekiel 31:3-14): in the last case the tree is the world tree and represents Assyria, the predecessor to Nebuchadnezzar's Babylonian empire). That the tree "reached up to heaven" surely recalls the Tower of Babel (Genesis 11:4: "a tower with its top in the heavens"). It is as though Nebuchadnezzar's empire, centred on the great city of Babylon that he had built (Daniel 4:29-30) and encompassing all nations (4:1), has resurrected the project of the builders of the Tower. For a while it looks to be carrying through that project more successfully.

Nebuchadnezzar thinks and behaves as though he were the highest power there is. This is why his own self-image as the beneficent monarch is only one aspect of the ambivalent image of the tree. What he is condemned for is the pride (4:37, cf. 29-30) that goes with forgetting that only God's sovereignty is absolute and eternal (4:3, 17, 25, 32, 34) and only God has the right to deal with his world as he will (4:17, 35). The narrative more or less takes it for granted that, given this attitude, Nebuchadnezzar has abused his power in high-handed and self-serving ways. But one reference makes this clear: Daniel urges him to repent by acting with justice and showing compassion to the poor and oppressed (4:27). Throughout the Bible justice and protection for the weakest in society are the primary purpose of and justification for political power. The Old Testament, which is very ambivalent about monarchy, tolerates or commends it only when the unique power of the monarch is used on behalf of the poor, enabling him to intervene to protect the rights of those too weak to resist the abuse of power by others of the king's subjects (e.g. Psalm 72). When kings or other powerful people do abuse their powers to oppress the weak, this is portrayed as the arrogance of people who think they can do what they wish with impunity and do not reckon with God's sovereign authority (e.g. Psalm 10). Every abuse of power has a whiff of self-deification about it.

This is why God characteristically dethrones the arrogant and puts the lowly into positions of power (4:37, 17; cf. Ezekiel 17:24; 1 Samuel 2:3-8; Luke 1:51-52). The latter, until they forget their humble origins, know their power is lent to them by God and remember that they are fundamentally the equals of all their people (Deuteronomy 17:20). Nebuchadnezzar can be made fit to rule only by being humiliated. Since, even after the dream and its interpretation, he fails to recognise his true position under God and alongside his subjects, God must humble him to the level of the humblest of his subjects—the wild animals. The one who exalted himself to heaven must be brought down literally to earth. His assimilation to the animals is carefully stated (Daniel 4:32-33). He does not become like the fierce predatory beasts that in Daniel's visions symbolise the human rule of the world empires (7:3-8). He does not resemble the lion that symbolises his own empire in Daniel 7:4. He is like the oxen and the birds. There is nothing derogatory in this reference to the animals. Presumably, if an ox could be king, he would be a better one than Nebuchadnezzar at the height of his pride. The ox knows its divine master, whom Nebuchadnezzar must learn to know by sharing the humble status of the ox.

Just as God's judgement at Babel proved good for humanity, so, rather remarkably, God's judgement on Nebuchadnezzar for his self-deifying arrogance is not destructive but redemptive. The story holds open the possibility of human power blessed by God when the powerful know their God-given limits and rule accordingly. We might compare the fact that, among the world empires to which Israel was subject, the Persian empire is portrayed with much less hostility than the others.[11] Among its characteristics was its benevolent tolerance of diversity among the peoples who composed it, of which its policy towards Judah (Ezra 1-7) was an instance.

The image of the world tree re-appears in Jesus' parable of the mustard seed. In his unique take on the image, it is from the mustard seed, the humblest of seeds, that the world tree grows (Mark 4:31-32). In its own way, this image is as bizarre and unlikely as the restoration of the lycanthrope Nebuchadnezzar to world-wide sovereignty under the King of heaven. But, more broadly than this, the whole complex of ideas about human and divine power and rule that Daniel 4 expresses has deeply informed the New Testament portrayal of Jesus and his exercise of God's sovereignty over the world. Jesus is the ruler whose kingdom does not reach up to heaven but comes down from heaven. Whereas Nebuchadnezzar had to be forced to share the condition of his lowliest subjects, Jesus voluntarily humbles himself as far as the slave's or the criminal's abandoned death. He is both the divine king who has the uniquely divine right to rule his human subjects and the human king who qualifies for his rule by self-denying solidarity with his human brothers and sisters (Philippians 2:5-11). In strictest fulfilment of Daniel 4:17, it is to the lowliest of all that God gives the kingdom. This is a form of globalization as far from domination as one could get.

At the Hub of the Global Market (Ezekiel 26-28)

The great superpowers of the ancient Middle East—Egypt, Assyria, Babylon, Persia, the Hellenistic empires, and Rome—are the Bible's paradigms of the global power that rests on military might and takes political form. But there is another sort of global power for which a different empire, a purely economic one, paradigmatically stands. This is Tyre, the city whose economic dominance is denounced in three remarkable chapters of Ezekiel's prophecy (26-28).[12]

The list of some forty peoples and places with whom Tyre traded (27:1-25)[13] reminds us again of the table of the nations in Genesis 10. Some names are common, others are different, but the global reach is comparable: from Spain (Tarshish) in the west to Persia in the east, from Armenia (Beth-togarmah) in the north to southern Arabia (Sheba) in the south. For all these places Tyre was the middleman,[14] facilitating world trade, creating, we might say, a global market. In this way Tyre enriched "many peoples", but especially, we should notice, the powerful elites: "the kings of the earth" (27:33). But, of course, Tyre's role at the hub of world trade especially enriched Tyre herself (28:4-5) and with wealth grew arrogance (28:5), that self-deifying *hubris* that drives conquerors, emperors, and multinational executives alike. It is not clear in what exactly "the unrighteousness of your trade" consisted (28:18), but "violence" (28:16) suggests more than corrupt dealings, perhaps piracy, perhaps brutal enforcement of excise duties. In any case, there is certainly the implication that Tyre's extraordinary economic success goes to her head: she thinks she can get away with anything. Her downfall is all the more unexpected and shocking (27:32-36). She sinks like one of her own ships, grossly overloaded with stuff (27:25-28).

The Destroyers of the Earth[15] (Revelation)

The Bible's narrative of globalization by domination and exploitation culminates in the book of Revelation's vividly imaginative portrayal of the Roman Empire. As well as the dragon, representing the diabolical power inspiring the system, there are three main symbols of earthly and globalizing power: the beast with seven heads, the second beast or false prophet, and Babylon the great city, the harlot. The seven-headed beast is the political power of the empire acquired and maintained by military domination. The false prophet is the political religion of the empire, the imperial cult, which maintains the power of the empire by ideology and propaganda. Babylon is the city of Rome, growing rich on the spoils of empire and worldwide trade.

One remarkable fact about Revelation's portrayal of this global system of domination is the pervasive allusion to Old Testament prophecy, which conveys the sense that Rome and her empire are the culmination of all the evil empires of history. The beast takes its place in the sequence of terrifying monsters that represent the world empires (from Nebuchadnezzar's Babylon onwards) in Daniel's vision (Daniel 7:2-8), summing up in itself the destructive qualities of them all (Revelation 13:1-8). In the vision of Babylon the great harlot and the oracle of destruction against her (Revelation 17-18), there are allusions to every one of the Old Testament's prophetic oracles against Babylon, as well as the two great oracles against Tyre (Isaiah 23; Ezekiel 26-28).[16] In fact, Revelation's Babylon is just as much a reincarnation of Old Testament Tyre as she is of Old Testament Babylon, and so represents Rome's economic dominance and exploitation, just as much as her military and political domination. Moreover, it is not difficult to see that her genealogy goes right back to Babel, and, while there is no clear echo of that story, there may well be an ironic allusion in the statement that Babylon's "sins are heaped high as heaven" (Revelation 18:5).[17] In Babylon's attempt to acquire divine status, only her sins reach heaven, whereas her opposite number, the New Jerusalem, comes down from heaven (Revelation 21:2, 10).

Thus, in chapter 13, Rome's power is portrayed as a marauding monster. The empire had survived a crisis in which it came close to collapse, and its survival (the healing of the beast's mortal wound) made it seem indestructible. Its deification was not only a matter of propaganda from the centre, but also the spontaneous response of all who observed its sheer, unchallengeable might: "they worshipped the beast, saying, 'Who is like the beast and who can fight against it?'" (Revelation 13:4). This is worship of power. But the beast also has a highly effective propaganda machine, the false prophet, which promotes the ideology of Roman power. According to the propaganda, Rome's conquests bestowed great benefits on the world, the famous *pax Romana*. Her subjects are thereby duped into welcoming rather than resisting the empire. But the empire appears in its true colours as the rampaging monster of John's vision.

The harlot Babylon, in chapter 17, is the city of Rome, unmistakably because she is seated on seven hills (Revelation 17:9). It is important to realise that the metaphor of prostitution does not here refer to false religion, as it does when, in the Old Testament prophets, it characterises Israel as God's faithless, promiscuous wife. Babylon is not God's wife. Rather prostitution here stands for trade, as it does in Isaiah's oracle about Tyre (Isaiah 23:15-18) and Nahum's about Nineveh (Nahum 3:4). But whereas Tyre's profits came from being the middleman of world trade, Rome was where all the goods of the empire (and beyond) ended up. It was for the city's own massive consumption of staples and extravagant luxuries alike that Rome exploited her empire economically (see the very accurately representative list of Rome's imports in Revelation 18:12-13). This is what Revelation calls the harlot Babylon's 'fornication' with 'the kings of the earth' (Revelation 17:2; cf. 18:3, 9). The phrase occurred also with reference to Tyre in Ezekiel (27:33); in Revelation it recognises that those outside Rome who did well for themselves out of her trade were the local elites in the provinces of the empire, as well as the ship owners and merchants (Revelation 18:15-19), not the common people. Finally, the inhuman exploitation that this economic system entailed is highlighted by the emphatic way that the list of imports to Babylon ends: "bodies, that is, human lives" (Revelation 18:13: a literal translation). "Bodies" is what slaves were commonly called, mere carcasses bought and sold in the slave markets as property like other consumer goods. Here it is pointed out that actually they are human beings.

At the height of her prosperity Babylon boasted: "I rule as a queen; I am no widow, and I will never see grief" (Revelation 18:7). This is the illusion of prosperity from which Ezekiel's Tyre also suffered. In literal fact it reproduces Rome's boast of being the eternal city. It is another form of self-deification: the system that feeds and fulfils the consumerist dream is the culmination of history and can be trusted to go on for ever.

Rome claimed to rule the whole inhabited world, a claim so patently untrue (the Parthian empire was a massive presence to Rome's east) that only those duped by propaganda or by their own infatuation with power could have believed it. The emphatically universal language of Revelation—all the inhabitants of the earth worship the beast (13:3), Babylon is the great city that rules over the kings of the earth (17:18) and all nations have drunk of her wine (18:3)—corresponds to Rome's claims and reflects the globalizing thrust of all such superpowers. But it can also be seen as pointing beyond Rome to later beasts and later Babylons, for whom there would be wider vistas of global opportunity. I do not mean that Revelation predicts one specific superpower, the mother of all superpowers, in the last period of history. That is not the kind of prophecy Revelation is. But the way that Revelation's images of evil gather up so many of the Old Testament precedents into something like a culminating case of global domination and exploitation suggests to me that they refer to Rome, not just in the very concrete character of the empire in which Revelation's first readers lived, but also as a model of where all such globalizing enterprises lead.

Jesus and the Kingdom of God

In many Old Testament passages, like the Psalms we quoted earlier, there is no doubt that the dominion of God over his whole creation is a present reality, but the prophets also look forward to the day when "the LORD shall become king over all the earth" (Zechariah 14:9). The latter relates to the acceptance of God's rule by all people. The God known to Israel as her God will become the God of all the nations. A kind of globalization of God's rule is envisaged, one that characteristically has a particular starting point in Israel and in Jesus, who embodies and enables Israel's vocation to be a light to all the nations.

When Jesus spoke of the kingdom of God he undoubtedly had this global future in mind. We have already mentioned the parable of the mustard seed, in which Jesus makes use of the image of the world tree:

> With what can we compare the kingdom of God, or what parable will we use for it? It is like a mustard seed, which, when sown upon the ground, is the smallest of all the seeds on earth; yet when it is sown it grows up and becomes the greatest of all shrubs, and puts forth large branches, so that the birds of the air can make nests in its shade (Mark 4:30-32).

Jesus contrasts the smallest of all seeds (as the mustard seed was proverbially thought to be) with the greatest of all shrubs into which it grows. But the sizeable shrub that the mustard plant actually is is so described as to suggest the mythical world tree that overshadows the whole world. In Ezekiel the birds that nest in its branches represent the nations that enjoy the blessings of God's global kingdom (Ezekiel 17:23; cf. 31:6). Characteristically Jesus expands a matter of common observation by his hearers into a way of talking about what God is doing in his ministry and in the global future.

The point of the parable is not to focus on the process of growth but to contrast the apparently insignificant beginnings with the astonishingly great end result. The modern ideology of progress tricks us into thinking all too easily of a steadily cumulative process by which either the church's missionary outreach or the values of the kingdom of God spread around the globe. But while there is, in God's purpose, a move-ment from the particular to the universal, a globalizing dynamic to his rule, there is no reason to see this as a single process that, even if there are also setbacks, generally progresses in a cumulative way. The hand of God in history cannot be plotted and calculated in such a way. Jesus' concern in the parable is rather to suggest that, insignificant as the signs of the kingdom occurring in Jesus' ministry might be, especially from a global perspective, in fact they really are the start of what will finally prove to be God's global rule.

If reference to the kingdom of God invokes the Bible's narrative of globalization, it is the globalization of blessing and salvation that is in view, not the globalization of domination and exploitation. Use of the image of "kingdom" or "rule" may rather easily obscure this difference, but there is much in the Gospels to suggest that Jesus was at pains to avoid the impression that God rules in the way earthly rulers do. It is a striking fact that, while Jesus speaks frequently of "the kingdom of God" he never calls God 'king',[18] while in his parables (which often begin, "The kingdom of God is like this") it is only rarely that a king appears as the figure who represents God.[19] Thus Jesus' use of the term 'kingdom of God' connects his teaching with the prophets and with later Jewish expectation of the coming of God's universal rule, but by avoiding the concrete image of God as king and preferring other im-ages, notably father, he shifts the focus much more to characterising God's rule as radically different from that of earthly rulers. The issue is not just that God's rule should replace the rule of the pagan empires, nor even just that God's righteous rule should replace the oppressive rule of the pagan empires, as many of Jesus' Jewish contemporaries hoped. More radically, Jesus wishes to portray God's rule as an alternative to earthly rule which is quite unlike all earthly rule.

The image of kingship—despite the Old Testament ideal of the king who secures justice for the oppressed—was hard to rescue from the sense of exploitative domination (cf. Mark 10:42). In the parables Jesus subverts expectations of kings and masters and employers by mak-ing the story turn on their surprising actions (e.g. Matthew 18:23-27; 20:1-15; Luke 12:37). Outside the parables, Jesus avoids calling God 'king' and privileges instead the other common Jewish description of God: 'Father'. The parabolic saying with which Jesus comments on the temple tax (the tax levied by the Jewish theocracy in God's name) is instructive: "From whom do the kings of the earth take toll and tribute? From their own children or from others?" (Matthew 17:25). The paral-lel which, for Jesus, illustrates God's relationship with his people is not with the way earthly kings treat their subjects (they tax them) but with the way earthly kings treat their own children (they do not tax them). The point is not that earthly fathers may not be oppressive, but that fathers function differently in relation to their family from the way kings function in relation to their subjects. Whereas the ancient political rhetoric of the king as father to his people would have meant little to Jesus' hearers, struggling to make a living and aware of government primarily as aggravating that struggle through taxation, the image of the father as generously providing for his children had reality (Luke 11:11-13). Whereas the king in the parable of the Unforgiving Servant acts as no one would expect a king to behave, the father in the parable of the Prodigal Son acts in a way that is just about understandable (though not expected) in a father, but would be incomprehensible in a king.

Related to this is the kind of social group Jesus expects his disciples to be, since they are the group who already live under the rule of God and instantiate its presence in the world. That they are to form a 'contrast society' (contrasting with many accepted ways and values) is evident in various ways, but for our purpose the extent to which Jesus fashions a radical alternative to domination is especially noteworthy:

> You know that among the Gentiles those whom they recognise as their rulers lord it over them, and their great ones are tyrants over them. But it is not so among you; but whoever wishes to be great among you must be your servant, and whoever wishes to be first among you must be slave of all (Mark 10:43-44; cf. Luke 22:25-26; Matthew 23:11).

Echoes of this theme are found in several places in the gospels, but most important is the scene in John 13, where Jesus himself adopts the role of the slave by washing his disciples' feet. Washing feet, a frequent, everyday menial task, was, more definitely and exclusively than any other task, the role of the slave. It was what every free person axiomatically regarded as unthinkably beneath their dignity. Jesus enjoins the disciples to wash one another's feet (13:14) not as a mere symbol of humility and not, as sometimes suggested, as a religious rite, but as a concrete instance, the most telling possible, of how the disciples should relate to each other. The ordinary everyday requirement of washing feet they are to do for each other. If this is not beneath their dignity, nothing is.

Also relevant are the ways in which Jesus in the gospels envisages the role of his disciples in the future. Their mission is certainly to be universal: "the good news must first be proclaimed to all nations" (Mark 13:10); "make disciples of all nations" (Matthew 28:19). But their role is not so much to achieve the universal coming of the kingdom as to proclaim it. They are to announce the coming of God's rule, to witness to it in signs, as Jesus did, to recruit disciples to the communities that God's rule itself creates as it comes.

Finally, there is a general feature of Jesus' ministry as portrayed in the Gospels that is usually taken for granted but that merits attention in the context of this essay. It is the small scale particularity of so much of what happens. The kingdom of God is a concept that projects a universal horizon, but in Jesus' understanding it never overrides or obscures the particular. God's rule takes effect in Jesus' healings and exorcisms, in which specific individuals are restored to well being, and in Jesus' very concrete personal association with all kinds of particular people. The story of Jesus is a collection of little stories, mostly about the sort of people who scarcely ever appear in historical accounts from the ancient world, because, compared with the movers and shakers of history, they were insignificant. The notion of globalization requires us to think in terms of the big picture, but God's movement from the particular to the universal, the story of the globalization of blessing and salvation, never leaves the particular behind. Real individual people, living communities of people, the concrete reality of their daily lives, are not dispensable for the sake of the grand scheme. If there is a grand scheme, it is precisely for their sake.

The Witnesses of Jesus (Revelation)

We could explore the theme of the church's worldwide mission in other New Testament literature, but within the limits of this essay it is important to return to Revelation, because there we see—it is a central theme of the book—how the two narratives of globalization contrast and clash.

The key words are "witness" and "conquer"—images drawn from the law court and the battlefield respectively. Both have Jesus and his followers as their subject, while only the second has the beast also as its subject. There is, however, a bestial counterpart to witness—"deceive". Revelation makes much use of the themes of truth and deceit. Jesus himself is "the faithful and true witness" (3:14; cf. 1:5) because of the witness he bore to God during his earthly life and his faithfulness in maintaining that witness even at the cost of his life. Jesus' followers are also "witnesses" (17:6; cf. 2:13); more specifically they are those who bear "the witness of Jesus" (12:17; 19:10). This phrase does not mean "witness to Jesus", but the witness that Jesus bore to God and that Christians continue to bear. This witness by Jesus and his followers to the true God and his righteousness serves to expose the falsehood of the beast's idolatry, his assertion of his own power as ultimate and divine. The "witness of Jesus" exposes this idolatry because the beast's power cannot overcome it, not even when it puts the witnesses to death. Quite the opposite: in their deaths Jesus and the martyrs witness to God's truth by not denying it even in the face of death.

When Revelation uses the image of messianic war, it certainly intends nothing in the least militaristic on the part of Jesus and his followers. Rather, it is by their faithful witness even, should it be necessary, at the cost of their lives that the followers of Jesus share in his own victory over evil and play their part in the coming of God's kingdom (12:11). Inevitably, they are involved in a "war" with the beast, which on his side involves brute force as well as propaganda, but on their side is fought purely by non-violent witness. When their witness proves convincing, the beast's deceits are exposed and people are won from serving the beast to worshipping the true God. Very revealing is the fact that the deaths of the martyrs, understood as witness, can be described both as the beast's victory over them (11:7; 13:7) and as their victory over the beast (15:2). From the beast's earthbound perspective he seems to have defeated them, but from the heavenly perspective that the book of Revelation allows its readers to share it is they who have won the real victory.

For our purposes in this essay what is most important is that the way in which followers of Jesus serve God's globalizing purpose of blessing and salvation for the world is by non-coercive witness to the truth. (Revelation stresses verbal witness, along with the suffering that results, but it also describes Christians as "those who keep the commandments of God and hold the testimony of Jesus" [12:17]. Their lives of obedience to God certainly assist their witness.) Because of the witness of Jesus' followers, a people he has redeemed "from every tribe and language and people and nation" (5:9) so that they may bear witness to "the people and tribes and languages and nations" (11:9), the book of Revelation holds out a real hope for the conversion of the nations to God. Triumphant over the beast in heaven, the martyrs sing: "All nations will come and worship before you" (15:4).

Consequent Reflections on Contemporary Globalization

It is not within the remit of this essay to engage contemporary globalization in the way that other essays in this volume do. Globalization is a multivalent notion. Many aspects of contemporary globalization, such as the speed of communication and travel, are historically unprecedented and not to be found in the biblical material we have discussed. Nevertheless there are important continuities, and doubtless, in some sort of hermeneutical circle, my awareness of contemporary globalization has already influenced the way I have read and presented the biblical material in this essay.

The biblical material suggests that human society and history have an inherent orientation towards the global that stems from the fundamental unity of the human race and its limitation to a common home on the earth. Ancient Israel's world may seem rather small to us, but it is notable how frequently the Scriptures that took shape within it open that world to its farthest known limits. Those Scriptures are alert to the complex economic, cultural, and political interconnections of that world, and they cannot, it seems, envisage a future destiny for Israel that does not also involve the nations. Even more importantly, and however Israel's faith in one God may have developed, historically, behind the texts, the God of the Hebrew Scriptures is not the God of Israel alone, but the Creator and Lord of the whole creation and all the nations. To think of this God is to think globally. But the Hebrew Scriptures go much further than this in envisaging a globalizing process: a divine purpose to bring blessing and salvation to all the nations in a way that started with Israel but is by no means intended to stop at Israel.

With such a background in the Scriptures of Israel, it should not be surprising that the New Testament, beginning with God's most particular presence in the world in the person of Jesus the Jew, projects a universal horizon for the salvation Jesus brings. The good news of Jesus, Saviour of the world, and the coming of God's rule in all the world, is of universal relevance and significance. His international people, the church, drawn from all the nations, has the commission to enlighten all the nations with this message.

The inescapably global dimension of human existence means that there is also another kind of globalizing impulse, one that is tainted by human sin. Indeed, as the Bible portrays it, it is driven by the primal and fundamental sin: the human desire to usurp divinity and achieve some sort of ultimate power and status for humans, an escape from finitude. This is idolatry. Inevitably its result is not the common good, but the domination of some, the powerful, over others.

That globalization risks idolatry can be seen very clearly in the contemporary world. The recent process of globalization has been driven by a very definite goal: the economic goal of a completely unfettered free market for the exchange of goods and commodities across all national borders. For the sake of this goal all other considerations can and should be overridden, because the free market is seen as the way of meeting all human needs. This is the latest version of the modern idea of progress, a metanarrative of salvation by the unrestricted pursuit of material wealth.

Like all idolatries, this one has turned out to be an ideology of domination: "Globalization has so far functioned predominantly as an enhanced opportunity for the economic, political and cultural outreach of the powerful."[20] It may have produced more wealth in aggregate worldwide, but in such a way that the rich have grown richer and the poorest poorer: "growing inequality is the most striking feature of the global economy".[21] This is economic growth at the expense of the poor. It is also at the expense of all other values in human life: face to face community, social solidarity, uncommercialised cultural diversity, and the preservation of the environment.

One way in which biblical faith comes into its own, even in the godless world of global economics and international politics, is in its critique of idolatry. A corollary of faith in the biblical God is alertness to every tendency to exalt something of the created world to the status that belongs only to God. Such tendencies are endemic in human life and need constantly to be exposed. When the failures of economic globalization—such as the failure to improve the lot of the very poor—are met with the explanation that the de-restriction of markets has not yet gone far enough and that poor countries are to blame for impeding the free play of market economics, we must surely suspect that the theory has become an idol. How far the current financial collapse and consequent world recession will prove to have permanently exposed the idol's feet of clay remains to be seen.

Much of contemporary Western society has been deeply infected with the belief that economic growth is the supreme good. There are other widely acknowledged values, to be sure, such as tolerance and respect for all, and the right of each to pursue happiness in their own chosen way, but economic growth seems to be necessary for the others to have any real substance. It is doubtful whether there is much precedent in history for such a scale of values in society at large (as distinct from the few who have always made their own economic aggrandisement their priority in life), but perhaps it would be most at home at the court and in the merchants' quarters of ancient Tyre.

The Bible certainly has one economic preoccupation, but it is with the plight of the poorest, the truly destitute. A core Christian criterion to assess any global development must be: does it benefit or further disadvantage the world's poorest people? This is a priority for the church because it is the biblical God's priority and an essential implication of God's love for all people. Love for all people requires special attention to the most needy.

So what of the contemporary church in a globalized world? It has to be said, first, that one of the great tragedies of church history has been a recurrent confusion of the church's mission with movements of global domination. Too often the church has appeared to ride on the back of the seven-headed beast, and in the modern era of imperialism and colonialism Christianity has not surprisingly been seen, all too often, as an aspect of Western aggrandisement and exploitation. In most recent history, radical Islamism has all too readily been able to portray Western dominance over the Islamic world as that of Christian over Muslim, and the indigenous Christians in Muslim countries have borne the brunt of this perception. (Their sacrificial loyalty to Christ has been a witness of incalculable value.)

Western missionaries have too often exported the peculiarly Western trappings of British, European or American Christianity, but it can also be said that over the long course of Christian history the gospel has taken root in a remarkably varied range of cultural contexts and borne fruit of similarly rich cultural diversity. The Bible, as we have seen, does value the diversity of human languages, histories and cultures. The way such diversity is affected by globalization is complex. Some see 'glocalization' occurring as a reaction to globalization, and it is apparent that globalization produces richly multicultural societies as well the homogenisation that derives especially from the world dominance of American popular culture throughout the world. In these circumstances the church must be true to its character as a rainbow people, called by God from 'every tribe and language and people and nation' in order to witness to 'every tribe and language and people and nation'.

The universal church, supposing it can truly recognise its essential unity in diversity, is the most international of all human communal identities (its international spread is greater than that of Islam or Buddhism). Its potential as a movement for resisting the evils of global domination and promoting instead a global solidarity of the prosperous with the needy and of the more fortunate with the more threatened (by global warming, for example) must be unparalleled. Its profile as such a movement by no means prejudices its mission to announce the good news of Jesus and the coming of God's kingdom, because such forms of global solidarity reflect what human life under the rule of God should be. The Bible's polarity between the globalization of domination and the globalization of blessing confronts believers with many concrete choices that must be made in our contemporary context.

....

RICHARD BAUCKHAM (Ph.D., Cambridge) is Emeritus Professor of New Testament Studies at St. Andrews University, Scotland, and Senior Scholar at Ridley Hall, Cambridge. His most recent books include *Bible and Mission: Christian Witness in a Postmodern World* (Baker, 2003); *Jesus and the Eyewitnesses: The Gospels as Eyewitness Testimony* (Eerdmans, 2006); *The Testimony of the Beloved Disciple: Narrative, History, and Theology in the Gospel of John* (Baker, 2007); *Jesus and the God of Israel: God Crucified and other essays on the New Testament's Christology of Divine Identity* (Eerdmans, 2008).

NOTES

[1] To my use of this word it might be objected that the Bible's usual cosmological picture envisages a flat earth, but I take it "global" no longer means "spherical" but "encompassing the whole world".

[2] F. Delitzsch quoted by C. Westermann, *Genesis 1-11* (tr. J. J. Scullion; London: SPCK, 1984), 528.

3   See also Deuteronomy 32:8, which may mean that there are seventy nations correspond-
    ing to the number of the children of Jacob according to Genesis 46:27; Exodus 1:5. See
    also Luke 10:1, where the seventy (or, in some manuscripts, seventy-two) sent out by
    Jesus may prefigure the Christian mission to all nations.

4   NRSV supplies this phrase (not in the Hebrew), conforming the formula to vv. 20 and 31.
    Some translations do not, connecting the rest of this sentence with v. 5a, so that it refers
    only to the descendants of Javan (v. 4).

5   The singular here in NRSV is misleading.

6   Ellen van Wolde, *Stories of the Beginning: Genesis 1-11 and Other Creation Stories* (tr.
    John Bowden; London: SCM Press, 1996), 159-160.

7   See also Daniel 3:4, 7, 29; 5:19.

8   "tribe" is equivalent to "family" in Genesis 10.

9   On the alternative translations, "in you all the families of the earth shall be blessed" and
    "by you all the families of the earth shall bless themselves" (NRSV and NRSV Mar-
    gin respectively), see J. Scharbert, "brk", in G. J. Botterweck and H. Ringgren (eds.),
    Theological Dictionary of the Old Testament, vol. 2 (tr. J. T. Willis; Grand Rapids, MI:
    Eerdmans, 1975), 297; J. Bailey Wells, *God's Holy People: A Theme in Biblical Theol-
    ogy* (JSOTSS 305; Sheffield: Sheffield Academic Press, 2000), 203-206; C. Westermann,
    Genesis 12-36 (tr. J. J. Scullion; London: SPCK, 1985), 151-152, who comments: "the
    reflexive translation ['shall be blessed'] is saying no less than the passive or receptive.
    When 'the families of the earth bless' themselves 'in Abraham', i.e. call a blessing on
    themselves under the invocation of his name . . . then the obvious presupposition is that
    they receive the blessing. . . . Where the name of Abraham is spoken in a prayer for
    blessing, the blessing of Abraham streams forth; it knows no bounds and reaches all the
    families of the earth" (152). Bailey Wells, on the hand, stresses the difference between
    the reflexive and the passive interpretations, both of which are possible, and distinguishes
    the reflexive interpretation as the meaning within the Hebrew Bible, the passive as the
    meaning when the promise is appropriated in the New Testament, though she notes that
    the passive meaning is adopted by the Septuagint (205-206).

10 In Daniel 4:4 it occurs in Aramaic; elsewhere in the Hebrew Bible it occurs as a Hebrew
    word.

11 See the books of Ezra, Nehemiah and Esther. Isaiah 45:1-13 portrays Cyrus as God's
    anointed, fulfilling God's purpose for his people, though Cyrus himself is ignorant of this.

12 See also Isaiah 23.

13 27:3-11 is a poetic description of Tyre imagined as a great and resplendent ship, while
    27:12-25 is a more prosaic account of Tyre's international trade.

14 Note the alternation of references to imports and to exports in 27:12-24.

15 The phrase is from Revelation 11:18.

16 There are echoes also of Old Testament oracles against Edom.

17 The primary allusion here is to Jeremiah 51:9.

18 The only exception is Matthew 5:35, a quotation from Psalm 48:2.

19 Only Matthew 18:23-34; 22:1-13; cf. Luke 19:12.

20 Frank Turner, "Globalisation From a Pastoral-Theological Viewpoint", *New Blackfriars*
    86 (2005), 184.

21 Ian Linden, "A New Map of the World", *New Blackfriars* 86 (2005), 146.

God, Globalization and Grace: An Exercise in Public Theology

by Jonathan Chaplin

Introduction: "Public Theology" as Response to Secularised Discourse

God *and* globalization? Many people at the start of the twenty-first century think they have enough on their plates coming to terms with the baffling reality of "globalization" without bringing "God" into the picture as well. Can a theme as complex and seemingly techni-cal and multifaceted as globalization adequately be addressed through the eyes of religious faith? The authors of the impressive series *God and Globalization*, published between 2000 and 2007, propose that it can *only* adequately be addressed through such eyes.[1] The series is a path-breaking contribution to an understanding of the relationship between globalization and religion. The four volumes—amounting to 1000 pages in total—are the outcome of an innovative project based at the Center of Theological Inquiry at Princeton Theological Seminary, led by noted theological ethicist Max Stackhouse who describes the enterprise as an exercise in "public theology". In this chapter I present an extended commentary on the series, posing selected questions generated by them and suggesting further pointers toward the goal of formulating a Christian reading of globalization. The first part of the chapter concentrates on the first three, multi-authored volumes, and the second assesses the fourth volume, authored by Stackhouse alone, in which a comprehensive theological vision against which to view globalization is presented.[2]

Stackhouse rightly observes that religion barely receives a pass-ing nod in mainstream discussions of globalization. He points out the absurdity of this neglect at a time when religion is reappearing as a major player all over the global stage—often beneficially, sometimes with a vengeance. It is worth pausing to reflect on why so many social scientists, and the policy-makers they influence, remain even today so blinkered when it comes to the influence of religion on the phenom-ena they engage. An obvious main reason is that the leading centres of social science remain located in the "secularised" West and still operate out of dated modernist assumptions about how science and reason have displaced faith as sources of reliable knowledge.[3] But it is now abundantly clear that "secularisation" is not a universal process to which all societies necessarily tend as soon as they become "modernised".[4] Indeed sociologists of religion have now awoken to the stubborn persistence of high-decibel religion in the most highly modernised nation in the world, the USA (how could they ever have slept through it?). It is therefore significant and salutary that a distinguished ecumenical and interdisciplinary team of international scholars should embark on an in-depth investigation of the relation between religion and globalization. Given the catastrophic global developments of the first decade of the new century—looming environmental catastrophes, forced migrations, regional wars, terrorism, economic collapse—it is hard to imagine a more timely enterprise.

Reading Globalization Theologically: "The Spheres of Life"

The term "globalization" acquired widespread currency during the 1980s as the name for a momentous development taking place in the world *economy*. As one representative definition has it:

> Globalization is the process by which nations and local communities become more economically and culturally integrated by relatively unimpeded flows of people, capital, goods and services, and ideas. As the world has become increasingly integrated, the globe has come to resemble a single large economy, with few barriers to economic and cultural flows across international boundaries.[5]

The definition mentions "cultural integration" but is essentially describing the emergence of a genuinely "global economy" in contrast to a merely "international economy"—one in which the majority of international economic activity is determined by processes occurring within national economies. Economic globalization is not simply the expansion of international trade (that is as much a symptom as a cause) but rather the incorporation of increasing numbers of trading partners into a world "single market".[6]

Unfortunately, the series nowhere gives economic globalization the serious theological and ethical treatment it deserves (it is addressed briefly and insightfully in volume 1, chapter 3, though not by an economist[7]). Its focus is rather "cultural" globalization in the broadest sense. Such a broad treatment has many advantages, as we shall see, but it is a significant deficiency to overlook what many regard as the principal driver of most other globalizing processes. I comment further on this below.

The subtitle of the series is "theological ethics and the spheres of life". The notion of "spheres" plays a crucial organising role in the volumes and is their most original contribution. In his Introductions to the first three volumes (amounting to over 130 pages), Stackhouse sets out a framework for analysing globalization in terms of a series of differentiated domains of social life—"*spheres* of dynamic activity"—which make up the modern globalized world. These spheres act as channels for "*powers*"—"moral and spiritual energies"—which drive the core "*principalities*" structuring human life in every society: the economy, the polity, the family and sexuality, culture and media, and religion. Stackhouse proposes that these are universally present; they reflect the deepest needs and capacities of human social life, and, he implies, they are grounded in our very created being.[8]

The modern world has also seen the emergence of specific "*authorities*" which have come to be differentiated from the principalities, including the classic professions of education, law, and medicine. A newer species of authority are the "*regencies*" of late modernity. These include familiar authorities such as science and technology.[9] These regencies are "seats of power . . . exercised in the various spheres of life by those principalities, authorities and dominions' possessing moral and spiritual legitimacy" (1:36). Finally, the "*dominions*" traverse and penetrate all the above. These are civilisation-wide religions like Christianity, Islam, Hinduism, Confucianism and Buddhism. A dominion is what "integrates the principalities into a working whole, and . . . gives distinctive shape to the development of authorities in complex societies . . ." (1:50).

Stackhouse's wider theological grounding for these notions is reserved for his final volume. But the salience and potential of this intriguing six-fold classification are clearly evident in the first three volumes. Many analyses of globalization are construed too narrowly. They concentrate on one "sphere" of human society at the expense of others, and so fall into various forms of reductionism: they shrink the full complexity and diversity of human life down to only one of its many dimensions. This, of course, is most apparent when globalization is seen as an *exclusively economic* process, at the cost of attention to the parallel and relatively independent transformations occurring in distinct social, cultural, intellectual, moral, and indeed religious dimensions, and which are not only effects of economic change. Some recent studies go some way to recognising the multi-dimensional character of globalization.[10] But no study I have seen offers an analytical framework with as much theological potential to resist reductionism as *God and Globalization*.

It can be noted that the notion of cultural "spheres" does not have immediate or exclusive relevance to a global context, nor to "globalization" *per se*. The "spheres", and the five other related entities, describe institutions or forces already long at work within nation-states. But Stackhouse's case seems to be that this set of categories is just as instructive for a non-reductionist assessment of globalization as it has been for such an assessment of single societies. His claim is that, just as a "sphere-based" analysis of societies within single nation-states has enabled Christian social theorists to carve out a "third way" between libertarian capitalism and state socialism, so a similar approach to globalization today can help them chart a distinctive route through the multiple analyses of globalization today.[11]

The first three volumes explore how globalization is operative in numerous diverse and interrelated fields and how religious resources in those fields might humanise it and steer it in wholesome directions. Volume 1 addresses transnational corporations (William Schweiker), war and peace (Donald Shriver), the family (Mary Stewart Van Leeuwen), and the media (David Tracy). Volume 2 engages education (Richard Osmer), law (John Witte), health care (Allen Verhey), science and technology (Richard Cole-Turner), ecology (Jürgen Moltmann), and morality (Peter Paris).

The exploration of the civilisational role of religious dominions and their relation to the spheres is reserved for the third volume. Following Stackhouse's introduction comes a critique of the Western Christian bias in definitions of religion operative in the "religious studies" guild (Diane Obenchain), a compelling argument for taking religion more seriously in international relations (Scott Thomas), and expert examinations of specific religions in the context of globalization: tribal religions (John Mbiti), Confucianism (Sze-kar Wan), Hinduism (Thomas Thangaraj), Buddhism (Kosuke Koyama), and Islam (Lamin Sanneh). These chapters disclose the varied senses in which the main global religions have come historically to exercise civilisational dominion by generating distinctive customs, moralities and institutions.[12]

These individual studies on world religions confirm Stackhouse's crucial proposition that the plural spheres of our differentiated society have not emerged, do not function, and cannot be sustained, in a spiritual vacuum. They challenge head-on the assumption that modern liberal institutions like the state, the market, the professions and the universities, must be insulated against religion. On the contrary, the authors argue, whatever virtues such institutions still possess will be sustainable over the long haul only insofar as they are opened up to the moral and spiritual reorientation which only religion can supply.

While Stackhouse obviously affirms proposals for an overtly Christian contribution, he presents these volumes as an exercise in "public theology".[13] Those wedded to the "secularisation" thesis regard the idea of "public theology" as a contradiction in terms. Theology merely vents the tribal faith-commitments of a particular social group and cannot hope to serve as a framework for debate in the public arena of society. Commendably, Stackhouse and other contributors challenge those who would thus confine theology to the private sphere, arguing cogently that to disqualify theology or religion in advance from participating fully in the public realm is not only arbitrary and intolerant but short-sighted. Religion is a universal human power, is deeply meaningful to many citizens across the globe and, for many, is the primary source of their personal and public identity. Religious believers are equally entitled and equipped to shape the destiny of our national and global public life as those who claim to hold no faith.

Indeed it is precisely because religion aspires to universal truth that theology must be "public". It is distinctive in that its subject-matter (that which is universal in religions) is public, its audience is public (it addresses, and offers normative guidance to, all humanity) (4:94, 109-110), and its methodology is public (it has to "meet the test of public reception" [4:84, 112]). Thus construed, public theology is the type of theology best-placed to contribute to the urgently needed debate about the religious orientation of a globalizing civil society (4:77).[14] And it is the distinctively *Christian* purpose of public theology to show how a pluralistic civil society could become the basis of a *global* culture (4:114).

Outstanding Questions

A series as ambitious as this inevitably evokes a huge range of questions. Here I concentrate on six which are of general significance for the series and the theme of globalization, passing by those that arise largely in relation to one of the many field-specific themes addressed. The first three are issues arising from Stackhouse's opening classification, and the next three address questions of method and perspective.

First, the connections between the spheres, powers, principalities, authorities, and regencies in each of the various fields are not stated precisely enough. For example, if the powers of regencies are, as Stackhouse suggests, exercised by principalities and authorities, how can they have come to be emancipated from the authorities? And how can dominions which are civilisation-wide religions also exercise the power of regencies? Are spheres more basic than powers, or vice versa? Drawing a Venn diagram of Stackhouse's six categories would be quite a challenge.

Part of the reason for the conceptual slackness in the framework may be because most of the terms used to denote the six categories of spheres arise directly out an exegesis of specific New Testament Greek words (e.g. "powers" is a rendition of *exousia*, "principalities" of *ar-*

chai). It is not clear, however, that such terms correspond sufficiently closely to the contemporary realities they are supposed to illuminate. Is "the economy" as a whole really what the word "principality" appropriately refers to today? Would not a transnational corporation or a currency market be a closer fit? Such biblical language may serve well the aims of theologians whose main focus is, rightly, the overall spiritual direction of such modern spheres. But social scientists and policymakers will want a more detailed and exact conceptual apparatus.

Second, the first three volumes seem to circle around but do not pay consistent enough attention to the centrality of *institutions*. Although Stackhouse tells us that the spheres include organisations and "clusters of institutions", none of the terms in his six-fold classification correspond exactly to specific entities like states, schools, corporations, hospitals, and families, or networks of structured interactions between them, such as markets, media domains or policy-making communities. Yet these are the actual centres of decision-making which are shaping globalization—or the vulnerable recipients of their effects.[15] What may be helpful here is the notion of the "irreducible responsibility" of an institution, its unique vocation to contribute to human society in a structurally specific way. This idea—associated especially with the pluralistic strands in Catholic and Reformed social thought—helps keep us alert to when institutions begin to stray from the vocation they are structured to fulfil.[16]

Third, there is no sustained critical assessment of modern capitalism in the volumes—a result of the neglect of the theme of economic globalization. Schweiker and Moltmann acutely raise some of the key questions, but a much more extensive treatment is demanded.[17] The series as a whole fails to convey the overwhelming power of the Western capitalist economy on the processes of globalization. The authors are certainly to be commended for resisting the narrowly economic focus of many secular studies of globalization. And it is also a welcome relief to read a Christian study of globalization which does *not* simply condemn economic globalization wholesale but seeks a balanced appraisal of its costs and benefits. Such an appraisal, however, cannot be attained without a thorough analysis of the depth of the transformations global capitalism is undergoing, a frank assessment both of the undoubted benefits globalization is bringing to many participants in the global economy but also of the economic distortions it is generating (such as the grotesque expansion of financial as against industrial markets, for which the world economy since the financial crash of late 2008 is paying a heavy price), and a much more comprehensive account of the devastating costs it is imposing on many vulnerable people, especially in developing countries.

Fourth, the series describes itself as an exercise in "theological ethics". But how does this sub-discipline of theology relate to social sciences like economics, political science, law or sociology? Of the twenty-three contributors, seventeen work in different areas of theology or religious studies, one is a philosopher, one is a historian, and four are social scientists (including specialists in psychology, law and international relations). The theologians seem well-versed in relevant aspects of social science (and *vice versa*). Yet this under-representation of social scientists and social theorists may explain why some contributors to the project seem to utilise too hastily the results of analyses produced by the seemingly "secularised" social science and social theory the project aspires to challenge.

A possible pointer towards an authentically Christian social theory of globalization appears in Stackhouse's introduction to the first volume. It arises from his posing of some fundamental theological questions: are the powers, principalities, and authorities somehow based in creation? If so, how radically have they diverged from their created purposes through sin? Can they be open to redemption? Volume 4 is his extended answer to those questions. But we also need to be able to link such basic theological affirmations more directly to social scientific and theoretic accounts of contemporary globalization, and so to suggest elaborations in the conceptualities of various social scientific disciplines. To do this we need to start from a biblically-guided account of *historical development* and the norms which should govern it. Such an account would seek to trace the ways in which the enduring designs of our social possibilities can be discerned historically through the enormous variety of particular practices and institutions in many different cultures and even amidst the deep distortions and oppressions caused by human sin. In the next section I build on the pointers offered toward such an account in the final volume.

Wisely, the series does not aspire to present a complete alternative to mainstream theories of globalization but only a "God-based framework for discernment, evaluation, and transformation" of globalization (1:18). However, to deliver even on this more modest goal involves more than the first three volumes offer. It requires more rigorous scrutiny of how such a framework could critically test mainstream social-scientific analyses which give no evidence of being intentionally shaped by Christian presuppositions. What the three volumes do provide is a thematically linked series of outstanding individual studies on various facets of religion *in a context of globalization*—perhaps not yet a "God-based framework" but certainly a "religion-sensitive" one. Given the current state of the debate, that is no mean achievement.

In the fourth volume, Stackhouse takes some further important steps in that direction. But already in the first three the issue of the distinctively "Christian" character of the proposed response to globalization appears. John Witte seems nearest the mark in pointing out that when religious believers participate in debates about global human rights, they should first dig deep into their own confessional traditions—"drink from their own wells", to adapt Gustavo Gutiér-rez's words—to find an authentic language in which to speak about human rights. Genuine consensus on a global human rights regime in the future may depend crucially on the empirical possibility that such a human rights hermeneutic within each religion can succeed.[18]

The invocation of explicitly Christian theological language also comes with potential pitfalls. To the degree that our elite cultures in the West remain dominated by those who believe public life should be rigorously secular, it may be counterproductive for religious citizens (or scholars) to *advertise* their contributions to public debate as "public *theology*". Non-Western contexts face different challenges. In societies like India or Malaysia where public religion is all too often experi-enced as a source of civil disorder, to offer what may appear to be a specifically "Christian" contribution to public life (as the word "theol-ogy" will often suggest) may be construed as mischievous. In majority world countries where Christianity is becoming the dominant public language, the problem is not only one of scepticism or division but also of the fear of a possible new hegemony.[19] The advocacy of "public theology", then, will require a demanding combination of confessional fidelity and nerve on the one hand, and context-sensitive communica-tive adroitness on the other. A cross-cultural, global Christian debate about *that* challenge would certainly make for interesting exchanges.

Finally, a far-reaching question about the scope of the term "religion" is insufficiently addressed in the series. The volumes rightly consider how the "traditional" global religions have come to shape major civilisations. They also record how Western civilisation has to a great extent been moulded by Christian religion. Stackhouse goes so far as to claim that "the socio-cultural forces that are most often associated with globalization . . . were formed by societies fundamentally stamped by Christian theological ethics" (3:12). That claim is assessed in the next section. Yet the first three volumes do not confront with sufficient robustness the question of whether the modern West has been equally, if not more, influenced by the *religion of secular humanism* and its offshoots in Enlightenment rationalism, liberalism and capitalism. Many would argue that this has been the most powerful of the "dominions" governing the modern world. There are some pointed but brief critical reflections on the influence of the secularist religion of modernity in individual chapters. But there is no dedicated chapter in the third volume, where it would have belonged, on the massive civilisational power of this secular religion of modernity. This is a significant lacuna, especially since a main indictment of the West by many non-Western religious believers is precisely the oppressive consequences of secular modernity on their own cultures. The final volume only partly remedies this deficit.

The Grace of Globalization?

Aside from serving as capstone to this series, Stackhouse's own volume, *Globalization and Grace*, can be viewed as the culminating statement of a lifetime of impressively wide-ranging and creative work in public theology. The volume is neither a summary nor a mere elaboration of the previous three, but rather an unfolding of the encompassing theological and methodological framework from which he himself proposes to understand globalization. I first present an overview of what is new in the argument of this book and then respond to Stackhouse's analysis of globalization by proposing a somewhat more critical reading of it.

What, then, is the phenomenon that a global public theology must address? Stackhouse defines globalization as an emerging "civilizational shift" of momentous proportions:

> [Globalization] involves the growth of a worldwide infrastructure that bears the prospect of a new form of civil society, one that may well comprehend all previous national, ethnic, political, economic or cultural contexts. It portends a cosmopolitan possibility that modernity promised but could not deliver, and thus can be considered as the most profound postmodernism (4:2).

Many observers have spoken of the appearance of a "global civil society" to complement (or combat) a globalized economy but few define globalization essentially as the arrival of a new form of civil society. What he seems to have in mind here is consistent with the definition he proposed in Volume 2, namely globalization as the "universalization of [the] authorities and regencies as they developed in the West" (2:2; see 4:216). He seems to have in view the global spread of the broader process of differentiation—the unfolding of the "spheres" (adapted in ways specific to particular cultural and religious contexts).

For Stackhouse, three factors compel a serious reckoning with globalization from the perspective of Christian faith. One, already well aired in earlier volumes, is that processes of globalization are themselves shaped deeply by the influence of religions. A second is that a new global civil society is bringing with it a new global public, one that "comprehends and relativizes all the particular contexts in which we live". In such a situation, "a new kind of particular context-transcendence is required" (4:77). The universal horizons of the world religions, especially Christianity, leave them well-suited to fulfil that role. Indeed, for Stackhouse the key question is not whether religion can shape globalization but which religion will and should do so (4:2,

6, 20, 56, 76). Third, and in partial answer to that question, globalization is the culmination of historical processes set in motion specifically by Christianity itself, which must therefore be both equipped to
address its own progeny and possessed of distinctive resources to do
so (4:6, 35). Other world religions can certainly make unique contributions to understanding and steering globalization but, finally, it is
Christianity that has the most adequate and comprehensive framework
for making sense of and directing it. Such is Stackhouse's claim.

The substantive content of Christianity's distinctive contribution
is set out in chapters 3-5 which treats, respectively, the doctrines of
creation ("the first grace"), providence ("the second grace") and salvation ("the third grace"). Here we see Stackhouse's own panoramic
framework for a public theological ethics on fullest display. No summary would do proper justice to these packed and insightful chapters;
and the questions I would wish pose to them are secondary to his main
interests in globalization (and mine). I highlight only those themes
pertinent to the remaining questions I will address.[20]

Creation is "the first grace" because it is "common" to all humankind (4:138-9, 150-1): it is the original gift of a meaningful, lawful
and knowable order of being in which human beings can respond to
the "cultural mandate" as God's image-bearers (4:131, 142). Unlike
in certain ancient religions, Christianity sees humans not as subordinate to nature but as entrusted with responsibility over and for it, and
so free to continually form and reform nature, history and society in
order to uncover, enjoy and extend its potentials, in ever wider social
and geographical circles. Modern science and technology are among
the principal blessings emerging from this project of human cultural
formation (4:126, 134, 142-3).

But the first grace has been "betrayed" (4:144). Creation is damaged and despoiled by human sinfulness, manifesting itself in myriad
distortions, deviations and oppressions. The cultural mandate now unfolds "out of the garden": the first city is built by Enoch (4:152, 154).
God's original action in bringing creation into being and his distinct
action in supervising the course of history are but diverse expressions
of (common) grace, of God's loving care for his creatures in all the circumstances of their tortuous yet potentially glorious historical destiny.
Providence is God's "surprisingly gracious" gifts to humans to aid
and protect them, and to encourage them to seek him, as they live in
a world of sin (4:160; 158). In the midst of sin, humans can nevertheless realise truth, goodness, compassion and community, and so build
sustainable societies.

Stackhouse gathers four central theological notions under the doctrine of providence: covenant, vocation, wisdom and hope. I comment
only on the first. Covenant is usually understood as a soteriological
rather than a providential idea, but Stackhouse emphasises the way in

which the gift of covenant serves to enable diverse and fractious human beings to come together in bonds of stable but open community among free equals (4:166).[21] The biblical authors "saw in the fabric of this pre-given yet freely chosen association an ordered liberty that interwove righteousness and power, stability and dynamic change, memory and promise, and, on the bases of these, formed a structured accountability that was intended to help all people to deal with one another, scarce resources and competing loyalties with equity" (4:163).

The remarkable cultural fruit was the emergence in the Christian West of a form of social ordering with far-reaching implications for the emergence of modern civil society: "[T]he idea of covenant . . . surpasses the herd solidarity of tribalism, racism, and classism with their subordination of the individual, the radical individualism of contractual voluntarism with its loss of community, and the various tyrannies that recur in societies on the basis of sexual, economic, political, cultural or elite professional dominations" (4:163). This is one of the tangible fruits of "providential grace".

But God's work goes beyond providence to repair and restore—the realisation of "a hope for a savior who could both restore the fallen fabric of creational grace, preserve the sustaining power of providential grace . . . and thus begin a new era that points proximately to a more just, loving and merciful reign of God in history, and ultimately toward a new civilization with a new heaven and new earth" (4:197). Stackhouse's account of the means of salvation—"the third grace"—is rather sparse.[22] But his main concern is rather with the historical fruits of salvation in the reformation of human societies. There is a need not only for individual conversion but also for "social conversion", involving the transformation of social arrangements under the inspiration of saving grace active in persons and institutions. To offer people the chance to leave the confines of their existing cultural traditions is an act of emancipation; to deny them that chance is to deny their humanity (4:206). The gospel contains a "mission to transform" cultures (4:201). Indeed it injects into historical cultures the possibility (perhaps for the first time) of liberating reform (4:206). And it opens societies to the possibility of a covenantal model of civil society, modelled on the church: the weaving of "a new social fabric . . . that reconstitutes civil society itself, incarnating the prospects of chosen communities of conviction" and laying "the seed-bed of a reformation of the whole of society, the social incarnation of true pluralism and freedom with a new order of discipline" (4:207).

Such a pluralistic, differentiated society of many associational spheres and vocations will, Stackhouse claims, need two kinds of integration if the common good is to be secured. It will need a horizontal integration among such spheres themselves, requiring "a network of associated spheres subject to a common sense of justice" (4:211; see also 4:212-214). And it will need an overarching and universal moral and spiritual framework that can only be supplied by religious faith (4:36, 51-3, 56, 213). For just as in the formation of great past civilisations, so today as a globalized culture emerges, religion alone can supply the integrative vision and the "the inner moral architecture" to hold the diverse parts of society together (4:217).

Today the adequacy of these visions is being tested as never before. Indeed, it is the strategic role of "public theology" to engage in "the comparative evaluation of the world religions" both to discern and affirm what may be common to many or all, and also to clarify what irreconcilable differences yet remain (4:217ff). For globalization is being received in diverse cultural contexts under the "dominion" of the religion regnant in that context, and the content of that religion will have a profound influence on the course and health of globalizing processes (4:56).

Stackhouse closes his account of a theological vision for globalization with an inspiring evocation of the coming Kingdom of God as the most adequate source of realistic hope and normative guidance for a world entering upon the new global civilisation (4:224-226). An outlook inspired by the Kingdom can supply "a recognition of the eschatological nature of the vision of the good for humanity, a demand for universal standards of right and wrong and an operational pluralism to sustain dynamic openness to those possibilities". Such a perspective testifies to "the final grace, inconceivable without a sense of common, providential [grace] and the special grace of Christ" (4:226).

But a question of huge import is raised by the foregoing theological account of the three forms of grace: how far is divine grace *already* present in globalization? Stackhouse emphatically rejects the religious anti-globalizers' view of "globalization as another fall" (4:235; cf. 21). Globalization may be fraught with peril and challenge, but fundamentally it heralds the promise of a beneficent new civilisation.[23] "Globalization is neither the Kingdom of God nor the New Jerusalem, but [its] dynamics . . . manifest the effects of Christ's inauguration of the Kingdom . . ." (4:228). This is not a utopian view but it is certainly a very optimistic one. It is based on a crucial judgement undergirding the whole series (though not necessarily endorsed by every contributor) that the processes of globalization today are substantially guided by the historical legacy of Christianity, indeed of the Western Christianity which, he insists, gave birth to "modernity", of which globalization is the most advanced manifestation.[24]

Stackhouse's concluding claim is as much that globalization is *in need of* grace as that it is *an effect of* grace. Yet many Christian commentators (even those who, like me, deny that it is simply "another fall") nevertheless see it as a profoundly distorted cultural development—not intrinsically evil, but, contingently, highly damaging in its present manifestation.[25] I now evaluate Stackhouse's positive appreciation of globalization in two steps: first, by questioning the understanding of "modernity" on which it rests; second, by elaborating a supplementary normative principle—"normative spatial disclosure"—by which it might be more precisely evaluated.

Globalization as "Hyper-Integration"?

Stackhouse is clearly unimpressed by totalising Christian modernity-critics like Alasdair McIntyre or John Milbank. Indeed he rejects generally, and in my view rightly, the "high contempt for modern culture" which he detects in "no few theological circles today" (4:37). Earlier I referred to the "religion of secular humanism" and complained that, as the leading "dominion" of the modern world, it deserved more searching critical analysis than it received in the first three volumes. Regrettably, however, this is not supplied in any sustained way in the fourth. Stackhouse certainly warns that we must not "make an idol" of modernity (4:85). And there are pointed critiques of the state imposition of the secular rationalism of the Enlightenment; the entire series is, as noted, essentially a critique of modernity's marginalisation of public religion. But the Enlightenment is presented not a radical departure from the Christian worldview but as profoundly continuous with it, as "rooted in great measure in the traditions of late medieval and Reformation thought . . ." (4:81). Stackhouse seems to be more interested in singling out for praise the *institutional* achievements of modernity, as seen especially in the process of societal differentiation (notably that between church and state), than in blaming modernity for its sceptical *epistemological* displacement of religion as a source of truth or its repudiation of the realist *ontological* assumptions on which pre- and early-modern Christian culture was built. Indeed the contributions of the Enlightenment "were often scientific or philosophical restatements of certain implications of the basic assumptions of previous theology" (4:82). One does not have to be a paid-up member of Radical Orthodoxy to baulk at this rather flattering depiction of the Enlightenment.[26] In my view this also leads Stackhouse to present an overly-favourable reading of contemporary globalization, which he sees as modernity's latest gift to the world.[27]

His somewhat uncritical embrace of secular modernity also shows up in his somewhat peremptory judgement that traditional minority cultural communities are foolish to resist the progressive advance of globalization even when it will mean the dissolution of their unique cultural identities (4:126-9). He does not seem to acknowledge the possibility that *some* aspects of traditional cultures may actually be morally *superior* to the culture of modernity. For example, attitudes of Aboriginal communities in North America or Australia to the natural environment may not be as adequate as that of a full-orbed biblical view of nature,[28] but they are closer to a biblical worldview than is the dominant view of secular modernity with all its devastating consequences for the destruction of nature (on which, incidentally, Stackhouse has rather little to say in any of the volumes).

The second step in assessing Stackhouse's notably positive embrace of globalization involves picking up my earlier suggestion of the need to formulate a biblically-guided, creation-based account of *historical development* and the norms which should govern it. Stackhouse certainly proposes a robust view of the *providential* activity of God witnessed in the historical evolution of particular kinds of social formation and institutional spheres. What may be helpful, in addition, is a conception of human history itself as the dynamic unfolding of cultural possibilities rooted in the creation order: a *creational law of cultural development.* I would wager that such a view can supply a deeper criterion by which major societal developments can be normatively assessed than is available in a merely providentialist or a soteriological view, since it points us to the most fundamental and original divine intentions for human social life.[29]

Using such an idea of cultural development, the Christian social scientist Bob Goudzwaard proposed a generation ago the idea of the "normative disclosure of society" as a framework for evaluating major historical transformations in social and economic life.[30] In later works he has ventured that globalization can be viewed in principle as a further normative historical disclosure of our created social possibilities, even though, in his judgement, its present course is being profoundly warped by the gross over-extension of the economic, and especially the financial, sphere.[31]

This promising suggestion invites us to regard ourselves and our communities, not as destined to remain confined within inherited territorial or tribal boundaries, but rather as created from the very beginning to aspire to mutual enrichment via global interdependence within God's one world. While this is broadly in line with Stackhouse's vision of globalization, on the basis of this notion we can go on to generate a more precise set of critical concepts by which to assess globalization.

Some ideas suggested by the neo-calvinist philosopher Herman Dooyeweerd might prove useful here. I suggest we define contemporary globalization as an advanced stage of the disclosure of the *spatial dimension* of our created social possibilities as they work themselves out in many spheres of human activity. We can thus speak of a process of "normative spatial disclosure" and reflect on how to correctly identify it and distinguish it from damaging spatial extensions. The notion does not endorse a process of endless or directionless forward or outward movement, but rather points to a normative vocation to advance human social well-being by widening the circles in which we cooperate for the common good of all God's creatures. How might we discern the shape of that "global common good"?

The core concept in Stackhouse's own account is the spatial expansion of processes of "differentiation": in hitherto traditional, tightly unified societies, free individuals, professions and autonomous institutions progressively emerge, as occurred in the modern West (4:147-152). The criterion of the global common good thereby implied is the extension of the processes of differentiation to more and more areas of the world, with all its attendant benefits of wider individual freedom, professional calling, and institutional pluralism. We might say that modern differentiation, infused and guided by a Christian public theology, will liberate individuals, professions, institutions and associations to discover and fulfil their various "vocations", for the common good. It aids an institution in discerning and fulfilling its "irreducible responsibility".

Dooyeweerd would likely agree with Stackhouse in characterising such a movement toward an emerging pluralistic global civil society as, in principle, a normative cultural development. Indeed Dooyeweerd operates with an essentially similar account of differentiation.[32] But he also proposes that differentiation does and should evoke its necessary complement in processes of societal "integration", serving to connect or reconnect what differentiation has quite properly distinguished. Integration is necessary so that differentiation does not produce mere fragmentation. Although Dooyeweerd did not employ the term "covenant" in his social theory, we can certainly see something like it at work in his view of social institutions (see his technical definitions of "community" and "association"), and implicitly in his "connective" view of societal integration.

His analysis (completed by the 1950s) was mainly confined to integration within nation-states. He did identify newly emerging cross-border processes of integration, but these were mainly examples of what Hirst and Thompson define as "inter-national" integration—not yet instances of contemporary "globalization". How then might he characterise the kind of integration occurring under contemporary globalization?

In my view he would likely not regard them as intrinsically damaging but rather as conditionally acceptable so long as they actually performed the connective or reconnective ("covenantal") functions they were supposed to serve. Thus the globalization of electronic communications through the Internet, for example, can be seen, in principle, as contributing to that connective goal (though it, too, can generate its own kinds of damage). The key test is whether such processes actually do serve to enhance the capacity of individuals and many types of societal institution to fulfil their own distinctive vocations, whether these are properly played out in local, regional, national or global arenas (thus, the test of "globalization" is not simply whether it protects "localism"—that is a romanticised view of human spatiality).

Not just any manifestation of global integration is warranted. Some kinds of integration, it turns out, can *actually undo the fruits of differentiation*, insofar as they undermine the fulfilment of the irreducible responsibilities of one or other types of institution (or those of individuals). One example would be the serious damage done to the irreducible responsibility of a family (i.e. to raise children in a context of material adequacy and social and moral stability), when a breadwinner is forced to migrate to find work after a transnational corporation suddenly shifts its capital elsewhere in order to maximise global shareholder value. Here we see the deleterious consequences of an advanced global "integration" of capital markets visited upon vulnerable institutions at their mercy. In this particular case, the "global integration" of capital presupposes the withdrawal of protective regulation (the "de-regulation") of labour markets, leaving employees over-exposed to the vicissitudes of "global competition".[33]

I suggest that what we are seeing today in contemporary economic globalizing processes (the most influential) is actually a form of "hyper-integration"—integration serving not to complement and protect appropriately differentiated institutions in the geographical locations which it is impacting, but rather to undermine and flatten them. This global hyper-integration suggests that contemporary economic globalization is better construed as a corrosive "hyper-modernism" than as a "most profound postmodernism", as Stackhouse proposes. Such economic hyper-integration undermines freedom and pluralism: it causes, not the *liberation* of the impacted sectors of global society but rather their *levelling*. It dissolves or pre-empts the covenantal bonds that should subsist between global economic agents. For example, the creation of a global capital market in which investments can be moved rapidly and unaccountably around the world too often creates a large pool of insecure migrant labourers in various regions of the world. This is not adequately characterised as a beneficent expansion of the blessings of Western differentiation, pluralism and freedom to formerly closed, traditional societies. Rather it is a process that can occasion the devastation of the only social and cultural infrastructure on which such labourers depend.

It is certainly true that a gradual extension of globally integrating processes such as world trade or new communication networks can assist in freeing up closed, authoritarian traditional cultures, and raise average levels of income and wealth; on that Dooyeweerd and Stackhouse would likely agree. But it is equally important that global integration should not outpace the capacity of differentiated institutions in the impacted regions to adjust to the destabilisation often thereby caused. *Normative* (covenantal) integration lends support to differentiated institutions, but what I am calling hyper-integration risks destroying the complex social ecologies on which such institutions depend.

Goudzwaard's judgement is that contemporary economic globalization over the last twenty years has been increasingly driven by what I am calling the hyper-integration of the global financial system with its highly fluid and volatile capital markets.[34] The process seems to have acquired a systemic dynamism—an automaticity—all of its own, irrespective of the long term needs of the "real economy" (e.g. the needs of most ordinary workers to find stable and rewarding jobs in businesses, farms and other producer units that serve local communities). The result is increasingly what Hirst and Thompson call a "disembedded" global economy, one whose systemic objectives are increasingly severed from the social institutions and relationships which any (normative) economic activity is intended to serve.[35]

The momentous expansion of "spatial disclosure" today, then, can be a creational good insofar as it serves to safeguard, support and extend the fruits of differentiation by making possible normative processes of societal integration, at every level of human interaction. I think this proposal is essentially in line with the thrust of Stackhouse's framework. The main way my proposal would modify his framework is by increasing its critical attentiveness to the disintegrative forces currently being unleashed by hyper-integration, especially in the global economy. Only if these disintegrative economic forces can be brought under control—and achieving that is a global project of major proportions—can the free, pluralistic global civil society toward which Stackhouse aspires, be approximated. Only then can globalization be "graced". To do so will require action in all the "spheres" (and principalities, authorities, and regencies) of global society, but today especially in the spheres of global governance and transnational corporations.

....

JONATHAN CHAPLIN (Ph.D., University of London) is the first Director of the Kirby Laing Institute for Christian Ethics, Tyndale House, Cambridge. He is author of *Talking God: The Legitimacy of Religious Public Reasoning* (Theos, 2009) and editor or co-editor of *Political Theory and Christian Vision* (UPA, 1994), *A Royal Priesthood: Using the Bible Ethically and Politically. A Dialogue with Oliver O'Donovan* (Zondervan, 2002), *God and Government* (SPCK, forthcoming), *God and Global Order: Religion and American Foreign Policy* (Baylor University Press, forthcoming).

NOTES

[1] Max L. Stackhouse with Peter J. Paris (eds.), *God and Globalization. Volume 1: Religion and the Powers of the Common Life* (Harrisburg, PA.: Trinity Press International, 2000). Max L. Stackhouse with Don S. Browning, *God and Globalization. Volume 2: The Spirit and the Modern Authorities* (Harrisburg, PA.: Trinity Press International, 2001). Max L. Stackhouse with Diane B. Obenchain (eds.), *God and Globalization. Volume 3: Christ and the Dominions of Civilizations* (Harrisburg, PA.: Trinity Press International, 2001). Max L. Stackhouse, *God and Globalization. Volume 4: Globalization and Grace: A Christian Public Theology for a Global Future* (New York: Continuum, 2008). Earlier versions of this chapter, written as review articles on the first three volumes, appeared in *Comment* Magazine, the opinion journal of Cardus: www.cardus.ca/comment (January 1, 2003); and in the British-based journal *Political Theology* 5, 4 (2004), 493-500.

[2] For a summary statement, see Max L. Stackhouse, "Public Theology and Political Economy in a Globalizing Era", in William F. Storrar and Andrew R. Morton (eds.), *Public Theology for the 21st Century: Essays in Honour of Duncan B. Forrester* (London: T & T Clark, 2004), 179-194.

[3] E.g., Elizabeth Shakman Hurd, *The Politics of Secularism in International Relations* (Princeton: Princeton University Press, 2008).

[4] José Casanova, *Public Religions in the Modern World* (Chicago: Chicago University Press, 1994). Peter L. Berger (ed.), *The Desecularization of the World: Resurgent Religion and World Politics* (Washington, D.C: Ethics and Public Policy Center/ Grand Rapids, MI: Eerdmans, 1999).

[5] Taken from the call for papers for a recent special issue of the American journal *Faith and Economics* on globalization.

[6] Here is a more technical definition: "[In a globalized economy] distinct national economies are subsumed and rearticulated into the [global] system by international processes and transactions. The inter-national economy, on the contrary, is one in which processes that are determined at the level of national economies still dominate and international phenomena are outcomes that emerge from the distinct and differential performance of the national economies. The inter-national economy is an aggregate of nationally located functions . . . The global economy raises these nationally based interactions to a new power. The international economic system becomes autonomized and socially disembedded, as markets and production become truly global." Paul Hirst and Grahame Thompson, *Globalization in Question* (Cambridge: Polity Press, 1996), 10.

[7] Unless otherwise indicated, subsequent references to the series will list volume number followed by page number or numbers, e.g. (1:3).

[8] See Stackhouse's crisp summary of these in "Public Theology and Political Economy", 182-189.

[9] Stackhouse also proposes that "nature" has come to exercise an authoritative hold over our late modern mind. And the heroic personal authority of figures such as Gandhi, Mandela and Tutu—in his chapter Peter Paris calls them "moral exemplars"—also hold regency-like sway over us (1:48-50).

[10] E.g. John Gray's *False Dawn: The Delusions of Global Capitalism* (London: Granta, 1998).

[11] He chides Christian theorists who depend uncritically on either neo-liberal (the "Chicago School") or on Marxist-inspired (Liberation Theology) analyses of globalization, both of which are reductionist—not least in ignoring the power of religion.

[12] The ringing title of this third volume—*Christ and the Dominions of Civilizations*— might lead some to expect to hear the claim that those dominions stand under the judgement of the Christ whom Christians confess as Lord *of all*. This claim, however, is not advanced in that volume.

[13] Here I refer to his accounts of this term both in the first three volumes and in the fourth.

[14] An additional reason is that "public theology" works most directly at the level of civil society in contrast to "political theology" which is too narrowly focused on the state: "Public theology tends to adopt a social theory of politics, and political theology inclines to a political view of society" (4:103); but the "public is prior to the republic" (4:100).

[15] Some individual chapters—notably Van Leeuwen, Osmer, Schweiker, Shriver— do, however, offer insightful treatments of institutions.

[16] E.g. Jeanne Heffernan Schindler (ed.), *Christianity and Civil Society* (Lanham, MD: Lexington Press, 2008); Jonathan Chaplin, "Civil Society and Christian Social Pluralism", *The Kuyper Center Review* (forthcoming, 2010).

[17] Stackhouse offers brief reflections at 4:15-16, 24-25.

[18] E.g. Max L. Stackhouse, *Creeds, Society and Human Rights: A Study in Three Cultures* (Grand Rapids, MI: Eerdmans, 1984); John Witte, Jr. and Johan D. van der Vyver (eds.), *Religious Human Rights in Global Perspective* (The Hague: Martinus Nijhoff Publishers, 1996).

[19] Isobel Apawo Phiri, "President Frederick Chiluba and Zambia: Evangelicals and Democracy in a 'Christian Nation'", in Terence O. Ranger (ed.), *Evangelical Christianity and Democracy in Africa* (New York: Oxford University Press, 2008), 95-129.

[20] In his accounts, Stackhouse instructively interacts both with other world religions and other worldviews.

[21] See Stackhouse's appealing rendition of the core moral content of covenant, the Ten Commandments (4:167-172).

[22] There is, regrettably, barely any mention here of salvation as atonement or reconciliation, of judgement on sin and triumph over evil, or their correlates: human ruin apart from Christ, human alienation from and accountability to God, and human spiritual death without Christ.

[23] The claim is carefully qualified: ". . . certain influences from the classic Christian traditions of theology and ethics are at least partly responsible for the patterns and deeper dynamics that are driving globalization" (4:35).

[24] In "Public Theology and Political Economy" he puts the point this way: "Globalization . . . is a by-product of a kind of pre-evangelization increasingly being adopted by much of the world in practice" (4:181).

25 For a wide range of Christian evaluations, see Peter Heslam (ed.), *Globalization and the Good* (London: SPCK, 2004).

26 Compare it, for example, with that presented in Herman Dooyeweerd, *Roots of Western Culture* (Toronto: Wedge, 1979).

27 Occasionally, there are also somewhat uncritical readings of America's role in the modern world which would be resisted by many outside the U.S. (and some within it) (e.g. 4:13-14). He is, however, alert to America's "temptation to imperialism" (4:12ff.), and critical of aspects of the foreign policy of the Bush Administration (4:3-4).

28 Stackhouse states this in chapter 3. In volume 2, Moltmann appeals to it in speaking more radically of the "boundless will towards domination which has driven and still drives modern [people] to seize power over nature" (2:171). See also Goudzwaard et al, *Hope in Troubled Times: A New Vision for Confronting Global Crises* (Grand Rapids, MI: Baker Academic, 2007), ch. 5.

29 See, for example, Dooyeweerd, *Roots*, whose creation-based account, however, is not without its own deficiencies.

30 Bob Goudzwaard, *Capitalism and Progress: A Diagnosis of Western Society* (Grand Rapids, MI: Eerdmans, 1979).

31 Bob Goudzwaard, "Globalization, Regionalization, and Sphere Sovereignty", in Luis E. Lugo (ed.), *Religion, Pluralism, and Public Life: Abraham Kuyper's Legacy for the Twenty-First Century* (Grand Rapids, MI: Eerdmans, 1998), 325-341; *Globalization and the Kingdom of God* (Grand Rapids, MI: Baker, 2001); Goudzwaard et al, *Hope in Troubled Times*, ch. 8.

32 Both reveal a dependency—arguably somewhat uncritical—on the work on Max Weber, the foremost theorist of modern differentiation. On Stackhouse's invocation of Weber, see 4:22, 30-31, 209 note 11.

33 For an excellent comprehensive, religiously-informed, analysis of globalization by a political scientist, see Eric O. Hanson, *Religion and Politics in the International System Today* (New York: Cambridge University Press, 2006).

34 Goudzwaard, *Globalization and the Kingdom of God*; "Globalization, Regionalization, and Sphere Sovereignty".

35 See also Schweiker, "Responsibility in the World of Mammon: Theology, Justice, and Transnational Corporations", in *God and Globalization*, (3:105-139).

Probing the Historical and Religious Roots of Economic Globalization

by Michael W. Goheen

Argentinian church leader Rene Padilla warns us that economic globalization is "the greatest challenge that the Christian mission faces".[1] Similarly Richard Bauckham says that, contrary to what many perceive, the major threat faced by the Christian church in the twenty-first century is not postmodernity that believes there are no true metanarratives; in fact, it is the grand story of economic globalization that threatens not only the Western church but also the whole world especially through the poverty and environmental destruction that comes in its wake. He says that "the reality of our world is not the end of grand narratives, but the increasing dominance of the narrative of economic globalization. . . . This is the new imperialism, an economic as distinct from the political and economic imperialism of the past, and representing, in fact, the domination of politics by capitalist economics."[2] If these comments are correct, it is incumbent on the Christian community to understand the powerful forces or processes that these authors label 'economic globalization'.

Often this reality is reduced to economic and technological forces. It is certainly true that the economic changes in our global world are the leading process in globalization. It is also true that the new global economic structures have been made possible by rapid technological innovation and development. However, this would be to misunderstand the broader cultural story of which economic and technological change are a part. Manfred Steger isolates and severely criticises the economic and technological forces in globalization. He refers to this process as the "new market ideology" and has harsh words for this phenomenon. However, at the same time he welcomes the progressive transformation of social structures that the modern story brings the global world insofar as it brings freedom and equality.[3] It is true that the spread of Western culture around the world has had both enriching and devastating effects, but it is doubtful that economic forces can so easily be separated from the whole process of modernisation.

It seems much closer to the truth to see economics and technology as embedded in a bigger cultural story[4] that finds its roots in the

Enlightenment. Bob Goudzwaard calls this story 'modern' and refers to the process of working out this cultural story and its beliefs in the structures of public life as 'modernization'.[5] He comments that globalization is "a form or method of modernization on a global scale".[6] The forces of modernisation in our global world come as a unified package; the economic and technological forces are part and parcel of a bigger worldview and story.

The 'economic' in 'economic globalization' cannot be separated from the broader cultural story of which it is part. But it is also true—and this is much more controversial but no less essential—that economic and technological change cannot be separated from the deeper *religious* forces driving the whole modern cultural story. Modern denotes not only social, economic, and political structures and processes, but a set of ultimate beliefs about the world that have been shaped by a long cultural story. These fundamental commitments unify, organise, provide direction for, and give shape to the various sectors of human life. Thus, "the word 'modern' is not neutral; it cannot be divorced from a specific view of life, humanity, the world, and ultimate meaning".[7]

Jonathan Chaplin also believes that the story which has shaped the West for centuries is one of the most powerful players in the global world today, and for him it is also fundamentally religious. What Goudzwaard calls 'modern', Chaplin labels the 'religion of secular humanism'. In his chapter in this volume that evaluates the ambitious and significant four book series *God and Globalization*, edited by Max Stackhouse, Chaplin notes that "the scope of the term 'religion' is insufficiently addressed in this series".[8] Religion is limited to traditional religions. For example, the third volume deals with the influence of Christianity on the West, tribal religions, Confucianism, Hinduism, Buddhism, and Islam which are all mined for their own unique resources to contribute to a more healthy globalization. However, as we noted in the introduction, Chaplin observes that the volumes "do not confront with sufficient robustness the question of whether the modern West has been equally, if not more, influenced by the religion of secular humanism and its offshoots in Enlightenment rationalism, liberalism and capitalism".[9] Secular humanism is, of course, not considered a religion by those who have been inculturated into its story and conditioned by its beliefs since birth. It is certainly not studied in the religious studies department of a university. The religion of secular humanism domesticates traditional religions that offer another view of the world by limiting them to the private domain of life, to the 'spiritual' and 'moral' areas of life. The religion of humanism that has shaped the West, and that is now a major player in the global world, is a story that simply eliminates rival truth claims and competing visions of the world by finding a non-threatening place for those rival stories in its bigger narrative. If one simply accepts this Western story, religion is, then, by definition private views of God and ethics.

Yet it is possible to define religion differently. Broadly we might see religion as our adherence to the ultimate truth of a universally valid story that commands our total commitment. That story narrates the world and gives to us our most basic beliefs, beliefs about the nature of the world, the nature and purpose of human life, the goal of history, the deepest problems of our world and how they can be remedied. These beliefs are held in faith and, like tectonic plates below the earth's surface, shape the whole of our communal lives. They offer hope as they define the goal of human life and the path to get there. Given this description, secular humanism is indeed a religion. It is this story and its ultimate beliefs about the world that have had significant formative influence on the whole social, political, legal, and economic life of Western culture. And this cultural and religious story remains very powerful today as one of the major actors in the global drama, not just because it is sweeping so many into its story, but also because its religious status is not recognised.[10]

The four part series on globalization edited by Max Stackhouse has gone further than others in recognising the shaping power of religion in the global world. Stackhouse employs a rather complicated, even unwieldy, framework derived from the New Testament language of principalities and powers.[11] As part of that framework, he speaks of the various 'principalities' at work in globalization—economics, politics, family and sexuality, media, and institutional religion. But further there are 'powers', moral and spiritual energies that give spiritual impetus to the various social spheres. He also speaks of 'dominions', religion that "integrates the principalities into a working whole, and what gives distinctive shape to the development of the authorities in complex societies".[12] It is in the third book that this series addresses these dominions, and surprisingly the spiritual impetus of modernity or humanism is not discussed! As we observed in the introduction, Chaplin notes this lacuna, and says that "many would argue that this [religion of secular humanism] has been the most powerful of the 'dominions' governing the modern world. . . . And it is the late-modern form of secular humanism that is driving the processes of globalization."[13]

If this is true, and I believe it is, then an analysis of globalization is severely hampered by the secular blinkers of the scholars who ignore these religious forces when they study globalization. The religious energy of the late-modern form of secular humanism that is one of the most powerful driving processes of globalism must be uncovered. One of the ways to unmask this religious motive is to look at its historical origins. Such a task is enormous and cannot be accomplished in one chapter. However, this chapter will briefly trace the humanistic seeds of globalization in the religious story adopted by the West in the 18th century Enlightenment, and then observe some of the ways that these seeds have developed to bear fruit in economic globalization today.

Early Roots of Secular Humanism

Humanism did not suddenly appear in the 18th century.[14] Its roots are found in religious choices made by people going back to the Greeks. The humanism of Greece and Rome was preserved in a synthesis with medieval Christianity for close to a millennium. The 15th century Renaissance was a hinge into the modern world as it purportedly "broke the shackles of tradition, religion and superstition with the hammer of a humanism forged in Greece and Rome".[15] Romano Guardini helpfully formulates three compass points of the modern world that emerged at this time: nature, subject, and culture.[16] The key to understanding all three of these concepts is *autonomy* by which Guardini refers to an understanding of creation, human life, and cultural development as existing apart from God and his authority. The non-human creation is removed from God's presence and rule, and is made independent. Thus, it loses its character as 'creation' and becomes 'nature'.[17] Likewise the person becomes a 'subject' as human life is defined apart from God's purpose and norms, and instead bears "the law of existence within itself".[18] 'Culture' is autonomous humanity's mastery of and domination over nature to shape it according to their will and for their purposes.[19] It will be this will to dominance, this penchant to define the meaning of human life in relation to the non-human creation that will lead to the idolatry of science, technology, economic growth, and material abundance in the coming centuries. Jürgen Moltmann summarises one of the beliefs that "rule our scientific and technological civilization".

> To put the answer simply, it is the boundless will toward domination which has driven and still drives modern men and women to seize power over nature. In the competitive struggle for existence, scientific discoveries and technological inventions serve the political will to acquire, secure and extend power. Growth and progress are still gauged by the relative increase of economic, financial, and military power.[20]

The scientific revolution gifted a method to the Western world that would enable it to realise their autonomy and control the world. At the beginning of the scientific revolution the Christian religious impetus was perhaps as culturally formative as the emerging humanism. However, by the end of this period humanism was the dominant faith that took up science into its stream. Contributing to this triumph of secular humanism was the reactionary opposition of the church to the original fathers of science which seemed to indicate Christianity's irrelevance to the emerging scientific world, as well as the religious wars of the 17th century that seemed to prove that the Christian faith was an unworthy cultural faith which only produced violence while science could achieve unity.[21]

As the scientific revolution drew to a close the "West had 'lost its faith'—and found a new one, in science and in man".[22] Scientific reason, as the light of the world, was rising quickly toward high noon. Alexander Pope catches this mood in his paraphrase of Genesis 1:3 and John 1:4-9.

> Nature and nature's laws lay hid in night.
> God said 'Let Newton be!' And all was light.

The Emerging Credo of Secular Humanism in the Enlightenment

During the 18th century Enlightenment this historical faith matured and the *credo* of modern humanism was forged. The dominating belief was a faith commitment to progress. Augustine's *City of God* had stamped upon Western culture a narrative shape to the world with the notion of the movement of history toward the city of God. The Enlightenment writers substituted the notion of civilisational progress for God's providential rule of history. Christopher Lasch summarises the fundamental difference between 'providence' and 'progress': ". . . [1] historical change comes from within history and not from on high and . . . [2] man can achieve a better life 'by the exertion of his own powers' instead of counting on divine grace".[23] Faith is placed in human effort and ability to build a better world. Ronald Wright refers to this faith in progress as "secular religion",[24] while Christopher Dawson believes that "progress is the working faith of our civilization".[25] And we must be clear that this is *faith*: "Progress of humanity belongs to the same order of ideas as Providence or personal immortality. It is true or it is false, and like them it cannot be proved either true or false. Belief in it is an act of faith."[26] And faith in progress fosters *hope*. Robert Nisbet argues that "no single idea has been more important in Western civilization. . . . This idea has done more good over a twenty-five-hundred-year period . . . and given more strength to human hope . . . than any other single idea in Western history".[27]

The impact of the Christian story also remains evident during the 18th century in the biblical images of paradise that shape the hopeful imagination of many writers during this time. Some of their descriptions of what humankind will build in their own strength sound like the New Jerusalem. And what is the primary characteristic of the good life in paradise? The French Enlightenment philosopher Mercier de la Rivière answers: "Humanly speaking, the greatest happiness pos-

sible for us consists in the greatest possible abundance of objects
suitable for our enjoyment and in the greatest liberty to profit by
them."[28] Adam Smith, the shaper of the economic vision which was
to have a powerful role in Western culture, along with the other classical economists of the day also believed that happiness depended on
material goods. Hla Myint notes that the "classical economists . . .
believed that quantities of satisfaction are proportional to quantities
of physical product".[29] Lawrence Osborn correctly observes that for
Enlightenment social and economic architects "progress is identified
with economic growth" and, therefore, "the economy [is] the chief
instrument in modernity's pursuit of happiness".[30] Material prosperity
and the freedom to pursue and enjoy it—this is the secular paradise
toward which the West is now directed.

How does one get to this paradise? The medieval notion of providence is replaced by an understanding that humanity is now the primary agent in historical progress: "Man's will, not God's, was the
acknowledged source of the world's betterment and humanity's advancing liberation."[31] The human capacity that can best get us to this
materially abundant world is reason. Humanity "is capable, guided
solely by the light of reason and experience, of perfecting the good
life on earth".[32] Scientific reason liberated from religion, tradition, and
faith can be employed to control, predict and shape the world according to humanity's autonomous will.

This better world is realised, first, as scientific reason discerns the
natural laws of the non-human creation and translates them into technological control. Both Francis Bacon and René Descartes urged the
union of science and technology so that humanity could be the "master and possessor of nature".[33] Enlightenment figures like the Marquis
de la Condorcet envisioned progress toward a materially prosperous
world constructed by science and technology.[34] But, second, if scientific reason could discern the laws of politics, society, economics, law,
and education, analogous to physical law, then those laws too could
be controlled to produce a more rationally ordered society. Bury describes the spirit in terms of a new social order that "could alter human
nature and create a heaven on earth".[35] Thinkers like Hugo Grotius
were architects of a rationalist, secular view of natural law that was
independent of God. In this new understanding of law there "was no
longer a divine law-giver whose commands are to be obeyed because
they are God's Laws but are necessary relationships which spring
from the nature of things (Montesquieu). As such they are available
for discovery by human reason."[36]

The view of natural law that develops at the Enlightenment is
thoroughly deistic. Deism is the transitional faith between Christianity and a secular faith. Deism retains the notion of creation order and
normative law for society but separates that law from God's immedi-

ate presence and authority. The laws are built in to the creation as parts are built into a machine. This deistic view of law for society functions on a "false analogy with physics".[37] The new physics of the scientific revolution proceeded by analysing the smallest units of matter and searching for laws that related those units. Thus both political and economic theory started with the autonomous individual—the smallest unit of society—and looked for necessary and mechanical laws that governed the economic or political relation between them. In economics, for example, the "basic unit of society is a human being, who, with single-minded purpose, seeks to acquire the maximum of goods and services with the minimum of effort".[38] The laws of supply and demand, for example, govern the economic activity of these individuals.

The Economic Dimension of Enlightenment Secular Humanism

Here we see the seeds of a vision of life that will grow into full-fledged cultural worldview in the West, and play a major role in globalization. The extended attention to the economic dimension of globalization in the current literature requires us to pause here briefly and draw attention to the centrality and nature of economics as it developed in this maturing Enlightenment vision. We have noted that economics begins to play a leading role in European social life since material prosperity was a primary goal of human life. In his popular book *The Making of Economic Society* Robert Heilbroner says that at the time of the Enlightenment "we begin to see the *separation of economic from social life*. The processes of production and distribution were no longer indistinguishably melded into the prevailing religious, social, and political customs and practices, but now began to form a sharply distinct area of life in themselves."[39] This could be taken to be healthy societal differentiation, in which a latent dimension of society that is creationally good is properly distinguished in its own right from other spheres. It could also point to an unhealthy development where the economic dimension of life begins to take an exalted place in culture overriding other societal spheres. Certainly in the years that followed, the economic sphere of life began to take this kind of totalitarian power distorting other social spheres in modern life. Goudzwaard offers a vivid illustration of this exaggeration of the importance of economic growth in the West, along with the way in which all other societal spheres adapt to this single focus—a beehive. The centre of a beehive is the queen bee whose task it is to produce eggs. This takes place only as she is surrounded by a hive in which everything is functionalised and directed toward her task. Likewise the centre of Western society would increasingly be economic and all other spheres would be shaped to contribute toward economic growth.[40]

Since economics as it developed at this time would increasingly play such a leading role in Western history and now in globalization, it is essential also to see the deistic context in which classical economics was forged. Remnants of that deism were clearly in evidence in the 1980s when we heard Margaret Thatcher say "you can't buck the market" and "there is no alternative" (TINA) to submitting to market forces. The deterministic language of necessary mechanistic economic forces to which we must simply acquiesce remains part of our world and is an important piece in understanding *economic* globalization.

In a deistic worldview where law is based on a false parallel with physics, economic law becomes mechanical. These laws are built into the creation just like various parts are built into a machine. These laws are inviolable just like the laws of physics. If I step off a 50th floor balcony, the laws of physics "kick in" and will make sure it is the last decision I make. You simply "obey" those laws or pay the price. Francis Bacon spoke of these natural laws when he said that "nature is only to be commanded by obeying her".[41] When the market and economic laws are understood in this false way, the market is no longer something that human society creates and moulds in a responsible way. It becomes an autonomous and neutral mechanism whose impersonal forces must simply be obeyed. Economics becomes "the science of the working of the market as a self-operating mechanism modelled on the Newtonian universe".[42] Newbigin has strong words of warning for this deistic view of the market.

> The idea that if economic life is detached from all moral considerations and left to operate by its own laws all will be well is simply an abdication of human responsibility. It is the handing over of human life to the pagan goddess of fortune. If Christ's sovereignty is not recognized in the world of economics, then demonic powers take control.[43]

In contrast to deism, God has ordered creation in such a way that human beings are given responsibility and are called to shape economic life and the market in a just and equitable way. The market is *not* an independent and mechanistic phenomenon but the way human beings steward the earth's resources and responsibly shape their economic life together. To abandon our economic life to "market forces" is tantamount to giving up our economic future to fate. Abdicating responsibility by relinquishing the market to autonomous forces will simply allow the market to be shaped by the most powerful economic actors. Markets *will* be shaped by human economic activity—of that we can be sure because this is the way God has made the world. The only question is whether they will be formed in a just or unjust, a sustainable or unsustainable way.

Adam Smith, an Enlightenment economic philosopher, constructs his economic theory in this context. He is a deist and his views of economics are shaped by a mechanistic view of natural law. In fact, he was first a moral philosopher, and one of his primary concerns in a situation of economic deprivation was to increase goods so that they could be distributed to the poor. For this to happen, two forces were necessary—division of labour and accumulation of capital. The market would be the mechanism that would coordinate these forces for the material betterment of humanity. Thus, the market becomes a key to the prosperous future of humankind.

It is Adam Smith's "invisible hand" that reflects his deistic view. The invisible hand was the mechanism of the market at work co-ordinating the actions of self-interested people to produce wealth and distribute it more fairly. A reference to an "invisible hand" reflects the fading memory of God's providential rule. Augustine had spoken of God's providence co-ordinating even conflicting individual activities in the same way a skilful composer resolves discordant sounds and harmonises them into a grand melody.[44] Augustine's active and present God is now banished in the thought of the deistic Smith.[45] The way the invisible hand worked was as individuals acted according to self-interest, there would be a harmony of conflicting interests that would produce wealth and prosperity. Gradually the growing bounty would trickle down to prosper the poor. "The rich are led by an invisible hand to make nearly the same distribution of the necessaries of life, which would have been made had the earth been divided into equal portions among all its inhabitants; and thus, without intending it, without knowing it, advance the interest of society."[46] Again it is a succinct couplet of Alexander Pope that captures this deistic viewpoint.

> Thus God and Nature formed the general frame,
> And bade self-love and social be the same.

Bob Goudzwaard and Harry de Lange suggest that Enlightenment culture made two gambles or calculations at this point. The first was the happiness gamble: If we have more goods produced by labour we will be happy.[47] The second was the market gamble: If we let the market be free for the economic self-interest of individuals then it will guide us to a better future for all.[48] These were faith commitments that would provide a direction for the development of Western culture.

In line with these gambles I would suggest that there are at least four religious choices in evidence at this point that would shape subsequent history. First, in keeping with Goudzwaard's happiness gamble, Enlightenment thinkers assume the goal or end of human life is material prosperity. This offers a vision for the good life, for what it means to be human, for what will satisfy our deepest longings. Second, this goal means that the relationship of humanity to nature would determine human life. Human beings have three relationships—to God, to each other, and to the non-human creation. Medieval culture focussed on the vertical relationship to God, and Asian and African cultures find a centre in horizontal social relationships. It is the relationship with the non-human creation that gives Western humanity their identity and resources for happiness. It would be the control of 'nature' that would give prosperity. This is why science, technology and the market would become such powerful idols or, maybe better, false messiahs: they are viewed as capable to bring about the goal of human life. Third, law was understood in a mechanistic fashion. Humanity has long been concerned to understand the lawfulness of God's world. How one understands order and law is not 'scientific' but a faith commitment bound up with one's broader worldview. Here law is understood as inbuilt regularities springing from the nature of things that must be obeyed. Finally, the deepest faith commitment of the Enlightenment is that human effort can solve the world's problems. As the committed humanist Corliss Lamont puts it, humanism "assigns to us nothing less than the task of being our own savior and redeemer".[49]

Goudzwaard summarises the growing faith commitment of the Enlightenment: "Growth in prosperity and scientifically founded technological progress are the two indispensable allies on the way to a better future. This is part and parcel of the Enlightenment creed."[50] This confessional vision has been transfused into the bloodstream of Western culture. It is this Enlightenment *credo*, with the leadership of neo-classical economics, which is playing a powerful role in globalization today. The market must be free from government interference; it is the mechanism that will produce wealth. Third world countries must participate in this market, which has now expanded to global proportions, if they want to prosper. The breakdown of the communist centrally-planned economies has made this vision even more plausible, perhaps beyond critique. This takes us into the 20th century but we must make a few observations on the 19th and early 20th century first.

The Nineteenth and Twentieth Century: Progress as Growing Material Prosperity

If the Enlightenment vision is true, if human beings truly are their own redeemers, if science, technology, a rational society, and a free market really are the keys to achieving material abundance which is the end of human life, then "the establishment of *new* social institutions is not a tedious, incidental task, but a dire necessity and a high ethical imperative. In that case, the narrow way to the lost paradise can only be the way of *social revolution*."[51] The revolutions of the 19th and 20th centuries—Industrial, French, American, Democratic, Marxist—sought to bring society into conformity with this Enlightenment faith.

The Industrial Revolution began to implement the Enlightenment economic vision of Adam Smith and the classical economists, developing science-based technology and the division and mechanisation of labour. The market expands significantly and plays an increasingly important role in the newly emerging social order. The Industrial Revolution did much more, however, than reorganise economic production; it shaped a new society around economic life, the world of industrial capitalism. About this emerging social form, David Wells says "capitalism has successfully reorganized the social structure for the purposes of manufacturing, production, and consumption. It has concentrated populations into cities and produced massive systems of finance, banking, law, communications, and transportation. In short, it has changed the shape of our world . . ."[52] It began to produce what the Enlightenment social visionaries were looking for: the market economy and industrial technology produced tremendous economic growth.

Confidence in progress toward material abundance and a growing economy through technological innovation and a free market hit its high point by the end of the 19th century. Morris Ginsberg tells us that the "culminating point in the history of the belief in progress was reached toward the end of the nineteenth century. . . . It owed its wide prevalence to the optimism inspired by the triumphs of applied science, made visible in the striking advances made in the technical conveniences of life."[53]

Yet the 20th century levelled some heavy body blows to confidence in progress, not least the destructive ideologies of the 1930s. Already before that in the early decades of the 20th century there were voices that began to disavow the utopian and paradisiacal versions of progress—the heavenly city of the eighteenth century philosophers as the goal of history.[54] Nevertheless, even while rejecting perfectionist and utopian interpretations, progress remained resilient in its socialist and liberal forms and remained the working faith of Western civilisation. Lasch analyses this interesting phenomenon. He suggests that "it is to Adam Smith and his immediate predecessors . . . that we should look for the inner meaning of progressive ideology".[55] Indeed, it is his notion of progress as the promise of universal abundance based on a self-regulating economy that would endure throughout the twentieth-century. Lasch writes:

> The concept of progress can be defended against intelligent criticism only by postulating an indefinite expansion of desires, a steady rise in the general standard of comfort, and the incorporation of the masses into the culture of abundance. It is only this form that the idea of progress has survived the rigors of the twentieth century. More extravagant versions of the progressive faith . . . collapsed a long time ago; but the liberal version has proven surprisingly resistant to the shocks to easy optimism administered in rapid succession by twentieth-century events.[56]

This, says Lasch quoting Horace Kallen, was because capitalism had "raised the general standard of living, . . . transformed scarcity into abundance, awakening wants where none had been before, multiplying few into many, bringing more and more varied goods to more people at lower prices, so that what had formerly, if at all, available only to a few . . . was now in reach of many . . ." Perhaps Lasch's next words offer insight into the global spread of this worldview: "It remained only to complete the capitalist revolution by making the 'blessings of leisure' available to all".[57]

The Religious Beliefs Shaping Economic Globalization

A major component of globalization is the global expansion of this religious story. To 'complete the capitalist revolution' means making the blessings of our story available to all the peoples of the earth. The 'capitalist revolution' harbours some deep faith commitments: faith in progress, the goal of progress is increasing material abundance which will satisfy the deepest longings of humankind, material abundance comes through economic growth, economic growth is facilitated by innovative technology and a free market. Economic globalization is not just the creation of a global market but it also involves the cultural and religious beliefs that have created and shaped the market.

Economic globalization does involve the creation of a global market stimulated by relaxed trade barriers and rapid developments in information technology. It is facilitated by multi- and trans-national corporations along with the development of global capital. Peter Heslam claims that "contemporary globalization involves the increasing integration of national economies into a global market, made possible by the rise of communication and information technology, air travel, large multinational corporations and financial capital".[58]

In principle, the Christian community should not oppose a global market or expanding global trade. If the market is responsibly shaped to provide goods and services for human well-being, then widening the market could be a source of good for more people. There are, however, deep distortions in economic globalization that threaten human (and non-human) well-being. It is not the global market as such, but the global market as it has been deeply distorted by the idolatrous beliefs of the broader humanist story that is producing growing poverty and ecological damage. One must distinguish *between* the creational potential of the process of globalization including the emergence of a global market *and* the way it has been twisted by idolatry. It is on this basis that the Christian community should be involved in the processes of globalization, seeking to seize the created potential and shape it in a healthy and life-giving way, while at the same time struggling against the debilitating and death-dealing distortions.[59] The remainder of this paper will observe the way that two foundational beliefs—a deistic view of the market and an idolatrous commitment to economic growth—have shaped an unjust global market contributing to massive poverty.

Global Market Ideology and Exclusion

Lesslie Newbigin is correct when he says that "free markets are the best way of continuously balancing supply and demand", but that in the "contemporary ideology of the free market . . . we have an example of something good being corrupted".[60] Newbigin's mention of 'ideology' reminds us that in the 1960s Daniel Bell proclaimed the end of ideology[61] and that more recently Francis Fukuyama celebrated its demise as well.[62] So to speak of the ideology of the free market, it is important to be clear what is meant.

Goudzwaard's analysis of ideology in *Hope in Troubled Times* is insightful.[63] An ideology absolutises a *societal end* or goal. These goals are legitimate human needs that take on exaggerated importance because of a certain context. For example, Adam Smith and the classical economists lived in a time of hunger, misery, grinding poverty, and economic need. They preoccupied themselves with finding economic solutions to the deprivation that afflicted their contemporaries. This legitimate concern became the determining issue that dominated their economic theory. This need captured the imagination of Western people and increasingly became the ultimate purpose around which they organised and structured their societal life. Indeed, long after human deprivation and hunger ceased to be a major problem in the

West, the goal remains deeply imbedded in the direction of Western society.

Moreover, an ideology selects certain *means or instruments* that will effectively enable society to reach that all-important end. An ideology's advocates "recruit and invest certain social forces with significant new power, and these forces then serve as the essential tools used to achieve the prized objective".[64] These social forces or institutions take on a messianic or idolatrous quality as they are invested with redemptive and liberating power because it is believed that they will effectively deliver the societal end for which humanity longs. In the case of classical economics technological innovation and the market freed from all outside interference are two of the primary means that would deliver the material abundance that had taken on such overriding significance for human life.

An ideology will seize control of an entire society, organising and unifying it in pursuit of the goal. It will also redefine norms and standards, ascribing evil to whatever blocks the way to that end, and assigning good to whatever helps to achieve that goal. Goudzwaard suggests that these ideologies take the form of stories that fill the spiritual vacuum created by the Enlightenment.[65] The story of progress toward material abundance accomplished by economic growth brought about by a free market and innovative technology has taken on the role of a global ideology in our day.

The global market that is emerging as the instrument of global prosperity, however, is an unjust market that is not leading to the material abundance for all. In fact it is impoverishing many leading to a growing gap between rich and poor. One of the reasons is precisely because the global market is being shaped by a deeper set of religious beliefs that twist it. Here I note at least two that have emerged in the Western story. First, a deistic and mechanistic view of the market that calls for our blind submission hides the fact that the market is something that must be shaped in a responsible way. Second, a fundamental commitment to economic growth leads those with economic power to shape the market for their own economic advantage.

The global market today exercises such far-reaching power that all countries are now included in its dynamics. However, at the same time that they are included in the global market, they are systematically excluded from many of the fruits of economic life. A market is being shaped in unjust and inequitable ways that systemically marginalises the poorer countries and people of the world. The market is not a neutral machine but a human social construction in response to God's normative call to stewardship that is being shaped in inequitable ways to maintain economic growth in the West. We can observe five different ways that poorer countries are unfairly excluded by decisions and policies that shape the global market.

First, they are *excluded from capital*. One of the remarkable changes in the last few decades is the meteoric growth of the financial sector of the economy. The financial sector (buying and selling money, options, futures, etc.) was originally created to aid the real economy (actual selling of goods and services). However, its rapid growth—17% annually while the real economy grows only 3%—has led to a situation where the financial sector now dominates and controls the real economy. Transactions in real goods fell from 90% in the early 1970s to less than 5% in the early 1990s![66] The primary motivation that drives this burgeoning financial sector is fast short term profit. This has serious repercussions for third world countries.[67] 1) Investment is concentrated in the wealthier countries. A disproportionate percentage of investment capital flows to the USA and Europe, and very little to the poorest countries of the world. For poor countries to attract capital they must pay higher interest rates. 2) Decisions about the flow of capital are not made on the basis of social usefulness and need, but rather on speculation as to where the fastest and greatest profit can be made. Large amounts of free-flowing currency can leave a country with the click of a computer key if a fraction higher return can be made elsewhere, and so poor countries must direct their economic policies, not for the needs of the population, but to keep precious little capital in their country. Even then third world countries are largely excluded from the capital necessary to participate equally in the global economy and share in its growing production.

Second, they are *excluded from currency*. The richer countries exercise control of the currencies that are used in international trade (the dollar, the euro, the pound, and the yen). Poorer countries who want to participate in the global market must borrow money from countries whose monetary unit is an accepted means of payment in order to purchase goods from other countries. They must pay interest just to secure the currencies they need to participate in the market. Clearly this puts these countries at a great disadvantage compared to those who do not need to borrow and pay interest.[68]

Third, they are *excluded from decision-making power*. The levers of economic power in the global economy are controlled by the wealthier countries whose policies, not surprisingly, are often self-serving. The International Monetary Fund (IMF) was formed to provide financial assistance for nations who could not make payments. The World Bank was founded to supply capital to poor countries. The policies of these institutions are controlled by wealthier countries who look after their own interests first. Poorer countries must acquiesce to the direction of these institutions if they are to receive money and participate in the global economy. To take one example: when poorer countries could not pay their debts at the end of the 1970s because of spiralling interest rates, the IMF and World Bank lent money, but for

those loans required "structural adjustment", a policy—still in place—
that required these countries to expand exports and slow imports. The
result: exports saturated the market, which drove prices down, and in
turn increased their debt.[69]

Fourth, they are *excluded from markets*. Even though the price
for receiving money from Western controlled banks was the opening
of their markets to the West, the response has not been reciprocal.
Even though the West has demanded that poorer countries take on a
policy of exports to service their debt, those same Western countries
have continued to prevent entry of products from other parts of the
world into their market through tariffs and other trade barriers. Joseph
Stiglitz, former vice-president and chief economist of the World Bank
refers to this as asymmetric globalization.

> . . . free trade has not worked because we have not
> tried it: trade agreements of the past have been neither
> free nor fair. They have been asymmetric, opening up
> markets in the developing countries to goods from
> advanced industrial countries without full reciproca-
> tion. A host of subtle but effective trade barriers have
> been kept in place. This asymmetric globalization has
> put developing countries at a disadvantage. It has left
> them worse off than they would be with a truly free
> and fair trade regime.[70]

One blatant example is that Western nations have consistently re-
fused to abandon their protection of domestic agriculture by offering
subsidies, effectively preventing "free trade" between Western and third
world farmers. These subsidies make it difficult for African farmers, for
example, to compete in world markets. This is just one way that 'free
trade' has been stifled by policies and structures in the global market. As
Stiglitz says, "The United States and Europe have perfected the art of arguing for free trade while simultaneously working for trade agreements
that protect themselves against imports from developing countries."[71]

Fifth, they have been *excluded from scarcities*. A fundamental
change has taken place in capitalism since the time of Adam Smith.
Smith was concerned to distribute scarcities to meet existing needs.
After all, when the rich had their needs for chairs met, say, increasing
production would mean that goods would trickle down to the poor
classes. However, sophisticated marketing tactics allied with incredibly powerful information technology attempt to influence consumer
demand by artificially expanding the needs of those who can afford
more. At a time when production could meet the basic needs of everyone, it is directed toward the artificially generated "needs" of the
wealthy. Maurice Strong says

> The response of our industrial machine is to expand
> its markets by creating new wants and new appetites
> amongst the people who can afford them. We are thus
> caught in a paradox in which we have created an in-
> dustrial system capable of meeting the basic needs of
> all the world's people but are in fact using it largely
> to foster further growth in the demand by the wealthy
> minority for goods and services well beyond what we
> need or is good for us.[72]

Thus the scarce resources of the world are channelled toward the
growing markets of the West that are artificially stimulated by powerful marketing techniques. There are only so many resources to go
around and so their deployment to meeting the contrived needs of the
wealthy mean they are at the same time directed away from the real
needs of the poor.

These exclusions have led to rising debt among the poorer nations
of the world. Much attention is given to the amount of aid money
that goes from wealthier countries to the Southern hemisphere. What
escapes notice is that the net transfer of money moves to the North.
That is, more money moves from the South to the North to pay debts
than the amount of money that flows to the South in aid. A growing
percentage of resources from third world countries are used to service
their debt rather than to provide basic services like health and education which are so desperately needed. Africa has been hardest hit
where in some countries the external debt is often much higher than
the value of all their exports. Even when these poorer countries are attempting to be fiscally responsible—and certainly there has been much
corruption and mismanagement in many of these third world countries
which may even be the primary problem—the structures and policies
of the global economy make it difficult to put a dent in the debt. These
exclusions make it clear that all the participants in the global market
are not equal partners; there simply is not a level playing field. And it
has led to crippling debt and massive imbalances of wealth, in which
the overfed live alongside the starving in the same world.

N.T. Wright speaks of the "massive economic imbalance of the
world" as "the major task that faces us in our generation" and as "the
number one moral issue of our day". With prophetic passion he goes
on to denounce it with very strong words:

> The present system of global debt is the real immoral
> scandal, the dirty little secret—or rather the dirty
> enormous secret—of glitzy, glossy Western capital-
> ism. Whatever it takes, we must change this situation
> or stand condemned by subsequent history alongside

those who supported slavery two centuries ago and those who supported the Nazis seventy years ago. It is that serious.[73]

Yet all of this is not to demonise the global market as such or vilify economic growth or simply offer protest against the globalization process. A global market can be structured in a just and stewardly way, responsible and sustainable economic growth may be a legitimate part of cultural endeavour, and globalization has the potential to be an enriching development. Moreover, undoubtedly the newly created global market has delivered economic benefits to poorer countries. These inequities are pointed out to observe the way our fundamental beliefs about the world shape our global economic life together. Treating markets as autonomous mechanisms and absolutising economic growth have detrimental consequences. If Christians are to know where to direct their attention and effort in order to have a transforming impact for the good of all people and all creatures, we must know how, where, and why the distortions have come.

Conclusion

Joseph Stiglitz identifies six areas in which globalization needs to be reformed: the need to address poverty, the need for foreign aid and debt relief, the need to make trade fair and equitable, the need to recognise genuine limits in the ability of poorer countries to open their markets, the need to address the environmental crisis, and the need for a healthy and just system of global governance.[74] Each of these issues is certainly urgent but they will not be resolved apart from addressing the deepest beliefs that give shape to the social and economic systems producing these problems. Thus, the neglect of the religious and spiritual roots of economic globalization in the current literature is not just regrettable, it is downright irresponsible.

MICHAEL W. GOHEEN (Ph.D., Utrecht) is Geneva Professor of Worldview and Religious Studies at Trinity Western University, Langley, B.C. Canada, and Teaching Fellow at Regent College, Vancouver, B.C. He is co-author (with Craig Bartholomew) of *The Drama of Scripture: Finding Our Place in the Story of the Bible* (Baker, 2004) and *Living at the Crossroads: An Introduction to Christian Worldview* (Baker, 2008).

NOTES

[1] Rene Padilla, "Mission at the Turn of the Century/Millennium", *Evangel*, 19, 1 (2001), 6.

[2] Richard Bauckham, *Bible and Mission: Christian Witness in a Postmodern World* (Grand Rapids, MI: Baker Academic, 2003), 94.

[3] Manfred D. Steger, *Globalism: The New Market Ideology* (Oxford, UK: Rowman and Littlefield Publishers, Inc., 2002), x.

[4] J. Richard Middleton and Brian Walsh speak of a twofold usage of the notion of 'story' in Alisdair McIntyre and other scholars. Story can mean a socially embodied narrative, which is an actual way of life of a people shaped by a common history. The second is a grounding or legitimating narrative which is the story they tell to account for and legitimate their way of life. I am using story primarily, though not exclusively, in the first sense. (*Truth is Stranger Than It Used to Be: Biblical Faith in a Postmodern Age* [Downers Grove: Intervarsity Press, 1995], 69-70).

[5] Bob Goudzwaard with Julio de Santa Ana, "The Modern Roots of Economic Globalization", in *Beyond Idealism: A Way Ahead for Ecumenical Social Ethics*; Julio de Santa Ana; Robin Gurney, Heidi Hadsell, and Lewis Mudge (Grand Rapids, MI: Eerdmans, 2006), 99.

[6] Bob Goudzwaard, Mark Vander Vennen, and David Van Heemst, *Hope in Troubled Times: A New Vision for Confronting Global Crises* (Grand Rapids, MI: Baker Academic, 2007), 142.

[7] Goudzwaard et al., *Hope in Troubled Times*, 143.

[8] Page 56 in this book.

[9] Ibid.

[10] If I can be permitted a personal story here: I remember the sense of liberation, even relief, expressed by a number of African leaders some years ago when during a seminar I led on the West and globalization, they began to realise that these Western forces shaping Africa where not just the way things should be, the expression of a neutral scientific perspective, a self-evident norm for public life. Rather they were religious beliefs, and were competing with other religious forces for the soul of Africa.

[11] There is a growing literature on this subject. See, for example, Hendrikus Berkhof, *Christ and the Powers* (tr. John H. Yoder; Scottdale, PA: Herald Press, 1962); Walter Wink, *Naming the Powers: The Language of Power in the New Testament. The Powers: Volume 1* (Philadelphia: Fortress Press, 1984); *Unmasking the Powers: The Invisible Forces that Determine Human Existence* (Philadelphia: Fortress Press, 1986); *Engaging the Powers: Discernment and Resistance in a World of Domination* (Minneapolis: Augsburg Fortress Press, 1992). For a brief discussion see Richard J. Mouw, *Politics and the Biblical Drama* (Grand Rapids, MI: Baker, 1976), 85-116. A large part of the reason this theme has emerged is to counter an individualistic understanding. See Newbigin, *The Gospel in a Pluralist Society* (Grand Rapids, MI: Eerdmans, 1989), 198-200.

[12] Max L. Stackhouse with Peter J. Paris (eds.), *God and Globalization. Volume 1: Religion and the Powers of the Common Life* (Harrisburg, PA: Trinity Press International, 2000), 50.

[13] Jonathan Chaplin, Review essay on Max Stackhouse et al, *God and Globalization*, Vols. 1, 2, 3 (Trinity Press International, 2000-2002), *Political Theology* 5, 4 (October 2004), 500.

14 Craig Bartholomew and I have traced this story at an undergraduate level in *Living at the Crossroads: An Introduction to Christian Worldview* (Grand Rapids, MI: Baker Academic, 2008), 67-106.

15 Philip Sampson, "The Rise of Postmodernity", in *Faith and Modernity* (Philip Sampson, Vinay Samuel and Chris Sugden [eds.]; Oxford: Regnum Lynx Books, 1994), 33.

16 Romano Guardini, *The World and the Person* (tr. Stella Lange; Chicago: Henry Regnery, 1965); originally published as *Welt und Person: Vesuche zur Christlichen Lehr vom Menschen* (Würzburg: Werkbund-Verlag, 1939).

17 Ibid, 11. Bernard Zylstra discusses a humanistic view of creation as 'nature' as "something that *the cause of its own existence in itself, can exist by itself, and exists for itself*" ("Thy Word Our Life", in *Will All the King's Men . . . Out of Concern for the Church: Phase II* [Toronto: Wedge Publishing, 1972], 156).

18 Ibid, 9.

19 Ibid, 11.

20 Jürgen Moltmann, "The Destruction and Healing of the Earth: Ecology and Theology", in *God and Globalization. Volume 2: The Spirit and the Modern Authorities* (Max L. Stackhouse and Don S. Browning [eds.]; Harrisburg, PA: Trinity Press International, 2001), 171.

21 See Goheen and Bartholomew, *Living at the Crossroads*, 89-91.

22 Richard Tarnas, *The Passion of the Western Mind: Understanding the Ideas that Have Shaped Our World View* (New York: Ballantine, 1991), 320.

23 Christopher Lasch, *The True and Only Heaven: Progress and Its Critics* (New York: W. W. Norton and Company, 1991), 45.

24 Ronald Wright, *A Short History of Progress*, CBC Massey Lecture Series (Toronto: House of Anansi Press, 1994), 4.

25 Christopher Dawson, *Progress and Religion: An Historical Inquiry* (Washington, D.C.: Catholic University of America Press, 2001; originally published 1929), 15.

26 J. B. Bury, *The Idea of Progress: An Inquiry into its Growth and Origin* (New York: Dover Publications, Inc.,1932), 4.

27 Robert Nisbet, *History of the Idea of Progress* (New York: Basic Books, 1980), 8.

28 Mercier de la Rivière, in Bury, *Idea of Progress*, 173.

29 Hla Myint, *Theories of Welfare Economics* (London: London School of Economics and Political Science, 1948), 9. Quoted in Bob Goudzwaard, *Capitalism and Progress: A Diagnosis of Western Society* (tr. Josina Van Nuis Zylstra; Grand Rapids, MI: Eerdmans, 1979), 23.

30 Lawrence Osborn, *Restoring the Vision: The Gospel and Modern Culture* (London: Mowbray, 1995), 46, 57.

31 Tarnas, *Passion of the Western Mind*, 323.

32 Carl Becker, *The Heavenly City of the Eighteenth-Century Philosophers* (New Haven: Yale University Press, 1932), 31.

33 René Descartes, *Discourse on Method*, 3rd ed. (tr. Donald A. Cress; Indianapolis: Hacket, 1993), 3.

34 In light of the discussion of classical economics below it is interesting to note that Adam Smith wrote much of his treatise *The Wealth of the Nations* in de la Condorcet's home.

35 Bury, *Idea of Progress*, 205.

[36] Lesslie Newbigin, *The Other Side of 1984: Questions for the Churches* (Geneva: World Council of Churches, 1983), 12. Newbigin's reference to Montesquieu (1689-1755) is from his famous first chapter in *De L'Esprit des Lois (On the Spirit of Laws)*, an essay on government, first published in 1748.

[37] George Soros and Jeff Madrick, "The International Crisis: An Interview", *The New York Review of Books* (January 14, 1999): 38. Cited in Bob Goudzwaard, *Globalization and the Kingdom of God* (James W. Skillen [ed.]; Washington, DC: Center for Public Justice; Grand Rapids, MI: Baker Academic, 2001), 24.

[38] Lesslie Newbigin, *Truth to Tell: The Gospel as Public Truth* (Grand Rapids, MI: Eerdmans, 1991), 77.

[39] Robert L. Heilbroner, *The Making of Economic Society* (Englewood Cliffs, NJ: Prentice-Hall, Inc., 1980), 70. His emphasis. The title is significant: *economic* is the primary adjective to describe Western society.

[40] Goudzwaard, *Capitalism and Progress*, 87-88.

[41] Francis Bacon, *Novum Organum*, book 1, aphorism 129.

[42] Lesslie Newbigin, *Foolishness to the Greeks: The Gospel and Western Culture* (Grand Rapids, MI: Eerdmans, 1986), 31.

[43] Newbigin, *Truth to Tell*, 79.

[44] For this image of melody in Augustine's thought see John Neville Figgis, *The Political Aspects of St. Augustine's 'City of God'* (London: Longmans, Green and Co., 1921), 40. This has been republished by Forgotten Books (2007), and the reference to the 'melody' image is on page 33.

[45] Werner Stark, *Social Theory and Christian Thought: A Study of Some Points of Contact. Collected Essays Around a Common Theme* (London: Routledge & Kegan Paul Ltd. 1958), 25-38. After quoting Augustine's *City of God* V, 11, he says: "It is a far cry from these sentiments, characterized as they are by the deepest faith in a personal God . . . to such deistical or atheistical writers as Adam Smith and Kant, or Hegel and Marx. Nevertheless, the structure of their thought is very close to, not to say identical with, that of Augustine. All four . . . were convinced that there operates in history and society a hidden law which coordinates and combines the disjointed and selfish actions of individuals into a great social order or process which achieves other, and indeed, better, in the sense of moral, effects than they have ever contemplated or desired" (28-30).

[46] Quoted by Andrew Skinner in his Introduction to Adam Smith, *The Wealth of Nations* (Harmondsworth: Penguin Books, 1970), 27.

[47] David Wells is one of many who believes that this gamble—or faith commitment—has failed: ". . . study after study conducted during this period [1945-1973] suggested that although newly prosperous Americans had the money and the leisure time to own and do a multitude of things that had been mere dreams for many of their parents, they were increasingly less satisfied with their lives" (*God in the Wasteland: The Reality of Truth in a World of Fading Dreams* [Grand Rapids, MI: Eerdmans, 1994], 13).

[48] Bob Goudzwaard and Harry de Lange, *Beyond Poverty and Affluence: Towards a Canadian Economy of Care* (tr. Mark R. Vander Vennen; Toronto: University of Toronto Press, 1995), 47-48.

[49] Corliss Lamont, *The Philosophy of Humanism*, 8th ed. (Amherst, N.Y.: Humanist Press, 1997), 309.

50 Goudzwaard, *Capitalism and Progress*, 49.

51 Goudzwaard, *Capitalism and Progress*, 50-51.

52 Wells, *God in the Wasteland*, 8.

53 Morris Ginsberg, *Essays in Sociology and Social Philosophy*, vol. 3: *Evolution and Progress* (London: William Heinemann Ltd., 1961), 8. Quoted in Goudzwaard, *Capitalism and Progress*, 81.

54 Cf. title of Becker's book. Cf. Lasch, *True and Only Heaven*, 40-41.

55 Lasch, *True and Only Heaven*, 54.

56 Ibid, 78.

57 Ibid, 78-79.

58 Peter Heslam (ed.), *Globalization and the Good* (Grand Rapids, MI: Eerdmans, 2004), xviii.

59 Heslam's edited volume mentioned in the preceding footnote proceeds in this way. Part 1 focuses on the *potentials* of globalization, part 2 a critique of the *distortions* of global capitalism, and in part 3 advocating practical ways to *reshape* the global economic process in a sustainable way.

60 Newbigin, *Truth to Tell*, 76.

61 Daniel Bell, *The End of Ideology: On the Exhaustion of Political Ideas in the Fifties* (Glencoe, IL: Free Press, 1960).

62 Francis Fukuyama, *The End of Ideology and the Last Man* (Toronto: HarperCollins Canada, 1993).

63 Goudzwaard et al., *Hope in Troubled Times*, 31-45.

64 Ibid, 39.

65 Ibid, 36-38.

66 Dieter Tober, "One World—One Vision for Business", in *Transition to a Global Society* (Suheil Bushrai, Iraj Ayman, and Ervin Laszlo [eds.]; Oxford: Oneworld Publications, 1993), 105.

67 Goudzwaard, *Globalization and the Kingdom of God*, 23. This trend has enormous repercussions for the environment as corporations sideline sustainable environmental policies to make more profit which in turn will attract more capital. Both countries and companies must shape their policies to attract capital.

68 Goudzwaard et al., *Hope in Troubled Times*, 151.

69 Leo Andringa and Bob Goudzwaard, *Globalization and Christian Hope: Economy in the Service of Life* (Washington, DC: Public Justice Resource Centre, 2003), 9-10.

70 Joseph Stiglitz, *Making Globalization Work* (New York: Norton, 2006), 62.

71 Ibid, 78-79.

72 Quoted in Gerald Vandezande, *Christians in the Crisis* (Toronto: Anglican Book Centre, 1984), 47.

73 N. T. Wright, *Surprised by Hope: Rethinking Heaven, the Resurrection, and the Mission of the Church* (New York: HarperCollins Books, 2008), 216-217.

74 Stiglitz, *Making Globalization Work*, 11.

The Emperor's (not-so) New Clothes: Postmodernity, Globalization and the "Triumph" of Modernity

by Craig G. Bartholomew

Introduction

Globalization is notoriously difficult to define and is clearly multi-faceted. Ulrich Beck distinguishes the following dimensions of globalization: communications technology, ecology, economics, work organisation, culture, and civil society.[1] Central to my argument is that John Ralston Saul is right when he asserts that, "you can focus on any piece of Globalization you wish, but in broader terms the argument always comes back to that of *viewing civilization as a whole through an economic prism*".[2] The evidence for this is available in Saul's writings and that of many others; suffice it here to note one of the damning pieces of evidence to support this contention: a multiplicity of international binding market-oriented agreements have been negotiated at the global level but not one in other areas of human life such as work conditions, taxation, health, the environment, child labour, etc.[3]

The New god: Consumerism or "Economics Becoming Religion"[4]

> I don't understand why the most important deity is the increase of gross domestic product. It is not about GDP. It is about the quality of life, and that is something else.[5]

It is my contention that *the* contender for the master-narrative of our day is precisely that pragmatic, consumer approach to life that is central to "globality".[6] One of the great characteristics of Western culture today is *consumerism* in which everything has the potential to become a consumer product. Susan White describes the spirit of consumerism as follows:

> If there is any overarching metanarrative that pur-
> ports to explain reality in the late 20th century, it is
> surely the narrative of the free-market economy. In
> the beginning of this narrative is the self-made, self-
> sufficient human being. At the end of this narrative is
> the big house, the big car, and the expensive clothes.
> In the middle is the struggle for success, the greed, the
> getting-and-spending in a world in which there is no
> such thing as a free lunch. Most of us have made this
> so thoroughly "our story" that we are hardly aware of
> its influence.[7]

The roots of consumerism go back to the commercial revolution of early modernity. Industrialisation played a key role in its development, and the development of mass production took place between 1880 and the 1930s. However it is only in the second half of the twentieth century that consumerism really took hold of Western society: the introduction of the credit card in 1950 may be seen as symbolically marking this transition.

Consumerism points to a culture in which increasingly *the core values derive from consumption rather than the other way around*. In principle everything becomes a product that can be bought and sold. As Don Slater notes, "If there is no principle restricting who can consume what, there is also no principled constraint on what can be consumed: all social relations, activities and objects can in principle be exchanged as commodities. This is one of the most profound secularisations enacted by the modern world."[8] Take sexuality for example. From a Christian perspective it is a profound gift of God to be fully enjoyed within marriage. Pornography has always turned sex into a marketable product but nowadays advertising and the Internet have intensified this process in an unprecedented way so that a huge variety of pornography from any country is immediately available for consumption. Little wonder that porn addiction is growing exponentially.

A consumer culture is furthermore one in which *freedom is equated with individual choice and private life*. Slater notes that freedom to choose whatever product you want in whatever area of life replaces the Enlightenment view of reason as a resource that the individual was encouraged to use against the authority of tradition, religion, etc. Freedom to choose which carrots you want is one thing, but the extension of this freedom into all spheres of life is quite another. As Zygmunt Bauman notes, those who resist the seduction of the market become the dirt of contemporary society. For the "seduced", consumerism becomes the source of liberty, but for the growing number of those who cannot afford this liberty, it becomes oppressive.[9]

Finally a consumer culture is one in which *needs are unlimited and insatiable.* This is ironic because while consumerism promises to meet our needs in an unprecedented way, its continued existence depends on our needs never quite being met: "market society is therefore perpetually haunted by the possibility that needs might be either satisfied or underfinanced".[10] As has often been noted the mall has become the cathedral of our day. However as Jon Pahl notes:

> The problem with the mall is that it actively encourages us to forget any ideals of collectively meaningful life beyond those that the market creates. The mall creates no enduring community, rests upon no tradition, and promotes no values beyond those determined by corporations to whom consumers are all but anonymous units or marks. We are 'united' by the place only in the hierarchy determined by our ability to consume. It is no coincidence that this hierarchy—where the rich get more and the poor get the door—also dominates American politics.[11]

Inseparably related to consumerism is *globalization*, facilitated by the communications revolution that has arrived with the Internet and intimately associated with the spread of free market style economics. Through this technology the big corporations of the day spread their influence around the world like the tentacles of a great octopus. The result is that malls throughout the West look remarkably similar and often the same chains and brands are found again and again.

At the heart of globalization is market economics, and this means that the market and thus economics are strong contenders for the centre of Western culture today. Consequently, if we are to understand what time it is in our culture today we need to look closely at the sort of economics driving the market that is embodied in consumerism. Economics is a complex science, and we cannot here explore it in detail.[12] Suffice it to note that the dominant form of economics today is called neo-classical economics.[13]

Classical economic theory, which is now two centuries old, laid the foundation for the economics that most of Western society now adopts. Two important principles of classical economic theory continue to wield great influence today. The first is *utilitarianism*, the view that human happiness is the result of adding up what is pleasurable (utilities) and subtracting what is painful (disutilities). Later classical economists saw the flow of all marketable goods as utilities and the labour used to produce these goods as a disutility. Utilitarianism led to the conclusion that human happiness is served best when a certain amount of labour produces as much output as possible. "And millions in the West today regard this conclusion, which would equate a rise in the productivity of labour with an increase in happiness, as self-evident."[14] From this perspective, the source of human happiness lies directly in the amount of goods and services produced and sold in the market.

The second principle from classic economic thought which is still dominant today is that we must follow the market wherever it leads because it will naturally guide us to a better future for all.[15] "Indeed, the free working of the market lies close to the centre of Western society's self-definition: in the West it is not government's place to tamper with the market, because this signifies a step away from a 'free-society' and towards a 'totalitarian society'."[16]

Modern neo-classical thought has been concerned not to be seen to recommend any specific direction for society. Thus "modern economics attempts merely to offer explanations, just as the natural sciences attempt merely to explain reality, as it searches for universally valid laws and undeniable facts that can be linked together in an objective and unbiased fashion".[17] The result is that human needs, motives and desires are deliberately excluded from economic calculations because "the economist must confine himself or herself to analysing strictly the processes of the market mechanism".[18]

Goudzwaard and de Lange rightly argue that the result is a terribly distorted worldview because it:

- merely accepts all needs as given
- believes that human needs are unlimited by nature
- sees nature and the environment as "data" and thus excluded from its domain of study
- reduces labour to nothing more than one of several production factors

Goudzwaard and de Lange's critique of this dominant economics is devastating:

> Because it operates in terms of market, it misses entirely the large shards of poverty that the market is unable to register; because it approaches scarcity solely in terms of prices, it cannot assess the economic value of the ecological problem; and because it views labour solely as a paid production factor, it bypasses the problem of the quantity and quality of work. Neo-classical economics was not designed to help solve these problems. It seeks to understand and support only that which relates to production, consumption, income, and money in a market economy.[19]

Our present economy is a "post-care" economy; in it
we engage in the highest possible consumption and
production and only afterwards attempt to mitigate
the mounting care needs with often extremely expensive forms of compensation.[20]

Post-Modernity?

The catch-all phrase which is used to name our time and place in
the West today is postmodernity or postmodernism. "Post" implies
"after" and, at least, denotes a fundamental critique of modernity. Two
world wars, the decidedly negative effects of communism, the holocaust, and large-scale environmental destruction created the context
for a radical questioning of modernity. *How then is it possible amidst
widespread post-modernism in the West that modern economics has
triumphed in the form of globalization?*
    The contemporary debate about postmodernism began in the
1950s and 1960s as a reaction to modernism in the arts.[21] This reaction
was soon extended to a critique of modern culture as a whole. This
does not of course mean that the postmodern debate has no earlier
roots. Little in theories of the postmodern is new, but it is the widespread disillusionment with modernity and the widespread embrace
of previously minority anti-modern positions that makes the present
different, at least philosophically.

Postmodernity in philosophy

In philosophy postmodernism involves a sense of a crisis in modernity or a reaction against modernity. Toulmin, for example, asserts
that, "[i]f an historical era is ending, it is the era of Modernity itself. .
. . What looked in the 19th century like an irresistible river has disappeared in the sand, and we seem to have run aground. . . . we are now
stranded and uncertain of our location. The very project of Modernity
thus seems to have lost momentum, and we need to fashion a succes-
sor program."[22] Neil Smith sums up the feeling of malaise and crisis
when he writes, "The Enlightenment is dead, Marxism is dead . . . and
the author does not feel very well either"![23]
    In this respect postmodernity is perhaps better described as *late
modernity*, for it can be read as the unravelling of tensions hidden deep
in modernity. Harvey observes in *The Condition of Postmodernity* that
modernity rejected tradition and religious authority but held on to the
hope that reason alone would lead us to truth. Postmoderns have given
up on the illusion that reason alone will lead us to truth, but they have
not recovered tradition and authority—instead they courageously cel-

ebrate and play amid our limitations and finitude, a sort of cheerful
nihilism. Indeed, by the end of the 20th century the hubris that the
20th century began with had been seriously undermined, at least in
philosophy.

The major post-modern thinkers such as Lyotard, Habermas,
Rorty, Derrida, etc., all acknowledge the crisis of modernity but their
responses differ. What we should note from them is that postmodern
philosophy challenges the foundations of modernity.

First, postmodern philosophy has raised all sorts of questions about
our capacity to know and how we know and whether we can accurately
represent reality, i.e. about *epistemology*. The possibility of universal
objective knowledge is considered by many to be impossible. Much
postmodern theory is strongly anti-realist and considers all knowledge
to be local, communal and a human construct. Such epistemological
scepticism is captured very clearly in Lyotard's notion of "incredulity
towards metanarratives". The corollary of this scepticism has been a
profound suspicion of the hidden agendas of "neutral" modern knowledge; what claimed to be objective and value free has come to be
seen by many as a mask for powerful ideologies.[24] The consequence of
this scepticism is an awareness of inevitable pluralism in knowledge
and consequent fragmentation. Certainty and truth are regarded by
many with great suspicion—paradoxically the one thing that radical
postmodern thinkers seem quite sure of is that there are no metanarratives or worldviews! There is widespread disagreement about the role
of rationality and whether or not knowledge can be grounded. Some,
like Norris, Habermas and Gellner seek to reconstruct the project of
modernity. Others would seek a genuinely post-modern position in
which rationality is always perspectival. Others like MacIntyre seek
to do justice to the perspectival nature of rationality while holding on
to more universal perspectives.[25]

Epistemology is closely related in the second place to *ontology*
and here too postmodernity has undermined the broad consensus of
modernity. A common ontological presupposition in postmodern theory is that language is the most fundamental aspect of reality. Derrida is
a good example of this view. Much postmodern theory has little room
for any notion of an order in reality existing apart from human construction through language. Scepticism about human knowing goes
hand in hand with a high view of the human community as constructing the worlds in which we live. This too reflects a particular ontology.

Finally, epistemology and ontology are inseparable from *anthropology* in the sense of the nature of humankind. The rationalistic autonomous view of the human which was so dominant in modernity has
been undermined and a plurality of alternatives proposed. Rorty, for
example, suggests that we should think of the moral self as "a network
of beliefs, desires, and emotions with nothing behind it—no substrate

behind the attributes. For purposes of moral and political deliberation and conversation, a person just *is* that network."[26] Foucault stresses the extent to which our view of the human person is a construct when he asserts that

> strangely enough, man—the study of whom is supposed by the naive to be the oldest investigation since Socrates—is probably no more than a kind of rift in the order of things, or, in any case, a configuration whose outlines are determined by the new position he has so recently taken up in the field of knowledge . . . man is only a recent invention, a figure not yet two centuries old, a new wrinkle in our knowledge, . . . that will disappear as soon as that knowledge has discovered a new form.[27]

If thinkers like Baudrillard play down the possibility of the human subject acting in any significant way, others stress the possibility of human self-creation.

Epistemology, ontology, anthropology: That so much postmodern philosophy is related to these areas indicates the extent to which the philosophical *foundations* of modernity are in crisis. Postmodern philosophy is characterised by pluralism, uncertainty, instability and fragmentation. The old certainties seem to have gone with no unified vision to replace them.

It is important to note however that the roots of modernity have been called into question by many of these postmodern philosophers, but not altogether abandoned. Mary Hesse's observation in this respect is acute: "The liberal consensus has so successfully established itself as the ideology of Western intellectual culture, that it has become almost invisible as the presupposition of every postmodern debate."[28] Human autonomy, for example, tends to remain as firmly entrenched as ever, the difference being that we now simply have to learn to live with the uncertainties. It should also not be forgotten that the nihilistic and relativistic side of postmodern theory is only one aspect of the contemporary situation. Other modern types of philosophy such as phenomenology and metaphysics continue to flourish.

Thus, within the pluralistic world of philosophy a plethora of worldviews compete for attention. The postmodern philosophers are the best known and it is their voices that mostly get heard in relation to the condition of our time as postmodern. This is helpful in the sense that important shifts *are* taking place and as Lyon says the concept of postmodernity is a valuable "problematic" that alerts us to key questions concerning our age:[29] "the question of postmodernity offers an opportunity to reappraise modernity, to read the signs of the times as indicators that modernity itself is unstable, unpredictable, and to forsake the foreclosed future that it once seemed to promise".[30]

Postmodernism and Other Disciplines

The postmodern debate is by no means confined to philosophy. Considering the way in which postmodernity has challenged the foundations of modern philosophy it is not surprising that postmodernism has spread like wildfire to the other subjects in the academy. From the arts and philosophy the debate about postmodernity has spilt over into every other academic discipline so that wherever you look in the academy you are likely to find titles with postmodernity in them.

We cannot here explore the impact of postmodernism in all the different subjects in the academy. But whether you are studying literature, psychology, art, theology, economics, law, history, science, medicine, drama, or any other subject you will find that there is now available a body of literature on postmodernism and your particular subject. For example, if you study English literature you will find courses available on critical theory which includes much, often impenetrable, postmodern philosophy. You will also likely find a course on the postmodern novel. In order to get a taste of what postmodernism means in a discipline we will take one example that is close to home for me, namely biblical studies. Nowadays there is a whole range of literature dealing with postmodernism and biblical studies in one way or another.

Postmodernism's effect on Old Testament interpretation has been to undermine old ways of reading the Old Testament and to introduce a smorgasbord of new and often zany ways of reading it. A prominent example of a postmodern Old Testament scholar is David Clines from Sheffield in the United Kingdom. In his early years of Old Testament scholarship Clines was a conservative proponent of the historical critical method, the "scientific" way of reading the Bible that emerged in modernity.[31] More recently however, Clines has shifted considerably from his earlier approaches towards a postmodern position which embraces textual indeterminacy—the view that a text has as many meanings as readers—and the view that the more ways we read the Bible the better. Cline's position is clearly articulated in his 1993 article, "Possibilities and Priorities of Biblical Interpretation in an International Perspective".[32]

Clines stresses the actual and, in his opinion, desirable pluralism in Old Testament studies nowadays. He used to think that Old Testament scholars were all doing the same thing in their scholarship but now he realises that different scholars have different goals.[33] In response to our changed context Clines proposes an end-user theory of interpretation. Clines says:

I want to propose a model for biblical interpretation that accepts the realities of our pluralist context. I call it by various names: a goal-oriented hermeneutic, an end-user theory of interpretation, a market philosophy of interpretation, or a discipline of 'comparative interpretation'. . . . First comes the recognition that texts do not have determinate meanings. . . . The second axis for my framework is provided by the idea of interpretative communities. . . . There is no objective standard by which we can know whether one interpretation or other is right; we can only tell whether it has been accepted. . . . There are no determinate meanings and there are no universally agreed upon legitimate interpretations.

What are biblical scholars then to be doing with themselves? To whom shall they appeal for their authorisation, from where shall they gain approval for their activities, and above all, who will pay them? . . . If there are no "right" interpretations, and no validity in interpretation beyond the assent of various interest groups, biblical interpreters have to give up the goal of determinate and universally acceptable interpretations, and devote themselves to interpretations they can sell—in whatever mode is called for by the communities they choose to serve. I call this "customised" interpretation.[34]

Such an end-user approach could entail recycling old waste interpretations which were thought to have been superseded by the progress model of modernity. These discarded interpretations could be revived in a post-critical form to stock afresh the shelves of the interpretational supermarket.

In Old Testament and biblical studies a great variety of postmodern readings of biblical texts can now be found. But once again it is important to note that the postmodern worldview—if for convenience sake we can call it that—is only one paradigm among many operating in biblical studies. Postmodern readers disagree among themselves—not all, for example, would agree with Clines that we should intentionally do readings that will sell!—old style historical criticism continues and there is also an encouraging trend developing which is called theological interpretation, which deliberately reads the Bible as Christian Scripture with the church in mind. As in philosophy we are in a pluralist situation in which a variety of worldviews compete as the framework within which to read the Bible.

You might think from the above that postmodernism is primarily an academic game. But this is far from the case. Postmodern trends are also found all over popular culture. Because of the great diversity that comes under this large umbrella of postmodernism, it is hard to characterise just what makes up the postmodern worldview. Indeed a celebration of diversity and a resistance to being pinned down are part of its ethos. But generally speaking we can see the following characteristics as central to the postmodern worldview:

- a reaction to modernity or the old ways of doing things
- a rejection of worldviews or comprehensive stories of the world which claim to tell the truth about the world—in place of this we find a celebration of our limitations or what has been called cheerful nihilism
- a confidence in ourselves to create our own meanings

In their resistance to worldviews postmoderns reject the possibility of discovering the truth about the world. Many would therefore claim strongly that they do not have a worldview but instead have a collage of elements that they use as they find helpful. But it is important to note that it is not so easy to escape having a worldview. Ironically, their very denial of worldviews conceals their own adherence to a very specific worldview. To assert, for example, that we cannot know the truth about the world is to put oneself in a position so as to be able to see that this clearly is the case! Under the guise of epistemic humility—we cannot ever know the truth—this approach turns out to be far from humble!

As an often fuzzy and contradictory worldview, postmodernism has slain its thousands, so much so that some think we have moved from modernity to postmodernity. But we need to stress once again that even though the postmodern worldview has spread throughout culture, in all the areas it is found we also find alternative worldviews competing for attention. Take English literature for example. Here again postmodernism has slain its thousands and attending a literature conference is often more like attending a conference on postmodern philosophy. Deconstructive and radical feminist and a smorgasbord of alternative ways of reading and writing novels abound. But, loads of English professors and lecturers and writers resist the postmodern approach to literature.

Postmodernism and Global Consumerism

We need to distinguish the increasingly convincing critique of the modern at the level of theory—notably

in the case of Heidegger, Lyotard, or Habermas—
from the fact that, at a practical level, we remain
thoroughly enmeshed in modernity, largely because
of the stranglehold that technology, the stepchild of
modernity, has on our daily lives.[35]

To return to our question posed above, how is it possible that the
postmodern critique of modernity has accompanied the triumph of
consumerism? Postmodernism has savaged modernity but without
ever abandoning the secular humanism at its roots. Take religion for
example: Derrida's, Vattimo's and other postmoderns' engagement
with religion is widely celebrated as a recovery of religion. There is
some truth to this and I for one welcome the way in which they have
put religion back on academic agendas. But it is crucial to note that the
form of religion advocated is invariably a post-Nietzschean, hollowed
out version of particular religions.[36] As Gadamer noted at the Capri
debate with Derrida, Vattimo, and others, they are all Kantian and the
old doctrines of the church are not recoverable.

The astigmatism of postmodernism is particularly noticeable in
its failure to engage with the renaissance of Christianity and Islam in
the two-thirds world where, unlike in the West, both religions are exploding and tend to be orthodox in their beliefs and capable of radical
social critique in their practices. Thus postmodernism has savaged its
own worldview while remaining adamant that there is no alternative.
Despite protests about the major ethical contribution of postmodernism the result has been a wounded modernity with little else to do
than what appears to work. In other words postmodernism has inad-
vertently opened wide the door for Western pragmatism of the worst
sort. With the restraints of traditional Western liberalism in tatters the
ground has been cleared for the triumph of technology and the market.

The variety and fragmentation that postmodernism has precipitat-
ed in our culture and its attack on modernity, especially at a theoretical level, leaves Western culture increasingly without an intellectual
centre from which to draw its meaning and practices. Several cultural
commentators have noted this, and here we refer to two evocative
examples. At the outset of his *After Virtue* Alasdair MacIntyre imagines a hypothetical scenario in which for various reasons the natural
sciences suffer a catastrophe.[37] Laboratories are burnt down, books
and libraries of science burnt, and scientists eliminated from society.
Later a reaction sets in and people try to recover science, "But all they
possess are fragments: a knowledge of experiments detached from any
knowledge of the theoretical context which gave them significance;
parts of theories unrelated either to the other bits and pieces of theory
which they possess or to experiment; instruments whose use has been
forgotten; half-chapters from books, single pages from articles, not

always fully legible because torn and charred".[38] Nonetheless the fragments are reassembled and the resulting "body" of knowledge is taught and learnt. People continue to use the vocabulary of science but the contexts of such knowledge has been lost so that their use of the reassembled knowledge is arbitrary and random. But essentially we are left with fragments and simply don't know how they fit together anymore. For MacIntyre this is an apt description of the situation of the world today in terms of *morality*:

> The hypothesis which I wish to advance is that in the actual world which we inhabit the language of morality is in the same state of grave disorder as the language of natural science in the imaginary world which I described. What we possess . . . are the frag-ments of a conceptual scheme, parts which now lack those contexts from which their significance derived. We possess indeed simulacra of morality, we continue to use many of the key expressions. But we have—very largely, if not entirely—lost our comprehension, both theoretical and practical, of morality.[39]

Our second example comes from Oliver O'Donovan's reflections on politics today. O'Donovan notes the challenge that modernity pre-sented to Christians:

> that crisis was precipitated by the presence of a rival confidence, a massive cultural certainty that united natural science, democratic politics, technology, and colonialism. Today this civilizational ice-shelf has broken up, and though some of the icebergs floating around are huge—natural science and technology, especially, drift on as though nothing has happened—they are not joined together anymore, nor joined to the land. The four great facts of the twentieth century that broke the certainty in pieces were two world wars, the reversal of European colonization, the threat of the nuclear destruction of the human race, and, most recently, the evidence of long term ecological crisis. The master-narrative that was to have delivered us the crown of civilization has delivered us insuperable dangers. So Western civilization finds itself the heir of political institutions and traditions which it val-ues without any clear idea why, or to what extent, it values them. Faced with decisions about their future development it has no way of telling what counts as

improvements and what as subversions. It cannot
tell where "Straight ahead" lies, let alone whether it
ought to keep on going there. The master-narrative
has failed; and even its most recent revised edition,
announced as "postmodern", which declares the collapse to be the glorious last chapter, and plurality to
be the great unifying principle, merely stands to the
failure as the angel in the famous Czech joke stands to
his own constant failures of prediction: "It's all in the
plan! Don't worry! It's all in the plan!"[40]

Postmodernity has reduced the grand story of modernity to disconnected fragments and icebergs. These are evocative images of how
the underpinnings of modernity at a worldviewish level are in bad
shape. But, just as in the Bible the casting out of a demon may create the space for seven more to return, the reality of postmodernism
should not for a moment make us think that modernity has vanished. A
vacuum at the centre cries out to be filled and there are ways in which
aspects of modernity, far from vanishing, have firmly occupied this
centre. As Heslam perceptively notes,

The irony of the present situation is that confidence
in the quest for the universal co-exists with a growing scepticism about the validity of the quest. As a
consequence, the universal is rapidly being replaced
by the much less well-defined concept of the global.
This concept, sometimes referred to as "globality",
lacks a grand scheme based on deeply held convictions and high ideals. It is about people all over the
world being able to eat the same kind of hamburgers,
drink the same kind of soft drink, watch the same TV
programmes and use the same software packages. .
. . The ascendant ideologies of capitalism and consumerism . . . are propounded as the only systems
that work, and it is "what works" . . . that is accorded
special status in the postmodern worldview.[41]

Our discussion above of David Clines' approach to biblical interpretation is particularly illuminating in this respect. Clines advocates
wild pluralism in biblical interpretation but in the name of this "liberty" ends up embracing a consumer approach to the Bible: "Do",
he tells us, "what will sell and what you desire". Richard Bauckham,
another biblical scholar, alerts us to the potential danger of postmodernism in relation to consumerism and globalization:

> The alleged incredulity towards metanarratives has a
> certain plausibility in contemporary Western society,
> but it can distract from the very powerful, late-mod-
> ern grand narrative of consumerist individualism and
> free-market globalization, which aims to subsume
> precisely postmodern plurality. It appears liberating
> in its valorization of consumer lifestyle choices but
> is oppressive in the much more realistic sense that
> affluent postmodern theorists are liable to ignore: it
> enriches the rich while leaving the poor poor, and it
> destroys the environment. In this way it continues the
> kind of oppression that the modern metanarratives of
> progress have always legitimated. . . . Postmodern
> relativism offers no cogent resistance to this metanar-
> rative, which is not threatened by diversity as long as
> its overarching framework of alleged economic real-
> ity goes unchallenged.[42]

Economist and sociologist Alan Storkey is far more direct: "postmodernism is consumption".[43]

The Emperor's Clothes

What are we to make of our new deity, our new emperor? It is a
mistake to write off all that globalization has achieved. Since 1950
world trade has increased dramatically—between twelve and twenty-
two fold. Production of technology has increased six times, international trade in technology nine times. In 1956 one could have eighty-
nine transatlantic telephone conversations at one time; today, care of
satellites and fibre optics, one million are available, plus faxes and
emails.[44] And of course global co-operation is potentially very good.

However, at present the cons far outweigh the pros. Stiglitz famously remarked that free trade has not failed; it has never been tried!
The geographer Harm De Blij points out that globalization has established a—predominantly northern—global core which contains fifteen
percent of the world's population but records nearly seventy-five percent of the world's annual income.[45] The inequality between rich and
poor, north and south continues to widen while increasingly a small
number of corporations dominate the economic wealth of the world.
"There is more than a hint of apartheid in the regional geography of
the world today."[46]

Not surprisingly the economic paradigm of globalization has not
been good for the environment. In his acute analysis of the ethics of
global warming, Northcott asserts that,

> At the heart of the present crisis is not a conventional empire but the global market empire fashioned by the United States and Europe in the last fifty years, as governments have deregulated money and trade and freed up economic actors and financial markets to enable maximal wealth accumulation by banks and corporations without regard to political sovereignty or territorial limits.[47]

In his analysis of factors leading to an end in the optimistic confidence in globalization Saul mentions in addition:

- The current mess the airline industry is in. The airline industry is an essential service but, "failure has been snatched out of the jaws of success by restructuring the whole thing through open-market forces into an oligopoly system dependent on the bargain-basement methods of shrinking margins, short term planning and long term instability".[48]
- The fact that globalization has led to a decline in healthy competition and the rise of oligopolies.
- The scandal of the appropriation of intellectual property by world trade.
- The commercialisation of pharmaceuticals: "The question is quite simple: How long will a handful of the most profitable joint stock corporations in the world, whose declared purpose is human well-being, be allowed to cause tens of thousands of premature deaths each year in the name of patent protection and stockholder interests? There are growing signs that the answer is not much longer."[49]

All in all our new emperor's clothes are not looking too good! But what should we do about them?

Scouting the Future

If our analysis of globalization is even close to correct what, from a Christian perspective, might we expect to happen? This is a vital question if we have any chance of getting ahead of the game, rather than proverbially bringing up the rear, as Christians are so prone to do. Are there any clues that will help us to scout out the future so that we can prepare ourselves for mission to our culture?

At a very basic level what we would expect from an overemphasis on the economic dimension of life is a kickback from the other aspects of life as God has made it. Intriguingly we are already starting to see such a reaction. Saul documents multiple signs of an end in the belief in globalization:

> None of this means that the global economy is coming to an end. What it does mean is that the Globalization model of the 1970s and '80s has faded away. It is now, at best, a regional project—that region being the West. But even there, the moves to regulation and the return of nationalism are carrying the twenty or so old democracies in quite unexpected directions. It could be said that American nationalism is the primary force in undermining the old Global project. Washington's lead role in inserting TRIPS [trade-related aspects of intellectual property rights] into the WTO [World Trade Organization], then defending the power of pharmaceutical transnationals over the desperate needs of countries caught in epidemics, then devaluing its dollar to try to solve national problems whatever the effect on other countries, have all demonstrated to weaker countries that nation-states and their own view of the national interest are still far more important than any international economic theory.[50]

As the reactions to globalization set in a real danger may be a new vacuum.[51] Christians have an opportunity to attend to the expected reaction to globalization and to help open the way to genuine global co-operation. How might we do this?

Firstly, Western Christians should develop a robust and nuanced critique of postmodernism. In brief, we can welcome much of postmodernism's critique of modernity but neither the autonomous humanism that remains deeply entrenched nor the nihilism and relativism that beckons, nor its failure to deliver healthy prospects for healing modernity. Too many Christians in the West have succumbed to the lure of postmodernism, being willing to disembowel their own tradition even while orthodox Christianity is exploding globally. As Plantinga, who describes postmodernism as creative anti-realism, perceptively notes,

> Creative antirealism is presently popular among philosophers; this is the view that it is human behaviour—in particular, human thought and language—that is somehow responsible for the fundamental structure of the world and for the fundamental kinds of entities there are. From a theistic point of view, however, universal creative anti-realism is at best a piece of laughable bravado. For *God*, of course, owes

neither his existence nor his properties to us and our
ways of thinking; the truth is just the reverse. And
so far as the created universe is concerned, while it
indeed owes its existence and character to activity on
the part of a person, that person is certainly not a *human* person.[52]

Secondly, in conjunction with Southern Christians we need to
develop far more nuanced analyses of what time it is in the West and
in our global culture today. So much Christian cultural analysis has
allowed Western postmodernism to set the agenda for contemporary
cultural analysis without noting, as Mary Hesse points out, the hidden
liberal assumptions framing the debate. Christianity is exploding in
the South and is of the sort that finds the arcane debates of postmodernism irrelevant while being focused on the very real economic and
political realities of development.

Thirdly, it is important to be critically aware of developments
in globalization. There is already a considerable body of literature
emerging that engages critically with globalization.[53] We need honed
Christian economic insight of the sort that Goudzwaard has provided
us with for decades and viable alternatives such as Goudzwaard and de
Lange's economy of care. A new generation of Christian scholars and
practitioners will need to take up this cause and to map out in detail
healthy ways forward economically. We also need non-reductionistic
theories of globalization which integrate the different elements and
resist the distorted reduction of globalization to neoliberal economics.
Christians have a particular role to play in repeatedly drawing attention to the crucial religious dimension of globalization, a dimension
that Western analysts still find hard to take seriously.

Fourthly, we must take whatever steps we can to resist the distortions of globalization. Western Christians are in the very orbits
of power from which the worst excesses of globalization are issuing
forth, and we need to find our voice and wallets in resisting these
excesses. *We* need to take the initiative in establishing alternative practices in the heart of globalization. We need to become implaced *locally*
so that we have a place from which genuine global co-operation can
take place.

Fifthly it is essential to take seriously the fact that the new centres of Christianity are now in the two-thirds worlds where population
growth is at its highest.[54] Most Christians now live in the countries
that will exert most influence in the century ahead, and Christians in
the West need to work *now* to develop co-operation with this mass of
vital Christianity and to attend together to the challenges of our world.
Christianity is possibly unique in the opportunity it has at present for
the development of genuine global co-operation.

CRAIG G. BARTHOLOMEW (Ph.D., Bristol University) is H. Evan Runner Professor of Philosophy and Biblical Studies at Redeemer University College, Ancaster, Ontario, and Director of the Paideia Centre of Public Theology. His most recent books are *Reading Ecclesiastes* (Baker, 2009) and, co-authored (with Michael Goheen), *Living at the Crossroads: An Introduction to Christian Worldview* (Baker, 2008) and *Drama of Scripture: Finding Our Place in the Story of the Bible* (Baker, 2004).

NOTES

1. Ulrich Beck, *What is Globalization?* (Cambridge: Polity, 2001), 19. Notably lacking from his—albeit incomplete—list, and from his discussion of globalization is religion.
2. John Ralston Saul, *The Collapse of Globalism And the Reinvention of the World* (Toronto: Penguin Canada, 2006), 20. Italics mine.
3. Ibid, 25.
4. See Saul, *Collapse of Globalism*, ch. 5. "A Short History of Economics Becoming Religion".
5. Vaclav Havel, interviewed in the *International Herald Tribune*, 22 October 2004, 1.
6. Beck defines "Globalism" as, "the view that the world market eliminates or supplants political action—that is, the ideology of rule by the world market, the ideology of neoliberalism" (*What is Globalization?*, 9).
7. Susan White, "A New Story to Live By?" *Transmission*, Spring 1998, 3-4.
8. Don Slater, *Consumer Culture and Modernity* (Cambridge: Polity, 1997), 27.
9. Zygmunt Bauman, *Freedom* (Milton Keynes: Open University Press, 1988).
10. Slater, *Consumer Culture*, 29.
11. Jon Pahl, *Shopping Malls and Other Sacred Spaces* (Grand Rapids, MI: Brazos, 2003), 79.
12. See Bob Goudzwaard and Harry M. de Lange, *Beyond Poverty and Affluence: Toward a Canadian Economy of Care* (Toronto: University of Toronto Press, 1995).
13. In what follows I am deeply indebted to Goudzwaard and de Lange, *Beyond Poverty and Affluence*.
14. Ibid, 47.
15. A key thinker in this respect is Adam Smith (1723-1790). In defense of Smith it should be noted that in his context he thought that the production of more goods and the opening of markets would lead to a trickle down effect which would raise the level of the poor. Sadly market economics has since developed such that the gap between the rich and the poor is widening so that it is clear that simply freeing the market does not lead to a trickle down effect.
16. Goudzwaard and de Lange, *Beyond Poverty and Affluence*, 48.
17. Ibid, 51.
18. Ibid, 53.
19. Ibid, 61.

[20] Ibid, 65.

[21] See Hans Bertens, *The Idea of the Postmodern* (London; NY: Routledge, 1995) 20, and Margaret A. Rose, *The Post-Modern and the Post-Industrial: A Critical Analysis* (Cambridge: Cambridge University Press, 1991) 3-20, on the earliest uses of the term "postmodern". Bertens points out that after the 1870s "'Postmodern' resurfaced in 1934, in 1939, and in the 1940s. From then on sightings began to multiply. There is, however, very little continuity between these early uses and the debate on postmodernism as it gets underway in the course of the 1960s."

[22] Stephen Toulmin, *Cosmopolis: The Hidden Agenda of Modernity* (Chicago: The University of Chicago Press, 1990), 3.

[23] Neil Smith, *Uneven Development: Nature, Capital, and the Production of Space* (First edition; New York: Blackwell Publishers, 1984), iii.

[24] See especially Michel Foucault in this respect.

[25] Alasdair MacIntyre, *Whose Justice? Which Rationality?* (London: Duckworth, 1988).

[26] Richard Rorty, "Postmodernist Bourgeois Liberalism", *Journal of Philosophy* 80, 10 (1983) 583-589; 585-586.

[27] Michael Foucault, *The Order of Things: An Archeology of the Human Sciences* (London: Tavistock, 1970), xxiii.

[28] Mary Hesse, "How to be Postmodern Without Being a Feminist", *The Monist* 77/4 [1994], 445-461; 457.

[29] David Lyon, *Postmodernity* (Buckingham: Open UP, 1994), 84-85.

[30] Ibid, 70.

[31] Its main methods are source, form, redaction and tradition criticism.

[32] David J.A. Clines, "Possibilities and Priorities of Biblical Interpretation in an International Perspective", *Biblical Interpretation* 1, 1 (1993), 67-87.

[33] Ibid, 71.

[34] Ibid, 78, 79, 80.

[35] Edward Casey, *Getting Back into Place: Toward a Renewed Understanding of the Place-World* (Indianapolis: Indiana University Press, 1993), 389, 390.

[36] See, for example, Gianni Vattimo, *Belief* (Stanford: Stanford University Press, 1999).

[37] For the details of his imagined scenario see Alasdair MacIntyre, *After Virtue: A Study in Moral Theory* (London: Duckworth, 2nd ed., 1985) 1-3.

[38] Ibid, 1.

[39] Ibid, 2.

[40] Oliver O'Donovan, *The Ways of Judgement* (Grand Rapids, MI: Eerdmans, 2005), xii, xiii.

[41] Peter Heslam, *Globalization: Unravelling the New Capitalism* (Cambridge: Grove, 2002), 7-8.

[42] Richard Bauckham, "Reading Scripture as a Coherent Story", in Ellen F. Davis and Richard B. Hays (eds.), *The Art of Reading Scripture* (Grand Rapids, MI: Eerdmans, 2003), 38-53; 46.

[43] Alan Storkey, "Postmodernism is Consumption", in Craig Bartholomew and Thorsten Moritz (eds.), *Christ and Consumerism: A Critical Analysis of the Spirit*

of the Age (Carlisle, Cumbria, UK: Paternoster Press, 2000), 115. This book is also online at http://www.reformationalpublishingproject.com/pdf_books/Scanned_Books_PDF/ChristandConsumerism.pdf (accessed 19 March 2009).

[44] Saul, *Collapse Of Globalism*, 21.

[45] Harm De Blij, *The Power of Place: Geography, Destiny, and Globalization's Rough Landscape* (NY: Oxford University Press, 2009), 13.

[46] Ibid, 18. See Saul, *Collapse of Globalism*, 184-187.

[47] Michael S. Northcott, *A Moral Climate: The Ethics of Global Warming* (Maryknoll, NY: Orbis Books, 2007), 5.

[48] Saul, *Collapse of Globalism*, 176.

[49] Ibid, 181.

[50] Ibid, 204.

[51] See Saul, *Collapse of Globalism*, ch. 23, "The New Vacuum: An Interregnum of Morbid Symptoms".

[52] Alvin Plantinga, "Advice to Christian Philosophers", *Faith and Philosophy* 1, 3 [1984] 253-271; 269.

[53] E.g. Saul, *Collapse of Globalism*; Beck, *What is Globalization?*; Colin Hines, *Localization: A Global Manifesto* (London: Earthscan, 2000).

[54] See Philip Jenkins, *The Next Christendom* (Oxford: Oxford University Press, 2002); *The New Faces of Christianity* (Oxford: Oxford University Press, 2006).

Globalization, Economics, and the Modern Worldview

by Bob Goudzwaard

Globalization is an undeniable and ongoing process in our reality; it is now fixed in the hearts and minds of many politicians and scientists. Yet even the word 'globalization' was not known forty years ago and certainly was not in use by economists. What has happened over that time—not only within the world-economy as a whole, but also within the reflections of economic science in relation to this remarkable new phenomenon? Was this outcome what economists expected or predicted forty years ago? I sincerely doubt that.

Let us therefore take as our point of entry the somewhat complex relationship between the factual process of globalization on one side and theoretical economic reflection on the other side. I begin by making a small but important comparison between the usual reaction of economists to the present process of globalization and the reaction to it from other social sciences, such as sociology, political science and social philosophy.

Globalization: Factual Process or Human Project?

Immediately we meet something that might surprise us: an initial comparison of the reactions to globalization already reveals a general divergence between the views of economists and that of other social scientists whose reaction is usually broader, sharper, and more colourful than that of most economists. The majority of Western-oriented economists approach globalization as a merely factual process of economic development. Of course, globalization is studied in terms of market behaviour and possible market equilibriums. From the viewpoint of welfare economics it is also analysed in terms of the final distribution of income and wealth. But for most Western economists, globalization belongs to the world of what is given—the world of objective facts and data that can be neither changed nor denied. This is significantly different from the usual reactions or reflections we encounter in the other social sciences.

I could give many examples—for instance by referring to the writings of Manuel Castells[1], Alain Touraine[2], and Pierre Bourdieu[3]—but I restrict myself here to one illustration. It is taken from *Postmodern Ethics*, written by the famous social philosopher and ethicist Zygmunt Bauman. In it Bauman discusses the influence of what he calls the "globalization of the economy"[4] upon present governmental behaviour:

> Whatever has remained of economic management in state politics is reduced to competitive offers of attractively profitable and pleasurable conditions (low taxes, low-cost and docile labour, good interest-rates and—last but not least—pleasant pastimes for all-expenses-paid travelling managers), hopefully seductive enough to tempt the touring capital to schedule a stop-over.[5]

What is remarkable in this quotation is firstly the wide framework of his reflection, much wider than economists usually adopt. For instance, he draws attention to the change in government behaviour by a critical identification of the growing volatility of capital-movements around the globe, which he dares to call "touring capital". But secondly, Bauman is also aware of the need to make a distinction between globalization as a factual *process* and globalization as a *project*, which is to say a plan or an intention in the heads and minds of many political and economic actors who have the conscious will to lead the world to a greater economic and financial market-oriented uniformity. *But you will look in vain for similar distinctions in the usual reflections that economists make on globalization.*

Now we might want to suggest that this other approach, here illustrated by Bauman, is merely an expression of the differences between economics and the other social sciences, that is, differences in the structure of their disciplines and in the methodology of their analyses. After all, economists are expected to study the economic aspect of globalization and not the entire phenomenon in all its aspects. That is no doubt true, but there is something else at work here that needs to be explained. In order to convince you that my intuition here is justified, we need firstly some kind of coherent interpretation of globalization itself, as a relatively recent empirical phenomenon. After that I will return more precisely to the usual way by which economists go about their investigations.

Describing the Orbit of Globalization

The process of globalization refers primarily to a shift that has taken place and is still taking place in the world today, a shift from local and national markets to regional and global markets. Or, to put it another way, it is about the mutual opening up of national economies to each other. This tendency is indeed undeniable. Consider this fact: since 1950 the real Gross Production in the world has increased by a factor of five, and at the same time the total export volume has increased by a factor of ten and the export of manufactured goods has even increased twenty-fold. A crucial role in this development continues to be played by the emerging transnational corporations. Their number has increased sevenfold within the last twenty-five years. Even the commodity trade of the countries of the South is now concentrated in the hands of a mere fifteen multinational companies. Globalization has thus from the beginning been not only a process, related to an increase in the volume of exports, trades, and flows of capital, but also has possessed an element of agency, related to a purposive increase in economic action. Increasingly, more producers and investors have begun to pursue business opportunities and possibilities in the so-called global market.

Further dimensions to globalization remain for us to disentangle. These come especially to the fore if we look for what is really new in this phenomenon. What is new is sometimes formulated as the addition of a layer of existence onto reality itself. At the very least globalization adds a layer to the common *perception* of reality. The international political and economic dimension is, of course, not new. It has existed for millennia. But in those past times, the wider world itself usually only came into sight as the end-point or the climax of local and national initiatives and activities. Increasingly now, the "global scene" itself functions as the starting point of numerous actions, present at the very beginning of many forms of human activity. Globalization refers primarily to those processes, which from the outset have a worldwide character. Globalization can therefore at best be compared to a kind of satellite, circling around the world in its own orbit, out of which it influences all citizens of all nations. Of course, globalization needed certain booster-rockets to arrive in its own orbit, like the Information and Communication Technology (ICT), the General Agreement on Tariffs and Trade (GATT) or the World Trade Organization (WTO), and the system of Bretton Woods. But it has now reached a sufficient height to maintain its own sovereign course around the world.

Let us briefly consider a few examples of this important shift:

1. Several multi-national companies had appeared already in the 1960s and 70s. Using their "motherland" as their home base, multinational companies opened up places of business as their "daughters"

in various other countries. In more recent decades we have witnessed the emergence of the "transnational" corporation. The transnational company has no specific ties to a mother country; it can easily move its main office when by reasons of efficiency it must do so. Rather than belonging to a specific country, the transnational corporation is a citizen of the world. It operates out of that global optic from the outset.

2. A second example is the rapid emergence of so-called global capital. Global capital circulates in enormous quantities around the world, in the form of short-run bank loans in foreign currencies, or in portfolio investments of a very speculative nature. If the prospects of profit making are favourable, global capital can arrive in a country in huge quantities. But it can also leave overnight, as Mexico and Argentina observed with much pain in recent times. Global capital constantly ricochets around the whole world, driven by its quest for maximum short term financial gain in a climate of always changing expectations. Indeed it belongs to an autonomous global circuit.

Venture-capital, in the form of private-equity investments, is a relatively new member of the same global speculative family. Here we find financial investment companies like Alpinvest, Capital Research and Centaurus, which try to make extreme worldwide profits in the shortest possible time by buying, controlling and selling company-shares. All this has led to an enormous expansion of the global financial markets, which, by approximation, have grown an unbelievable 120% over the past three years. The remarkable degree of vulnerability of most "real economies" to the whims of "virtual" global capital has now indeed become quite apparent. *The Economist* recently highlighted the growing subordination of national political and economic life to the regime of the global financial markets in the following words: "The financial markets have become the judges and the juries of all economic policies."

3. A third and last example of the new global dimension lies in the patterns of consumption and communication. Internet is, by nature, a global network. Globally specific symbols of consumption have now materialised. Globalization, for example, has been called "McDonaldization", (George Ritzer's term). Popular culture has also become partially global: there are universal "Top 40 hit parades" and blockbuster movies that are released simultaneously around the world. Such standardised popular culture is now the order of the day.

Globalization as Systematic Modernisation

Let me try to summarise. Globalization, seen as one of the most dominant empirical processes of our time, is primarily a market and money-oriented dynamic phenomenon. It is also, therefore, very much

geared to technological and financial impulses. But the world of global finance is most dynamic of all those dynamic processes. It is not by
accident that it has gradually become the heart of the present process
of globalization. And thirdly, globalization is full of the will to transform existing economic realities by modernising them. Globalization
is obviously a systematic method or effort towards an ongoing modernisation of all cultures—surely not only the Western ones.

With this last remark we reach a very interesting point in our whole
investigation. Usually we use words like *modern* and *modernisation*
only as catchwords. They stand for everything that involves a departure
from former traditions and long-established institutions. We also use it
in that way for the development of theories. I would argue that those
words, *modern* and *modernisation*, are far from devoid of any content,
but are thoroughly Western. And so, for the sake of making our argument complete by locating the roots of the present process of globalization, we need to reflect for a short while upon the history of Modernity
itself, a concept which was born in the heart of Western culture.

Most philosophers consider the origins of Modernity to be found
in the 16th and 17th centuries, quite shortly after the start of Western
colonial expansion, but some time before the outbreak of what is now
called the Enlightenment. A deep sense of insecurity prevailed at that
time in Western society. There was a lot of political and religious un-
rest, with constantly changing loyalties facing ordinary citizens. But
there was also a growing awareness of the existence of ancient non-
Western societies, which shook the confidence of the West, since the
West believed that no alternatives to its own God-given social order
could be stable or viable.

Last but not least, a doubt grew about the reliability of the senses.
What is still secure in the universe if it is the earth that goes around
the sun—so clearly opposite of what you see with your own eyes? So
a deep desire—even a basic hunger—grew for re-establishing a realm
of new undoubted security. It was also at that same time that Descartes (1596-1650) established this new type of security, centred on
the individual human reason or ratio (the *more geometrico*): "*I think,
therefore I am.*" Only a few years afterwards, Thomas Hobbes (1588-
1679) found his security in the achievements of the natural sciences,
which demonstrated so clearly the truth of mechanical, natural laws,
which rule the universe.

So Modernity arose as a reaction to one of the deepest existential
human problems: the problem of fear, of insecurity. Modernity, we
can say, reinstalled human security, first in the domain of logic and
in the certainty of mathematical and mechanical laws. Later on, and
this is for us the most important point, it also sought to overcome this
insecurity by a rational and systematic effort to reorganise and recre-
ate human society. So, from the outset, Modernity was taken up with

developing mechanisms, with forming them and developing obedience to them—which includes the emergence of and the obedience to
the market-mechanism and of the democratic mechanism! For both
could be seen and valued as a rational expression of the full liberty of
the autonomous individual will. It is this concept of Modernity that increasingly became the context for the way Western humanity thought
and also that dynamically acted in a manner that was perceived and
accepted as true historical progress.

Why is all this important? There are at least two reasons. The first
is that, as far as globalization can be seen as a modern phenomenon, it
also involves the persistent effort to modernise the world in a dynamic
way according to the laws of functional mechanisms. However, looking to these distinct cultural roots means that globalization can in no
way be analysed as a neutral, purely factual, value-free phenomenon!
Globalization is basically founded in a Western humanistic type of
rationalism, individualism and a sense of autonomous freedom, which
supports also the desire to extend this message to the whole world for
the wellbeing of all.

The second reason for referring to this historical background relates to the fully modern character of mainstream economic *theory*
today. Like globalization, mainstream economics is modern, and in a
similar way. Economic theory is modern in its systematic effort to be
seen and valued as entirely neutral or value free. It is also and even
more modern in its deep attachment to both individual values and opti-
mal working mechanisms! So both the factual process of globalization
in concrete reality and the foundations of classical and neo-classical
economic theory share to a large extent the same foundational roots:
the roots of Modernity. No wonder, therefore, that the economists of
today who work and think in that modern tradition have so few things
to say, and even less to criticise, about the present process and project
of globalization! For more than any other social science, the science of
economics was and is deeply rooted in Western Modernity. And that is
the major reason why, in my view, modern economics is usually so flat
and lacks sufficient depth in its analysis of globalization.

Broadening the Economic Analysis of Globalization

This no doubt audacious hypothesis needs at least one critical test:
if modern economic science and globalization are so very near to each
other, just like twins, then we should also expect that the opposite
is true—namely that a broadened and deepened view of economic
science can and should lead to a broadened and deepened economic
appreciation of the process of globalization itself. And to meeting that
challenging test I devote the remainder of my chapter.

The position from which I will try to meet this challenge is a reformed Christian tradition of philosophical and economic thought. From this position I identify and here explain three elements of my own economic reflection on globalization, which I believe could have a broadening and deepening potential in broader academic understandings of this process.

In summary:

1. *Firstly, I wish to refer to the* inner normativity *of the word economy or* oikonomia *over against the tendency to see and evaluate globalization only in terms of a given and neutral dynamic development.*

2. *Secondly, I want to say something about* markets as social and cultural institutions *that are broader than their usual perception as global mechanisms.*

3. *And thirdly, I wish to make a plea for a further reformation of economic thought in terms of a* broadened concept of causality, *also in our treatment of the process of globalization itself.*

1. The word 'economy' has, as we all know, very old Greek roots. It is used and explained by Aristotle, but is also present in the New Testament. Let me draw your attention to the fact that the word *oikonomia* consists of two small Greek words: *oikos*, which means household, and *nomos*, which is the rule or law of good behaviour. Economy, from its origins, has thus an undeniable *normative* flavour, the flavour of personal but also communal *good stewardship*. Let me put it in another way. The norm of *oikonomia* is not only oriented to the need to sustain life by the production of a sufficient level of commodities and services, it is also a norm of preservation, of administrative care for nature and of all other life-supporting scarce entities. These entities include not only land and other material resources, but also the social framework or organisms of society as the treasure of human health.

The character of an economic good is therefore insufficiently described by restricting the term to *objects of use*, which owe their value to the fact that they can be destined for (further) production or consumption. Economy implies the need for preservation and thus leads necessarily to the notion of *objects of care*. To give an example: human health is usually seen as no more than an economic need, which need is satisfied by food and good medical treatment. Yet human health is also an economic object, namely an object of preventive care. If health is squandered, then also the possibilities for human labour are partially lost. This insight, by the way, is the element of truth in Marx's idea of the production costs of human labour.

This kind of normative economic approach is, in my view, essential if we wish to deepen and widen our economic evaluation of the present processes of globalization. Since, as we have seen, this process is rooted in the Western ideas of Modernity and of modernisation, in practice, globalization tends always to glorify its own dynamic progress. Thus it also tends to neglect systematically its economic shadow-sides, sides which relate to a lack of careful preservation of what is valuable in nature, culture, and human health. Globalization seen as an economically responsible process needs a fundamental injection of the value and significance of economic *care*.

A concrete illustration of that can be found in the remarkable change that the World Bank had to adopt in its basic calculation-scheme in the last decade of the previous century. Up until 1995 the World Bank used so-called structural adaptation schemes in its programmes with the countries of the South. They were based on the premise that the main goal of development had to be higher economic growth, especially export growth in the fight against all forms of poverty. On the basis of that perspective, Structural Adjustment Programs were implemented which not only cut government consumption, but also involved restraints on wage increases and asked for privatisation and a devaluation of the currency. Particularly in Africa, however, this policy contributed significantly to the so-called disasters of the eighties, sometimes called "the lost decade". Hospitals were closed, schools had to increase their school-fees—and as a result often stood empty—and at the same time the degree of erosion and desertification grew significantly. The price of this export-oriented growth became so high that a turn had to be made.

From 1995 on the World Bank started to use another calculation scheme, in which the public expenditures for health, natural preservation, and education were no longer categorised as governmental consumption but seen as a form of 'public investment'. At first sight this is only a change of words, but it had remarkable consequences. Since that moment, all public expenditures that were destined to uphold and preserve human health, education, and the environment received from the World Bank the equal value and identical significance given to investments in so-called physical capital. Such expenditures left the soft domain of consumption, which you could cut endlessly, and entered the domain of investments in human capital, social capital, and natural capital. (This scheme, by the way, is still not used by the International Monetary Fund. The IMF still sticks to the old formulae and calculation schemes.) This change has to be applauded, but we should not forget that much pain was needed, especially in Africa, before the World Bank was willing to admit that it had been led by a too-narrow economic perception that, to some extent, had become economically destructive. This begs the question: how much unnecessary pain is still caused in the process of globalization by those many economic actors who still travel the same paths of implementing narrow investment and development-schemes. Economic development should always give sufficient attention to potential losses to the existing human, social and natural capital.

2. A similar truth is found in the restrictive or narrow way in which markets are treated, as much in economic theory as in economic practice. The project of globalization has namely an inbuilt tendency to reduce all markets to just and only dynamic mechanisms of exchange. But markets are far more than that. Markets are forms of human interaction, so they must have an ongoing social aspect. They also function in the context of rules of law, so they exist with a juridical aspect. Good market-behaviour points to the presence of a moral aspect. And finally markets always take their form from the culture in which they exist. An African market is different from a traditional Mexican market, and surely they are both different from a Japanese or a North American market. Mainstream economic science, however, has no idea how to handle all those aspects and differences. For Modernity, as we saw, has always involved an artificial self-constructed mechanistic view of reality which is basically designed by the equilibrium-analyses of the natural sciences.

Even more than some kind of theoretical reduction has taken place. In the practice of globalization, new markets have been introduced and shaped in a similar way. The ideal format or model for new markets in neo-classical thought is still pure competition: an anonymous, working feedback mechanism, which is viewed as far more advanced and efficient than the living markets of the past. My question is, does competition always and everywhere bring real progress? There are grounds for sincere doubt, especially when we consider the present growth and expansion of the so-called financial markets.

Money, from the viewpoint of the norm of *oikonomia*, of good stewardship, is of great use in facilitating human economic interactions. But money is not an original part of God's good creation like birds and trees and minerals. Humans had to develop money. We put monetary values on things when we exchanged two turtledoves for a dozen pears and then three rocks for a turtledove. Money, then, is just a peculiar kind of utensil in the service of what we correctly call the real economy, which includes the production, consumption and exchange of real commodities and services. In Modernity, though, there is no view to restrain serviceability in referring to the role and the place of money—and thus, no reason to fear a full implementation of financial markets as mechanisms that are allowed to steer and rule the entire real economy.

In the present pattern of globalization, financial markets indeed expand continually in size and significance and, in their turn, are strongly dominated by the interests of speculative investors and private equity funds. Companies increasingly have to obey the claims of short term maximum shareholder profitability, even if that implies mergers and buy-outs with important losses of employment. This is not only morally doubtful but is also a basically un-economic devel-

opment: the real economy should have priority in economic development, and each living economy needs therefore to be protected from
the dominance of the artificial financial markets. Such a view is not
just an abstract wish. If this principle is rejected, it can also cause a
great deal of economic harm, because if financial market-mechanisms
are built on the weak foundation of human subjective expectations
they will also show an extreme degree of volatility. Just listen to the
words of one of the biggest speculators of the last decade, George
Soros, who wrote that "equilibrium theory in economics is based on a
false analogy with physics".[6] Further he makes the following remarkable empirical observation:

> The rethinking must start with the recognition that
> financial markets are inherently unstable. The global
> capitalist system is based on the belief that financial
> markets, left to their own devices, tend towards equi-
> librium. This belief is false. Financial markets are
> given to excesses. Instead of acting like a pendulum,
> financial markets have recently acted more like a
> wrecking ball, knocking over one economy after an-
> other. Indeed, that unbelievable, but also unnecessary,
> harm has already become an undeniable part of the
> recent history of globalization.[7]

3. I now come to the last part of my plea for a broadened and deepened economic analysis of the process of globalization, and this part
is devoted to possibly one of the most difficult and abstract themes in
economic philosophy, namely the concept of economic causality. A
discussion about causality seems at first sight unrelated to the turbulent practice of the present globalization, but I have strong hopes of
converting you with these final words. Economic causality is highly
relevant for our own subject because the question of economic causality reminds us of our scientific presuppositions, which include the
framework in which cause and effect are experienced by us. Let me
therefore start with a question.

We all know that if any event takes place in reality, then somehow
there is or should be always one or more factors that caused this effect to happen—maybe another event or circumstance, but of course
also of some kind of human action. Now the question is, what is the
reason that especially in the explanation of economic events, such as
growing unemployment or rising price levels, economists are always
inclined to ask *what* could have caused this to happen but never *who*
has caused it? For instance, we economists address unemployment
through causes like a decrease of the investment level, or a lack of
aggregate demand, or a decline in the export markets. But we seem

to systematically ignore or avoid the question of "who?" Asking "who?" uncovers the specific contributing role of a whole range of actors such as governments, labour unions, employers, speculators, and international organisations, who could all be involved in causing those real things to happen. Is it possible that a presuppositional stand in economics has established the habit of leaving the human actor, the steward, the one called to care for his or her neighbour, the *imago dei*, out of the picture for theoretical analysis? Of course I am aware of the actor-oriented approach in modern game theories, where the behaviour of one or more actors is analysed in a standardised or simulated way, an analysis which thus takes place in some kind of virtual reality. But the question of "Who?" in real economic life is different; namely, it requires us to also identify the non-standardised behaviour of real agents as I just indicated. Is it our fear of being accused of partiality that explains this hesitation? Is it that we want to avoid being involved in a 'blame game' quarrel or being accused of making subjective value judgements? No doubt all these elements have a part in our avoidance of the "Who?" question. But from a scientific standpoint it is, of course, simply not permissible to systematically ignore the possibility that some kind of economic result, good or evil, has its roots, its main cause, in the actions of one or more actors, which for instance may be under-reacting or overreacting to a specific economic impulse.

It is the famous Dutch reformed philosopher Herman Dooyeweerd who pointed to the error in this alleged scientific attitude already some fifty years ago. His view was that, if the fullness of God's creation demonstrates a variety of aspects, such as the physical aspect, the aspect of biological life, the social aspect, the juridical aspect, the economic aspect, and so on, then the study of reality from the viewpoint of each of those aspects will involve its own concept of causality. Causality in biology should, for instance, be centred on the possibility of life, the growth of life and the maintenance of life, and will therefore be different from the type of mechanical causality we study in physics.[8] Economic causality should be, in Dooyeweerd's view, always related to criteria for economic accountability, because human economic actions are always taking place in a context of one or more human responsibilities. Therefore, economists, in this view, should address the "Who?" question in looking for economic causes of economic problems—not in order to make any kind of moral judgement, but to be able to explain what really happened.

The reality is that economists usually ignore that type of causality, and I may add, continue to do so in their study of the consequences of globalization. The question of why this is so is answered in the best possible way by Nobel Prize winner John Hicks, who wrote an important book about this subject under the title *Causality in Economics*.[9] Hicks begins his book by digging into the past, explaining to the reader that since medieval times the study of economic events mainly took place by using the "Who?" type of causality question. The increase of the volume trade, for instance, was explained in terms of good entrepreneurship or in terms of the positive role of governments. This "old causality", as Hicks calls it, broke down fully in the seventeenth and eighteenth centuries—especially after the great mid-eighteenth century earthquake that ruined Lisbon. Questions like "Who caused that earthquake?" can only lead to supernatural causes, like an action of God. Such an answer is not acceptable in any social science. Hicks continues: "The solution was found by the philosophers of the Enlightenment, Hume and Kant. It was the 'Old' association between Causality and Responsibility which had to be rejected. Causality is a matter of explanation; but when we explain, we do not necessarily praise or condemn. Their 'new causality' was a permanent acquisition."[10] Since that day, Hicks concludes, economics has been committed to the New Causality.[11]

I have quoted Hicks so extensively because what he says here is very important. To evade questions of a "supernatural" nature in order to be a modern science and "explain" without any reference to God or beliefs, economists deliberately choose for a type of causality which systematically refrains from asking the "Who?" question, restricting itself to "What" causes. In their analyses of economic problems the question of which agent caused something to happen is now no longer asked.

A question I wish to ask is, does not this deliberately chosen position contain within it the possibility of also causing *harm* in our world of ongoing globalization? In the process of globalization we see many economic actors—transnational companies, governments, international institutions, labour unions and venture capitalists—all of whom play diverse and important roles. Their actions sometimes have economically positive consequences, but they are also sometimes economically very wasteful. Ours is a reality in which human enrichment at a personal or collective level can easily cause forms of great impoverishment elsewhere, and only fools can and will deny that. Economists should, therefore, not avoid the "Who" question in the analysis of the process of globalization, but be aware of how economic actors use their economic power in several concrete critical situations—again, not to make moral judgements, but with the singular purpose of having a better analytical insight into present economic reality.

You may ask, is such an approach that focuses upon the "Who?" question still possible? Does this normative approach not imply per definition a departure from good standards of academic impartiality? I do not think so, and my best witness here is another Nobel Prize winner, Amartya Sen. One of his main early publications was the book *Poverty and Famines: An Essay on Entitlement and Deprivation*.[12] Sen is a thorough, accurate, and impartial economist, but in this remarkable book he presents a comparative analysis of the causes of three so-called natural disasters: the great Ethiopian famine of 1972-74, the famine and great drought that afflicted the African Sahel region 1968-73, and the 1974 famine in Bangladesh. In his analysis, Sen comes to some unavoidable conclusions in terms of a "Who" type of causality. He proves that the main cause of the Ethiopian famine can only be found in the reduction of the food supply and the increases in food prices which landowners demanded; in the Sahel it was the too rapid introduction of cash crops which was one of the main causes of growing hunger and poverty; and in Bangladesh, Sen even points his finger to the partiality of many local authorities and the rapid alienation of the land of small landowners. Sen correctly received the Nobel Prize for this and other studies about economic entitlements, never avoiding the actor, or "Who?" perspective when he discusses economic causation. If we are to develop a comprehensive economic explanation of what occurs in the present world he confirms that economists never should ignore the role of human differentiated responsibilities.

Sen has opened up a new scientific way of discussing economic causation that seems to be consonant with what Dooyeweerd hoped for, fifty years ago, when he made his plea for a distinctively economic concept of causation. Sen's approach is also very similar to Adolfo Garcia de la Sienra's recent statement about "a new agenda for economic theory". He says: "In opposition to current economics, I would like to point toward an economic theory in which human behaviour is not understood as blind and mechanical, but as obeying moral standards, (in accordance) with God's norms for creation."[13]

Conclusion

I hope to have proved in this article that modern globalization and modern economic science demonstrate similar traits that hamper most economists from giving an appropriate appraisal of the process of globalization. In defending this broader and deeper perspective, I need to be quite clear that it is not my intention to encourage economists to reject or throw away *a priori* factual processes such as globalization. Neither should economists be led by the desire to stand as judge over concrete actors for possible abuses to their stewardship. That is not our competence as economists, reminding us of the need to always be self-critical in our theoretical work. The main task and obligation of economists is always to look for the truth and nothing but the truth. We may never avoid analysing the real causes—the "Who" causes and the "What" causes of what happens and what is at the point of happening—even if our analysis is going to make some people or actors very angry. For it is only when that search for truth prevails in our scientific efforts that we really do serve. As Lord Keynes once said during a table speech, when he referred to the role and the tasks of economists: *Economists are the trustees, not of civilisation, but of the possibility of civilisation.*

....

Bob Goudzwaard (Ph.D., Erasmus University) is professor emeritus of economics and cultural philosophy at the Free University of Amsterdam, and advisor to the Department of Justice, Peace, and Creation of the World Council of Churches. A few of his more recent publications are *Hope in Troubled Times: A New Vision for Confronting Global Crises* (with Mark Vander Vennen and David Van Heemst) (Grand Rapids, MI: Baker, 2007) and *Globalization and the Kingdom of God* (Grand Rapids, MI: Eerdmans, 2001).

NOTES

[1] Manuel Castells, *The Information Age. Volume I, The Rise of the Network Society* (Oxford: Blackwell Publishers, 1996), 97-99.

[2] Alain Touraine, *La Séparation de l'Etat et de la Nation* (Paris: Cahiers de l' Urmis, 2001), 6, 28. Touraine also wrote about globalization in its ideological aspects in *La Globalización como Ideologia* (El País, 1996).

[3] Pierre Bourdieu, "The Politics of Globalisation" in *Global Policy Forum* 2, 1 (2001), 1; *Acts of Resistance: Against the Tyranny of the Market* (Cambridge: Polity Press, 1998).

[4] Zygmunt Bauman, *Postmodern Ethics* (Oxford: Blackwell Publishing, 1993), 224.

[5] Ibid, 232.

[6] George Soros, *The Crisis of Global Capitalism: Open Society Endangered* (New York: PublicAffairs, 1998), xxxiii.

[7] Ibid, xiv.

[8] Herman F. Dooyeweerd, *A New Critique of Theoretical Thought (I,II,III)* (Amsterdam: H.J Paris; Philadelphia: The Presbyterian and Reformed Publishing Company, 1953), II, 182; III, 159.

[9] John R. Hicks, *Causality in Economics* (New York: Basic Books, Inc., 1979), 6-9.

[10] Ibid, 6-7.

[11] Ibid, 7, 9.

[12] Amartya Sen, *Poverty and Famines: An Essay on Entitlement and Deprivation* (Oxford: Oxford University Press, 1981).

[13] Adolfo Garcia de la Sienra, "A New Agenda for Economic Theory", response to Bob Goudzwaard, *Globalization and the Kingdom of God* (Grand Rapids, MI: Baker Books, 2001), 88.

Globalization and the Logic of Capitalism

by Paul Spencer Williams

"Globalisation has become the *primary* idea by which we understand the transition of human society into the third millennium."[1]

Despite, indeed perhaps because of, its importance, 'globalization' is a good candidate for being what the German linguist, Uwe Poerksen, describes as a *plastic word*—one that displaces more precise terms with words that sound scientific but actually blur meaning and disable common language.[2] Plastic words include, for instance, *development*, *strategy*, and *project*. Such words are malleable and can be used in a number of different ways depending on the context. 'Globalization' functions in this way. It is used to describe almost everything that seems different since the 1960s—changes in information technology, global warming, genetics, the growth of air travel and so on. Everything appears to be 'globalizing'—a phrase which 'helpfully' means, "*to render global*".

Globalization is also a term that is subjected to a great deal of ideological scrutiny. It "is convenient shorthand for *de facto* exclusion", says Susan George of the Jacques Maritain International Institute.[3] It is a myth. It is a synonym for neo-liberalism. It is simply the extension of the American 'empire'. Or according to Alex Singleton of the London-based Globalisation Institute, it is "a force for good", because "only by integrating the poorest into the world economy can we put an end to the poverty that still blights much of the world today".[4]

Globalization is therefore doubly confusing. It not only functions with a malleable meaning but also exists within multiple ideological frameworks. This essay will attempt to dispel some of this confusion by arguing that though globalization might impact on all areas of life, it is primarily driven by the logic of capitalism. Considering globalization through the lens of capitalism enables the possibility of speaking meaningfully about the future of globalization and provides a clear focus for a constructive Christian response. The remainder of this essay is structured according to a set of straightforward questions: What is globalization? What is driving it? Where is it headed? How do we evaluate it? How do we respond as Christians?

What is Globalization?

Globalization can be described as the process by which market economies, governments and cultures are becoming increasingly inter-linked and integrated across the globe to an extent that fundamentally undermines "territoriality as an organising principle for social and cultural life".[5] This results in a growing global consciousness which impacts significantly on cultural behaviour. Definitions of globalization differ as to whether economic, political or socio-cultural causes are given primacy. I will argue that whilst all of these concepts and causes are indeed important aspects of globalization, they do in fact arise from an underlying process that is fundamentally economic in nature.

In order to understand globalization it is insufficient simply to describe its outcomes. Rather we must understand the process at work and what drives that process. The individualistic and systemic logic of capitalism is the main driving force behind globalization and this economic driver is responsible also for the major political and cultural changes that are often identified with globalization. Relative to the underlying logic of global capitalism, in other words, all other aspects of globalization are secondary or tertiary effects. This becomes clearer as we trace the integration and inter-linking that constitutes globalization in its economic, political and cultural dimensions.

Economic integration occurs as capitalism transects national boundaries, extending transportation and communication infrastructures, expanding markets, and enlisting greater tranches of labour power throughout the world. Globalization is more than the idea that a capitalist form of economic activity spreads to more countries. Instead it relates to the functional integration of local, regional and national economies at a global scale so that an increasing proportion of global wealth is produced and distributed within a unitary system of globally connected firms. For example, it is not that whereas in the past Britain, Germany, the USA and Japan had a car industry and now many other countries around the world have car industries. Rather, it is that the organisation of the car industry takes place on a global, not a national scale. The various elements of the manufacturing process, such as design, component manufacture, assembly, marketing and sales are functionally and geographically separated and take place in the most advantageous part of the world for that function, all within a highly co-ordinated corporate system. For instance, design might be undertaken in Munich and component manufacture in China, South Africa and Argentina. Assembly might take place in each continent near to the final customer and sales operate through a network of local dealerships. In what sense then can we describe this entity as, say, 'German' if most of the vehicle is made, and most of the firm's activities occur outside of Germany? Typically we do so on the basis that its head office is in Germany and it is quoted on the German stock exchange. Of course its shareholders may include only a minority of Germans.

Such transnational corporations that operate increasingly independently of political arrangements and can even achieve economic domination over them have progressively dominated the global economic landscape. The Global Policy Forum estimates that of the top one hundred largest economic entities in the world, only around one half of these are countries.[6] The annual global revenue of General Motors, for instance, is larger than the annual GDP of Thailand, and sales of the Shell oil company are greater than the GDP of Greece.[7]

This expansion of an increasingly efficient capitalist mode of *production* is matched by the development of a new global market for *consumption*. As international communications and economic exchanges extend, a new global market develops. Management theorists Yongjiang Shi and Mike Gregory describe this in an article on international manufacturing networks:

> This global market is based on the shared and common demands of different countries. It integrates different national preferences into a core entity and presents this as a fundamental and non-differentiable market requirement. To satisfy the growing global market, the traditional products and related development strategies are clearly not enough to satisfy companies' internationalization. Trans National Corporations are therefore keen to learn about and develop global or world products and to restructure their worldwide manufacturing systems.[8]

In other words, it is in the interests of global firms to improve their own efficiency by selling the same product throughout the world as much as possible, rather than having to bother with different national tastes or preferences. The result of this economic integration is that increasingly the globe is constituted as a single market for commodities, capital and labour.

The *political* integration of nation states as embodied in organisations like the World Bank, the International Monetary Fund (IMF), World Trade Organisation and the European Union is a phenomena that, whatever separate rationale it may have, is fundamentally driven by the need for transnational political co-operation in the face of widespread economic integration. Government policy has become increasingly directed toward the international economy. Political decisions that promote foreign investment and liberalisation both facilitate globalization and are required by the powerful capitalist logic of economic integration. An efficient globally integrated manufacturing system, for instance, requires access to target countries in order to buy or lease land, import machinery and hire workers and, depending on the industry, sell products. It also requires capital and tax arrangements that facilitate the flow in and out of the country of working capital and profits and the avoidance of double taxation.

It is this logic that leads the IMF to require developing countries to deregulate their markets, allowing unrestricted access to international mobile capital, and to remove any protective barriers to their consumer markets from outside competition. Former Chief Economist at the World Bank, Joseph Stiglitz, summarises this approach as follows:

> Rapid . . . liberalisation, in the manner pushed by the IMF, amounted to setting [developing countries] off on a voyage on a rough sea, before the holes in their hulls have been repaired, before the captain has received training, before life vests have been put on board.[9]

However, it would be a mistake to think that global markets bring pressure to bear only on small developing countries. Even the wealthiest countries are involved in what has been described as a 'race to the bottom' as governments attempt to make their societies as attractive as possible to mobile companies. Taxes are cut, social welfare programmes abolished and environmental regulations removed, all in an attempt to maintain an attractive environment for mobile capital. In order to protect themselves from this process, governments cede regulatory power to international institutions on the grounds that if a large number of states agree to a given standard then mobile capital cannot play them off against each other. This is the context for the development of bodies like the European Union, or agreements like the Kyoto protocol on climate change. The effect of this political response to economic integration is that we are moving from an international system of states to the global integration of political power.

Finally, *cultural* integration occurs as this economic and political integration leads to a compression of cultural and societal relations arising from the growing interdependence of the different parts of the international system. Cultural integration—as well as economic and political integration—has been dramatically accelerated by the development of modern information and communications technologies. Virtually instant communication with any part of the globe is now not only possible but routine. Access to global media of all kinds means that there is now a truly global consciousness in a way that has never before been possible. The coherence and continuity of a culture is maintained, in part, through cultural symbols or 'signs' that represent facts, preferences, tastes, beliefs and values. The rise of global consumerism has exposed all cultures to an invasion of foreign ideas, customs and values. In itself this could be a positive thing, but as a result of the compelling logic of capitalism, these ideas and customs are increasingly separated from their local context, commodified and marketed within the emerging 'global village'. For instance, the presence of Tibetan prayer flags on clothes lines in North America represents not only the postmodern spiritual milieu of North America but also the erosion of Tibetan culture.

What is Driving Globalization?

At the heart of the globalization process I have described is the logic of capitalism. It is this logic that is the driving force of globalization and in this section I identify two main aspects of its operation.

The first concerns its *utilitarian individualism*. In mainstream economic theory, the human person is modelled as an abstract individual, who is the locus of rational choice, and the goal of the economic system is to maximise the range of choices available to individuals so that each can optimise individual utility or happiness. The Canadian philosopher, Charles Taylor, describes the utilitarian self thus:

> The aim of [utilitarianism] was precisely to reject all qualitative distinctions and to construe all human goals as on the same footing, susceptible therefore of common quantification and calculation according to some common 'currency'.[10]

This focus on procedural rationality, argues Taylor, is a consequence of rejecting any source external to the individual to serve as a basis for morality, a rejection itself arising from the Enlightenment notion of freedom as individual autonomy. So whilst a moral good, namely 'happiness', is recognised, Taylor argues, "this is characterised by a polemical refusal of any qualitative discrimination. There is no more higher or lower; all that belongs to the old metaphysical views. There is just desire, and the only standard that remains is the maximisation of its fulfilment."[11]

Supported by these economic constructs, capitalism offers the individual the prospect of freedom from the constraints of tradition in order to maximise individual happiness. An ideology of progress and consumerism is harnessed to offer the prospect of happiness through material wealth and liberation from social constraint. The individual is 'liberated' from the past, tradition and social custom and encouraged to view these as consumption choices, chosen on the basis of whether they contribute to 'individual happiness'. Happiness, or 'utility' can be measured monetarily in that each individual's choice reveals a preference and consequently an expression of their pursuit of happiness. In any transaction, an individual is thus revealing a value of one thing in terms of another. The price system allocates a monetary value to this transaction and the sum total of all transactions thus represents or proxies the total utility or happiness in an economy. The goal then simply becomes the maximization of this total utility, or in modern parlance, the pursuit of economic growth measured in terms of Gross National Product.

The fundamentally mistaken utilitarian anthropology that underlies this vision is not only false but also dangerous. Charles Taylor again notes that "instrumental-rational control of the world in the service of our desires and needs can just degenerate into organised egoism, a capitulation before the demands of our lower nature".[12] Contrary to Christian and indeed many other religious and philosophical understandings of the self, the rational utility maximiser of capitalism knows of no distinction between a higher and lower nature.

The economists Peter Buckley and Mark Casson have argued that the absence of any conceptualisation of a higher nature in economic theory supports a weakening of the degree of self-control exercised in a society.[13] There is less restraint on producers to avoid deception or exploitation. Consumers and borrowers lacking self-control and self-awareness become easy targets for the selfish manipulation of producers and lenders. Advertising that offers instant credit, or that promotes products as instruments of sexual seduction, directly undermines the individual consumer's self-control.

The systematic use of mass marketing to undermine consumer self-control enables producers to generate the tastes and preferences for goods and services via advertising, and to supply the purchasing power to buy them by stimulating a growing supply of debt to the consumer. In this context, the following observation of the economist turned theologian Lesslie Newbigin is particularly incisive:

> The economic system is no longer directed to meeting needs . . . manufacturing industry does not exist to meet the needs of people; on the contrary, wants are manufactured to meet the needs of industry. Its growth therefore, far from being a sign of health, may be essentially cancerous—the multiplication of cells as an end in itself.[14]

The individualist logic of capitalism that points to the maximisation of individual happiness is related to a second *systemic* aspect of capitalist logic. Capitalism is concerned to maximise the outputs of the economic system as a whole. *Economic growth* is the goal, and growth requires market scale for efficiencies to be realised. Capitalism as a system, and the mainstream economic theory that underpins it, insists that all barriers to the creation of the largest possible market be removed. The language of capitalism describes such barriers as 'regulations', 'customs' and 'restrictions' that are to be removed by markets, governments and societies in order for growth to be realised. These 'barriers' include any impediment to the free movement of goods and services, capital and labour—including familial or communal customs that limit labour mobility, or notions of nationhood that seek to limit foreign ownership of national assets. All such 'barriers' are regarded as limitations on the development of an efficient market. The systemic logic of capitalism undermines the connections between people and places. In doing so, it also encourages the objectification and use of the environment as nothing more than a resource to serve the consumption needs of humanity.

In order for the market to deliver the maximum possible economic growth, the free movement of labour and capital is required in order to ensure the allocation of resources to their most efficient use. Such use will pay slightly higher wages or interest rates in order to attract the right labour or capital. Consequently, wage rates, labour, interest rates and capital must all be completely free to adjust or move in response to changing market conditions and price signals. Government policies to de-regulate financial and labour markets, to enable high levels of capital mobility, and to make hiring and firing easy for companies are all guided by this theoretical requirement.

Yet the de-regulation of labour and financial markets also leads to increased inequality and instability. Increased inequality occurs largely as a result of agglomeration economies in which the returns to capital and skilled labour are concentrated around major metropolitan hubs at the expense of more peripheral areas and unskilled workers. Increased instability arises directly from increased labour and capital mobility in the form of uncertain job prospects and destabilising speculative capital flows. These processes operate within and between countries and actively undermine the possibility of rooted communities.

Both the systemic and individualistic logic of capitalism thus act to reinforce one another in undermining the connections between people and places on the one hand (by encouraging mobility and generating instability) and people and the past on the other (by encouraging an individualism at odds with tradition and social ties). This separation of people from time and space is what the British sociologist Anthony Giddens describes as 'distanciation'.[15] Accelerated by modern telecommunications technologies, globalization 'disembeds' social relations from local contexts and restructures them across time and space so that 'symbolic tokens' representing tastes and cultural preferences can be rapidly deployed in other contexts where often the original meaning is lost or radically reinterpreted.

Moreover, the failure to adequately conceptualise the need for self-control within human nature tends to accelerate a separation of people from *themselves*. This materialist reductionism at the level of the person is mirrored throughout society as the imperialistic logic of capitalism extends itself. Those who consider that economics is the social science that examines how we organise money and wealth in all its forms are mistaken. Rather, as the classic definition of the subject given by Robert Mundell states, "Economics is the science of choice."[16] The vision of individual freedom embodied in capitalism's utility-maximising rational consumerist anthropology does not stop at the boundaries of the physical needs of life. Instead, a constant process of commoditisation goes on in which ever broader areas of social life become monetised. All areas of life are reduced to what sociologist Craig Gay has called the Money Metric.[17] Decisions about marriage, health care, which political party to vote for, education and so forth are increasingly made as if civic values, learning, care-giving, marital fidelity, and sexual orientation are just like any other good or service. By disembedding cultural values and then placing them in the service of consumer markets, capitalism gradually reduces all values, all beliefs, and all meaning to a matter of taste, preference and consumption habit.

Clearly this imperialistic capitalist logic has profound and disturbing implications for human communities, depending as they do on a continuity of people in a place having shared histories and meanings. Mobile international capital and the consumerism that it stimulates is gradually undermining the nature of 'places' and creating a borderless world in which everyone belongs equally anywhere but nobody is at home in community.

It is this disconnection of space and time, of people and places, that is the fundamental cause of the economic, political and cultural problems commonly associated with globalization. To recap, these problems include but are by no means exhausted by, the following:

- Economic instability arising from huge global capital flows: For instance, in 1998 the hedge fund 'Long Term Capital Management', a company of only 200 employees and $3.6bn in capital, was caught in an adverse market holding in excess of $1 trillion in derivative exposure (roughly equivalent to Canada's annual GDP) and nearly brought the entire financial system on Wall Street to its knees. More recently we are witnessing the systemic instability of global financial markets in the current worldwide economic crisis and downturn, triggered by defaults on highly leveraged 'sub-prime' borrowing and associated financial derivatives. The trading and speculation taking place in these complex financial products illustrates well the increasingly disembodied and anonymous nature of the global market. Unlike traditional lending, based to a high degree on personal relationship and trust, these transactions have thrived on anonymity and indeed the deliberate passing of risk onto those in a poor position either to evaluate it or to care about the impact of their profit-seeking activity on others;

- Rising inequality of income: Since 1960, the poorest 20% in the world have seen their share of global income fall from a little over 2% to less than 1%, while the richest 20% have seen their share rise from 70% to 90%. These *inter-country* comparisons are significant, but of equal significance is the inequality and social exclusion occurring *within* countries. Whether in London or Lagos, capitalism allows some to live like kings while others struggle to survive.

- Environmental degradation: Rapid losses of rain forest, desertification, exhaustion of groundwater, loss of biodiversity, global climate change and pollution are all effects made possible largely by the social separation of economic activity from a rootedness in the places on which it depends.

- Corrosion of civic integrity: Described most forcefully by Kenichi Ohmae as the "end of the nation state",[18] the process of globalization is undermining traditional political stability. The growth of giant corporations and the corresponding growth of increasingly powerful but un-elected supra-national institutions results in a disturbing democratic deficit and loss of accountability as these huge institutions have a growing impact on our daily lives. The growing voter apathy measurable in all major democracies is a sign of the sense of helplessness concerning the possibility of meaningful change taking place through the normal political process.

- Cultural breakdown: The widespread fragmentation of local cultures and family structures, whether we are thinking about rural cultures in Europe and North America or traditional cultures in Africa, the South Pacific or elsewhere, continues to fuel the cultural resistance to globalization. Increasingly, this resistance is taking on violent forms.

Where is Globalization Headed?

I have argued that globalization is driven by the compelling logic of capitalism. Visions of globalization's future have a remarkable degree of coherence with this logic, even though the visionaries themselves embrace these visions with wildly differing degrees of enthusiasm. Globalization theorist Malcolm Waters envisages the future as one in which a single society and culture occupy the entire planet. Culture will be unified only at an extremely abstract level, expressing toler- ance for diversity and individual choice.[19] This sounds remarkably like a globalized Western liberal democracy. This vision is similar to more explicit globalization 'enthusiasts', who argue that what we need is the de-regulation of all markets, the commodification of every part of the planet including the eco-systems, and then all problems will be solved by private business and the market.

However, almost all of the prophets of capitalism—whether Adam Smith, Alfred Marshall or Freidrich Hayek on the right, or Joseph Schumpeter and John Maynard Keynes from the political centre, or Karl Marx on the left—predict that capitalism will eventually be its own undoing. In other words, there is a high degree of unanimity amongst political economists that capitalism is *self*-destructive and, according to many of these theorists, that some form of substantial governmental intervention or regulation of the economy will be necessary. This is in significant contrast to most of the major social, political and economic theorists of globalization.

The basic reason for this view is that all the problems identified and foreseen concerning global capitalism—economic instability, inequal- ity of wealth and power, widespread ecological damage, and the grow- ing commoditisation of life—all arise from within the system itself. The only solution seems to be for the state to intervene and manage the problem from outside of the system. Unfortunately it is already a moot point as to whether government is any longer 'outside' of the system. But in any event we have seen that global capitalism is tend- ing to undermine the power of national governments and moreover that many of the major problems facing global capitalism are indeed global in scope. This is why many commentators and theorists argue for the creation of ever more powerful structures of world governance and regulation. What seems likely then is that, left unchecked, globalization is taking us toward an unprecedented centralisation of power in which world governance structures are needed to regulate the behaviour of giant transnational corporations and manage the growing instability and unpredictability of globally integrated financial markets.

How Do We Evaluate Globalization?

In evaluating globalization, it is important to clearly state what is, and what is not, being critiqued. Capitalism as described in this essay is not to be equated with the market economy. Although the two are deeply intertwined, the market is a mechanism for organising exchange whereas capitalism is an ideology that has infused and colonised that mechanism with its own peculiar vision for society. Similarly, when we loosely equate capitalism with free markets we need to be very careful to distinguish which markets we are talking about. Adam Smith advocated a free market in the trade of goods and services. He assumed that capital markets remained localised. It is the de-regulation of capital markets allowing firms and speculators to move capital freely between regions and countries that is the most problematic functional feature of capitalism, though the unequal power relations that result do distort the operation of trade, usually to the disadvantage of developing countries. With these brief caveats in mind, we can observe then that globalization, driven by the logic of capitalism, is essentially:

A *homogenising* force—it spreads a mono-cultural version of Western consumerist society around the world that is based on a fundamentally flawed model of the human person.

A *centralising* force—it tends to concentrate power in the hands of the owners of capital and, in response to its effects, the purveyors of international political power.

A *relativising* force—it reinforces a postmodern confusion by reducing cultural symbols of belief, value and meaning to matters of taste and preference.

Biblical Help in Evaluating Globalization

For biblical help in evaluating globalization we turn first to consider the institutions, norms and practices associated with the Jubilee, as recorded in Leviticus 25 and related passages on debt cancellation, and the banning of interest in the Deuteronomic code. Taken together, these laws constitute an alternative socio-economic paradigm designed for the context of sinful humanity. They are not idealistic but nor do they constitute direct commands to us today. However, as Richard Bauckham points out in his excellent book on hermeneutics, these provisions are certainly *instructive* for us in understanding God's wisdom for the economy.[20]

The over-riding objective of these provisions is to ensure the permanent socio-economic inclusion of each Israelite family in the community and to establish a relation between community and place. The Jubilee sets out to provide a secure place of relationship in the land of God's provision that cannot be destroyed by economic hardship or greed. Each Israelite family was granted a land-holding following possession of the land. The Jubilee laws are designed to ensure that each family continues to maintain such ownership over time, so that the relationship between God, a worshipping community and the stewardship of God's land, is not broken. The Jubilee laws would prevent the accumulation of ownership in the hands of a few wealthy farmers and the permanent alienation of any Israelite families from the economic and social foundation of their society.

Clearly the economics of the Jubilee embody a completely different socio-economic vision to that of capitalism, despite the fact that the Old Testament basically supports markets and private property. Unlike that of capitalism, the systemic logic of the Jubilee is explicitly relational and linked closely to notions of physical place that centre the theological concepts of home, belonging and dwelling with God and God's Creation. The system exists to protect the ability of people to serve God in community and recognises that persons have their identity in community, not in isolation from others. Its logic is completely contrary to the individualistic and systemic logic of capitalism.

As an alternative socio-economic vision to capitalism, the Jubilee certainly provides the basis for a relatively negative critique of global capitalism, but perhaps the most compelling biblical critique of globalization derives from the Babel narrative in Genesis 11 and its theological pairing with the coming of the Holy Spirit at Pentecost in Acts 2.

God's intervention at Babel demonstrates both His opposition to an oppressive conformity and an affirmation of diversity. Both judgement and mercy are combined in the enforced scattering of humanity that returns them to the original creation mandate to be fruitful, multiply and spread throughout the earth.

At Pentecost, the homogenisation and confusion of Babel is transformed not into an organised mono-culture, but rather a unified multi-culture. The gift of tongues, in which "all heard in their own language", affirms the linguistic and cultural diversity of peoples, all of whom have a place in the redeemed community which finds its unity not in organisational power structures but in relationship with Christ. There is in globalization both the modernist tendency toward cultural homogeneity and the centralisation of power, as well as a reinforcement of the post-modern babble of confused voices. Both are subverted at Babel. Both are redeemed at Pentecost. Walter Brueggemann captures the biblical vision beautifully in his commentary on Genesis:

> God wills a unity which permits and encourages scat-
> tering. The unity willed by God is that all of human-
> ity shall be in covenant with him and with him only,
> responding to his purposes, relying on his life-giving
> power. The scattering God wills is that life should be
> peopled everywhere by his regents, who are attentive
> to all parts of creation, working in his image to en-
> hance the whole creation, to bring 'each in its kind'
> to full fruition and productivity . . . The purpose of
> God is neither self-securing homogeneity as though

God is not Lord, nor a scattering of autonomous parts as though the elements of humanity did not belong to each other.[21]

How Do We Live?

Let me conclude by suggesting some positive ways forward for us as Christians. Responding theologically to globalization concerns, among other things, a renewed understanding of the significance of our occupational life, an ecclesiological response and a re-framing of global mission.

Renewed Faith

When confronted with the reality of globalization, there is obviously the need to respond in the arena of personal decisions regarding lifestyle and seek to live as responsible stewards in the ways we use resources and influence the behaviour of others. However, this is not likely to be sufficient, nor does it really fulfil our responsibility as those sent as witnesses of the gospel into the world. We are in need of a conversion not just in our behaviour as consumers but also in our occupational life. When the people came to John the Baptist asking what 'fruit in keeping with repentance' actually was, his answer involved a conversion in their working lives (John 3:11-14). He told the tax collectors to stop extorting people and the soldiers to be content with their pay. Zaccheus is a clear example of such occupational conversion resulting from Jesus' ministry. *What we do* with our lives is of crucial missional importance. We need a conversion in our role as producers as well as our role as consumers.

Church as a Community of Hope

The process of globalization can be seen as a type of over-realised eschatology. Globalization is the attempt to realise the eschatological future of the complete unity of humankind in the here and now through purely human means. As has been argued, this has had and is having disastrous consequences. One of the saddest is the growing loss of hope that anything can change. Increasingly, the most effective defence of globalization is the claim that there is no alternative. Yet the church is called to witness in its common life to God's alternative future. The unity of humankind is only possible through the redemptive work of Christ and the church is called to be the eschatological sign of this future hope. In the church there is "neither Jew nor Gentile, neither slave or free, neither male nor female, for you are all one in Christ Jesus" (Galatians

3:28). There is, in this sense, a very different kind of 'globalizing' that is taking place in the church. This type of unity is not homogenising, centralising or relativising. Christ's work of unifying—the way of the cross—is profoundly different to the imperial and violent attempts at unity that are attempted through purely human means. A key missional task of the church is to embody this alternative understanding of 'globalization' and at the same time re-constitute an expression of local and particular community embodiment in contrast to the universalising claims of globalization.

Re-framing Global Mission: Love in Action

Finally, these first two together actually constitute a biblical church. That is, one that understands itself both as *gathered* together to worship a Trinitarian God and live out the life of God in its midst and then is *scattered* by the Holy Spirit throughout society and the world, throughout our myriad occupations and neighbourhoods, to witness further to what God is doing to bring about his Kingdom. When the Church does this it is in its being and nature missional. We then can better discern a different kind of globalization—namely the integration of human communities that is taking place around the world in Christ. We need to be willing to give weight to Christian voices from cultures other than our own and not to allow our relative wealth in the West to deceive us into thinking that we are also spiritually wealthy. Paying attention to my particular local neighbour, and recognising this alternative countercultural global community, is God's way of transforming the world. "This is how men will know that you are my disciples: that you love one another" (John 13:35).

....

PAUL SPENCER WILLIAMS (M.A., M.Sc., Oxford; M.C.S., Regent College), is David J. Brown Family Professor of Marketplace Theology at Regent College, Vancouver, Canada. He is also the Leadership and Executive Director of the Regent College Marketplace Institute as well as the Director and Economic Advisor to DTZ, a multinational real estate consulting and investment banking group headquartered in London, UK, for whom he has worked extensively throughout Europe, Asia and North America. He has over 18 years experience acting as a strategic economic advisor to a wide range of major international companies and British and international government departments and agencies, particularly in the areas of competitiveness, globalization and sustainability.

NOTES

[1] Malcolm Waters, *Globalization* (London: Routledge, Chapman and Hall, 1995), 1.

[2] Uwe Poerksen, *Plastic Words: Tyranny of Modular Language* (tr. Jutta Mason and David Cayley; University Park, PA: Penn State University Press, 1995).

[3] Susan George, "Globalisation: A Challenge for Peace Solidarity or Exclusion?", available from http://www.tni.org/detail_page.phtml?act_id=1489&username=guest@tni.org&password=9999&publish=Y&print_format=Y (accessed 11 March 2009).

[4] See http://news.bbc.co.uk/1/hi/england/4123222.stm, (accessed 13 March 2009).

[5] Waters, *Globalization*, 5.

[6] Sarah Anderson and John Cavanaugh, "Top 200: The Rise of Global Corporate Power", *Global Policy Forum* (2000), available from http://www.globalpolicy.org/socecon/tncs/top200.htm (accessed 11 March 2009).

[7] Anderson and Cavanaugh, "Top 200".

[8] Yongjiang Shi and Mike Gregory, "International manufacturing networks—to develop global competitive capabilities", *Journal of Operations Management*, 16 (1998): 195-214, 196.

[9] Joseph Stiglitz, *Globalization and its Discontents* (New York: Norton and Company, 2003), 17.

[10] Charles Taylor, *Sources of the Self* (Cambridge, MA: Harvard University Press, 1989), 22.

[11] Ibid, 78.

[12] Ibid, 364.

[13] Peter J. Buckley and Mark C.Casson, "The moral basis of global capitalism: Beyond the eclectic theory", *International Journal of the Economics of Business*, 8, 2 (2001): 303-327.

[14] Lesslie Newbigin, "The Welfare State: A Christian Perspective", *Theology* 88 (1985): 175.

[15] Anthony Giddens, *Modernity and Self-Identity: Self and Society in the Late Modern Age* (Stanford, CA: Stanford University Press, 1991).

[16] Robert Mundell, *Man and Economics: The Science of Choice* (New York: McGraw-Hill Book Publishing, 1968).

[17] Craig Gay, *Cash Values: Money and the Erosion of Meaning in Today's Society* (Grand Rapids, MI: Eerdmans, 2003), 40.

[18] Kenichi Ohmae, *The End of the Nation State: The Rise of Regional Economies* (New York: Free Press Paperbacks, 1996).

[19] Cf. Waters, *Globalization*.

[20] See Richard Bauckham, *The Bible in Politics: How to Read the Bible Politically* (London: SPCK, 1989), 6.

[21] Walter Brueggemann, *Genesis* (Atlanta: John Knox, 1982), 99.

From Shock and Awe to Shock and Grace: A Response to Naomi Klein's *The Shock Doctrine*[1]

by Brian J. Walsh

Shock and Awe

In 1996 the US military released a document entitled *Shock and Awe: Achieving Military Dominance*. In that document the authors articulate a military policy in which an invading force should "seize control of the environment and paralyze or so overload an adversary's perceptions and understanding of events so that the enemy would be incapable of resistance".[2]

It is not enough to simply seize control through swift and efficient military strikes. An enemy can regroup and begin to launch counter measures even under these circumstances. No, you must seize control of more than just the battlefield, the transportation and communication lines and the energy resources—you must also "overload an adversary's perceptions and understanding of events" because only by doing so will you render the enemy incapable of resistance. Overload perceptions and understandings. It is not enough to take captive territory, you must also take captive the imaginations of the vanquished people.

This is an old strategy and has been the common practice of all imperial forces throughout history. "Resistance is futile" not just because of the empire's superior military strength, but more importantly because of the empire's control of perception. Why resist an empire that has the blessings of the gods? Why resist an empire that has the very force of history behind it? Why resist an empire that brings nothing but blessing, security and economic growth? Why resist an empire that has the sheer force of nature, indeed the very laws of nature, on its side? It would be as futile as resisting the law of gravity.

But people will resist such imperial force. People will stubbornly hang on to their old ways, their old perceptions of reality, their old worldviews. So the empire must use shock therapy. So shock and awe the opponent that the change in their reality is so quick, so radical and so thorough that old ways of thinking, old perceptions simply can't account for the new reality. Create such a deep experience of disorientation that the old ways, the old perceptions, the old worldview, the previous orientation simply cannot cope and the people, the nation, are left paralysed in the face of it all.

This, says Naomi Klein, has been the strategy of Friedmanite economics since its first experiment in the coup in Chile on September 11, 1973. Milton Friedman, the father of what has become known in the US and the UK as neoconservative economics, but is aptly named neo-liberalism everywhere else; the granddaddy of what is also known as the "Chicago School" or the "Chicago Boys" once said that "only a crisis—actual or perceived—produces real change. When that crisis occurs, the actions that are taken depend on the ideas that are lying around. That, I believe, is our basic function: to develop alternatives to existing policies, to keep them alive and available until the politically impossible becomes politically inevitable."[3]

But what were the existing policies that needed to be overthrown? Generally speaking these would be policies of a mixed economy in which the state is active in controlling, stimulating, directing and regulating the economic life of the nation. Policies like taxation to pay for education, health care and social welfare protection. Policies like allowing the state to own and operate certain sectors of the economy—from transportation to oil production to communications, health care, education, prisons, policing, etc.

But these are all, in the perspective of the radical laissez-faire economics of the Chicago School 'unnatural' interventions in the free and natural functioning of the market. And so it is part and parcel of the Chicago ideology—an ideology that has dominated the World Bank, the International Monetary Fund, the US Treasury and Foreign policy since at least the Reagan years—that economic reform must include cuts in taxation for the richest people in a society, the liberalisation of trade laws to allow for so-called 'free trade' between nations (especially free access to resources and markets in the impoverished South for the wealthy North), the privatisation of most government functions (including health care, education, communications and transportation), the privatisation of all nationalised business operations (especially in the energy sector) and, interestingly, an increase in tax-based military expenditures.

Now remember that Friedman said we need a crisis, or a shock, to occur before such policies could be implemented. Why? Because only in such a crisis will the "politically impossible become the politically inevitable".

But why would these policies be politically impossible? Isn't this vision of life all about freedom? Hasn't the mantra always been that political and economic freedom go hand in hand? Hasn't the mantra always been that democracy and free market capitalism always come together? And if this is true, wouldn't it suggest that not only is such an economic system economically inevitable (it is, after all, simply the natural way to organise an economy), and politically inevitable, but that it would also be politically desirable and therefore eminently possible?

Well the answer is, no. We didn't need Naomi Klein to tell us that wherever this kind of economic ideology has raised its head, wherever it has come to political dominance it has been accompanied by dictatorship, violence, and the repression of political, social and even religious freedom and rights.

Just think of the places:[4]
> Chile
> Uruguay
> Argentina
> Guatemala
> Brazil
> Indonesia
> China
> Russia
> South Africa
> Poland
> Iraq
> Sri Lanka
> UK
> USA

Just think of some of the names:
> The Shah of Iran
> General Pinochet
> General Suharto
> Colonel Castillo
> Rios Mont
> Boris Yeltsin
> Deng Xioaping
> Margaret Thatcher
> George Bush
> Paul Bremner

The politically impossible must become the politically inevitable.

But why is it politically impossible? This kind of economic revolution is politically impossible for one very good reason: there are more poor people than there are rich people. This is an economics that cannot be democratically maintained because poor people are hurt in it and the rich benefit.

Who benefits from taxing the rich? Who benefits from free public education? Who benefits from state sponsored heath care? Who benefits from public control over public resources? Who benefits from trade laws that will privilege local producers and protect the local market from being flooded with goods produced elsewhere? Who benefits from investment laws that limit foreign investment and control?

Who benefits? Those who cannot afford to pay for education and health care benefit. Those who somehow believe that the resources of their nation should serve the needs of their community benefit. Those who need protection because they don't have the economic or political power to protect themselves benefit.

No wonder these radically laissez-faire economic reforms are politically impossible. No wonder you need shock therapy to so disorient the society that you can then institute these reforms with rapid speed without democratic consent. The majority of people would never accept such changes. Eliminating the public sphere, providing free reign to corporate power, and reducing social spending to a skeletal level are not the kinds of things that most people would vote for.

And no wonder, these changes come with an increase in military spending. You need a strong and repressive military force to pull off this kind of stuff.

The Shock Doctrine

Naomi Klein's book is deeply disturbing. Her thesis is as simple as it is devastating. Shock takes three stages: first put the entire population in a state of collective shock through some kind of crisis (whether it be a coup, a terrorist attack, market meltdown, war or a natural disaster, doesn't really matter); then, in that brief moment of societal confusion and disorientation move quickly to radically reform the economy, and other social and political structures in a way that will institute Chicago school economic policies; and then, if there is opposition, if people arise out of their confused state and begin to protest what has gone on, begin to militate against the new regime . . . well then the third level of shock is necessary and out come the electric shock cables, out come the implements of torture, people start getting 'disappeared', mass graves need to be dug, the society must be cleansed of the filth, the garbage, the pollutants that will stand in the way of what is politically and economically inevitable. What once was thought of as democratically impossible must now engage in such repression that there will be no imagination left, no perception left, no reorientation possible that would allow for dreaming of new possibilities beyond the repression.

Klein argues that this pattern has been seen over and over again over the last thirty-five years—from the Southern Cone to the former Soviet Union, to South Africa, to China, to post-tsunami South East

Asia, to post-Falklands Thatcher's UK, to post 9/11 America and the rise of the national security industry.

And sometimes, while reading the book, I would turn the page and say to myself, "not again! Surely this pattern didn't repeat itself in post-Solidarity Poland, surely not in post-apartheid South Africa! Surely that isn't what happened in post-Katrina New Orleans!" But Klein's argument is compelling and her evidence is exhaustive and at times emotionally and intellectually exhausting.

The matters before us in *The Shock Doctrine* are not of mere intellectual curiosity. They are matters of life and death. They are matters of ideological power wielded over the lives of billions of people, nations, economies, indeed the planet itself. As Ericka Stephens-Rennie has put it, this is a story of rape—a story of deep and violent penetration, a story of sexual assault on a massive, indeed global, scale.[5] And Klein is telling the story.

It is a story of empire. If empire is a matter of systematic centralisation of power secured by structures of socio-economic and military control, legitimated by powerful myths and sustained by ubiquitous images that seek to capture the imaginations of subjugated people, then 'disaster capitalism' well names this corporatist empire and the shock doctrine is foundational to its imperial ideology.[6]

Klein insists that "certain ideologies are a danger to the public and need to be identified as such". Specifically, "these are the closed, fundamentalist doctrines that cannot co-exist with other belief systems; their followers deplore diversity and demand an absolute free hand to implement their perfect system". In such ideologies, "The world as it is must be *erased* to make way for their purist invention."[7]

This is a purified vision of the world, and all who oppose this vision are filth who have no legitimate voice or place in this reborn world. If they cannot be cleansed, if they cannot be re-educated, re-indoctrinated, re-formed, then they cannot be saved and they must be cast out.

And Klein is pretty sure that this kind of an ideology has roots in biblical religion. And it is not just the fact that many of the proponents of this ideology happen to be right wing Christians (Donald Rumsfeld certainly comes to mind), but it has more to do with the inherent mythological foundations of the ideology. Again, she writes: "Rooted in biblical fantasies of great floods and great fires, [this ideology has] a logic that leads ineluctably toward violence. The ideologies that long for that impossible clean slate, which can be reached only through some kind of cataclysm, are the dangerous ones."[8]

I come to this book from the perspective of Christian faith, and perhaps Klein's deep aversion to certain kinds of biblical faith gives me an entry into the conversation. While we might want to argue that biblical kinds of faith are not the only options for legitimating a clean-slate-purity kind of ideological violence (can we blame the Bible for Stalin, Mao, Suharto and all other ideological genocides?), it is clear that Klein is decidedly worried about such biblical metaphors of a flood that cleans all things for a fresh start, or language of a new creation, or apocalyptic images of cataclysmic fire. And I'll return to all of that in a moment.

Notes Between the Bars

Before we go there, however, I want to say something more about what Klein is up to in this book. In the last chapter she writes:

> A state of shock, by definition, is a moment when there is a gap between fast moving events and the information that exists to explain them. The late French theorist Jean Baudrillard described terrorist events as an 'excess of reality;' in this sense, in North America, the September 11 attacks were, at first, pure event, raw reality, unprocessed by story, narrative or anything that could bridge the gap between reality and understanding. Without a story, we are, as many of us were after September 11, intensely vulnerable to those people who are ready to take advantage of the chaos for their own ends. As soon as we have a new narrative that offers a perspective on the shocking events, we become reoriented and the world begins to make sense once again.[9]

Narratives make sense of reality. Without narrative there is deep confusion and disorientation, and in such a situation we are intensely vulnerable. That is why the CIA torture manual makes it clear that you separate the prisoners. Take away all stimuli that can help orient the prisoner to what time of day it is, to where he is, or to what is happening to him. And don't let prisoners talk to each other, because they will then compare notes, help keep each other oriented, share stories.

And what prisoners try to do in such a situation is "to pass notes between the bars". Pass notes, share stories. You aren't crazy: this has happened to me as well! And Klein's book is one large note passed between the bars. It is a long note that tells a new narrative and offers perspective, perhaps provides orientation in the midst of the disorientation of the shock therapy.

"All shock therapists", writes Klein, "are intent on the erasure of memory".[10] But shock therapy—either on psychiatric patients, or in the torture cell, or in the machinations of the economy—can never totally erase memory. "(R)ecollections can be rebuilt, new narratives can be created. Memory, both individual and collective, turns out to be the greatest shock absorber of all."[11]

And that is why, in the end, Klein is decidedly anti-revolutionary. The Friedmanites are the revolutionaries. Bush is a revolutionary. Pinochet and Suharto were the revolutionaries. They are all about erasing memories and creating clean slates. They all want to start again "from scratch". Klein says that subjugated peoples, awakening from the shock-induced amnesia of their oppression, do not start from scratch again, but begin to start from the scraps. They start to pick their way through the rubble of their lives, the rubble of their economies, the rubble of what is left after the shock of war or water has hit, the rubble that is left after the shock of military intervention or market meltdown has played itself out, and they rebuild. They pick up the scraps of memory that remain and begin to piece together the story.

I think that this is profoundly right and deeply problematic. Profoundly right because it is out of the rubble that life is rebuilt—there are no blank slates, there is no tabula rasa, there is no pure state from which to begin. We are in the rubble—of our own lives and of the sheer brokenness of our world.

Rebuilding requires memory. Rebuilding requires a narrative that will make sense of our lives and give us orientation and direction in how we go about rebuilding our lives. And this book of passing notes between the bars, of telling the story of shock capitalism, is indispensable, indeed liberating in that rebuilding process.

Liberal Memories?

Klein's narrative of shock capitalism, however, must itself be rooted in a larger narrative. There is an operative metanarrative at work in Klein's book that gives her the perspective to discern and deconstruct the metanarrative of the Chicago Boys. There is a memory, a story at work here that she believes is a more healing narrative, a narrative that provides memories that can be foundational to the reconstruction of our lives post-disaster capitalism.

And that narrative, that vision, is nothing more radical than the kind of New Deal economics that we saw arise in the midst of the Great Depression. That vision is the liberal economic vision of John Maynard Keynes—or Keynesian economics. On one level, this is a non-controversial policy of nationalising certain key sectors of the economy, investing in education and health care, and allowing the government to regulate the economy, even stimulate the economy for the sake of the broadest public good.

This is a liberal narrative, I say, because it does not radically depart from the fundamental principles of capitalism. While it promotes a mixed economy that allows for market freedom within the broader context of national economic policy, regulation and controls, it nonetheless is a capitalist economy that will attempt to direct the operations of the market in ways that will be least damaging to the environment and the social fabric.

If post-disaster capitalism is a salvage operation, then is there enough to salvage here? Do the scraps of this older Keynesian economic vision, the memories of these older ideas and systems, provide us enough resources to engage in the rebuilding project in front of us? Is this memory, this liberal worldview, this story, deep enough, dense enough, thick enough to sustain us in the wake of the tsunami of the neo-liberal disaster?

I don't think so. My argument isn't with mixed economies per se (indeed I believe in a mixed economy, especially if it focuses on local economic sustainability)—no my problem is with the narrative underlying this Keynesian vision. This narrative, which is foundational to Klein's alternative story, is, I think too shallow, too thin, and lacks the kind of weight, substance and moral vision that we need in our times. Let me explain this a little further.[12]

The moral consternation of much "liberal" analysis of the neo-liberal disaster is rooted in memories of post-Depression industrial economies that attempted to shape economic life in a way that the most vulnerable were not constantly discarded and dismissed. But if we are to understand what happened between the demise of this liberal worldview and the present neo-liberal regime, then we need to ask questions of why that older liberal vision collapsed. Why did the liberal worldview that brought us the New Deal, together with state intervention to alleviate things like poverty and homelessness by means of a social safety net collapse? Is the shock doctrine sufficient to explain the shift?

There are many reasons why the welfare state was untenable, but I want to focus only on one—it was rooted in a thin narrative. The narrative of the kind of liberalism that brought us mixed economies and national economic policies was deeply rooted in a faith in economic growth. Bob Goudzwaard and Harry de Lange have described the welfare state as a post-care society.[13] The first priority of society is to seek economic growth in the forms of ever increasing processes of production and consumption and an increase in the Gross National Product. At this point, liberalism and neo-conservatism are in agreement. But liberalism acknowledges that there will be casualties of economic growth. Not everyone will benefit equally from this growth and the "invisible hand" will not, on its own, raise the standard of living of all people. So there is a role for the state to care for the poor and to make sure that there is at least a modicum of income distribution so that the disadvantaged also may benefit from the economic growth of society as a whole. Neo-conservatives have greater faith (against all the evidence, as far as I can see!) in the powers of the market. Nonetheless, this liberal vision of the welfare state is a "post-care" society, because "care" comes only *after* economic growth. And here is its greatest weakness. The foundational assumption of a liberal welfare state is that economic growth and abundance is a never-ending dynamic of a capitalist society. As long as the economy is growing we can afford to redistribute wealth in small ways, we can afford to give everyone a chance to fulfil the "American dream", we can afford to intervene when the invisible hand of the market economy doesn't seem up to the job. But what happens when there is an economic downturn? What happens if things like the OPEC oil embargo, rising inflation and the success of the Asian economy in the 1970s occasion an economic recession in the early 1980s? What happens to our public responsibility to the poor when there is not the same kind of economic abundance to be spread around? What happens when the boom markets of the Asian tigers, or the slow but secure markets of Chile or Argentina experience radical melt down? What happens? Responsibility evaporates, liberalism dies, and neo-conservatism takes its place.

Naomi Klein's friend, Linda McQuaig argues that the recession of the early 1980s resulted in an exaggerated sense of scarcity and powerlessness.[14] As government deficits increased it was concluded that we could no longer afford those earlier social welfare programmes. A self-secure culture of affluence and liberal largesse was replaced by a culture of perceived scarcity which itself bred a sense of economic insecurity. In such a culture the habits of social responsibility and care (albeit in a post-care approach to society) dissipate together with the liberal narrative that gave them their cultural legitimacy.

The problem with the liberalism of the past was that it was *too shallow*. It was *too thin* of an ethic to sustain a sense of civic solidarity and responsibility to the poor when it was perceived that we couldn't afford such responsibility anymore. Rooted as it was in an individualistic understanding of society, when the going got tough, self-interest again raised its ugly head. If Michael Walzer is right in saying that home is "a dense moral culture", then the problem with Western society—whether liberal or neo-conservative—is that it has no density, no foundation for an economics of care, an economics of justice.[15]

If it was an economic downturn that made the whole culture lose its ethical nerve and gave entry to neo-conservatism, then why doesn't an economic upturn result in a return to the ethical principles that for a while seemed too expensive? This would seem to be at the heart of much liberal consternation. It is no longer the early 1980s; we are no longer in recession. At least in Canada there have been budgetary surpluses not deficits. So why don't we reinstate the programmes that were dismantled? The money is there, the analysis is done, and we know that real people are in need of these programmes. Don't we have a "moral obligation"? And the answer is, no. The economic growth of the last ten to fifteen years has done little to change the cultural mood regarding responsibility to the poor. That older liberal ethic, rooted as it was in assumptions of economic growth, has proven itself too shallow to sustain any kind of a renewed civic sense of responsibility that could creatively and ethically respond to the crisis of disaster capitalism. Once that liberalism died at the hands of the recession and the prophets of neo-conservatism, it would not rise again. The culture of fear has given birth to an ethos of individualism, scarcity, survivalism and withdrawal from social responsibility.[16]

Klein could well respond to my concerns by insisting that she does not believe in a liberal individualism, but in a collectivist vision that insists upon communal responsibility and care. So do I. But the problem is that Klein hasn't provided us with a narrative that is rich enough to sustain such a vision, praxis and morality. I'm not saying that she couldn't—only that she hasn't.

Biblical Fantasies Revisited

Klein is clear, however, that anything like a biblical faith, rooted in Hebrew and Christian scripture, is definitely not the answer, but part of the problem. Remember that quote about biblical fantasies of great floods? Well, the very first words that we meet in this book—before Klein has told us any part of her story—is the epigraph that opens the first chapter:

> Now the earth was corrupt in God's sight, and the earth was filled with violence. And God saw that the earth was corrupt; for all flesh had corrupted its ways upon the earth. And God said to Noah, "I have determined to make an end of all flesh, for the earth is filled with violence because of them; now I am going to destroy them along with the earth."

Klein doesn't begin her book with Genesis 6:11-13 for a little religious inspiration. No, she is arguing that this text, and texts like it provide mythic/symbolic legitimacy for the purist and fundamentalist ideology that she is exposing. Indeed the only other biblical text she quotes comes later in the book and it is from Revelation 21:5, "See, I am making all things new."

The suggestion is clear. From Genesis to Revelation, we meet a faith of destruction, or wiping slates clean in order to make all things new—a mythic worldview tailored for an ideology of radical economic purification!

The problem is that language of newness, language of a shifting of things so that the old order, the old status quo will be overthrown and real newness will be experienced in peoples' lives, tends to be received as good news by those who are most oppressed by the present order. Images of a new creation, a new day, a new order, indeed even a new city that replaces the old city—a New Jerusalem that replaces the repressive world of the old Babylon—are images of hope for the oppressed. These are images that subvert empires—whether Babylonian, Roman or corporatist American—precisely by proclaiming that these regimes are not eternal, they are not secure before the power and sovereignty of God. Empires don't really like newness. They like the same old thing. That's why in all of the regimes that Klein discusses, constitutional reforms are imposed that guarantee the economic structures of neo-liberalism even after potential political change.

But Klein is enough of a chastened leftist to know that such language of revolutionary newness is a double-edged sword. This is dangerous language and can be easily employed in the interests of violently imposed economic and social oppression. Perhaps she can see this so clearly in Friedmanite economics because she has seen it happen in the economic revolutions of the left as well.

Nonetheless, if we are to engage Klein from a biblical perspective, then perhaps her citing of Genesis and Revelation gives me permission to revisit some of the bits of this narrative that are found in between.

My argument is simple. Klein's liberal, Keynesian narrative is too thin and not substantial enough to sustain the kind of economic restoration that she envisions and hopes for. My question is whether a biblical narrative might just be a thicker memory with more weight and more depth, and that it just might be able to sustain a vision, praxis and morality of economic justice and restoration. So let me make just a few observations.

God Says "Oops ..."

First, the difference between God's notion of a clean slate and Milton Friedman's is that God recognised that it didn't work. Friedman, and most of his disciples, never said "oops". They never looked at the wreckage of the economies that they had revolutionised or the lives that they had decimated and said, "well that didn't work". Nor did they ever say that they are sorry.

The God we meet—even in this ancient narrative of the flood—is precisely a God who says, "oops". Really briefly, in Genesis 6 the narrative says that God saw in his own heart that there was nothing but violence and wickedness in the human heart and therefore decided that he would 'blot them out' from the face of the earth. Corruption this deep, this evil, needs to be cleaned out. Here is the clean slate ideology that Klein so despises.

But listen to what happens when the flood has been accomplished. Looking over the results of the flood, the results of the cosmic clean up campaign, God says, "I will never again curse the ground because of humankind, for the inclination of the human heart is evil from youth; nor will I ever again destroy every living creature as I have done" (Genesis 8:21).

As far as I can see, God says, "oops". If the same reason that God had to destroy the earth—namely the evil of the human heart—is the reason he gives for never doing that again, then the implication is clear: the flood didn't work. Clean up campaigns like this don't work because the issue is deeper than can be rectified by such destruction. The issue is the human heart, and floods, shocks, economic liberalisation, war, torture and privatisation can do nothing about that heart.

Covenant and Rape

So, second, what does God do? God makes covenant. God enters into a relationship with the human creature; God unites his already deeply grieving heart with the heart of the human creature that is full of nothing but the imaginations of evil. God enters into a relationship that is likely going to be an abusive relationship where God is the abused partner.

Let's put it this way. If the imaginations of evil that Genesis describes are to take socio-historical and economic shape today, then it is likely to take the shape of shock torture of people's bodies and the body politic of nations. The imagination of evil takes the shape of violent abuse. The imagination of evil, the need for a shock that will 'penetrate' ever deeper into the body of a people's psyche, economy and literal bodies, will take the shape of massive gang rape. And I think we could say that the Chicago Boys, with their third world lackeys, and their Washington power brokers, are a violent gang who have been fucking the world for thirty-five years. Always penetrating more deeply! The Shock Doctrine is a legitimation for rape.

And here's what going on in Genesis 6. God sees that the human partner is a violent rapist and decides to enter covenant with such a violent partner. God enters into covenant, marries, a partner who is likely to do nothing but fuck around, do nothing but abuse him. I can see the future of this relationship and it is violence, it is murder. But God is not the perpetrator of this violence, God is the abused lover.

In the largest picture of the biblical narrative (and I acknowledge that there are bits that I am leaving out) the God we meet is a covenantal God who bears abuse at the hands of his covenant partner. God is an abused lover. And this God bears such abuse, bears such suffering precisely because this is a story that insists that the violence of the human heart, the violence that has captured the imagination of the human subject is overcome not through more violence, but through suffering love. Not the suffering love of passive recipients of injustice, though. No, this is the suffering love of God himself.

But this perhaps takes us too far afield. Let's think for a minute about the implication of covenant for economic life.

Sabbath and Jubilee: Shocking the System

My third observation is that the story of God in covenantal relationship with humanity is a story not of clean slates but of liberation. This is a God who hears the cries of disenfranchised slaves labouring under the impossible brick quotas of the empire and acts in history to set them free. This is a story of slaves set free.

This story of exodus liberation then gives birth to a covenantal understanding of economic life. You see, liberated people still have hearts filled with violence, they are still self-interested, and have imaginations taken captive by greed. So even in a community of liberated slaves there will still be oppression. Brother will oppress brother and sisters and mothers will be sold into slavery. Any economy in which broken, self-interested and sinful human beings are involved will in one way or another succumb to ideological violence.

So Israel's Torah proposes an alternative economics. Not a naïve economics of purity, but an economics that recognises the propensity of the powerful to oppress the weak and sets out to restrain such oppression. It is called the Year of Jubilee.

In brief, here is how it works. Every seventh year in Israel is called a sabbath year.[17] On the sabbath year the land is given its rest. Note that this is an economics that begins with land. How you treat the land will give a clear indication of how you will treat the inhabitants of the land. So the legislation begins with land. Every seventh year the land is to receive its rest. Rest for regeneration, rest from being subject to ceaseless production, rest to enjoy being the land. Why should land get its sabbath? Because all land is covenant land. God's covenant established back in that Noah story wasn't just with human beings but with all of creation.

So what kind of an economics is this? It is an economics of respect for the land. It is an economics of rest, not ceaseless toil. And it is an economics of trust. If you don't plant crops in the seventh year then you have to have a deep trust in the covenantal God that your faithfulness in granting the land its rest will be blessed with an economic abundance in the sixth year that will carry and sustain you through the seventh year and until the harvest at the end of the eighth year.

And if you are going to have such an economics of trust, rest and respect, then it will have to be an economics of enough. This kind of an economic vision can't be driven by an insatiable desire for never ceasing growth precisely because the sabbath year puts a radical check on any such aspirations for limitless growth.

All of this would be radical enough, but so far we have only talked about land. We have only talked about the sabbath year. Here's the kicker. After seven sabbath years, that is 7 x 7 years, that is after the forty-ninth year, then the fiftieth year is proclaimed as the sabbath of sabbaths. Upon the blowing of the horn to proclaim the Day of Atonement, in the fiftieth year, Jubilee is proclaimed and all who have lost their lands or who have been sold into slavery are to receive their land back and be set free from slavery.[18]

The Day of Atonement and the year of Jubilee that it announces is a day of forgiveness of all debts. This is the day, and this is the year, of return: return to their God, return to their land, return to economic liberty, return to covenantal life in the land, return to an equal standing in the community. Atonement is about setting things right; setting all things right. And when people are restored to community and when economic relations are set right again, then the master/slave distinction must collapse, the unjust division between rich and poor must be overthrown and the reality of some folks having possession of land and the resources for economic well-being while others are dispossessed and left destitute must be rectified through a radical economic redistribution.

Let there be no mistake. This is something of a shock doctrine. The economy is radically shocked. This is not a shock to institutionalise further oppression, however, but a shock that creates a level playing field, restrains the appetites and power of the rich, and provides new economic opportunity for the poor. This, says the Torah, is how we provide for the redemption of the land. This is, if you will, not shock and awe, but shock and grace—a shock to the economic system precisely to create space for grace, for forgiveness, for new beginnings.

This is, of course, an audacious vision. This is an economics that recognises self-interest and puts covenantal checks and limits on that self-interest. This is a redemptive economy in the face of business as usual.

Of course the question that invariable comes up is, did this ever happen? Did they ever actually practice Jubilee in ancient Israel? And I find it interesting that this is the first question. I think we want to hear that it never happened precisely so we can discount this accounting of economic life as impractical.

The more important issue is that such a vision of life was imaginable in ancient Israel. It was imaginable precisely because it arose out of the experience of a Creator God who created a good creation, a covenant God who promised to bring *shalom*-blessing in all of life, and a liberating God who sets slaves free. This story gives rise to this kind of economic vision. It is precisely this kind of Jubilee vision that then functioned as the basis for judgement on oppressive economic structures as they arose in Israel, and as the basis and foundation for hope when Israel found itself subject to one more empire after another.

The Jesus School of Economics

When Jesus came to his hometown synagogue in Nazareth and they handed him the Isaiah scroll he took a few minutes to find the place in the scroll where the prophet employed Jubilee language to provide hope for his community labouring under the shock and awe of the Babylonian empire.[19]

And Jesus read from Isaiah:

The Spirit of the Lord is upon me,
    because he has anointed me
    to bring good news to the poor.
He has sent me to proclaim release to captives
    and recovery of sight to the blind,
    to let the oppressed go free,
    to proclaim the year of the Lord's favour.

And then he rolled up the scroll gave it back to the attendant and sat down. And everyone in the synagogue was looking at him. What would Jesus say about this prophecy? Here is a word that all the oppressed folks in Nazareth had hung their lives on. Here was a social and economic vision of liberation. Here was that old vision of Jubilee voiced again in the midst of oppression, voiced again in the midst of disorientation and confusion, voiced again to a shocked people awed by the military might and economic control of the Roman empire. What would Jesus say about this vision?

He sat down and said, "Today this scripture is fulfilled in your hearing."

Today, he said. Today is the year of the Lord's favour. Today is the year of Jubilee. Today, in my presence and in my proclamation, is Jubilee. The poor hear good news, captives are set free from prisons, and the oppressed are set free. Today, the shocked and awed people of South American hear good news. Today, the prisoners at Guantanamo Bay and Abu Ghraib are set free. Today, those who have been oppressed by IMF structural adjustment programmes, trade liberalisation, privatisation and exclusion from economic life . . . today they go free.

Well you can imagine the response. Isn't this Joseph's son? Isn't this one of our local lads whose done good? Wasn't that wonderful? Wasn't that profound, exciting and gracious? Liberation is at hand, our oppressors will be defeated, some Roman heads are going to roll, some business executives are going to die in the World Trade Centre, we are going to make America crumble and beg for mercy . . .

Wait a minute. Jesus didn't say that. In fact, if I listen closely enough I notice that he dropped something from that Isaiah's reading. Didn't Isaiah follow that line about the favourable year of the Lord, that reference to Jubilee, with something about a day of vengeance? Doesn't Jubilee redemption and liberation require a settling of accounts? Don't we need a clean slate? Don't we need to purify covenantal life by getting rid of the pollution of the empire? Don't we need to see some vengeance on Rome, on the IMF, on America? Where's the vengeance stuff? Why did he drop the line of vengeance?

And where did that line about giving sight to the blind come from? Isaiah didn't say that. Why did Jesus add that into his reading? What game is he playing here? Is it possible to have an economic revolution, a Jubilee shocking of the economic system without there being the vengeance of wiping the slate clean?

And the answer is, not in the way that Jesus enacts Jubilee. If Friedmanite economics is about cleaning out the impure, then the economy of Jesus is found in his embracing of the unclean, his fraternisation with the impure, his partying with the excluded. If shock capitalism is about taking control of the economy for the benefit of the rich and the violent exclusion of the poor, then the economy of Jesus is about throwing parties and inviting those who are never invited. His is an economy of radical generosity. His is an economy that tells the rich man to sell everything that he has and give it to the poor. His is an economy of radical inclusion. His is an economy that prays, "forgive us our debts as we forgive our debtors". His is an economy of enough that tells the rich man who keeps building bigger and bigger barns to horde his wealth that he is a fool. His is an economy of the kingdom of God, which says that those who are first will be last, that to be great in this kingdom is to be the servant of all.

But what about that violent heart? What about that violent covenant partner? What's going to happen to the violence? Okay, so Jesus won't allow for a kingdom built on vengeance, he won't allow for a kingdom of violent exclusion of anyone, even our oppressors. But what can he do about the violence in the human heart? Where is all that violence going to go? Where is that human propensity to shock and awe each other with sheer power, and violent control, going to finally play itself out.

Well, it plays itself out on the cross. The economy of Jesus is an economy of violence. But it is not the violence of God set up to clean up an impure world. It is the violence of the world poured out on the holiest of all. It is the violence of the empire that does it worst by putting our covenant lover on an imperial cross.

Tom Wright puts it this way: "The cross was not the defeat of *Christ* at the hands of the *powers*. It was the defeat of the powers at the hands—yes the bleeding hands—of Christ."[20] Or consider the way Andrew Lincoln, puts it, "The powers of evil are defeated not by some overwhelming display of divine power, but the weakness of Christ's death. . . . the death of the victim, who has absorbed the destructive forces of the powers, becomes precisely the point at which their domination is decisively brought to an end. Their claims, their accusations, their oppressive and divisive influence have all been subverted by a very different power: the power of the victim on the cross."[21]

I am prepared to say that the powers of disaster capitalism are powers of domination.[22] They are powers of oppression and division. What we need is a story more radical than theirs. What we need is a narrative that can see the defeat of these powers, not by violent power defeating violent power, but by the power of self-sacrificial love defeating the power of oppression. The shock of the cross meets the grace of God. The shock of the empire is overthrown by radical love. The shock doctrine is transformed by Jubilee.

What we need is an economy of care. What we need is an economy that says that care for the earth, care for the human community, careful stewardship of common resources for the benefit of all are foundational requirements of all economic life. What we need is an economy that begins with care—a pre-care economy rather than a post-care economy. A pre-care economy that reverses the relationship between economic growth and care for the vulnerable by prioritising justice over narrowly conceived notions of economic efficiency: A pre-care economy that is rooted in an economics of respect, rest, trust and enough; An economy that considers justice, compassion, community, good work and ecological responsibility as points of departure for economic life, not as (necessary) afterthoughts.[23]

Such an economy is impossible, however, without a transformation of the violence of the human heart into a heart of love, a heart of communal care and solidarity. Such an economy is impossible as long our imaginations are held captive by self-interest and narrowly conceived economic growth. What we need, I believe, is a transformed imagination. An imagination reshaped in the image of the one who bears the image of God. An imagination transformed through sacrificial love. An imagination shaped by the story of Jesus.

Milton Friedman is right: "only a crisis—actual or perceived—produces real change". Indeed, it is precisely his kind of economics that has helped to create the kind of economic, ecological and geo-political crises that characterise our time. And he is also right when he says that "the actions that are taken depend on the ideas that are lying around". But he wasn't thinking of ideas in the rubble. He wasn't thinking of reaching back into deeper memories of liberation. He wasn't thinking of tapping into the deepest longings of the human heart for homecoming, for return, for justice, for equality. Perhaps, just perhaps, there are some biblical ideas lying around in the rubble. Perhaps lying around in the rubble of the church we might find some stories, some ideas, some vision that will not legitimate ideological clean-up campaigns but will engender a rebuilding rooted in memories of sacrificial love, memories of Jubilee.

....

Brian J. Walsh (Ph.D., McGill University) is the Christian Reformed Church Campus Minister at University of Toronto. He is coauthor (with Richard Middleton) of *Transforming Vision: Shaping a Christian Worldview* (IVP, 1984), *Truth is Stranger than it Used to Be: Biblical Faith in a Postmodern Age* (IVP, 1995), (with Sylvia Keesmat) of *Colossians Remixed: Subverting the Empires* (IVP, 2004), and (with Steven Bouma-Prediger) of *Beyond Homelessness: Christian Faith in a Culture of Displacement* (Eerdmans, 2008).

NOTES

[1] First presented at "Empire Remixed", University of Toronto, November 26, 2007 and "Theology in the Pub", University of Western Ontario, November 28, 2007.

[2] Naomi Klein, *The Shock Doctrine: The Rise of Disaster Capitalism* (Toronto: Alfred A. Knopf Canada, 2007), 176.

[3] Cited by Klein, *Shock Doctrine*, 166.

[4] I am indebted to Ericka Stephens-Rennie for these lists. "Plots, Pressures and Penetrations: Neo-Conservative Economics and the Injustice of Rape". A presentation at Empire Remixed, University of Toronto, November 26, 2007. http://empireremixed.files.wordpress.com/2007/11/esr-shock-doctrine-final-edit.pdf (accessed 11 May 2009).

[5] Stephens-Rennie, "Plots, Pressures, and Penetrations".

[6] See Brian J. Walsh and Sylvia C. Keesmaat, *Colossians Remixed: Subverting the Empire* (Downers Grove, IL: InterVarsity Press, 2004), 31.

[7] Klein, *Shock Doctrine*, 22-23.

[8] Ibid, 23.

[9] Ibid, 551-552.

[10] Ibid, 557.

[11] Ibid, 557.

[12] This critique of liberal economics is based upon Steven Bouma-Prediger and Brian J. Walsh, *Beyond Homelessness: Christian Faith in an Age of Dislocation* (Grand Rapids, MI: Eerdmans, 2008), 108-109.

[13] Bob Goudzwaard and Harry de Lange, *Beyond Poverty and Affluence: Toward a Canadian Economy of Care* (tr. Mark Vander Vennen; Toronto: University of Toronto Press, 1995), 64.

[14] Linda McQuaig, *The Culture of Impotence: Selling the Myth of Powerlessness in the Global Economy* (Toronto: Penguin, 1999).

[15] Michael Walzer, *Interpretation and Social Criticism* (Cambridge, MA and London: Harvard University Press, 1987), 16.

[16] Whether we will see a revival of this kind of liberalism in the administration of Barack Obama in the United States remains to be seen. I am convinced that Obama will need a deeper and more biblical narrative than classical liberalism has offered in order to address the economic, social, environmental and military crisis that he has inherited.

[17] See Leviticus 25.

[18] The Jubilee year is another sabbath. As such this kind of an economic vision of homecoming requires an even deeper trust than we have already seen is the case for the regular sabbath years. By proclaiming Jubilee, by providing for atonement throughout the economy, the community must trust that God will bless the crops of the forty-eighth year so that the community will be sustained for three years, that is, until the harvest of the fifty-first year.

[19] This story comes from Luke 4:16-30. The text that Jesus quotes is from Isaiah 61:1-2.

[20] N.T. Wright, *Following Jesus: Biblical Reflections on Discipleship* (Grand Rapids, MI: Eerdmans, 1994), 19.

[21] Andrew T. Lincoln, "The Letter to the Colossians", in Leander Keck (ed.), *The New Interpreter's Bible* (Nashville: Abingdon, 2000), 11:628.

[22] See Walter Wink, *Naming the Powers: The Language of Power in the New Testament* (Philadelphia: Fortress Press, 1984).

[23] Again, I am indebted to Goudzwaard and deLange, *Beyond Poverty and Affluence*, and these ideas are developed at greater length and with specific reference to issues of homelessness in Bouma-Prediger and Walsh, *Beyond Homelessness*, ch. 4.

Commercial Entrepreneurship for the Good of People and Planet

by Peter S. Heslam

> *... the family, the business, science, art and so forth are all social spheres, which do not owe their existence to the state ... Neither the life of science nor of art, nor of agriculture, nor of industry, nor of commerce, nor of navigation, nor of the family, nor of human relationship may be coerced to suit itself to the grace of the government. The State may never become an octopus, which stifles the whole of life.*[1]

Poverty has always been with us but in recent years it has risen to a new level of public consciousness. This is reflected in the fact that gatherings of the world's political leaders regularly devote significant debating time to this issue; courses and programmes in international development have proliferated; and books on development frequently become best-sellers. The focus tends, however, to be on aid, debt relief and the reform of international economic institutions. While these are important, the danger is that the potential of the commercial enterprise is overlooked or downplayed. After fifty years and more than a trillion dollars spent on international development, almost half of the world's population still lives on less than US$2 per day. Yet flourishing and responsible entrepreneurial business can deliver the kind of economic growth that lifts people out of poverty, giving them hope for the future and a vision of dignity and well being that can be realised through dint of their own honest endeavour. The experience in recent decades of low-income countries such as India and China confirm that there is no more effective way to alleviate poverty than through the vigorous growth of enterprise. This has been true for every rich country, and it's true for every poor one now.

One reason why the vocation of commercial entrepreneurship to alleviate poverty is so often overlooked is the focus of the development community on definitions and causes of poverty. Even if a decisive definition of poverty could be found, and the causes of poverty properly understood, it is questionable how useful this knowledge would be compared to rigorous answers to the question, 'what causes wealth?'[2] While attention is often drawn to the fact that nearly half the world's population lives on less than US$2 dollars per day, the solutions-oriented question 'what happened to the other half?' is rarely asked, despite the significance of its answers to addressing poverty. To address poverty effectively, the solutions-oriented approach implied by this question is crucial to addressing poverty. The problem of poverty, in other words, is the problem of poverty, whereas it needs to become the problem of wealth—how is it best created? While vast numbers of people were mobilised, with the help of celebrities, to support a global campaign in 2005 called Make Poverty History, the effectiveness of the campaign would significantly have been increased had its working paradigm, if not its slogan, had been inverted to 'make wealth the future'. All attempts to solve poverty need to start by seeking to understand the creation of wealth.

Without this, development thinking remains tied to a belief in the effectiveness of aid, despite all evidence to the contrary. This is reflected in the Millennium Development Goals (MDGs), on which much of the development community is focused. These goals, and the non-governmental organisations (NGOs) that so vigorously promote them, appear to underestimate how much enterprise development is needed to achieve them. To provide clean drinking water, for instance, in support of these goals will mean that approximately 270,000 households per day need to be connected to clean water supplies over the next fifteen years. This will require thousands of engineers, builders and plumbers to lay the necessary supply infrastructure, the vast majority of whom will come from the private sector.

Business, in other words, is indispensable to the very goals it is so often assumed are achievable merely through public and charitable initiatives. To promote the MDGs without the promotion of private enterprise and economic growth is to implement a model that has long been tried but has almost always failed. Charitable donations and government aid may bring short term improvements, particularly in situations of economic crisis. But over the long term they tend to create dependency and victimise the poor. A more sophisticated approach to development is needed that recognises that foreign direct investment has become the largest source of funding in the developing world, and that vast numbers of poor people are dignified, resilient and creative entrepreneurs and value-conscious consumers.[3] Development agencies need to be encouraged to direct more aid towards catalysing, creating and facilitating enterprise development in poor countries. This is sufficient to indicate that business is vested with unprecedented opportunities to be an agent of positive social transformation in the world today. No account of globalization, theological or otherwise, is adequate, therefore, if it fails to understand the purpose, potential and constraints of the commercial sphere.

Reasons abound why theology, in particular, should engage with business. They are not restricted to the sphere of poverty alleviation but include issues such as vocation, purpose, creativity, human flourishing, work and leisure, responsibility and freedom. But a basic starting-point in applied theology is the conviction, held widely across the faiths, that poverty is not part of the divine plan for human beings. Within the biblical traditions, human beings are made in the image of God and as such are destined for *shalom*, a form of well-being that is as much physical as spiritual. Because poverty scars that image, it must be overcome. God has, therefore, a 'bias to the poor', which for Christians is embodied in the life, death and resurrection of Jesus Christ, whose message to the poor is one of good news. For this reason, material poverty is a theological as well as a socio-economic scandal.

Commercial entrepreneurship is the primary means by which, in the redemptive purposes of God, this scandal is addressed. This is because material wealth is the only solution to material poverty, and the only sphere that generates such wealth is business. This ought to mean that being pro-poor (as all people of faith must surely be) is tantamount to being pro-business. In reality, however, this is far from the way things are, at least in rich societies. Contrary to popular perception, it is people in poor countries who are generally most alive to the benefits of wealth.

Business alone is not enough to achieve prosperity, of course. This requires two particularly important factors that are frequently overlooked: first, the social institutions that characterise all free societies, such as property rights, the rule of law, an independent judiciary and a free press; and second, the cultivation and exercise of virtue beyond the requirements of the law. These elements have strong biblical foundations, and provide the context in which business can flourish.

Basic conditions such as these aside, there is simply no other way to banish poverty in the long term than through the commercial operations of private vigorous growth of enterprise. Why then is this so often ignored or denied, not only by the development community but also in the media, academia and civil society in general? One reason is the negative attitude towards business that is so prevalent in the churches, which have played a key role in highlighting the plight of the world's poor. Inasmuch as Western culture has been radically influenced by Christianity over the past 2000 years, this attitude can also be found in wider culture, though the traffic in attitudes flows in both directions— there is good evidence that the church's attitude grew out of its wider cultural context during the early centuries of its history.[4] However, insofar as the contemporary blind spot towards the potential of business is attributable to Christian teaching, this chapter seeks to make the case that at least part of the remedy is the development of a theology of business, and that such a theology has greater prospects, both in theory and in practice, if it is based on the theological paradigm of *transformation* rather than the one on which it has been based ever since the advent of liberation theology in the 1960s, which is *liberation*.

There is, however, a major barrier to the call for a positive transformational theology of business: the widespread suspicion, intensified in the wake of the credit crisis of 2008-09, that business is unable to act as a moral agent because it is inevitably indifferent or hostile to virtue and to the claims of the environment. Newspaper columnists, political pundits and other opinion formers have, in fact, gone further, vociferously claiming that business appeals to some of the lowest human vices, such as avarice, greed and exploitation, all of which dissolve the moral fabric of society. It is, therefore, the duty of the state to impose ethical behaviour on business, by means of regulation.

This chapter accepts as a starting-point that state does indeed have a regulatory role—libertarianism is only alive in textbooks. As the leading Cambridge economist John Maynard Keynes (1883-1946) is famous for having argued, the invisible hand of the market needs assistance from the visible hand of the state. The state must, for instance, try to prevent certain markets emerging (such as those in dangerous drugs, prostitution and slavery), and to keep business away from those areas of human life in which it has neither legitimate role nor competence. Regulation is necessary for human beings to be able to exercise freedom, including the freedom the market brings. There are good reasons, however, why regulation is unable to secure an ethical market economy and why it *is* possible to look to business as a valid agent of the moral capital required to achieve and sustain prosperity. This chapter will summarise four of these reasons before taking a look at the area in which the relationship between the commercial and political sphere is often portrayed as highly contentious—responsibility towards the environment. Hopefully this exercise will help stimulate the development of conceptual frameworks and practical models that will help bring greater clarity not only to the currently highly vexed and contorted issue of corporate freedom and state regulation but to the primary role of business, the service of people and planet.

Business as moral agent

The first reason for confidence in the moral identity of business is that the quest for profit, rather than disqualifying business from moral agency, is its first and foremost moral obligation. Business has a legitimate role to generate wealth, on which the whole of society turns. Indeed, it is only if this obligation is fulfilled that business can make any further contribution to moral capital, or to any other kind of capital. Whereas many virtues are recognised as such because the source of their authority is clearly based in moral or religious tradition, the specific virtues necessary for good business are no less moral because they have to do with satisfying customers, promoting innovation and generating new wealth, all with a view to turning a profit. While profit is not an end in itself, it is a vitally important means of serving what *is* the end of economic activity: human persons and the natural environment, for the glory of God. It can, therefore, act as a valid measure of how well this end has been served. Profit is neither immoral nor amoral. Because it is gained through human relationships, results from certain choices, serves as a measure of stewardship, and has the potential to service human and environmental needs, it is intensely moral.

Enterprise, secondly, is capable of inculcating and promoting ethical behaviour. The market economy ought not to be regarded, as so often it is, as the key driver of rampant consumerism, uncontrolled greed, environmental destruction and family breakdown. Such things merely reflect the fact that market freedom, like any other freedom, gives people opportunities both for virtue and for vice. As Lord Acton famously argued, 'liberty is not the power of doing what we like, but the right of being able to do what we ought'. This is why not all young people exposed to tobacco advertising start smoking, or why, though the entertainment industry may constantly expose them to the glamour of sexual promiscuity, some decide on one partner for life. In other words, freedom, which is the very destiny of people and the environment, contains an inbuilt moral challenge. So too, by extension, does the so-called free market. Business faces this challenge on a daily basis and needs to be inspired, incentivised and resourced in order to meet it. Substituting this for legal coercion is misguided not because it imposes too much on business, but too little. It also assumes that business cannot be a moral agent without such coercion. Whatever the failings of particular banks and corporations, business can and does provide a fertile context for people to acquire and convey moral competence. Such competence is more important than the law as a source of justice, reflected in the fact that businesses frequently will not do things which are legal but are not moral, even when this may not appear to serve their best financial interests.

The moral role of business is revealed, thirdly, in the relationship between economic growth and moral development. The Harvard economist Benjamin Friedman has recently provided a rigorous analysis of this relationship. A growing economy, he argues, has the potential to improve the environment, reduce poverty, and promote democracy, openness and tolerance.[5] The extent to which he considers this impact to be inevitable is, however, unclear. Surely it is only ethical business that is capable of such positive returns, which then raises the question of causation: which is prior, ethics or enterprise? Much more detailed research is needed to shed light on this issue. In the meantime, Friedman's core thesis is plausible and indeed has precedents in the work of the Nobel Prize-winning economist Simon Kuznets. It may even find support in the encyclicals of Pope John Paul II, in which he wrote: "The advancement of the poor constitutes a great opportunity for the moral, cultural and even economic growth of all humanity."[6] The Pope's perspective represents not only a departure from the zero-sum economics that typifies ecclesiastic perspectives on economics but also a recognition that economic and moral growth go together. This is borne out later in the same encyclical, where John Paul II makes clear that he sees "the training of competent business leaders who are conscious of their responsibilities' as a way in which rich countries can help poor ones".[7] The Pope would have been gratified to see that the moral dimensions of operating in developing countries are attracting growing attention amongst business leaders, partly as a result of increased globalization. This is indeed good news, for the pathway out of poverty for almost all the world's people—private enterprise—is only likely to succeed if the thinking and actions of business leaders are infused with norms, values and virtue. A commercially successful company with such leaders at the helm is likely to be a company that is high in moral capital, with the potential to disseminate that capital within the communities in which it operates, while strengthening the moral capital that already resides there.

Trust, fourthly, is a virtue of particular importance to the ways in which business can contribute to the moral capital required for economic development. Indeed, this virtue helps explain why so many countries have failed to achieve a developed market economy. If trust is limited or confined to familial or tribal relationships, trading opportunities are lost and the need for state regulation increases, thus raising transaction costs. High levels of trust, on the other hand, which depend on a robust institutional framework, encourage strong private sectors in which large companies can grow. Such companies are often wary about doing business in low trust societies, due to the associated risks and costs. The consequences for economic development are serious, given the important role played by private enterprise in tackling poverty. It is important, therefore, to gain a better understanding of the role of business in promoting trust. Communication methods must be central to this investigation, given that recent research indicates that the top performing companies are those that are most effective in communicating the company's moral values and guiding principles.[8] It is also important to explore how a company can ensure its operations reinforce whatever indigenous networks of trust there are that extend beyond familial and tribal loyalties. What mechanisms can be put in place to ensure that infringements of ethical behaviour are met with the social disapproval and peer pressure that come from within the host community, rather than relying on legal pressure imposed from outside? Addressing such questions will help business live up to its potential as a purveyor of moral virtue through its core operations. The analysis has to shift, however, from the constraints ethical behaviour imposes to the market opportunities it creates. Where opportunities are limited, due perhaps to pressure from shareholders or competitors, the possibilities companies have to cut the costs of ethical behaviour need to be explored.

Business as environmental agent

Conserving the environment through a reduction in carbon emissions provides a good example of how both the reduced costs of ethical behaviour and a robust legislative framework can serve business interests by increasing competitive advantage. Energy prices are in a state of flux in the midst of the current economic turmoil. But over recent years they have been under upward pressure due to rising demand from the emerging economies. This means that there is an economic as well as a moral and environmental case for greater energy efficiency and for the development of alternative energy sources. By themselves, however, rising energy prices will not be enough to drive investment away from cheap, carbon intensive energy sources towards more sustainable alternatives, many of which, initially at least, will be more expensive. It appears, therefore, that the establishment of a meaningful price for carbon is necessary—one that will drive new investment into low carbon products and services.

The world's largest mechanism for delivering this is the European Emissions Trading System, which caps the overall level of emissions that are permitted, allowing participating companies to buy or sell emission allowances so that cuts can be achieved in the most cost efficient way. This major political achievement would not have been possible without companies and business associations such as the Confederation of British Industry (CBI) agitating for it. One of their aims in doing so has been to achieve greater certainty, for the sake of business planning. It has also been to show that emissions can be reduced without damaging competitiveness, and to support the growth of international carbon markets. For the business sector, the longer it takes for a carbon trading system to emerge, the costlier their environment-friendly investments will be.

Business has, therefore, a leadership role to play in this field. Not only can it provide innovative solutions and drive green change through its supply chains, it can also provide customers and employees with the information and incentives they need to make greener

choices. Business can also reach out to policymakers to help develop
rules and standards, and encourage investment in green technology.
The Energy Technology Institute, a UK-based joint venture between
public and private finance, is one example of what is possible. Likewise, developing carbon capture and storage appears to have caught
the imagination of both policy makers and energy companies. The
CBI has also taken a lead in creating a Climate Change Board with a
view to developing policy, promoting best business practice and holding both government and business to account. This Board will seek
to collaborate with all of the UK's main political parties to exchange
ideas and information about the development of environmental policy.
It aims thereby to green the current tax system; to provide a set of
proposals to support new low carbon technologies coming to market;
and to develop consensus on a standard methodology for reporting
corporate carbon emissions.[9]

Many people, including many church leaders and theologians, respond to such demonstration of environmental concern on the part of
business with cynicism or suspicion. Emboldened by the anti-business
sentiments of the media, they tend to regard business only as part of
the problem of climate change, rather than as part of the solution. The
commitment of business to securing a sustainable future is dismissed
as mere 'greenwash', motivated not by concern for the health of the
planet but by naked profit. But those who turn to environmental cam-
paigning often find that those they considered culprits are actually
fighting on the same side. Three events during 2006 serve as examples:

- the chairman of the Virgin Group Sir Richard Branson declared that he will commit all the profits from his transport
  companies over the next ten years—a projected US$3bn
  (£1.6bn)—to develop renewable forms of energy;
- the US President George W Bush, a former oil magnate, challenged his country's 'addiction to oil' and pledged massive
  financial support for research into cleaner fuels.[10]
- a consortium of British big-business leaders sent an open letter to the Prime Minister urging tougher regulation of carbon
  emissions and the CBI significantly steps up its activism in
  this area.[11]

People with an understanding of the opportunities, rather than
merely the constraints, of commercial enterprise are less likely to
be bewildered by such developments, or to stigmatise such apparent
changes of heart as attempts by wolves to don sheep's clothing. For
many business leaders make the case that greater curbs on CO_2 emissions would encourage innovation and increase their company's competitiveness in the global marketplace. There is a secret here that those

who align themselves too uncritically with the green movement often fail to grasp: business is generally only too willing to change the way it operates in accordance with the social and environmental concerns of consumers, because doing so increases its market opportunities. That is, after all, how big business stays big.

It is also the reason why oil companies are no longer interested solely in oil. Hydrogen energy is a major concern for Shell, for instance, and BP now stands for 'beyond petroleum'. Car companies, similarly, are engaged in a frenetic race to develop cheap and reliable clean-fuel vehicles. It is not merely the depletion of oil reserves that motivates such companies. They want to get ahead of demand so that they can capture new markets. That is why they regard regulation as a guarantee that, in the long run, their investment in green technologies will pay off. While cynics claim that economic recession will bring an end to business' purported concern for the environment, corporate leaders are increasingly regarding the green economy as one of the most promising routes to recovery. In a recent research report from the Economist Intelligence Unit, forty percent of respondents said their firms had developed new products and services in the last two years that help to reduce or prevent environmental problems. Nearly a third confirmed that this type of new product development will be a high priority over the next couple of years.[12] The demand for lower carbon emissions is creating a plethora of new business opportunities that may represent the first green shoots of recovery.

Whatever transpires, Richard Branson's putative $3 billion is not, in fact, a donation. It is an investment in his renewable-energy enterprise, Virgin Fuel. That is why his announcement is good public relations (PR), even though it cannot be dismissed as *merely* good PR. Poachers are turning to game-keepers as they discover the vision and commitment to convert an inconvenient truth, as Al Gore would have it, into a convenient one.[13] Inhabiting a moral universe means that what is good for people and the environment turns out to be what is good for the bottom line. There is, therefore, a transformative power in enlightened self-interest and it is this that will help save our planet. Whatever truth there may be in the claim that the operations of business are largely responsible for the degradation of the environment, it would be foolhardy, in view of this transformative power, to assume that solutions can be found that ignore or disqualify commercial interests.

But the plea not to rule the interests of business out of the picture puts things too negatively. If the above argument has any validity, there is every reason to believe that business is well qualified to share some of the responsibilities that are often assumed only to be those of government or the 'third sector'. Should the profit motive really be a bar to social and environmental good, human beings would inhabit a strange moral universe, for most of the good that human beings can do for one another and for the world they inhabit is related in some way to the operation of that motive. Even such rudimentary elements as bread and wine are the work of human hands—hands that are animated by a mixture of impulses. Even if all the motives involved in producing such elements were to be entirely honourable, they would not necessarily be entirely altruistic. Self-interest, which is not the same as selfishness, is integral to human (and indeed animal) existence and cannot be assumed to be a part of what theologians have traditionally called the Fall. Indeed, self-interest is so basic to earthly existence that it governs anatomical reflexes over which human beings have no control but which are essential for sustaining human life. While the profit motive occupies a central place in the sphere of commerce, the motive of self-interest is common to all institutions of society. All social institutions are thereby equally bound to operate morally, to ensure that this motive is counterbalanced by other-regarding motives.

It is, therefore, entirely appropriate to expect business to operate morally and to encourage those within this sphere to work towards this goal, rather than assuming that another sphere—the state—needs to impose morality on it or implying that the not-for-profit norms of the third sector need to be made central to business. As noted earlier, the state does have the privilege and duty, as the argument in Romans 13:1-7 appears to imply, to impose legislation on other spheres, including business. But the state, similarly to business, needs to operate within the limitations and boundaries, as well as the obligations and duties, of its role. For government to meddle in the sphere of business is as problematic as business meddling in the sphere of government. While the credit crisis is widely thought to prove the case for the moral bankruptcy of the commercial sphere, it may in fact have at least as much to do with governmental pressure on the banking sector to extend home ownership opportunities to those on low incomes, in an effort to win votes and bolster social stability. Appropriate state interventions notwithstanding, the spheres of society require freedom to flourish, though each sphere is to avoid the danger faced by the early church of using freedom as a licence for evil (1 Peter 2:16). The liberty enjoyed in free societies is, rather, a licence for virtue and it is to the inspiration of such virtue that the efforts of all Christian leaders need to be committed, not least in response to the current economic downturn. The virtues, particularly the virtues that underlie trust, such as thrift, are the foundations on which the market economy was built. Whatever short term fixes of the crisis are found, long term economic prospects depend on a recovery of such virtues. Only with such a recovery will a healthy balance be found between corporate freedom and state regulation.

Transformative business

Hopefully, sufficient rationale for the moral and environmental agency of business has now been given to open up the possibility of a positive theology of business based on the paradigm of transformation. There are many reasons why such a theology has so much to commend it, though this chapter only allows space to deal with two. Before doing so, it is important to stress that 'transformation' is not so all-encompassing to be the only paradigm with which business can adequately be addressed. It is, rather, one that is sorely needed in developing a theology of business that resonates both with those in poverty and with those in business. A theology of business and poverty needs simultaneously to be a theology for business people and for people in poverty (most of whom are involved in some form of commercial enterprise). Given that entrepreneurship offers the best hope for such people, this theology needs to be a theology for entrepreneurs.

The Latin roots of some of the key words used in commercial entrepreneurship suggest that there are good grounds for confidence in the credibility of this project. The word 'company' derives from *cum* and *panis*, which when compounded mean, 'breaking bread together'. The word 'corporation' comes from *corpus*, meaning 'body', and 'credit' comes from *credo*, 'I believe (I will be repaid)'. The word 'commerce' comes from *commercium*, meaning exchange, not only of goods and services but of opinions and attitudes. The intimacy in communication and relationship implied is reflected in its use to denote both a traditional academic feast known at universities in most Central and Northern European countries and sexual intercourse (the latter in Shakespeare, for instance). These meanings are deeply suggestive of the way in which contemporary business can be a transforming agent in society, helping to build credible, meaningful and inclusive patterns of community based on trust. They even suggest that in doing so they manifest a form of sacramentality. This certainly corresponds with the experience of many Christian business people, who find that their workplaces provide a relational context for exercising their gifts and ministries that is deeper and more effective than those provided by their church.

A single example from history is sufficient to highlight the transformative potential of an inclusive approach to business. Liberation theology assumes that the task of social revolution is the preserve of those excluded or oppressed by the wealth-creating processes of contemporary economies. The history of Marks & Spencer suggests, however, that business itself can be a vehicle of such revolution, by way of its inclusivity. By the mid-1920s, the four brothers-in-law who ran the company, which had begun penny bazaars in Manchester in 1884 and variety stores in 1915, had turned the company into a major chain of variety stores. At this point, they could have decided to sit back and enjoy their considerable wealth. Instead, after visits made by Simon Marks to US retailers in 1924, they decided to re-think the overall objective and mission of their business. The purpose of Marks & Spencer, they decided, was not retailing but 'social revolution'. It would seek to subvert the class structure of Victorian England by making goods of upper-class quality available to the working and lower-middle classes, at prices they could easily afford. This vision influenced the company's decision to concentrate on clothing, as, in the England of the time, what people wore was the most visible of class distinctions.

Instead, therefore, of seeing business as the power from which we must be liberated, it may be more fruitful if we were to hold business organisations in similar regard to the way we hold our churches, neighbourhoods, voluntary organisations, schools and hospitals. We may even grow to love business, though to do so we would need to make concerted efforts to understand it and become more familiar with its constraints and opportunities, for as St. Augustine wrote: "you cannot love what you do not know". This need for understanding is well expressed by two Roman Catholic writers, who call for, "intellectual caution by religious thinkers when speaking about anything as complex as modern business. The theologizing is bound to be better if there is a comprehensive understanding of what it is businessmen and women do."[14]

If we were to do this, we would still find plenty wrong with business. But the attitude of trust that would spring from such love would mean that any judgements and moral demands we make are far more likely to be heeded and acted on by those within the business sphere. The prophetic, in other words, needs to be balanced with the pastoral. To fail in this would be to allow the role of the church to be banished yet further from the mainstream of society. As Ronald Cole-Turner writes: "It is altogether too likely that the church will marginalize itself in the role of chaplain, picking up the pieces, caring for the bruised, mopping up the damage, but never engaging the engines of transformation themselves, steering, persuading and transforming the transformers."[15] Change will come only when this work of engagement and transformation comes to be seen as a sacred task. Though sharply critical of the market for substituting God's economy of gift with an economy of exchange, Bishop Peter Selby writes: "Those who engage with the business of economic transformation, which is the opening of the world to justice and the freeing of the world to a future of hope, are in my view doing work that is not just good but sacred."[16]

Without developing a transformative theology of business, it is doubtful, indeed, whether the church will be able to construct a viable vision for the strengthening and renewal of civil society, as business has become the chief agent of social transformation. It is also the social form distinctive of an increasing amount of cooperative activity outside the family, government and personal friendships. As such, it is a cornerstone of society. Estimations as to which sector of society is most fundamental have often been exaggerated, of course, with damaging effects. For Hegel it was the state; for Marx, the commune; for Lenin and Hitler, the political party. Earlier estimations have included the church, the feudal lords and the monarchy. Each of these suggestions reflects the historical context in which they were forged. Today, however, there can be little doubt that it is business that has become the pre-eminent social sphere in most of the Western world. Whatever the pros and cons of this situation, it does seem generally to hold true that where opportunities to form businesses are constricted or the skills needed to sustain them are deficient, societies stagnate and remain materially deprived. The converse is also true—many countries in Asia, most notably India and China—are undergoing vigorous development in circumstances in which the amount of red tape surrounding the formation of businesses has been considerably reduced.[17] The US and Canada now have more inter-corporate trade with Asia than with Europe, reflecting the fact that the focus of global commerce is shifting from the Atlantic community to an emerging Asia-Pacific community of nations. And despite the ongoing vigour of liberation theology in Latin America, the larger nations of that region are turning to a renewal of democratic patterns of governance, with an increased role for business.

Business is clearly a social institution to which more and more of the world is becoming committed. The biblical message needs, therefore, to be dynamically reconceived in social and economic environments far removed from those of biblical times. This task is at least as important to the future of humanity as today's theologies of sexuality and biomedical ethics. The biblical, doctrinal, ethical and interpretive resources of the churches have more to offer contemporary culture by means of a focus on entrepreneurship than has yet been seen to be the case. A rediscovery of these resources is the first requirement of all Christians and church communities that wish to speak with social and ethical relevance in today's rapidly changing culture.[18] The second requirement is to listen carefully and humbly to entrepreneurs, who often face ethical dilemmas from which theological ethicists are generally protected. Otherwise there is a danger that the church's teachers will become like the lecturer in liberation theology encountered by Laura Nash, a Harvard academic. When she asked him whether he had ever engaged in a discussion with managers of multinational corporations with responsibilities in developing countries, he answered with surprise, 'Why should I do *that*?' He was quite certain that he understood the psychology of business people, which was bound by selfishness and greed and lacked theological grounding.[19]

A second key advantage of the transformative paradigm is that it takes account of the biblical story of Creation, Fall, Redemption and Consummation. It is thereby able to avoid extreme positions that either denounce business as irretrievably corrupt or embrace it as synonymous with God's kingdom. Unlike a liberational perspective, a transformational one advocates the reform, rather than replacement, of the means of production. The market economy, existing as it does under the sovereignty of God, is an arena in which Christians can confidently participate, affirming and strengthening what is good, mitigating the effects of the Fall, furthering the effects of Redemption and anticipating the coming new order.

A transformational perspective allows business to be seen, therefore, as one of the foundational spheres of human life that provide the moral framework for human flourishing. This sphere is constituted and shaped, at least in the current era, by market-oriented institutions and practices—in a similar way to which, in the political sphere, at least in high-income countries, democratically oriented institutions and practices are predominant. Just as democracy has proven, in theory and practice, to offer the best prospects for human flourishing over other systems of government, the same is true of the market economy. Both 'systems' should, therefore, be accorded the kind of qualified ethical affirmation given in the papal encyclical *Centesimus Annus*.

This is not to suggest that the market principle, any more than the democratic principle, should be read back into the pages of scripture in an effort to gain blanket biblical endorsement. It is to suggest, however, that in developing a Christian ethical view of the role of business, the positive as well as the normative is important (the way things are, not just the way things should be). It follows from this that, if democratic and economic freedom can be shown to contribute to human well being, this is of moral significance; the empirical is not necessarily antithetical to the ethical. Business can and should be seen as a key agent of moral and environmental good, and Christians ought therefore to be committed to it, striving to provide moral guidance, inspiration, challenge, admonition, support and friendship for those who work within it.

The positive impact of such action would be felt on many levels, contributing to the reform not only of business but of society at large. As two leading proponents of 'relationism' argue: "Reform seeks to create an environment in which it is easier to live righteously. It is both reasonable and right to mould society so as to minimize the conflict between Christ and culture. . . . Transforming society is about getting relationships right."[20] It would, moreover, help to maximise the potential of business to help extend the kingdom of God. This kingdom is breaking into the created and fallen world through the redeeming work of Christ, even in instances in which Christ is not named. In words from the Second Vatican Council: "Earthly progress must be carefully distinguished from the growth of Christ's kingdom. Nevertheless, to the extent that the former can contribute to the better ordering of human society, it is of vital concern to the Kingdom of God."[21] Whether the extension of God's kingdom through business occurs in explicit or implicit ways, Christian mission and development agencies are gradually waking up to this potential. Some are beginning to encourage entrepreneurs and other business professionals to use their commercial skills to bring both spiritual and material uplift to needy countries. This new model of mission reflects the fact that business is becoming a transcendent global culture. Through their involvement in it, business people are finding that otherwise impenetrable societies are opening up to Christian witness *and* experiencing increasing economic well-being.

Again, this global business culture has great potential for ill as well as for good. It can be used to dominate, exploit and demean, as neo-Marxist post-colonial intellectuals are often swift to point out.[22] The principle of reciprocity must always be maintained, therefore, as a safeguard against abuse. In other words, the transformers need the consent of those whose lives they propose to help transform. It is arguable, however, that markets based on free exchange provide a rudimentary form of reciprocity. Many people in poor countries are finding, moreover, that business, though having the potential to exploit, can be a vehicle of social justice, dignity and freedom from oppression. Indeed, a recent Globescan survey commissioned by the Commission for Africa found that most Africans lay the primary responsibility for the problems in their countries at the door not of global business, nor of former colonial powers, but of their own national governments.[23] One of the challenges of globalization is the opportunity it gives for those with commercial skills to follow Christ into the global marketplace, seeking to pervade every area of business with his truth, liberty, creativity and justice. As Richard Harries writes:

> We need a new vision of capitalism existing for all God's children. Such a vision and the determination to bring it about is the work of Christian discipleship in the social, economic and political spheres. The risen Lord, whom Christians seek to serve, calls us to follow him not only in our personal lives but by denying ourselves, taking up our cross and following him into the companies, markets, exchanges and parliaments of the world. If we do this we are bound to come up against vested interests, and deeply ingrained forces of institutional self-interest as well as personal selfishness. But in suffering with Christ on

behalf of the poor we will enter more fully into the
joy of the resurrected life.[24]

For the call to seek first the kingdom of God (Mt 6.33) is not just
for ministers and professional missionaries, leaving business people
merely to support them financially. Rather, in the 21st century, business
holds a vital key to unlock societies to the freedoms and joys of the
kingdom of God. Countries that have closed the door to traditional
missionaries are competing with each other to attract entrepreneurs
who can help grow their economies. Taking the opportunities for
Christian witness that are naturally available in commerce is a vital
and strategic means of co-operating in God's mission to the world.

This mission involves bringing salvation, healing and *shalom* to
every sphere of society. The impact of the Fall is waiting to be undone.
Because of the Cross and Resurrection, evil can be overturned and the
scourge of poverty can be addressed. History is replete with examples of
how Christians have picked up this challenge—through the political and
economic framework of the Roman Empire, the trade relations of the Age
of Exploration, the invention of the printing press, even through the colonial apparatus, and, most recently, through global business enterprise.

Christians at work in the global economy are uniquely placed to bring
transformation to the circumstances of the world's poor. As they do so,
they are ensuring that globalization works as a blessing, rather than as a
curse. They are helping to realise globalization's potential to bring social
uplift, serve the common good and even help protect the environment.
While the emphasis in liberation theology on seeing the world from the
perspective of the poor is to be cherished, its economic dogmatisms have
to be set aside in favour of a rigorous and theologically balanced engagement with the transformative role of business in today's world. Without
this, it is not obvious that the church will have a sufficiently compelling
vision to allow it to 'make a difference' in contemporary culture. For a
reconstruction of its theology will require a major shift in orientation
and tone. But such a reconstruction is an important first step in making
poverty history by making true wealth the future.

....

PETER HESLAM (DPhil, Oxford) is a Fellow of the Faculty of Divinity Faculty
and Director of Transforming Business at the University of Cambridge. He
is also a Fellow of the Royal Society of Arts and an Adviser to the Centre for
Entrepreneurial Leaders at Trinity Western University, Langley, Canada. His
publications include *Creating a Christian Worldview: Abraham Kuyper's
Lectures on Calvinism* (Eerdmans, 1998), *Globalization: Unravelling the
New Capitalism* (Grove Books, 2002), and *Globalization and the Good*
(Eerdmans, 2004).

NOTES

[1] Abraham Kuyper, *Lectures on Calvinism* (Grand Rapids, MI: Eerdmans, 1931, 1987), 90, 96.

[2] I argue elsewhere that Pope John Paul II's willingness to ask this question makes his encyclical *Centesimus Annus* of 1991 distinctive in Catholic Social Teaching, www.stthomas.edu/CathStudies/cst/conferences/thegoodcompany (accessed 4 April 2009).

[3] Whereas annual Official Development Assistance to developing nations remained flat at US$53 billion between 1990 and 2000, net private capital inflows to developing nations nearly quadrupled, from $44 billion to $154 billion over the same period (Institute for International Finance, *Capital Flows to Emerging Market Economies*, 2007, www.iif.com (accessed 4 April 2009).

[4] For an exposition and evaluation of the key teachings on wealth and poverty of the patristic period, see Peter S Heslam, "Can Christianity Give a Positive Value to Wealth? An Engagement with the Early Church Fathers", www.transformingbusiness.net (accessed 4 April 2009).

[5] Benjamin Friedman, *The Moral Consequences of Economic Growth* (New York: Alfred A. Knopf, 2005).

[6] Pope John Paul II, *Centesimus Annus*, #28.

[7] Ibid, #35.

[8] Keith Leslie, Mark A. Loch and William Schaninger, "Managing your organization by the evidence", *The McKinsey Quarterly*, 3 (2006).

[9] The CBI brought out a report on climate change towards the end of 2007, which called for urgent action to cut greenhouse gas emissions by means of a partnership between government, business and consumers. See *Climate Change: Everyone's Business*, available at www.cbi.org.uk (accessed 4 April 2009).

[10] See George W Bush's State of the Union address in 2006, available at www.whitehouse.gov (accessed 4 April 2009). The Climate Change Technology Programme (CCTP) was keenly supported by the Bush administration—see www.climatetechnology.gov (accessed 4 April 2009).

[11] This culminated the following year with a report published by the CBI that called for urgent action to cut greenhouse gas emissions by means of a partnership between government, business and consumers. See *Climate Change: Everyone's Business*, available at www.cbi.org.uk (accessed 4 April 2009).

[12] Economist Intelligence Unit, *Countdown to Copenhagen: Government, Business and the Battle Against Climate Change*, www.carbontrust.co.uk (accessed 4 April 2009).

[13] Former US Vice President Al Gore has produced both a film and a book entitled *An Inconvenient Truth* (London: Bloomsbury, 2006). For an account of how Sir Richard Branson was 'converted' to environmentalism over a breakfast he had with Gore, see www.abcnews.go.com (accessed 4 April 2009).

[14] Oliver F. Williams and John W. Houck (eds.), *The Judeo-Christian Vision and the Modern Corporation* (Notre Dame: University of Notre Dame Press, 1982), 23.

[15] Ronald Cole-Turner, "Science, Technology, and the Mission of Theology in a New Century", in Max L. Stackhouse with Don S. Browning (eds.), *The Spirit and the Modern Authorities* (Harrisburg, PA: Trinity Press International, 2001), 143.

[16] Peter Selby, *Grace and Mortgage: The Language of Faith and the Debt of the World* (London: Darton, Longman & Todd, 1997), 168.

[17] Registering property in Norway requires one step, but 16 in Algeria. To incorporate a business takes two days in Canada, but 153 in Mozambique. In Sierra Leone it costs 1,268 percent of average income, compared with nothing in Denmark. These and other regulatory and bureaucratic obstacles can be found in the World Bank's *Doing Business* reports, www.doingbusiness.org (accessed 4 April 2009).

[18] Max L. Stackhouse and Dennis P. McCann, "Post-Communist Manifesto: Public Theology after the Collapse of Socialism", *Christian Century*, 16 January 1991, 1, 44-47. Reprinted in Max L. Stackhouse, Dennis P. McCann and Shirley J. Roels (eds.), *On Moral Business: Classical and Contemporary Resources for Ethics in Economic Life* (Grand Rapids, MI: Eerdmans, 1995).

[19] Laura Nash, "How the Church has Failed Business', in *The Conference Board Review* (2007), available at www.conference-board.org (accessed 4 April 2009). For further examples of this attitude, see Laura Nash and Scotty McLennan, *Church on Sunday, Work on Monday: The Challenge of Fusing Christian Values with Business Life* (San Francisco: Jossey-Bass, 2001).

[20] Michael Schluter and John Ashcroft (eds.), *Jubilee Manifesto: A Framework, Agenda and Strategy for Christian Social Reform* (Leicester: Intervarsity Press, 2005), 26-28.

[21] *Gaudium et Spes*, section 39. Cited in John Paul II's *Laborum Exercens*, section 27.

[22] See, for instance, Michael Hardt and Antonio Negri, *Empire* (Cambridge, MA: Harvard University Press, 2000). See especially sections 3.4 and 3.6.

[23] The results showed that 49 percent blamed their own politicians; 16 percent blamed former colonial powers; and 11 percent blamed other rich countries. In other words, three times more Africans blamed their own countries than former colonial powers. See Commission for Africa, *Our Common Interest: Report of the Commission for Africa* (London: Commission for Africa, 2005), 41. Available at www.commission-forafrica.org (accessed 4 April 2009).

[24] Richard Harries, *Is there a Gospel for the Rich? The Christian in a Capitalist World* (London: Mowbray, 1992), 175-76.

Canada's Oil Sands Developments as Icon of Globalization[1]

by John L. Hiemstra

A "black gold rush" has transformed the Canadian province of Alberta into "the poster child for what a red-hot economy looks like".[2] Fuelling this massive set of industrial developments is a novel form of petroleum initially named the "tar sands" but more recently given the more environmentally friendly moniker the "oil sands". In fact, the oil sands developments are a typical example of globalization with its astonishing negative and positive impacts on our economic, social, and environmental life. Not only is it reshaping Alberta and Canada as a whole; it is impacting all of North America, since Alberta now supplies more oil to the United States than any other single country. The effects of the tar sands boom now also echo around the world, impacting climate change, resource depletion, capital flows, income disparities, social breakdown, technological innovation, consumption patterns, and human migration!

This article argues that the tar sands developments, with all their contributions, complexities, costs, and contradictions, are best understood as an icon of globalization. An icon symbolises something of greater significance through a literal or metaphorical depiction, often something of deep religious, cultural, political, or economic importance. Alberta's oil sands are an icon of globalization in two closely related ways. First, they are an astonishing 're-presentation' of most of the vast technological and economic processes, as well as common social, economic and environmental challenges, associated with globalization. This argument meshes well with much of the literature on globalization. Many of the common scholarly approaches to globalization, however, tend to be reductionistic in that they focus almost exclusively on the technological and economic processes and structures of globalization. They tend to underplay, or fail entirely to address, the underlying dynamics that direct and shape globalization. The second argument of this article, therefore, is that the tar sands developments are an icon of globalization because they also signify the deeper spiritual thrust of the interlocking and dynamic processes of globalization. When we look at the oil sands developments, we see an icon of the vision of life that pervades the structures and processes of globalization, that is, the Enlightenment faith in progress.

Before proceeding, I note that the terms 'tar sands' and 'oil sands' are highly charged terms and part of an ideologically loaded discussion of the oil sands developments today. The material extracted, of course, is technically neither oil nor tar but rather bitumen. In order to remain open to "hearing and engaging" arguments and evidence from all corners, and not to prematurely shut down sorely needed dialogue, I use both terms interchangeably.

Alberta's Black Gold Rush

When any state, province, or region experiences the highest levels of economic growth in a country, attracts massive levels of global investment, and sets records for new job creation, our secular mainstream culture recommends that we respond with joy and celebration. Over the last decade, before the global economic slowdown began in 2009, most citizens of Alberta took this advice. The province went crazy about the black gold rush. Alberta had the highest consumer spending in Canada, the highest personal savings, and soaring population growth. Albertans bought more hi-tech gadgets and consumer goods and services than in any other province. Wages were skyrocketing. They enjoyed the lowest unemployment rate in Canada, which until recently, sank below 4 percent. Immigration of skilled workers from other provinces and countries could not keep up with labour demand. The Alberta government ran billion-dollar budgetary surpluses each year and proudly proclaimed itself the only debt-free province in the country. Alberta was the centre of international attention as its oil-driven economic growth powered the entire national economy and began to play a significant role in the energy and economic futures of the USA and the world.

What did Alberta have to thank for these economic 'blessings'? Although its conventional oil and gas reserves were depleting, Alberta's oil sands contain petroleum reserves second in size only to Saudi Arabia. At least 175 billion barrels can be recovered from the oil sands with existing technology, and with new technologies under investigation the recoverable reserves might swell to as much as 2.5 trillion barrels! Current production from the oil sands is just over 1 million barrels a day, projected to reach 3 million by 2015, and 6 million barrels by 2030. Most of this production is shipped directly to the United States, which, former President George W. Bush admitted in 2006, "is addicted to oil".[3] Significantly, America's addiction has become Alberta's prosperity, and Alberta is now the new 'supplier' on the block!

Development of the oil sands took off exponentially when oil prices spiked after 2006 to well over $100 US per barrel. Production from the oil sands had generally been profitable at around $35 US per barrel, according to Canada's National Energy Board. Oil sands extraction plants that are already established and running, like Syncrude and Suncor, were making a profit at prices as low as $25 per barrel. While per barrel costs have risen dramatically, due to spiralling construction costs generated by intense growth rates, large transnational energy corporations were making mammoth profits from the oil sands until the economic collapse of 2009. During this boom period, investment in the oil sands has jumped to $90 billion dollars in current extraction and plant construction, and projections showed up to $100 billion of investment was planned over the next decade.

Tar Sands Exhibit the Structures and Processes of Globalization

How are we to understand this amazing 'black gold rush'? In this section, we explore how the tar sands developments can be understood as an icon of globalization, in the sense that they contain the widely acknowledged technological and economic features of globalization. The oil sands developments are enabled by, and serve to perpetuate, the new forms of communications, transportation, and information processes that characterise globalization. They clearly depend on the massive capital flows, complex production processes, world trade patterns, and enormous transnational corporations that globalization has spawned.

Globalization has produced typical urban and suburban landscapes and associated ways of life. It has spawned intricate national and international transportation systems and given rise to the complex world-wide trade processes we now take for granted, even though they demand massive quantities of transportation fuel to operate. Since various petroleum products—such as gasoline, diesel and jet fuel—are still the pre-eminent and preferred transportation fuels of our societies, globalization requires a persistent and ongoing hunt for new and larger reserves of petroleum. The explosive growth in the tar sands developments is a direct result of this critical and increasingly desperate need built directly into the fabric of globalization. As world demand for petroleum increases, we are forced to search for and recover more and more remote, marginal and technically complicated sources and forms of petroleum.

As an extremely difficult and costly form of petroleum to produce, however, the tar sands are further linked to globalization because they require massive amounts of investment, technology, energy and expertise to exploit. The tar sands have become a 'viable' source of petroleum for a globalized world only because of the capacities developed within globalization itself! To restate this another way, the tar sands are considered an excellent international investment and viable energy source only because of the complex technical processes, massive industrial projects, giant transnational corporations, and mega-project designs that globalization itself has generated! The oil sands developments are *iconic* of globalization, therefore, in both supplying the needs of, and in being dependent on the technological and economic processes of globalization.

The Oil Sands Developments

The oil sands deposits are essentially oil-soaked sand found at or near the surface of the earth. Technically, they are "deposits of bitumen, heavy black viscous oil that must be rigorously treated to convert it into an upgraded crude oil before it can be used by refineries to produce gasoline and diesel fuels".[4] The best way to describe bitumen is "a thick, sticky form of crude oil, so heavy and viscous that it will not flow unless heated or diluted with lighter hydrocarbons. At room temperature, it is much like cold molasses."[5] These oil sand deposits cover nearly 149,000 square kilometres of Alberta, which is a quarter, or 23 percent, of the province,[6] an area larger than the state of Florida.

The energy in the oil sands can only be recovered with immensely large and technically complex extraction, upgrading, and refining processes. David Suzuki, a Canadian award-winning scientist, environmentalist, and broadcaster, describes the two main types of extraction processes:

> A film of water surrounded by oil coats each grain of sand. The bond has to be broken by an energy-intensive hot water process. There are essentially two methods of extraction. If it's a deep deposit, steam to liquefy the oil must be piped underground. The oil seeps like molasses into wells where it can be pumped to the surface. For shallower deposits, they dig giant open pit mines, 100-metre deep holes, as big as 100 square kilometres. In one day, one oil sands mine processes a staggering 450,000 tonnes of earth.[7]

You are probably starting to imagine the immensity of these operations, but let's take a closer look at some remarkable oil sands facts that underline its vast scale.[8] It takes two tonnes of sand to produce one barrel of oil. For the open pit mines, the so-called "overburden" is scraped off; then the oil sands layer is removed and trucked to plants that separate the bitumen from the sand and water. Currently, "oil sands producers move enough overburden and oil sands every two days to fill Toronto's Skydome or New York's Yankee Stadium".[9] Imagine the largest dump trucks in the world, twenty-two feet tall and forty-eight feet from front to back, weighing 400 tonnes, and costing US $6 million each. These trucks carry loads of bitumen-soaked sand to extraction plants. The oil sands operations currently use two times the water used by Calgary, a city of 1 million people. The magnitude of these operations is highlighted by the fact that one of the toxic-tailings ponds is held back by the second largest dam in the world! All of the oil sands projects officially proposed at this time would produce open pit mines 2000 square kilometres in size. The natural gas that will be used to extract the bitumen, when the forecast oil sands developments are in place and production of 5 million barrels per day is achieved, is enough to heat every home in Canada. At the geographical location of the oil sands, the village of Ft. McMurray has grown from 1,500 people in the 1960s into a city of over 70,000 today.

The awesome scale of the oil sands operations and the incredible scientific and technical expertise required to extract this oil show the tar sands developments are centrally connected to globalization. This is further illustrated by the widely held assumption that tar sands exploitation is enormously and automatically beneficial, an assumption frequently held about globalization. For the first years of the current boom, the stance of many Albertans could be summarised by the (perhaps mythical) bumper sticker slogan that appeared just after the collapse of the last 1980s oil boom: *"God, give me another oil boom, and I promise not to blow it this time!"* This attitude reflects the belief that basically everything was positive with the last oil boom in Alberta, except some people failed to profit as much as they had wanted. Recently, however, the assumption of beneficence has been tested by a small but growing sense of disquiet at the margins of Alberta society. New mega-projects may have been driving unprecedented levels of economic growth, but the ecological destruction, social dislocation, and economic problems that are swirling in its wake are becoming more and more troubling.

Media Analyses: "Potholes on an Economic Superhighway"

In spite of growing disquiet in the province, popular media reports during the boom continually underscored the boom's benefits and argued that the economic *benefits* clearly out-weigh the other costs and problems. In a 2006 pull-out section of the *Edmonton Journal* dedicated to oil sands,[10] for example, Gary Lamphier uses the metaphor of "an economic superhighway" to describe the explosive money-making activity around these developments. He celebrates the fact that Alberta's $187 billion economy is "poised to widen its economic and competitive lead against the rest of the nation" as it stands on the "brink of

an era of unprecedented prosperity". He repeats the commonly recited
proofs for economic benefits: the oil sands are producing opportunities
for businesses to *invest*, to create high-paying *jobs*, to generate abundant wealth, and to painlessly multiply government revenues.

In the context of celebrating these positives, Lamphier does touch
on some problems. The way in which he frames them, however, reveals
a lot about his perspective on the tar sands development. Gleaned from
interviews with "some of Canada's best and brightest commentators",
Lamphier outlines five key challenges which, I add, are all integrally
linked to larger processes of globalization: shortages of skilled workers in almost every sector of the economy; a critical deficiency of
infrastructure (roads, bridges, schools, hospitals, etc.); a general over-
dependence on commodity prices and associated "lack of (economic)
diversification"; the lack of a provincial government "spending plan" (it
is too freewheeling in spending the royalty and revenue windfalls); and
the fifth and presumably the scariest challenge, the threat of "outside
economic risks", such as the US, the major consumer of Alberta's oil
and gas products, slipping into an economic slump. These problems are
then portrayed by Lamphier as "potholes", that is, as mere fringe phenomena on an otherwise healthy, vibrant, and vigorous economic superhighway. Significantly, Lamphier's report represents the tenor of most
mass-media coverage of the oil sands economy. Potholes may cause
inconvenience and discomfort, but they are not understood to signal
any fundamental problems with the superhighway itself. The pothole
metaphor implies that the superhighway is itself sound and its bearing
is in the correct direction. Globalization, along with its step-child of oil
sands development, is assumed generally to be a healthy, economically
advantageous, and an obligatory or even fateful course of action.

Scholarly Analyses: Narrowly Disciplinary and Interest-Based Studies

The size, scale and structure of the oil sands developments clearly
place them in the orbit of globalization. Scholarly and think-tank studies confirm this by showing how globalization's capital flows, labour
movements, production processes, trade patterns, and transnational
corporations are transforming the ways that bitumen from the tar sands
is extracted, transported, upgraded, and refined. These scholarly studies also recognise that problems have emerged and, like the popular
literature, tend to downplay their significance by conceptualising them
as mere technical problems on an otherwise successful mega-develop-
ment. Time and space do not permit a full exploration of this category
of studies. In this section, we examine only three *problem* areas, e.g.

economic, social, and environmental, within the oil sands as well as the correlating sets of *solutions* served. The way academic and think-tank literature frame their understandings of the problems and solutions in the oil sands offer further insight into how the oil sands fit the patterns of globalization.

Economic Problems

Economic studies of the oil sands identify a growing list of problems. For purposes of illustration, we identify four. First, some studies focus on the serious shortage of skilled labour and trades people caused by the oil sands boom in Alberta.[11] Skyrocketing economic growth exposed major problems with labour mobility, the introduction of foreign workers from around the world into Canada, and official recognition of off-shore professional and trade credentials. The same studies propose solutions to these problems, such as developing training for aboriginal peoples, so that they can also participate in oil sands jobs, and creating a more systematic and stream-lined credentialing system for foreign workers.

Second, economic studies also show that during the boom Alberta's consumer prices and costs of living spiralled upwards.[12] Wage increases, mounting consumer demand for goods and services, housing shortages, and a rising consumer price index combined to make Alberta a more and more expensive place to live. Poor people were especially vulnerable to rising rental rates, the shortage of homeless shelters, increasing prices, and the dilemma of fixed social incomes. But all Albertans were affected by these trends. Wealthier Albertans faced increased renovation costs as inflation and house prices doubled in only a few years. All levels of government faced rapidly rising construction costs for public infrastructure, schools, and hospitals, as well as spiralling costs for public services. Albertans may have become *richer*, but they were also paying more for private and public goods and services. One solution commonly recommended for these problems is to slow down the rate of expansion of the oil sands development and thereby cool inflation, lower construction costs, and ease pressures on the economy.

Studies also identify a third problem: the low level of government royalties collected from corporations that exploit the oil sands.[13] In Canada, natural resources on crown land are owned, controlled, and administered by provincial governments on behalf of their citizens. Corporations may receive permission to extract these resources in exchange for paying royalties. A royalty is not a tax but a fee paid in exchange for the right to develop and sell a publicly owned resource. Studies argue that the government has exercised poor stewardship of this non-renewable crown resource by failing to collect a fair share of royalties. They note that Alaska imposes a higher royalty rate on oil companies. In relation to the oil sands, Alberta charged a royalty rate of one percent of gross revenue until initial plant construction is paid for, then a 25 percent rate based on net revenue once a company starts to produce oil and make money in its operation.[14] Some studies suggested that this royalty policy amounts to *giving oil away* in order to finance the initial construction and operation costs of plants owned and operated by profitable, transnational oil corporations. Furthermore, the royalty rate stays at 25 percent of profits even in the case where oil prices sky-rocket, producing windfall profits. In response to public pressure, the Alberta government marginally increased the royalty rate on bitumen in 2008, but the rates stay well below what it should charge for a non-renewable heritage resource. A common solution proposed for this problem is that Alberta raise its royalty rates on non-renewable oil sands, save excess revenues, and invest in future generations.

Fourth, economic studies inspired by Canadian nationalism[15] argue that trans-national oil companies are, and others plan to, piping the unrefined bitumen products extracted from the Canadian oil sands directly into the USA for upgrading, refining, and production of end-products. This means Canada forgoes the associated benefits of investment, jobs, and other economic spin offs. Studies propose Alberta adopt regulations requiring companies to upgrade and refine bitumen in Canada leaving more economic benefit in Canada.

An Emerging Pattern

The scholarly and think tank literature on economic problems and solutions teaches us a great deal about select costs and benefits associated with speeding down this *economic superhighway*. Before exploring social and environmental facets of the tar sands boom, we pause to examine how these economic problems are framed, and ask how this discloses important assumptions underlying these studies. Three assumptions stand out.

First, these studies frame problems primarily as *technical issues* that can be addressed and resolved through appropriate applications of new science and technology. Problems in the tar sands are seen as instrumental side-effects of a larger beneficial process of economic development. These scholarly and think tank studies fail to explore the overall thrust of the oil sands boom, and do not ask why it was occurring, or investigate whether on balance it was an overall healthy or destructive event. Instead, they narrowly focus on problems as fragmented phenomena that can be studied and understood in isolation.

Second, based on this type of narrow, technical definition of problems, these studies tend to propose *solutions* that are conceptualised and formulated as *technical adjustments* aimed to repair individual problems or at least mitigate their worst side effects. The solutions that are commonly proposed in this literature tend to be framed as technical adjustments to what is considered a generally beneficial and required set of oil sands developments. They seem to assume that new communication, transportation, and information technologies of globalization can be adopted, adapted and adjusted to resolve these problems, reduce unwanted costs, and mitigate undesired outcomes.

This brings us to a third assumption, namely the belief that oil sands development is essentially a necessary development, on balance sound and beneficial, and in any case, inevitable and fated to continue unfolding in the same general direction. These studies do not investigate economic problems in the context of the deeper vision of the world that drives these developments. It does not consider or reconceptualise problems nor does it formulate solutions in the light of the overall dynamic of the oil sands boom. Consequently, this literature does not entertain the possibility that solutions for oil sands problems might involve taking steps that redirect, turn-around, or outright halt these developments. Nor does it ask how any proposed solution might contribute to this sort of re-orientation of oil sands developments.

A holistic approach to understanding Alberta's massive tar sands developments and how they relate to the larger phenomena of globalization must, I believe, penetrate far deeper than the structures and processes of globalization—deeper than narrow problem definitions and technical-adjustment solutions—down to the deepest spiritual dynamics. As we now examine scholarly and think tank studies of the social and environmental dimensions of the oil sands developments, we look for further evidence of this pattern of narrow problem definition, of technical-adjustment type solutions, and of failure to assess the big picture in which this boom is occurring.

Social Problems

Recent analyses of the oil sands developments show that not everyone shares in the prosperity, a pattern of income distribution often associated with globalization.[16] I briefly introduce three of the problems identified in this literature, moving from those experienced most immediately—aboriginal peoples—to problems impacting people globally—especially the poor in the global south.

First, studies show that some First Nations living near the oil sands operations in Fort McMurray are unhappy with the way these developments are disrupting and destroying their traditional way of life and undermining their inheritance of land, air, water, wildlife and ecology.[17] While some proposed policy solutions seek to curb and diminish these negative side-effects, the more common solution for this problem is to replace traditional lands and lifestyles with jobs and business opportunities for native peoples in the oil sands operations.

Other studies focus on the stubborn persistence of poverty across the province of Alberta in spite of the boom. They show that the gap between rich and poor is actually growing. In 2004, when the oil sands boom was in full swing, the Edmonton Social Planning Council (ESPC) reported that 350,000 Albertans lived in poverty. More than 100,000 of these were children (14.1 percent).[18] In 2007, ESPC Research and Policy Coordinator John Kolkman noted that little had changed: "Despite a booming economy with record low unemployment and labour shortages—Edmonton's social health index is mixed with some indicators up, others down, and a modest increase of 10.95 percent since 1993". On the down side, he elaborates, ". . . there is growing inequality in incomes and wealth. There are more low-weight babies, increased incidence of sexually transmitted diseases, and higher rates of family violence. These negative trends show that we have a long way to go to improve social health in our community."[19] Key suggestions for dealing with these problems include increasing official minimum wages, raising income transfers, and improving social services. To deal with the growing problem of homelessness, studies propose adjusting the market so that it provides more homeless shelters and low-cost housing.

Third, impacts of the oil sands developments surprisingly reverberate into the global south as well. Alberta anticipates $100 billion in oil sands investment over the next decade so that it can supply energy for what amounts to excessive and artificial *wants* of the global north. At the same time, the genuine and pressing *needs* of the poor in the global south fail to attract significant if any private or public investment.[20] Genuine human needs of clean water, malnourishment, poverty, mal-development, environmental destruction, disease, and poor health simply fail to attract private international investors. The solution, studies tell us, is to attract investment to the global south either by increasing foreign aid or by structurally adjusting southern government policies so that their economies are more attractive to market investment.

These analyses of the social impacts of the oil sands developments, as with the previous economic studies, often can teach us some important things. The same assumptions emerge in these studies, however, including the narrow confining approach to problem-definition and the constricted view of solutions as technical-adjustments. Can technical adjustments to the existing system of exploiting the oil sands actually transform it into a healthy form of development? We need to ask ourselves whether these studies and their proposed solutions really offer a new hopeful trajectory of development, or do they simply assume that fate dictates we continue along the same problematic track?

Environmental Problems

Studies of the environmental problems arising from the tar sands reflect the same patterns as above, and add to the growing lists of problems.[21] These studies catalogue problems relating to resource waste, loss of habitat, pollution, health problems, climate change, the loss of future possibilities, and loss of clean air, water, and soil. We briefly explore only three of these problems.

First, water-related problems are growing on all fronts of the oil sands operations. Both the open pit mining and in situ [steam injection] forms of bitumen recovery use huge amounts of fresh water. The level of the Athabasca River, the main source of fresh water in the region, is dropping; and water levels have not returned to their predevelopment levels. Local aquifers are also being drawn down at a rapid rate. Extraction processes produce water pollution and place huge demands on waste-water treatment. The steam-injection approach to extracting bitumen produces saline water as a by-product. The open-pit mining operations leave behind vast toxic tailing ponds. The Pembina report makes a number of very helpful suggestions, including a general call for reduced energy use. On the whole, however, many environmental studies recommend overcoming water-related problems by discovering new technologies to conserve and recycle water.

Second, damage to land and ecology is a staggering problem in the oil sands region. Current and planned open-pit mines would cover 2000 square kilometres. This is comparable to 28,465 National Football League fields, three times the size of the City of Edmonton, or five times the size of Denver. The overall area now leased to oil companies has grown to 32,000 square kilometres. The physical lay and quality of the land and environment is totally transformed by these developments. The oil sands deposits in northern Alberta are covered by the Boreal Forest, which wraps the entire northern region of the globe. Surface oil sand mines cause massive disruption and loss of habitat. Furthermore, 40 percent of the Boreal Forest is wetlands, and notably 35 percent of the world's wetlands are located in Canada's portion of the Boreal Forest! Even if an area is developed by the steam-injection process rather than strip-mining, the ecology of the area is still severely damaged by the fragmentation of forests caused by roads, seismic exploration lines, pipelines, drill sites, power lines, and other infrastructure. To repair this damage to the land and ecology of the region, commentators propose developing new knowledge and technologies to prevent this damage or to devise better practices for restoring and rehabilitating mining and in situ sites.

Air pollution is a third problem identified in the reports. Oil sands developments release a variety of toxic and other pollutants, making Alberta the number-one acid-rain polluter in Canada today. Alberta's

3 million people now pollute more than industrialised Ontario with 11 million people. Large amounts of fossil fuels are burned to extract, upgrade, refine, and transport oil sand products. Green house gas emissions per barrel produced from the oil sands exceed those of any other form of energy! In this era of heightened awareness over global warming, the oil sands developments will continue to push Canada well beyond its Kyoto Treaty obligations. Studies propose that we invest in new technologies and develop better regulatory regimes for reducing pollutants, minimising acid rain, and diminishing and disposing of green house gases.

In a pattern similar to the above social and economic analyses, these environmental studies also tackle the oil sands phenomenon in ways that do not adequately address the overall character and thrust of the oil sands developments. The environmental literature offers a range of solutions that, while well intentioned and helpful in many ways, tend to technically adjust this massive development process.

Modernist Analysis and the 'Spirit' of the Oil Sands Boom

Scholarly studies of tar sands developments do provide us with helpful insights into the technological and economic processes shaping the oil sands. But, this literature fails to recognise the underlying 'thrust' of these developments or to open our understanding to the deeper beliefs and commitments shaping them. Most of this scholarly literature is framed without considering the visions of life influencing and directing the agents and institutions currently developing the oil sands. Why?

Some initial reasons are provided in the highly controversial essay "The Death of Environmentalism: Global warming politics in a post-environmental world",[22] published by Michael Shellenberger and Ted Nordhaus in October 2004. While not wanting to downgrade or ignore the past achievements of the environmental movement, the authors focused their essay on its failings, in particular on its ineffective approach to *global warming*. Recent USA policy shows, the authors claim, that "modern environmentalism is no longer capable of dealing with the world's most serious ecological crisis". The environmental movement is failing, Shellenberger and Nordhaus argue, because it relies on the view of scholarship and policy action that dominates society. The Enlightenment belief in rationality and human mastery completely dominates our contemporary politics, culture, and academia. It tells us three things: first, problems should be defined according to our interests, that is, as "environmental" or social, or cultural, or economic interests. Second, we should craft "technical" remedies to these problems "based on sound science". Finally, we should "sell" our solution—through interest group lobbying and media campaigns—as the proper technical solution for legislators to adopt.

Significantly, the authors' critique of contemporary environmentalism on global warming illuminates the approach to scholarship and policy action found in much of the tar sands literature. Participants, and even some critics, tend to define economic, social, and environmental problems narrowly, often in terms of one or another interest. They craft and propose technical solutions for their problem in order to adjust the overall development processes and thereby to reduce the problematic side effects. Finally, they lobby government to adopt their peculiar policy adjustment solutions.

Shellenberger and Nordhaus' conclusions also apply to the oil sands. The approach to scholarship and policy action which they identified fails, they argue, because problems such as climate change are not narrowly 'environmental problems' at all. To speak of the environment in this way transforms it into a 'thing', an object for which 'interests groups' can devise technical solutions and then politically lobby for their adoption. This approach is too reductionistic, fragmented, and compartmentalised. The environment is us too, the authors argue, climate change is integrally linked to our entire way of life and built into our societal institutions and core values. They observe that "not one of America's environmental leaders is articulating [in public campaigns on climate change] a vision of the future commensurate with the magnitude of the crisis. Instead, they promote technical policy fixes like pollution controls and higher vehicle mileage standards—proposals that provide neither the popular inspiration nor the political alliances the community needs to deal with the problem." This observation is also eerily on target for Alberta's oil sands boom.

Modernist Science Obscures the Oil Sands Thrust

The approach to scholarship and policy action which Shellenberger and Nordhaus identify and critique is known in various contexts as the modernist or Enlightenment approach to science, or the "naturalism-empiricism-positivism tradition".[23] This reductionistic approach to analysis disaggregates the phenomena it studies into smaller and smaller disciplinary and sub-disciplinary elements. Scholars focus their attention on problems within their highly focused expertise—in the tar sands, for example, the focus is on water, labour shortages, housing and rent problems, GHG emissions, tailings ponds reclamation, infrastructure shortages, governance, or another issues—and then research and analyse them. This narrow, fragmented focus is acceptable to the modernist proponents of this approach precisely because they assume that the resulting insights will automatically cohere into a unified body of knowledge that accurately portrays, even predicts, events in the larger whole. They consider it as a rational and objective approach which transcends divisions of belief, ideology, class and religion around the world. Everyone can use the resulting body of knowledge, proponents argue, to "unlock the secrets of nature" and to achieve major increases in "human health and wealth".[24]

The economic, social and environmental costs of developing the tar sands, which we inventoried above, suggest something far deeper is going on. The modernist method of analysis simply doesn't allow or encourage us to ask any deeper questions of the oil sands developments. Instead, oil companies, government regulators, and even some oil sands critics, use the fragmented knowledge produced by this modernist approach both to narrowly identify problems, and to devise solutions, without analysing the whole or discerning the thrust of the overall boom. Solutions end up being structured as *technocratic adjustments* to the overall process of exploiting the oil sands. Fragmentary knowledge results in actions that lack insight into the interplay of parts as well as the dynamics shaping the whole. This has far ranging consequences. Technocratic solutions often end up tackling symptoms of the larger oil sands developments and, in some cases, paradoxically can produce newer and often more-perplexing problems.

The Spiritual Drive of Globalization

This narrowed approach to analysis along with the technocratic adjustment manner of solving problems, so commonly seen in the tar sands operations, are also characteristic in the development and functioning of globalization. While this approach to analysis is considered by proponents to be neutral, objective and universal, closer examination suggests it is deeply stamped by the Enlightenment faith in progress.[25] Since this modernist approach to analysis is blind to the particular beliefs and convictions that shape its own functioning, it should not surprise us that this approach is also blind to the spiritual thrust behind its objects of study, including human society, the tar sands operations, and globalization.

In their examination of global warming, Shellenberger and Nordhaus also conclude that we need to "take a collective step back to rethink everything". The environmental movement must "tap into", they conclude, "*the creative worlds of myth-making, even religion*, not to better sell narrow and technical policy proposals but rather to figure out who we are and who we need to be".[26]

A sensitive discernment of the deeper thrust of globalization shows that the same convictions animating the modernist approach to analysis also animate globalization. Bob Goudzwaard argues in *Globalization and the Kingdom of God*, that the structures and processes characterising globalization are not fate but are shaped, deep down, by convictions that dominate our times. At heart, globalization "proceeds on the basis of the conviction that the fittest should survive, that victory should go to the strongest, and that might makes right". Consequently, contemporary globalization directs "human economic activities" so that they blur "all distinctions among the different spheres of life worldwide".[27] These characteristics of globalization are organised by the Enlightenment ideology of progress. This ideology can be summarised as follows: humans can exhaustively understand nature through reason and science, they can use this resulting knowledge to create technologies that allow us to completely master and exploit nature, mastered nature can be shaped to generate continuous economic growth, and increasing our material prosperity will guarantee human happiness.

The Tar Sands as Icon of Globalization

This spiritually deepened evaluation of globalization helps us understand why the tar sands developments are, at their deepest level, *icons* of the 'faith in progress' now driving globalization. The tar sands developments are being shaped by the same progress myth that animates globalization. Many Albertans, as with most Canadians, are so obsessed with achieving the goal of material prosperity that they allow the market unrestrained freedom to develop the oil sands with the blind hope that in the end—guided and corrected by a series of technical adjustments—these developments will produce prosperity and happiness. This is the Enlightenment ideology of progress in action. It is linked to a reinforcing ideology which promises that single-minded confidence in scientific development and technological innovation will push society further along the route of progress. The tar sands symbolise and depict the economic and technological patterns of globalization but, more significantly, the deeper ideological or religious thrust of globalization. This is the most profound sense in which the tar sands development functions as an icon of globalization.

We pause before closing to consider briefly whether the ideological thrust shaping both the tar sands and globalization really ought to be referred to as a 'spiritual' or 'religious' thrust? I argue that if an ideology urges people to replace their faith in God with faith in idols, this ideology is for all intents and purposes functioning like a pseudo-religion. Only human creatures can generate ideologies which lead them to breathe life into idols. When humans become so obsessed with achieving one of their central *goals* that they begin placing ultimate trust in one or another *means* in creation—a good created thing, process, or institution—to ultimately deliver the goal to them, they generate an idol.[28] The Enlightenment ideology of progress has given birth to various contemporary forms of idolatry. It is responsible for transforming potentially good elements of creation—such as science, technology, market and the state—into institutions before which entire societies bow and ultimately hope for their security, provision, salvation or future wellbeing.[29]

Another biblical characteristic of idols reinforces this conclusion that the ideological thrust shaping the tar sands boom and globalization ought to be referred to as 'religious'. The adherents of idolatry are described as becoming deaf, dumb and blind, just like the idol itself (Psalm 135: 18). The Enlightenment ideology of progress also produces this effect in society. Relentless pursuit of progress is accompanied by a general form of hypnosis—that is, the single minded pursuit of a goal increasingly closes down the awareness we have of our surroundings. This type of 'hypnosis' leaves us blind to the real effects and genuine problems generated by our obsessive pursuit of our goal. This, the Bible suggests, is one of the main reasons humans fail to act justly, to love mercy and to walk humbly with God (Micah 6:8). In the oil sands developments we see this hypnotic effect causes us to repeatedly profess that 'problems' can be adjusted away and that continuing down the track of progress is in actual fact fate. Significantly, technical adjustment solutions often fail to work as they cause new and larger problems, but most significantly, the rapid development of the oil sands is not fate. Notably, this same characteristic of hypnosis also prevails in the processes of contemporary globalization.

Recognising that the deepest drive of globalization and the oil sands are religious opens up a remarkable insight. Christian faith need not be ignored in analyses of globalization and the tar sands but can, instead, function as a liberating and revealing force. The distinction between Creator and creation, for example, suggests that no force in creation is capable of *autonomously* directing human lives. God alone is the sovereign creator and redeemer. This revelation awakens us to examine more accurately, and to understand more holistically, the ways humans contribute to the creation of problems within the oil sands developments. It encourages us to notice intrinsic connections between novel problems and the human obsessive pursuit of goals. A distinguishing feature of Christian scholarly and social action, therefore, at minimum ought to involve *unmasking* idolatries that masquerade as pseudo-saviours in any part of societal, political, or economic life.

Conclusion

The modernist approach to analysing globalization tends to address tangential problems but misses the indispensable heart of the matter. In particular, it fails to plumb the spiritual and religious depths of events like oil sands developments, overlooking their deepest religious-ideological currents. The stakes are high indeed in properly understanding the tar sands developments as icon of the heart of globalization. Nothing less than the character and direction of our society's participation in these massive developments is at stake.

When a modernist approach to analysis is adopted uncritically within Christian higher education—or Christian social action organisations or overseas development agencies—they tend to fail to identify and critique the central religious thrust of culture, economy, politics and society.[30] The church and Christian agencies need to develop alternative approaches to analysis that are characterised by a vital openness to the spiritual thrust of human activities—that is, to the intention of people to direct their developments by an ultimate love of God or by a love of another creature. In Augustinian sense, Christian higher education needs to encourage society and the academy to discern the deepest love out of which human activities spring. What love directs the unfolding of the structures of globalization and the oil sands developments?

When confronted by events within globalization, such as the tar sands developments, we can respond in various ways. We can adopt a stance of silence, thereby implicitly endorsing and participating in the reigning survival of the fittest, dog-eat-dog vision currently powering the oil sands boom. In this mode, they would simply continue the use of technical adjustment steps to direct the oil sands down the pathway of presumed progress. We can also, however, engage the 'icon of globalization' in our backyard by discerning the underlying obsessions with wealth, progress, science and technology. By exposing these ideological preoccupations, the limiting hypnosis of society can be countered. Technical adjustment solutions can be rethought and replaced with re-orienting steps that redirect oil sands development, as well as our materialistic, self-centred and globalized way of life, into new life-giving paths. Global economic activity can be unfolded, Goudzwaard reminds us, so it "honors the worldwide diversity of God's good creation and prefigures the reign of the coming Lord—the good Shepherd-King—who will do justice to the weak, protect the poor and take care of the land".[31]

John L. Hiemstra (Ph.D., University of Calgary) is Professor of Political Studies and Dean of the Faculty of Social Sciences, The King's University College, Edmonton, Alberta. He has published a wide variety of articles on faith and public life, and *Worldviews on the Air: The Struggle to Create a Pluralistic Broadcasting System in the Netherlands* (Lanham, MD: University Press, 1997).

NOTES

[1] This article is a reworking of an article "Alberta's Oil Sands Boom: A wake-up call for Christian scholarship?" published in *Pro Rege* XXXVI, 3 (March 2008), 15-27. It is based on the speech "Hypnosis, the Myth of Progress, and Our Christian Scholarly Calling" presented during Justice Week at Dordt College, Sioux Centre Iowa, 2 November, 2006.

[2] Gary Lamphier, "Paving the road ahead", *Edmonton Journal*, 11 March, 2006, F1.

[3] President George Bush, "State of the Union Address", Washington, D.C., January 31, 2006. Bush further asserts that "The best way to break this addiction is through technology".

[4] Alberta Government, "What is Oil Sands", http://www.energy.gov.ab.ca/OilSands/793. asp (accessed 31 December 2008).

[5] Ibid.

[6] Dan Woynillowicz, Chris Severson-Baker, & Marlo Raynolds, *Oil Sands Fever: The Environmental Implications of Canada's Oil Sands Rush*, The Pembina Institute: http://www.pembina.org/pub/203 (accessed 1 November 2005), 1.

[7] David Suzuki, "When less is more", *The Nature of Things*, CBC television, air date: Sunday, August 13, 2006, transcript: 3. Dr. Suzuki has a Ph.D. in genetics, is co-founder of the David Suzuki Foundation, and is an award-winning scientist, environmentalist, and broadcaster.

[8] The statistics in the next paragraph are drawn in part from Suzuki, "When less is more", 3-15.

[9] Alberta Government, "What is Oil Sands".

[10] Lamphier, "Paving the road ahead".

[11] Alberta Employment, Immigration and Industry commissioned a report examining worker needs and shortages in the Regional Municipality of Wood Buffalo where most of the oil sands extraction occurs. Applications Management Consulting, *Wood Buffalo Labour Market Information: Worker Needs and Shortages Analysis*, (Final Report), prepared for: Alberta Employment, Immigration and Industry, December 2007. http://www.woodbuffalo.net (accessed 11 February 2008). Alberta Employment, Immigration and Industry also issues periodic reviews of labour market, see: *Annual Alberta Labour Market Review*, 2006, http://employment.alberta.ca/cps/rde/xchg/hre/hs.xsl/67.html (accessed 11 February 2008), and the *Annual Alberta Regional Labour Market Review, 2006*, http://employment.alberta.ca/cps/rde/xchg/hre/hs.xsl/67.html (accessed 11 February 2008). For a critical perspective, see Alberta Federation of Labour, "Another Perspective on the Labour Shortage", *Labour Economic Monitor*, Fall 2007, http://www.afl.org/publications-research/econ-monitor/default.cfm (accessed 11 February 2008).

[12] See Statistics Canada, "Consumer Price Index, February 2007", The Daily, Tuesday, March 20, 2007, http://www.statcan.ca/Daily/English/070320/td070320.htm (accessed 11 February 2008). Longer term trends are explored in Statistics Canada, "Consumer Price Index, annually, by city, 2003-2007", table: 326-0021, last modified: 2008-01-29. http://www40.statcan.ca/l01/cst01/econ45a.htm (accessed 11 February 2008).

[13] See Amy Taylor, *Royalty Reform Solutions: Options for Delivering a Fair Share of Oil Sands Revenues to Albertans and Resource Developers*, Oil Sands Issue Paper, No. 5, (Pembina Foundation: May 2007). See this report, and a series of other studies on Alberta

Royalty reform, at http://www.pembina.org/pubs?filterCategories=11 (accessed 11 February 2008). The government-commissioned study of royalty rates issued the report: Bill Hunter, Chair, Royalty Review Panel, *Alberta Royalty Review Panel Final Report*, 2007, http://www.albertaroyaltyreview.ca (accessed 11 February 2008). The Alberta Premier Ed Stelmach responded with a new royalty rate in Alberta's New Royalty Framework on October 25th, 2007, http://www.energy.gov.ab.ca/About_Us/1293.asp (accessed 11 February 2008).

[14] Alberta Energy, "Royalty Information Briefing #3 – Royalties – History and Description", Alberta Royalty Review 2007, http://www.energy.gov.ab.ca/Org/pdfs/InfoSeries-Report3-Formulas.pdf (accessed 11 February 2008).

[15] See, for example, Hugh McCullum, *Fuelling Fortress America: A Report on the Athabasca Tar Sands and U.S. Demands for Canada's Energy* (The Parkland Institute and Polaris Institutes) March, 2006. http://www.ualberta.ca/PARKLAND/research/studies/Fuelling%20Fortress%20America%20WEB.pdf (accessed 22 October 2007); and Gordon Laxer, *Freezing in the Dark: Why Canada Needs Strategic Petroleum Reserves* (Edmonton: Parkland Institute, January 31, 2008); http://www.ualberta.ca/PARKLAND/research/studies/index.html (accessed 11 February 2008).

[16] See, for example, Anette Wickenheiser, author, John Kolkman (ed.), *Tracking the Trends, 2007 Edition* (Edmonton: Edmonton Social Planning Council, 2007). Also see statistics based on the Market Basket Measure, MBM, from Edmonton Social Planning Council, National Election News Release, May 23, 2004.

[17] Involvement of aboriginal groups with the oil sands varies greatly. Many first nations are being left out in the race to develop the tar sands, see http://www.tarsandswatch.org/tags/aboriginal-rights. A high profile dispute concerns the effects of pollution on aboriginal nations living near the oil sands. See, for example, Dr. Kevin Timoney, "A Study of Water and Sediment Quality as Related to Public Health Issues, Fort Chipewyan Alberta", (Nov. 7, 2007), http://www.tarsandstimeout.ca/images/resources/fcreportupdate-part1.pdf (accessed 11 February 2008). Commissioned by the Nunee Health Authority of Fort Chipewyan, this study looks into the health effects on aboriginal communities downstream of the oil sands mines and upgraders. Graham Lanktree, "Oilsands whistleblower MD cleared: Government charge of 'undue alarm' from cancer warning remains". *National Review of Medicine*, Vol. 5, No.1, Jan. 15, 2008.

[18] See statistics based on the Market Basket Measure, MBM, from Edmonton Social Planning Council, National Election News Release, May 23, 2004.

[19] Wickenheiser, *Tracking the Trends.*

[20] See for example, Bob Goudzwaard, "The Need for Churches' Involvement from an Economic and Theological Perspective", position paper for the conference "Towards a just international financial system" (Frankfurt, Germany, 2000); and Bob Goudzwaard, Mark Vander Vennen, and David Van Heemst, *Hope in Troubled Times: A New Vision for Confronting Global Crises* (Grand Rapids, MI: Baker, 2007).

[21] Woynillowicz et al., *Oil Sands Fever*, 19-58; David Suzuki, "When less is more"; and Ann Bordetsky, et. al., *Driving it Home: Choosing the right path for fuelling North America's transportation future* (jointly produced by Natural Resources Defense Council, Western Resource Advocates, and Pembina Institute, 2007). The information in the following environmental paragraphs is drawn from these reports.

22 Michael Shellenberger and Ted Nordhaus, "The Death of Environmentalism: Global warming politics in a post-environmental world", released at the Oct. 2004 meeting of the Environmental Grantmakers Association. http://thebreakthrough.org/images/Death_of_Environmentalism.pdf (accessed 4 July 2007). These arguments have been helpfully explored in more depth in Ted Nordhaus and Michael Shellenberger, *Break through: from the Death of Environmentalism to the Politics of Possibility* (New York: Houghton-Mifflin, 2007).

23 Donald Polkinghorne, *Methodology for the Human Sciences* (Albany: State University of New York Press, 1983), covers the empirical approach in chapters 2 & 3, and "briefly reviews" it on 201-203. He cites Kockelmans on the names of the 3 basic approaches to human sciences.

24 J. R. McNeill, *Something New Under the Sun: An Environmental History of the Twentieth-Century* (New York: W. W. Norton, 2000), 328.

25 For example, see Herman F. Dooyeweerd, *Roots of Western Culture: Pagan, Secular and Christian Options* (Toronto: Wedge, 1979); Polkinghorne, *Methodology*; Lisa Anderson, *Pursuing Truth, Exercising Power* (New York: Columbia University Press, 2003); and Bob Goudzwaard, *Capitalism and Progress: A Diagnosis of Western Culture* (Grand Rapids, MI: Eerdmans, 1979).

26 Michael Shellenberger and Ted Nordhaus, "The Death of Environmentalism", [my emphasis]. To this they add, incidentally, that the environmental movement needs to create "new institutions and proposals around a big vision and a core set of values".

27 See Goudzwaard's argument along this line in *Globalization and the Kingdom of God* (Grand Rapids, MI: Baker Books, 2001), 22.

28 Note that both the *goal* of "guaranteed material prosperity" and the *means* of market exchange can be considered good possibilities within God's creation. It is our obsession with this goal and over reliance on market means that can distort them and structure them in oppressive and destructive ways. Other elements of creation that people can improperly call on to deliver to them their obsessive goals—like "fail-safe survival of our nation" or "guaranteed security"—are the "state", "law and order", and "revolutionary change".

29 The centrality of the theme of idolatry within the Bible is evident by the fact it is discussed in 213 scripture passages: 172 on 'idols' and another 41 on 'idol'. See John Mihevc's (1-4) and other references to idolatry in *Jubilee, Wealth & the Market* (Toronto: Canadian Ecumenical Jubilee Initiative, 1999). The definition of idolatry in this paper is similar to what Kairos (Canadian Ecumenical Justice Initiatives) refers to as "the consequences of unbridled human activity (alias sin)" http://www.kairoscanada.org/e/ecology/climateChange/turningUpHeat.asp.

30 See, for example, Bob Goudzwaard, *Capitalism and Progress*, 117.

31 Goudzwaard, *Globalization and the Kingdom of God*, 22.

The Challenge of Islam's
Critique of Technology[1]

by Egbert Schuurman

The recent rise of Islamic terrorism has brought to the forefront of global discussion tensions between the Western world and the Islamic world, worlds which share a great deal of history. In these tense times I would like to consider a question that is rarely raised today but that may be relevant to the topic of globalization and quite revealing: What attitude do these two worlds take toward technology? And might the overlap between these perspectives provide us with possible directions for the future?

Any attempt to examine the first question in historical perspective cannot ignore the religious underpinnings of technology, both in the Islamic world and in the West. Tellingly, the themes of religion and technology are very popular today: we note a renewed interest in the vitality of religion around the world and in the arguments regarding its influence on culture,[2] and especially in the historical development of technology. Let me be clear, though, what I mean by the term 'religion'. When the media addresses 'religion' they usually treat it as one of many factors or variables in human life, distinct from and equal to, say, sport, politics or science. If, however, we look carefully at religious communities and various types of societies around the world we can see that religion is not just a typical function among others but is, rather, the *root* from which the different branches of life sprout and grow and from which they are continually nourished. Religion is of *radical* and *integral* importance to culture: it concerns the deepest root of human existence and integrates human life into a coherent whole.

With that assumption in mind this article explores the opening questions in the following steps: First, I briefly sketch the history of technology in the Islamic world, after which I shall try to clarify the background of the mounting tensions between Islam and the West. To do so I review several Islamic ideologists in whose thinking on science and technology play a big role.[3] Islamic critique of technology comes from two sides: from the spiritual, peace-loving Muslims and from the radical, violent branch of Islam. I shall try to explain the challenges this poses for the West by looking at the tensions internal to Western culture itself. These turn out to be related especially to technology. Such tensions have been present for a long time already, but they have been growing in intensity ever since a formerly Christian culture was secularised under the influence of the Enlightenment, an intellectual movement which eschewed religion yet which nonetheless has had an integrating effect of its own and whose relation to Christianity has become increasingly strained. The Enlightenment represents the religion of the closed material world that is blind to the non-material dimensions of reality. Understanding the Enlightenment in this way broadens our analysis so as to gain more accurate insights into the nature of the tensions amongst Islam, Christianity and Enlightenment in connection with technological development.

Both the critique of technology found in Christian philosophy and the critique of technology found in Islam challenge Western culture to change. A turnabout is needed in the West's dominant cultural paradigm—in the ethical framework within which Western culture has been developed. Such a turnabout is crucial in light of many global issues and may also lessen tensions with several currents within the Islamic world. I would note, though, that Islamic terrorists will not be satisfied with such an ethical and technological turnabout because their attitude—as they themselves tell us—concerns a non-negotiable religious position. At best such a turnabout can reduce the winds that encourage the sails of violence.

Technology in Islam

What place does the Islamic world assign to science and technology? After the death of Mohammed in the year 632, early Islam was strongly influenced by the Greek-Hellenistic world. This created an atmosphere conducive to the development of a distinctively Islamic pursuit and promotion of science.[4] The pursuit of science was viewed as taking place within the universe created by Allah, a universe that displays order and equilibrium and thus constitutes an aesthetic unity. Philosophy and science based on this view experienced a long period of florescence that lasted for more than 500 years, reaching its zenith in the Arab civilisation of the 9th and 10th century and getting further enriched by knowledge imported from Persia, India, and even as far away as China. Scientific growth was in keeping with the lifelong duty of every Muslim to increase in knowledge, and Islamic scholars were already well acquainted with scientific experimentation and technological research. In pursuit of these activities, care for nature was deemed as important as a one's care for family. It gave a boost to the economic sectors such as trade and commerce, which in turn fostered further progress in science and technology. Historians speak of a symbiosis at that time between the Islamic religion and (applied) science, as graphically illustrated by the construction in desert countries of monasteries, mosques, schools and irrigation works.

During the Middle Ages the Islamic world clearly led the West in science and technology. At the start of the Middle Ages, Islam even mediated between the ancient world and the West. In other words, the West owes a great deal to the Arab world for its scientific development. Following the eleventh century, however, the pursuit of science in Islamic countries entered a time of stagnation. For a variety of reasons—mostly political and socio-economic—it went into decline. Since then, the Islamic world has increasingly been characterised by traditionalism and isolation, attended by a loss of political power and a decline in material prosperity. The earlier, positive appreciation of science and technology even turned negative.[5]

In later times as well, during the industrial and post-industrial eras, Arab countries contributed little to science and technology apart from improving the exploration and marketing of crude oil and refining the weapons technology imported from other countries. There are, however, Islamic scholars today who—as we shall see in a moment—wish to promote modern science and technology in the light of Islam's own past and its original sources.[6] Their critique is not so much directed at science and technology as such, but rather at the "technological culture" of the West—in other words, at the Western *ethos* of technology.

The Influence of the Enlightenment in the West

Meanwhile the West, under the influence of its belief in progress, particularly in the Age of the Enlightenment, fuelled the prejudicial view that the Islamic world per definition erected more and more roadblocks to impede the development of science and technology. Scholars blamed this on Islam's contemplative nature and Arab fatalism. That ethos, although at variance with its original attitude, did indeed acquire much influence in the Islamic world. It even reinforced the Islamic world's resistance to Western science and technology. A reversal did take place in the 20th century as a result of the process of globalization. Arabic universities were established, borrowing heavily from the West.[7] However, it seems as though modern technology is appreciated only insofar as it can be made to serve Islamic religion. Science and technology, it is said, must be brought under the Islamic banner. This goal has not been entirely successful: Western technology comes hand in hand with Western ethos, which continues to meet with resistance. Acceptance of scientific and technological knowledge—modernisation—stands in sharp contrast with resistance to Westernisation, secularism, materialism and Western profanity.[8] Islam will have to furnish modernisation with a moral compass.[9]

Reactions inside Islam

It is important, meanwhile, to distinguish among different Islamic reactions to the Western ethos. In the case of more than one Islamic country, those reactions go back to the period of colonialism. On the one hand exists a radical, violent, fundamentalist current that rejects science and technology as well as Westernisation—the ethos of the Enlightenment. On the other hand exists a current that accepts both elements from the West. It is mostly found among those who have political and economic power, but sometimes also among Muslim scholars.[10] Understandably, the first current can target the second. This is the reason why terrorist activities occur just as often in Islamic countries as in Western countries.

A third current Huntington calls the reformists.[11] The reformist's public image is of being spiritually-minded and peace-loving. They accept modern developments in science and technology short of the dominant Western ethos. They hold that as the Islamic world embraces Western science and technology a thoroughgoing process of rationalisation will have to be accompanied by profound spiritual convictions.[12] Often they advocate a similar approach to adopting a Western-style democracy.[13]

Ideological differences and growing tensions among these three currents may well cause violent protests against the West to escalate as well as heighten cultural tensions within the West, which is being populated by Muslims in ever greater numbers. The choices of the smallest group, the fundamentalist Muslims, pose a violent threat to Western culture and cast a sombre shadow over the world.

Hatred of the West

This destructive urge is explored in a recent study by Buruma and Margalit.[14] They use the term "occidentalism" to refer to the demonisation of the West by its enemies. The West, led by the United States, has blanketed the globe with industrialism, capitalism and economic liberalism. Fanatic Muslim groups regard this "Americanisation" as a machine civilisation that destroys cultures. And globalization only reinforces this destructive civilisation of machines, which is cold, rationalistic, mechanical and without a soul. Granted, the spirit of the West is able to develop technology and raise it to ever-higher levels for realising ever-larger economic successes; but it cannot grasp the higher things of life because it is woefully lacking in spirituality. It is helpless and hopeless in the very things which humanly speaking are important, nay all-important. What the spirit of the West exports is *scientism*—the belief in science and technology as the only way to acquire knowledge.[15] In the eyes of Muslims, the religion of the West is materialism, and this religion militates against the worship of the Divine spirit.

The hostility that is directed at the West, according to Buruma and Margalit, is rooted in this resistance to the "technological culture". The Western spirit suffers from a grave mental illness: it is arrogant, shallow, irreverent, merely efficient, like a computer. Western culture, accordingly, is a spiritless, superficial, materialistic culture of technological presumption, power hunger and greed—a brutish and decadent culture, a culture that deserves to be destroyed. Suicide terrorism has catapulted this hostility against the West to new heights. The suicide bombers, as worshippers of the Divine spirit, send the worshippers of earthly matter to their death with this slogan on their lips: "Death for the sake of Allah is our supreme ambition."[16] Their war against the West is a holy war.

Islamic Terrorism and Dialectic Tensions in Western Culture

In their analysis of occidentalism, Buruma and Margalit try very hard to understand those who act on their hatred of the West. They write: "Unless we understand why they hate the West so much, we need not nourish the illusion that we can keep them from destroying mankind."[17] More than once, as I studied Islamic analyses of Western culture including Baruma and Margalit's search for the reasons behind hatred of Western culture, I was reminded of what Reformational philosophy has come to see as the dialectical tension within Western culture. It is striking how often these authors look for an explanation in the internal tensions within Western "technological culture" itself. In the context of globalization, these are tensions that are felt worldwide. Whereas, until recently, reactions against this culture were confined to the West itself, counter-movements are today found around the world. Jihad terrorism is only the most powerful and the most dangerous expression of it and often uses critiques of culture borrowed from Western writers. Popular with many radical Muslims, for example, is the critique of "technological culture" levelled by Martin Heidegger.[18]

But what exactly is meant by "dialectical tensions" in Western culture? My first inaugural oration dealt with the cultural tension between technocracy and revolution.[19] Since that time, the dialectic tension or inner conflict in culture, with its constantly altering forms, has been a recurring theme in my lectures. Identifying the dialectic allows us to see what is going on in our culture at a deeper level. It helps us to see the inherent problems, their gravity, but also—understanding their origin and historical development—how they can be, and must be, contained.

Dooyeweerd located the origin of the Western dialectic in the pretended autonomy of humanity, of the human being who is sufficient unto himself, of humanity without God. Pretended human autonomy produces an experience of reality as a closed, human-centred world, and history as a purely man-made process. Because our culture is shut off to the transcendent God, humanity is thrown back on a this-worldly reality. This dependence, which can occur in a variety of ways, ultimately results in an orientation to *this* world as the only reality. Western humanity attempts to realise the idea of self-glorifying autonomy by means of science and subsequently to confirm it by means of technology: modern technology can bring us the perfect humanity and the perfect world. This whole development calls up forces that create tensions of gigantic proportions. The ideal of unprecedented material well-being may have been realised in part, but at the same time it is clear that this prosperity has been attained at the price of human freedom and at the expense of the biosphere, and that with all our prosperity we are standing on the edge of a volcano that is about to erupt. Western culture is a culture that is internally divided. Absolutised freedom is in tension with the absolutisation of scientific-technological control, and vice versa. It is a tension that shapes the history of our time.

The Development of Dialectical Tensions

Initially, the dialectical tensions—which are at their roots religious in nature—were confined to philosophical theories. Under the growing influence of the Enlightenment they have entered culture under full sail. It is entirely in the spirit of the Enlightenment, after all, not only to understand reality in terms of rationality, but also to shape the world rationally. The Enlightenment project aims at using the instrument of reason to create a society in which human freedom can be enjoyed to the full. The actual situation, however, is that the objective structures which autonomous reason designs and then implements take on a life of their own, independent of humans, and as such turn against cultural freedom. That threat is all the more menacing as the forces to contend with are developing with accelerating dynamics and increasing complexity, so that people can no longer size them up, let alone alter them.

Throughout my course on Currents in Modern Philosophy at University of Wageningen I demonstrate how the powers of science, technology and economics have been recommended and reinforced by dominant philosophical currents like positivism, pragmatism and systems theory. These currents do so especially because they think newer technologies are needed to solve the cultural problems created by the technologies that are now outdated. Opposed to this way of thinking are the philosophical currents representing the dialectical counter-pole: Existentialists point out that in a technological society, human freedom suffers as humanity is reduced to an object for techni- cal manipulation. Neo-Marxists call attention to the fact that the ongo- ing development of science and technology augment and affirm the influence of economic and political powers, threatening humans as bearers of culture and agents of politics. Environmentalists and eco- critics demand attention for the oppression of nature and therefore argue for technologies that protect the environment against pollution and destruction. New Age thinkers protest against materialism and argue for a more spiritual approach to life. Finally, naturalists ("deep ecologists") emphasise the meaning of nature as an integral whole, over against the impersonal, artificial and abstract nature of technol- ogy.[20]

All the while, there is not one person living in the technological culture who does not feel the tension, mentally and viscerally. The tension is mounting by the day between infinite technological expan- sionism and the finite nature of creation and its inherent potentials.

Why is it that human pursuit of mastery and control always seems to win out over that other pole in the cultural dialectic, namely the ideal of freedom? The reason is that the mastery pole utilises the *objective* powers that manifest themselves in new scientific and technological possibilities such as systems theory, information science, computer technology and genetic manipulation. And economic powers only reinforce that process. However much the critiques are mounting, a turnabout of culture has become almost inconceivable. The cause of that lies especially with economic powers that know no bounds, and a public that is caught in consumerism and repeatedly takes the side of the dominant cultural trend in the hope and belief that even more blessings of science and technology will come their way.

The Gravity of the Current Dialectic

It is essential that we emphasise the increasing seriousness of this historical process. Modern technology and the wholesale application of what it can do is going through unprecedented growth and taking on a despotic character. Its mastery and control of the whole world not only curtails human freedom but also threatens to deplete natural resources, pollute the environment, and damage nature beyond repair. Of late, increasing attention is being paid to climate change as well. The unbridled scientific-technological dialectic defies natural, ecological, social and energy limits, causing clashes which, owing to the absence of sufficient concrete outlets for the rising tensions, can rapidly escalate into open conflicts.[21] The impact of globalizing technical and economic development in the Third World often gives rise to deep feelings of political impotence, combined with a sense of ongoing economic neglect. It does not take long before people experience this as a direct form of humiliation. Western science and technology, riding the current of globalization, put enormous pressure on other cultures. The dialectic easily translates into culture wars, ethnic strife, and international standoffs. Thus political catastrophes may boil over and cultural cataclysms may detonate.

A *new* element in the current situation of the cultural dialectic consists of two components. Thus far, as we have seen, resistance has remained confined to *subjective* resistance. Because people did not have objective cultural power at their disposal, their resistance could not succeed in changing—at best only in adapting—the "technological culture". Now the first new component of that resistance to the "technological culture" is coming from the outside, from Islam. In fact the resistance of Islam also comes from within Western culture, and at the same time—this is the second new component—it makes use of *objective* cultural power. Terrorism is all too real. A Western philosopher like Waskow, a revolutionary utopian, was still able in the sixties to exclaim that the technical culture had to be violently overthrown,[22] but he could get no further than words. Present-day terrorists have a great deal of cultural power at their disposal, including technical possibilities, and form a worldwide network by means of technology—for example, the Internet, precisely the kind of thing they oppose. The attack on the Twin Towers makes clear that they are able to destroy technology with other technology. Events like these are rightly a grave cause for concern. How do Muslim ideologists respond to the current cultural situation?

The Critique of Islamic Ideologists

One of the most influential Islamic thinkers of the past century, the Egyptian writer Sayyid Qutb, championed a pure Islamic community as a defence against encroaching Americanism which he interpreted as the empty, idolatrous materialism of the West.[23] In the course of his life, the behaviour of the West made him more and more bitter, causing him to be opposed to every form of accommodation. Like all dreams about purity, his ideal of spiritual communion was a fantasy bearing within it the germ of violence and destruction. Qutb became the founder of an Islamic ideology that challenged the main ideologies of the West. His rejoinder to Western arrogance was Islamic intolerance.[24] His objectives were the purity of Islam and the destruction of the West. Qutb is a representative of radical Islam that does not flinch from the use of violence in opposing the West—and in fact advocates it.[25] In him, the cultural dialectic has become the engine of destruction.

Fortunately there are also reformists—that is, Muslims who aim at harmonious co-existence. One of them is Mohammed Iqbal, a writer from Pakistan. Iqbal is no occidentalist. He critiques the West from a Muslim perspective, in particular the unbridled development of science and technology, the financial power of capitalism, the inherent forms of economic exploitation and the secularism attendant upon it. He blames Western influence for detaching people from Allah—thus putting his finger on the worst effect of the Enlightenment—and causing them to serve idols of their own making. Hence he is very critical of Western arrogance, Western imperialism, and public morality in the West. Nevertheless, Iqbal does not take distance from science and technology.[26] On the contrary, he bases his evaluation of them on the familiar Muslim concept of the Unity of Allah. That unity has to be reflected in human society in the form of harmony, expressed in justice, equality, solidarity and care for nature and the environment. Thus, in keeping with the spirit of early Islam, he advocates important reforms in science and technology, hoping in this way to reduce the cultural tensions.[27]

In the same vein, the Pakistani Muslim Mohammed Abdus Salam, a winner of the Nobel Prize for physics, has made a plea for accepting technology. In a very readable paper of 1983 he states that Allah has placed everything on earth "at the service of" humanity.[28] Muslim scholars are to acquire insight into the world and thus into Allah's plan. Science must be an integral part of the human community for the purpose of promoting material well-being. Accordingly, Salam orients himself to the universal value of science and technology. Their successes should be a cause of gratitude to Allah and of greater conformity from now on to Allah's will. In order to learn about the proper motives for pursuing science and technology, Salam wants to go back to the early beginnings of Islam, when the torch of scientific and technical development was passed on from generation to generation. For him, therefore, Islamic faith is essential for the correct motivation and ethics of science and technology. Salam is one Muslim scholar who has spoken about the relation or interaction between religion and technology in words which are new in the present-day Muslim world and which are seldom if ever heard in the Enlightenment thinking of the Western world.

Christian Philosophy and the Critique of Technology

That said, reformist Muslims do have a one-sided opinion of Western culture. It is a matter of historical record that the Enlightenment has Christian roots. But this intellectual-spiritual movement, which arose in the eighteenth century, has increasingly taken distance from Christianity, has in fact more than once repudiated it. Accordingly, it is not right of Islam to make little or no distinction between the influence of Christianity and that of the Enlightenment, as if the two would necessarily lead to a similar ethics for technology.[29] On the contrary, Christianity, as I have shown, levels a profound criticism at the dialectic tensions inherent in the Enlightenment worldview. In the course of the twentieth century, both ideals of the Enlightenment— the ideal of human freedom and the ideal of scientific-technical control—have reached a crisis that may have disastrous consequences for global culture. Dialectical tensions in culture are building up. Radical and violent Islam is offering ever-stronger resistance. In other words, Western culture is increasingly being exposed to threats by internal and external forces alike. No one less than Habermas, at heart an Enlightenment philosopher, has recently shown that the "failed Enlightenment" needs religion.[30] Huntington argues that the clash between Islamic and Western civilisations is due to the weakening of Christianity as the central component of the West.[31] The question is pressing: Can a culture that has lost its religious roots survive?[32] A renewal of Western culture would mean that Westerners return to the religious well-spring of the Christian religion and that Christianity embraces its cultural calling, even actively pursuing it. Christianity, on the basis of a powerful conviction, ought to appeal earnestly and emphatically for a turnaround of Western culture. Thankfully, that call is being answered today from all sides. I am thinking here of the effort of the theologian Hans Küng to arrive at a "global ethics" for science and technology.[33] World organisations of churches, too, have published reports in which developments in Western culture are heavily criticised.[34]

I see much value in these calls for change. I do think, however, that they trace the problems and tensions of our culture too much as a disruption of economic relations and view them too little against the backdrop of the twin ideals of the Enlightenment. Those ideals are in tension with each other. How can that tension be eased? By replacing autonomous freedom with a freedom that answers to values like order, discipline, authority, respect, trust, mutual help, human solidarity, freedom can be linked to responsibility. In addition to easing that tension, a new motivation for science and technology is needed. Dominating power must make way for serviceable power with a view to global justice. The norms and values for technology should no longer be derived from the scientific-technological worldview, which leads ultimately to developments without purpose or direction. This realisation is essential, because it is precisely technology that lies at the basis of many cultural activities. And to resort without question to technological solutions for problems occasioned by technology is to pre-programme, as it were, new problems and threats. That is why a different view of technology opens up the possibility of reducing or even resolving our cultural problems. The lofty flight of technology needs a transcendental anchor. But how?

My proposal for a way forward begins by acknowledging God as the origin of all things and recognising human beings as responsible creatures, made in the image of God and commissioned to unfold God's creation with all that has been gifted, including science and technology. Such a recognition makes the meaningfulness of science and technology subservient to the divine meaning and purpose of history, namely the coming of the kingdom of God.[35] The dominant worldview of the Enlightenment must be replaced with an orientation to the unfolding of creation as disclosure of its potentials, an historical process that began in a garden and will end in a garden-city.[36] A sustainable and durable society cannot do without religion and spirituality. In short, in its desire for a transformation of "technological culture" Christianity opposes the "religion of matter" as much as does reformist Islam.

For that matter, happily, there are plenty of people outside Christianity and Islam who are keenly aware that Western culture is in need of a fundamental change, a radical shift in direction. A radical change is needed, as we saw, because of gathering clouds within and threats from without, like those from radical Islam. As we work toward this goal, we may expect additional help—despite big differences with Christianity—from reformist Islam on account of its ethos, its care for nature and the environment, and its concern for social justice. Mutual support of this kind could be very useful in bringing about the much needed *paradigm shift* away from "technological culture".

The Paradigm Theory of Thomas Kuhn

To make the notion of a "paradigm shift" somewhat clearer, I shall give as an example Thomas Kuhn's paradigm theory of scientific development. Kuhn has demonstrated on the basis of the *actual* growth of science in history that scientific theories can ultimately be explained in terms of sociological, psychological, economic and even religious factors. His theory explains not only the continual growth of scientific knowledge but also and especially its development in spurts. The continual development of science exhibits stability and consensus among scientists. Whenever it reaches a crisis, however, the basic framework—or paradigm—within which science is practiced alters. That is to say, the reigning paradigm will be exchanged for one with greater explanatory power. Not until the new paradigm is firmly established will the crisis in science be resolved, followed by a new period of "normal" scientific work. Simultaneous to such a paradigm shift, the truth claims of science are considerably relativised.[37]

Kuhn shows that during crises in the formation of scientific theories big fundamental questions are abruptly pushed to the surface. The old scientific beliefs are shaken to their foundations. Old assumptions are questioned. Community among scientists erodes. Consensus about values crumbles. The "tacit knowledge" shared by like-minded scholars begins to totter. The old paradigm has had its day. A new development gains ground.[38]

Could the necessary change in the cultural paradigm be analogous to Kuhn's view of paradigm shifts in science? Analogies can be helpful but they also have their limitations. Science, for example, is only a branch or component of culture. Culture comprises so much more than science. Yet we have good reasons, precisely because our culture is more and more seen as a "technological culture" or a "scientific culture", to allow ourselves to be inspired by Kuhn.

The Transformation of "Technological Culture"

One wonders: could a relativising and eventual transformation of the current cultural paradigm happen in the present cultural development? The reigning paradigm poses many problems in the West, and we are trying to solve these problems by the same means and the same methods that have called them into being in the first place! The solutions turn out to be, owing to economic and political support, part of the problem. Slowly but surely we are beginning to realise that this cannot go on. Is there a possibility that the crisis will help us find the way to a new phase of culture in which the problems of "technological culture" can really be pushed back?

Any cultural revolution or turnaround, by analogy with a scientific revolution, will be accompanied by tense discussions that ultimately hark back to what people believe and what they consider to be true. The part that religion plays in all this will become unmistakably evident. Religion, or religions, will offer different critiques of culture or technology, as is the case with Christianity and Islam. The challenge will be to come up with a different cultural paradigm that reduces the cultural dialectic and curtails or even resolves present problems and threats. That will not be easy, because the representatives of the old culture model will not give up on it so quickly: they will hold on to it with a kind of grim stubbornness. I am speaking of economic, political and cultural counterforces. Yet at the same time, the longer current developments continue, the clearer their weakness will become. Surely that is patently evident in the mounting consequences that stem from current scientific-technical-economic thought and that are threatening the whole world?

Nevertheless, there are possibilities. One concrete example today of a cultural transformation, both in the West and in the Muslim world,[39] is the contest—successful or not, convincingly argued or not—between organic farming and industrial agriculture. The latter is giving rise to more and more problems. Chances are that these problems will be taken more seriously and solutions pursued more earnestly as a growing number of opponents of industrial agriculture and proponents of organic farming enter into dialogue with each other and an increasing number of successful alternatives are realised within the as yet vague contours of a new paradigm. Conversely you hear defenders of industrial agriculture arguing for more environmentally friendly ways of farming. Either way, it is evident that people are facing up to existing problems and are searching for new, more sustainable methods of agriculture.[40]

Cultural Turnaround

Similar turnarounds should address the whole of "technological culture". Owing to looming problems, we are witnessing a growing interest among politicians and economists in cultural alternatives, sustainable development and socially responsible corporate behaviour. The socio-economic climate is becoming more favourable for drastic change. Recent reports to government from the world of business state that more needs to be done to tackle environmental pollution and climate change.[41] Another catalyst for developing new cultural alternatives is the latest UN Report on Climate, compiled by a global consortium of 2500 researchers who finger humanity and human technology, economics and consumption as the chief culprits of the enormous emissions of greenhouse gases, with all the risks that this entails.

Attention to climate change, rise in sea levels, shifting climate regions, disruption of ecological systems, loss of biodiversity, new tropical diseases, and so on—all present a case for a change in our cultural ethos. So do the activities deployed by men like Bill Clinton and Al Gore. Nor should we underestimate the impact of the many years that the Greenpeace movement has been active. More and more eyes are beginning to see the need for a new cultural paradigm. More and more people are realising that modern society with its patterns of producing, mastering and consuming is inherently, not coincidentally, unsustainable.[42] These emerging factors are now undermining the very cultural patterns that exist at the moment. And to the degree that governments work seriously toward levels of sustainability—by introducing the precautionary principle for example—and thus do not allow sustainability to become a mantra or a myth, to that degree the public will begin to doubt whether the prevailing culture is at all sustainable. In this way politics can contribute positively toward a change in attitude toward culture. And if in addition consumers begin to realise how new approaches can help them escape certain dangers and how their quality of life can be improved, conditions will be favourable for a cultural crisis. The much needed cultural turnaround will then become a realistic prospect, with greater attention for the life of future generations and for the rich variety of countless fellow-creatures, hence for true sustainability. A realistic prospect as well will be that more attention will be paid to the promotion of justice in the face of the injustices intrinsic to current trends in globalization.

Accordingly, it is of paramount importance that the post-industrial culture assists in reducing and resolving the problems and threats of industrial culture. That will have to be a learning process of small and large steps, a process in which serious attention is paid to things that have been blithely ignored in the past or are conveniently being overlooked in the present. I suspect that the heightened interest in religions at the moment has everything to do with it. Those religions put long neglected but fundamental questions back on the table. What is the essence of human life? How do we understand the meaningfulness of culture, technology, the economy? Proceeding from these fundamental questions—from the religious roots of cultures—the consequences are being examined for all culturally formative sectors. In Kuhn's terminology, we can speak by analogy of the great need of a "gestalt switch", a "turnaround", a "revolution". What is needed is nothing less than a "leap". Justly so, for it is "time to run". The cultural experiment that was grounded in the Enlightenment, it is patently clear everywhere, has failed. We need not deny the many good things it has brought us to conclude that, in the large, as a whole, it is leading us to disaster. The tensions and menaces need to be turned back if civilisation is to survive. For that to be possible, a firm basic orientation, a fixed anchor—in other words, a meta-historical compass—is required.

Content of a New Cultural Paradigm

But what should the new cultural paradigm look like? What would it be, essentially? It will have to differ from the previous one and yet incorporate the old in a process of transformation. In the old cultural paradigm, nature is seen as lifeless and, given that framework, is exploited by unbridled manipulation. Thus, if until recently nature, humanity, environment, plants and animals were viewed from a technical perspective—the so-called "machine model"—now the overriding viewpoint in cultural formation will have to be the protection of *life*. Science and technology and economics should no longer destroy life in all its multiplicity and rich variety of shapes and forms but, on the contrary, stand in the service of it. When that is done, technology and economics will be able to answer better to their intrinsic meaningfulness. Proceeding from different religious perspectives, Christianity and Islam, however widely they differ religiously and—I emphasise this—however unbridgeable these differences will remain, both also have much in common, enabling them to get along in working toward such a cultural turnaround.[43] The garden model suits both Christianity and Islam.[44] Both seem to concur with this confession: "We love all creation because of the Creator."[45] Christian and Islamic cultures, in their own ways, can contribute to a globalizing culture in which life is not threatened but enriched and in which greater justice and righteousness is done to ease tensions. For all their great differences, together they can work for greater social cohesion and mutual peace. Christians should be eager to promote forms of collaboration like this, for they are called to be peacemakers.[46] If, however, Christians lack the power of faith and fail to conclude a moral pact with reformist Islam, then a transformation of culture will not succeed. Then the battle between the competing claims of Enlightenment and radical Islam will intensify and Muslim violence will increase. Then there will be reason enough to remain pessimistic about the future.[47]

Summarising Conclusions

Technical thinking predominates in industrial society. Virtually everything is viewed in terms of the technical model or—more broadly—the machine model. Neither of these models has any room for life as a fundamental and decisive factor. They have guided the application of the power of technology in a tyrannical way. Huge problems have been the result. Today we can see how the "technological culture" threatens *life* itself, to the point of destroying it. A solution to these problems of modern culture is impossible so long as we continue to think and act within the parameters of the technical model. In the new phase of culture and civilisation, however, we shall not say farewell to technology as such but we shall have to put it in the service of life and human society. Reality must no longer be viewed as providing mere objects for technical manipulation but must instead be received in love as a prior given, as a divine creation, as a gift from God. Such an attitude will require respect and awe for the Owner of all things;

it will call for openness, humility, meekness, wonder, reverence and care. Our appreciation of technology will change completely if the will to power and mastery will be exchanged for respect for all that lives, in all its multi-coloured variety and multiplicity. It will also alter our attitude toward our fellow man and foster love of the worldwide community of man. The aim of technology should become, not to break down in order to master and control, but to unfold and cause to flourish. For a healthy disclosure of the creation, both Christianity and reformist Islam nurture the perspective of the living and vibrant garden-city, of a culture that takes care of nature and the environment. The preservation of life and well-being is worth more than material prosperity.

A culture whose basic categories are life and love and whose mission is to promote and strengthen the cause of justice and right-eousness in the world will orient itself to supra-subjective normative limits. This will make possible a more balanced, sustainable, peace-able and also richly varied development. When people learn to prac-tice moderation tensions and threats will subside, not only within the West itself but also in Western relations with Islamic culture. Given its ethos, it must be possible to win over reformist Islam for a turnaround of culture. To the extent that radical, violent Muslims and syncretical-ly-Westernised Christians refuse to go along with this development, political measures will have to cut them off from the objective cultural powers of science, technology and economics, from financial funds and subsidies, and from weapons. In light of the perspective here sketched, world problems and global menaces can be pushed back, terrorist threats can be combated more effectively, and a more durable and just global development can be realised as we move toward the second decade of the twenty-first century.

....

EGBERT SCHUURMAN (Ph.D., Free University of Amsterdam) is Professor Emeritus of Philosophy at the Technical University of Eindhoven, Technical University of Delft, and the University of Agriculture at Wageningen. He is the author of a number of books, including *Reflections on the Technological Society* (Wedge, 1983), *Faith and Hope in Technology* (Clements, 2003), and *The Technological World-Picture and an Ethics of Responsibility: Struggles in the Ethics of Technology* (Dordt, 2005).

NOTES

1   The present essay is an edited text of my ex-augural address delivered at the University of Wageningen on 20 September, 2007, on the occasion of my retirement from the endowed chair in Reformational Philosophy. The original translation is by Harry Van Dyke.

2   Jürgen Habermas, *Zwischen Naturalismus und Religion* (Frankfurt am Main, 2005).

3   I thank my student and fellow philosopher Mohammed Balali from Iran for his critical comments on the text and for his advice about recent Islamic literature on the subject.

4   Ansgar Stöcklein et al. (eds.), *Technik und Religion* (Düsseldorf, 1990), 102.

5   Ahmad Y. Al-Hassan, "Factors Behind the Decline of Islamic Science after the Sixteenth Century", Epilogue to *Science and Technology in Islam* (UNESCO, 2001); Pervez Hoodbhoy, "Science and the Islamic World—The Quest for Rapprochement", *Physics Today* (August 2007): 49–55.

6   N. Abu Zayd, *Reformation of Islamic Thought: A Critical-Historical Analysis* (Amsterdam: Amsterdam University Press, 2006), 31–35.

7   Samuel Huntington, *The Clash of Civilizations and the Remaking of World Order* (New York: Simon and Schuster, 2001), 70; Abdolkarim Soroush, *Reason, Freedom and Democracy in Islam* (Oxford: Oxford University Press, 2000).

8   Soroush, *Reason, Freedom and Democracy in Islam*, xvii.

9   Wetenschappelijke Raad voor het Regeringsbeleid (Thinktank for Public Policy), *Dynamiek in islamitisch activisme – Aanknopingspunten voor democratisering en mensenrechten* (Dynamics in Islamic Activism: Points of Contact for Democratization and Human Rights) (Amsterdam: Amsterdam University Press, 2006), 38f. Hereafter cited as WRR.

10 Hoodbhoy, "Science and the Islamic World", 55.

11 Huntington, *The Clash of Civilizations*, 118ff.

12 Riffat Hassan, "Religion, Ethics and Violence: Developing a New Muslim Discourse", in Berma Klein Goldewijk (ed.), *Religion, International Relations and Development Cooperation* (Wageningen Academic Publishers, 2007); Abdolkarim Soroush, "Ethics and Ethical Critiques", (2004), www.drsoroush.com (accessed 4 April 2009).

13 Soroush, *Reason, Freedom and Democracy in Islam*; WRR, 29–58.

14 Ian Buruma and Avishai Margalit, *Occidentalism: The West in the Eyes of Its Enemies* (New York: Penguin, 2004).

15 Ibid, 76, 96.

16 Cited in Buruma and Margalit, *Occidentalism*, 73; see also Abd Al-Hamid Al-Ansari, "The Roots of Terrorism Is the Culture of Hate", (2007), www.memri.org/bin/opener-latest.cgi (accessed 4 April 2009).

17 Buruma and Margalit, *Occidentalism*, 17.

18 WRR, 45; Zayd, *Reformation of Islamic Thought*.

19 Egbert Schuurman, *Reflections on the Technological Society*, 2nd ed. (Toronto: Wedge Publishing, 1983), 1–25.

20 Egbert Schuurman, *Faith and Hope in Technology* (Toronto: Clements Publishing, 2003), 135–61.

21 Koo van de Wal and Bob Goudzwaard, (eds.), *Van grenzen weten: Aanzetten tot een nieuw denken over duurzaamheid* (Budel, 2006), 223.

[22] See A. I. Waskow, "Creating the Future in the Present", *Future* 2, 4 (1968).

[23] Buruma and Margalit, *Occidentalism*, 36, 116 f., 124 f., 131.

[24] Huntington, *Clash of Civilizations*, 333.

[25] Sayyid Qutb, *Milestones* (Indianapolis: American Trust, 1990).

[26] Buruma and Margalit, *Occidentalism*, 122, 152.

[27] Mohammad Iqbal, *The Reconstruction of Religious Thought in Islam* (Lahore, 1971); see also Richard C. Foltz, et al., (eds.), *Islam and Ecology: A Bestowed Trust* (Boston: Harvard University Press, 2003).

[28] Mohammed Abdus Salam, "Science and Technology in the Islamic World", keynote address delivered at the Science and Technology Conference, Islamabad, 1983.

[29] Buruma and Margalit, *Occidentalism*.

[30] Habermas, *Zwischen Naturalismus und Religion*.

[31] Huntington, *Clash of Civilizations*, 335.

[32] Russell Hittinger, "Christopher's Dawson's Insights: Can a Culture Survive the Loss of Its Religious Roots?" in *Christianity and Western Civilization* (Ft. Collins, CO: Ignatius Press, 1995).

[33] Hans Küng, *Weltethos für Weltpolitik und Weltwirtschaft* (Munich, 1997).

[34] Hans Opschoor, "'Wealth of Nations' or a 'Common Future': Religion-based Responses to Unsustainability and Globalisation", in Klein Goldewijk (ed.), *Religion, International Relations and Development Cooperation*, 247–81.

[35] Jack Clayton Swearengen, *Beyond Paradise: Technology and the Kingdom of God* (Eugene, OR: Wipf & Stock, 2007), 271ff.

[36] Egbert Schuurman, *The Technological World-Picture and an Ethics of Responsibility: Struggles in the Ethics of Technology* (Sioux Center, IA: Dordt College Press, 2005).

[37] Thomas S. Kuhn, *The Structure of Scientific Revolutions* (Chicago: University of Chicago Press, 1962).

[38] Herman Koningsveld, *Het verschijnsel wetenschap* (Amsterdam, 2006), 110ff.

[39] Foltz et al., *Islam and Ecology*, 3ff.; Attilio Petruccioli, "Nature in Islamic Urbanism: The Garden in Practice and in Metaphor", in Foltz et al., *Islam and Ecology*, 499ff; Schuurman, *The Technological World-Picture*, 49ff.

[40] Petrus Simons, *Tilling the Good Earth: The Impact of Technicism and Economism on Agriculture* (Potchefstroom, 2007), 63, 240ff., and 374ff. See also Schuurman, *Faith and Hope In Technology*, 102ff., and Schuurman, *The Technological World-Picture*, 49–59.

[41] Rein Willems et al., *Pleidooi voor een kabinet met een mondiale visie op natuur- en klimaatbehoud* (Plea for a cabinet with a global vision for the preservation of nature and the climate). Open Letter to party leaders in the Dutch parliament, The Hague, Dec. 2006.

[42] Van de Wal and Goudzwaard (eds.), *Van grenzen weten*, 8ff.

[43] Günter Rohrmoser, *Islam, die unverstandene Herausforderung* (Bietigheim, 2006).

[44] Petruccioli, "Nature in Islamic Urbanism", 499ff.; Schuurman, *The Technological World-Picture*, 37ff.

[45] Foltz et al., *Islam and Ecology*, 29.

[46] Cf. Jeremiah 29:7 and Romans 12:18.

[47] Bruce Bawer, *While Europe Slept: How Radical Islam Is Destroying the West from Within* (New York: Doubleday, 2006).

Islam and the USA: Contrasting Visions of the End of History

by James W. Skillen

The title of this essay is admittedly odd. Islam is a world religion; the United States of America is a modern state. Islam has shaped much of the world for nearly 1500 years; the USA is not yet 250 years old. The *umma* (the Muslim community) is not a "spiritual" institution distinct from institutions of political governance; the USA, by contrast, is a modern state distinct from various religious communities that exist within it and around it. What, then, is the reason for putting the two up for comparison and contrast?

The argument that follows is that Islam's vision of world history, which has been carried forward in important ways by different kinds of political and legal institutions, finds some parallels in the American civil-religious vision of the USA's God-ordained role to lead the world to its true destiny of freedom and democracy. If Islam is a religion embracing political-legal means, then the USA is a political entity carried along by a religiously deep identity and purpose. There is no all-encompassing symmetrical comparison between the two. However, an understanding of comparable factors can illuminate, among other things, some of the reasons for the considerable antagonism of today's radical Islamists toward the United States as well as the religiously deep meaning of the Bush administration's "war on terrorism". And even if in the years ahead, radical Islamism were to disappear and American administrations were to quit fighting a "war on terrorism", the similarities and differences between Islam and the USA will remain significant for understanding two of the world's most important shapers of our shrinking globe.

The Dar al-Islam and the Dar al-Harb

Founded by Muhammad in the seventh century after Christ, Islam emerged and grew as a community (*umma*) called to submit itself fully to Allah (God). As Islam grew, the territory it embraced was called the *Dar al-Islam*, the House of Islam, the arena of submission to Allah, the realm of peace. Central to Islam was the mission to promote submission to Allah throughout the world, because the whole world is Allah's. Pursuit of this mission entails *jihad*—exertion in, or along, the path of Allah. *Jihad* amounts to more than warfare, for it is supposed to characterise the whole of life, similar in some ways to what Christians call discipleship—following Jesus, following in the path of obedience to God in all of life. The world outside the realm of the *Dar al-Islam* is the *Dar al-Harb*, the arena in which submission to Allah has not yet become reality, and thus it is the land of conflict or the House of War. In its broadest sense, then, Islam is a mission to bring the *Dar al-Harb* into submission to Allah and thus to make it part of the *Dar al-Islam*, which, in the end of history, will fill the whole earth.[1]

The full scope of Islam is not our concern here. Rather, we want only to identify its broad mission and the basic distinction between the *Dar al-Islam* and the *Dar al-Harb*. Moreover, it is important to emphasise that for most of its history the mission of Islam has included, quite legitimately, the use of force to expand the territory of the *Dar al-Islam*. There is plenty of evidence that the prophet Muhammad and his followers were influenced by Roman imperialism, as was early Christianity.[2] Thus, the expansive religious mission, entailing *jihad*, to bring the whole world into submission to Allah came to have a strong territorial, political, and legal meaning even though the *umma*'s identity was broader and deeper than a territorial, political entity. According to Efraim Karsh,

> Muhammad expanded Islam from a purely Arab creed to a universal religion that knew no territorial or national boundaries. He also established the community of believers, or the *umma*, as the political framework for the practice of this religion in all territories it conquered; and he devised the concept of jihad, "exertion in the path of Allah", as he called his god, as the primary vehicle for the spread of Islam. Muhammad introduced this concept shortly after his migration to Medina as a means to entice his local followers into raiding the Meccan caravans, developing and amplifying it with the expansion of his political ambitions until it became a rallying call for world domination. As he told his followers in his farewell address: "I was ordered to fight all men until they say 'There is no god but Allah.'"

> In doing so Muhammad at once tapped into the Middle East's millenarian legacy and ensured its perpetuation for many centuries to come. From the first Arab-Islam-

ic empire of the mid-seventh century to the Ottomans,
the last great Muslim empire, the story of Islam has
been the story of the rise and fall of universal empires
and, no less important, of imperialist dreams.[3]

Insofar as Christianity—both Western and Eastern—also absorbed
and adopted Roman imperial characteristics, it too came to be strongly
identified with political territory—the territory in which the Roman
Catholic Church (in the West) or the Christian emperor (in the East)
held sway. The realm in which Christianity held sway was called
Christendom; outside Christendom were the barbarians who should
be brought under Christendom's banner by evangelisation and other
means.[4]

In the centuries following Muhammad's death in 632, various
divisions within Islam, most notably that between the Sunni and
Shia,[5] often produced conflict and war within the *Dar al-Islam* itself.
Furthermore, the Muslim *umma* was organised in different tribes
and under different regional leaders, caliphs (deputies or successors
to Muhammad), and imams (heirs of the prophet). On the one hand,
therefore, the practices of political governance in the Muslim world
were diverse, often at odds with one another, and sometimes exercised
by authorities who were not fully observant Muslims. On the other
hand, the idea of the Muslim *umma* as an undivided people was not
relinquished or reduced to a merely "spiritual" entity. Therefore, even
though a distinction has been made within the *umma* between political
rulers, on the one hand, and the leaders who rightly interpret the Koran
and apply Muslim law, on the other hand, the *Dar al-Islam* was never
understood in a way that allowed for the distinction between a "religious" *umma* and "secular" political governance outside the realm of
Allah's sovereignty.[6]

Part of what sparked the rise of radical Islamism in the twentieth
century, however, was what they judged to be Islam's gradual, historical accommodation to the West and its loss of a faithful way of life
characterised by comprehensive *jihad*. For example, the complaint of
Sayyid Qutb, one of the intellectual founders of the Muslim Brotherhood in Egypt and an inspiration of al Qaeda, was that Muslims
were succumbing to the West's splitting of reality between the sacred
and the secular. Consequently, the revival of Shi'ism, the Khomeini
revolution in Iran, and subsequent radical movements, including those
employing terrorism, have manifest the desire and driving ambition
to purify Islam and to resist, if not defeat, all the forces of the *Dar
al-Harb* that are infiltrating and threatening the *Dar al-Islam*.[7]

One of the enduring questions within Islam is that of the specific normative role of political rulers. Prior to the rise of the modern
Western state, Islam was carried by various regimes—Umayyads,

Abbasids, Ottomans—and resisted by many non-Muslim empires, including the Christian Byzantine Empire and Western Christendom. In modern times, Islam has been carried and/or resisted by different kinds of states: Turkey, Egypt, Iran, India, Indonesia, Pakistan, Russia, and China, to name a few. Moreover, the Muslim obligation of *jihad* continues to be upheld even without a general consensus among Muslims about when and how force should be used against enemies. Consequently, the meaning and identity of the *Dar al-Islam* has become fragmented and threatened both from within and from without. There is no Muslim consensus today about the legitimacy and role of the modern state, which Islam had little or no hand in creating. Thus, even though Muslims throughout the world now live and work in the context of states, Muslim understanding of personal responsibility and the *umma*'s ultimate fulfillment does not yield a consensus on what the state's role should be in the achievement of the *Dar al-Islam*.[8] Nevertheless, the end and goal of history is still believed to be the realisation of the whole world's submission to Allah.

Western Christianity and the Rise of Enlightenment Secularism

Because of conflicts between imperial and papal claims to supremacy during the growth of Christianity in the declining Roman Empire, a rather clear distinction eventually came to be adopted in Christendom between ecclesiastical authority and political governing authority. The chief dispute was over which of these should be supreme. In the West, ecclesiastical (papal) supremacy eventually took hold with the consequence that a hierarchical social order was established in which superior *religious* vocations were distinguished from all those responsibilities that pertained to life in this world—the *saeculum*—from which our word "secular" is derived. The *saeculum* was not considered disconnected from, or unrelated to, God, but rather was recognised as having its relation to God through ecclesiastical mediation, particularly by way of the participation of laypeople in the ecclesiastical sacraments.[9]

When the political and social world of Western Christendom collapsed under the impact of the Renaissance, the Reformation, and the rise of the modern state, most non-ecclesiastical institutions gradually came out from under the Roman Catholic Church's moral and legal supervision. "Secular" then gradually came to mean "not religious": firstly in the sense of not being mediated by, or deriving its authority from, the church, and then, secondly, in the sense of being autonomous—entirely independent of any divine agency or authority. Under the impact of the Western Enlightenment, the driving ambition of which was to achieve human autonomy and liberation from ecclesiastical and aristocratic authority, the so-called secular world increasingly came to be understood as the realm of purely human self-governance and rational authorisation. Newly emerging political regimes, which aimed to promote freedom and enlightenment usually allowed for the continued existence of churches, but "religion" was relegated to the private sphere by a tolerant, secular public. The reversal was rather dramatic: the church was no longer recognised as delegating the "earthly sword" to subordinate authorities within Christendom; instead, the supreme authority of the people (or of a rational, secular government) now made room, by its "grace", for the practice of religions in private.

Against this backdrop, we can easily recognise the modern, secular character of the USA. Its political institutions—beginning with the Constitution—were grounded in the sovereignty of the people. No church or religion was established. Religious practice becomes a matter of personal freedom and private association. However, this supposedly secular, enlightened character of America's political institutions does not provide a sufficient description of the self-chosen identity of the American people. The latter, even in their secularising political tendencies, had, by 1776, also taken to itself an identity that originated with the New England Puritans. The American founders, who were establishing government on the basis of popular secular sovereignty, also understood themselves, at the same time, to be a new Israel, a people in special covenant with the god who had shepherded them to independence and had set them in a new Promised Land as a City on a Hill to be a light to all nations. Call this a *secular* religion or a modern civil religion, if you like, authorised only by the claims of the human organisers who initiated the covenant with America's god, but it is a religious vision and self-understanding nonetheless.[10]

Although the institutions of church and state were separated in a modern way in the US Constitution, the American people saw themselves, in a *national political* sense, as an "exceptional nation", empowered with a divinely ordained mission. The mission was not to usher in the ultimate kingdom of God beyond history, nor was it to extend the US government's control directly over all nations by imperial conquest. Instead, the mission was, and still is, to be both the leading example and the vanguard of freedom and self-government for the whole world. The ideal of human autonomy is the universal, undivided goal of history in this framework; the realisation of that ideal will come when every person and every nation makes freedom its own, as the USA has done. This vision is rooted in the conviction that America's god ordained it to be both the prophet and the vanguard of the goal of history. Compared with Islam, this is quite a different vision of the end of history and of the means of arriving at that goal. Yet there are many parallels as well.

The Third Rome

While the primary purpose of this chapter is to compare and contrast two visions of the end of history, namely those of Islam and the USA, our purpose can be enhanced by drawing in, tangentially, the Soviet communist vision that derives from another wing of the civil-religious secularisation of Christianity. Modern Russian nationalism emerged from, and helped to expand, the Russian Empire of the tsars. In the sixteenth century, Russia's Ivan III declared that Moscow would henceforth serve as the Third Rome of Christian Orthodoxy, succeeding Rome and Constantinople. In 1547, Ivan IV declared himself Tsar (Caesar) of All the Russians, thus assuming Caesaropapist leadership of the Orthodox Church as well as of Russia and holding out the vision of the completion of Christ's rule over the earth through Russian imperial mediation.

By the late nineteenth century, under the impact of modern, secularising nationalism, the Christian element of Russian imperialism was weakening in relation to the nationalist element. And when the democratic movements in Russia began to gain strength at the turn of the century, the ground was fertile for a coup by Lenin's Bolshevicks, who displaced the Tsar with a new dictatorship and a new vision of the end of history, namely, Karl Marx's secularised Christian vision.

Whereas the American experiment featured a secularisation of the Protestant Puritan idea of a new Israel in covenant with God, Lenin's Marxist vision represented a secularization of Caesaropapism that had been carried by the Russian Tsar. If the American nation as a whole was identified as a new Israel, Russia was identified by Lenin and then Stalin as the socialist carrier of the Communist Party's mandate to lead the way to the end of history. The Communist Party claimed to be the vanguard of the proletariat, the latter being (according to Marx) the true (messianic) carrier of the revolution that would usher in a communist end of history. Lenin identified himself as the leader of the Communist Party, the supposed vanguard of the proletariat, but he functioned more like a secular Tsar of Russia.

The USA: Making the World Safe for Democracy

The joining of an Enlightenment ideal of freedom to a Puritanised new-Israelitism gave shape to a small American republic at the end of the eighteenth century. By the end of World War I, that small republic was on its way to becoming a colossus. The international position of the United States among the world's states at the end of World War I, and its even more formidable position as sole superpower after the collapse of the Soviet Union, came about not by the conquering achievements of imperial legions but by a combination of American participation with allies in world wars it did not start and by building alliances and cooperative international organisations during and following the two world wars and the Cold War.

The outcomes of the two world wars appeared at the time to many Americans to be evidence of God's continuing providence in leading America to global preeminence and the world to freedom and democracy. America was simply playing its humble part in carrying out a divine mission. This view of historical events helps to explain why most Americans continue to think of themselves as non-aggressive, non-imperial innocents living in a dark and dangerous world. President Woodrow Wilson had tried for as long as possible to keep the USA out of Europe's war. When he finally asked for Congress's authorisation to enter the war, his rationale was defensive—to help save the world and America from disaster and to keep the way open to freedom. Through the League of Nations, Wilson believed the American government would continue to exercise an essentially defensive function: to protect free and self-governing peoples.[11] Every American military foray into the world was, by definition, therefore, only a response to evil, a reaction to threats from the outside, in order to defend the light of democracy shining from the American City on a Hill out to the world.[12]

As it turned out, by 2001, the front lines of America's *defense* forces could be found in the farthest corners of the globe. One consequence was that immediately after 9/11, the cry went up in the USA for "homeland defense" (later changed to "homeland security"). This was quite an irony given the hundreds of billions of dollars spent each year by the US Department of Defense. Yet America's major military forces were (and still are) positioned so far away and in so many parts of the world that an American citizen could feel inadequately defended within the actual borders of US territory. That irony helps explain American blindness to the hegemony and imperial reach of their country. Why is this the case? The peculiarity originates in the earliest self-interpretation of the nation as a City on a Hill, whose calling was to bear witness to the universal political destiny of the world. America's calling was not to try to achieve that goal by military conquest but to do so by example. Yet insofar as America's civil-religious calling bears witness to a universal goal, then the US must always keep in view the entire world as the field of opportunity for freedom's expansion and remain ever prepared to defend against threats to freedom's survival. Non-imperial America must, therefore, be prepared to fend off all imperialist ventures by those who would threaten the progress of freedom and who could thereby destroy America and its unique vocation. Niall Ferguson calls this the "imperialism of anti-imperialism". When, at the end of World War II, the USA succeeded in helping Japan and Germany rebuild, it was motivated in large part by "the fear of a rival empire", and that fear continued throughout the Cold War and after 9/11. "For an empire in denial [the US], there is really only one way to act imperially with a clear conscience", says Ferguson, "and that is to combat someone else's imperialism. In the doctrine of containment, born in 1947, the United States hit on the perfect ideology for its own peculiar kind of empire: the imperialism of anti-imperialism."[13]

Contrasting Soviet Communism, Islam, and the USA

The peculiarity of America's civil-religious mission to make the world safe for democracy can now be compared more closely with Islam's mission. And that comparison can be enhanced by comparing both to the Soviet communist mission. The comparable factor that can be found in Islam, the USA, and Soviet communism is the conviction that history is moving toward the fulfillment of a universal human destiny and the primary historical force authorised to lead the world to that destiny is a specially chosen vehicle (Islam, the USA, or the communist proletariat), which must overcome diametric opposition in order to fulfill its mission.

Soviet communism began with the 1917 Russian Revolution at about the same time that the Ottoman Empire was collapsing and America was beginning to fill the void of the declining and collapsing western European empires. The war and these consequences constituted a great setback to Islam. Communist ideology *secularises* Russian Caesaropapism into a dictatorship by the leader of the Communist Party and *sacralises* the proletariat for a messianic role in bringing about the final world-historical revolution. For early Christianity, the mission of Christ's disciples was to bear witness through their way of life to Christ's coming kingdom and the fulfillment of history. For the Russian Orthodox Church, which supported the tsar headquartered in Moscow, the movement toward the City of God was supported by a centralised, hierarchical, Caesaropapist empire. In Lenin's and Stalin's hands, Russian Caesaropapism was transformed into the Communist Party's dictatorship, which purportedly represented the worldwide proletariat as its vanguard. According to Karl Marx, the worldwide proletarian revolution was supposed to produce the "new man" as an outcome of a final judgement—the communist revolution. That final judgement was to come about through the liberation from Capitalism achieved by the proletariat, a revolution that would bring an end to the state as well as to capitalism. Western capitalist countries, like the USA, were considered reactionary bastions of oppression that had to be kept at bay or destroyed. All traditional religions were seen as historically obsolete and as nothing more than an opiate for the people.

However, the Russian communist attempt to foment a worldwide proletarian revolution was directed not as Marxist theory said it would be by the working classes in all countries but by the Russian imperial state, renamed the USSR (Union of Soviet Socialist Republics). Consequently, contradictions and inconsistencies appeared in the Soviet Union's actual practices, because the effort to advance Russian state interests in a global, balance-of-power system frequently ran counter to the communist ideology's goal of uniting the working classes throughout the world and dissolving the state altogether. Thus, the communist proletarian vision was not carried forward by an independent, working-class organisation but was only promised and anticipated by the powerful Soviet-bloc states and various revolutionary movements supported by those states. The Soviet Union and its allies were confronted chiefly by American and European states that cooperated to deter and contain the Soviet Union. In the end, a worldwide proletariat never materialised. With the collapse of the Soviet empire, achieved in part by the efforts of Muslim opponents in Afghanistan and elsewhere, communist ideology suffered a major if not fatal setback. Communism's vision of the end of history is now generally judged to have been a false hope generated by a failed ideology.

Islam and the USA, by contrast, are still very much going concerns and their competing quests to bring about history's fulfillment are shaping history today. Muslims, as we saw earlier, anticipated the progress of Islam as an unstoppable expansion of the *Dar al-Islam*, which would eventually overcome the oppositional *Dar al-Harb*. The forward movement of history would be powered and defended by *jihad* in its broad sense of a personal and social struggle for god. For Muslims, including radical Islamists, this human struggle is a divine mandate. America's self-perception and sense of mission appear to fall somewhere between those of Soviet communism and Islam. For many if not most Americans, Providence is somehow both behind and ahead of vanguard America, just as Allah is behind and ahead of the progress of Islam. However, in contrast to Islam as well as to Christianity, the goal trumpeted by the USA is this-worldly in character. In that respect, its mission is more like the Soviet communists'. The worldwide American mission anticipates a future when the peoples of the world are all self-governing and democratic, trading freely and living prosperously in peace with one another. American civil religion does not strive for a final renovation of the world by means of either a holy war or a proletarian revolution. Moreover, the American civil religion is tied to a particular polity—the United States. Americans believe in political liberty and democracy (and thus in a modest and limited state) and many want liberty precisely in order to be able to express their private faith in the coming, transhistorical kingdom of God. American opposition to Nazi and communist totalitarianism arose in

large measure because of antagonism toward the universalist, undifferentiated, revolutionary aims of those ideologies. The American
mission is, therefore, quite distinct from both the Russian communist
and the Islamic missions.

The missions of Islam and the USA have been carried forward by
different sacral *carriers*. Islam's carrier is a community whose crisis
of identity today is due, in part, to the fact that it has lacked significant
visible unity since the end of the Ottoman Empire and has not been
witnessing the ongoing expansion of the *Dar al-Islam*. Radical Islamist movements are fueled in part by disgust with the accommodation
of Muslims to political leaders who cooperate with infidels and fail to
promote jihad for the cleansing and advancement of the *Dar al-Islam*.
Thus, the worry that burdens many contemporary Muslims is whether
the end of history as they envision it will be achieved and whether
their mission will succeed.

The American civil-religious mission is carried by a particular
state on behalf of the whole world. In contrast to the carriers of the
communist and Muslim missions, the American carrier is still very
much intact. Yet the growth of democracy throughout the world has
not been uniform and seems less certain of realisation today than it did
fifteen or twenty-five years ago, especially because of American failures in Vietnam, Iraq, and Afghanistan. Those failures, coupled with
the rise of China, still controlled by the Communist Party, and the
reinvigoration of Russian authoritarianism, have led many countries
in the world to conclude that the USA is the carrier of little more than
its own interests. There now appears to be more reason to doubt the
American vision of the end of history and to wonder how much longer
America's preeminence in the world will last.

The *realm* in which the Muslim, American, and Soviet communist
missions have expected to find their fulfillment is nothing less than the
whole earth; all three missions are universalist and exclusive in this
sense and are thus destined for conflict with one another. Prior to the
triumph of the universal good that each anticipates they all expect conflict between good and evil, truth and error. The realm of truth, goodness, and righteousness for Muslims is the *Dar al-Islam*. The realm of
truth, goodness, and righteousness for the Soviet communists was, we
might say, the *Dar al-Communism*. And for the American republic, the
earthly realm of truth, goodness, and righteousness we might call the
Dar al-Freedom or the *Dar al-Democracy*. Each of these "holy lands"
is challenged or threatened by a diametric antagonist—a *Dar al-
Harb*—which needs to be converted or overcome. Historically speaking, Islam's *Dar al-Islam* kept expanding for several centuries but
subsequently suffered setbacks of major proportions. Islam remains
a compelling way of life for millions of people today even if many
Muslims are perplexed and angry about why Islam has lost some of its

ground and become fragmented. The *Dar al-Communism* projected by the USSR expanded rapidly (in the guise of state socialism and Soviet imperialism) into vast territories, but it collapsed almost as quickly— all in one century. There are very few communities of communist faith left in the world today.

The American-sought *Dar al-Freedom* began its expansion much later than Islam's *Dar al-Islam*, yet more than a century before the rise of Soviet communism. Today, it is the progress of the *Dar al-Freedom* that appears to be the most rapidly expanding political realm in the world, having withstood Russian communist imperialism and, thus far, the most threatening forces of radical Islamism. Yet the USA appears to be losing its preeminent status in the world, as we noted, and Islam remains a force to be reckoned with. In addition, we might ask, is it even correct to identify the United States as the vanguard of the *Dar al-Freedom*? Is it not the mistaken belief of American religious mythology rooted in the original understanding of the nation as a new-Israel? There are, after all, many other democracies in the world. Moreover, as was evident in Wilson's foreign policy, the American state does not always choose as its first priority to advance freedom and democracy in the world. Sometimes the USA chooses to work with and support illiberal and even anti-democratic states (such as the Soviet Union in World War II, Iran under the Shah, Egypt, and Saudi Arabia today) in order to advance its own interests, which, from its point of view, are always ultimately good for the world and for the ultimate advancement of freedom and democracy.

The vanguard of world progress, in American eyes, is certainly the USA, whose state interests and balance-of-power politics must often take precedence over the promotion of democracy elsewhere and may also take precedence over American support of other self-governing states, including other democratic states. After all, from the viewpoint of America's civil religion, if the US were ever to be dealt a lethal blow, then democracy and freedom everywhere would be threatened. The future of the world would be in doubt. If the exceptional nation fails, from whence comes salvation and the fulfillment of history?

Conclusion

In this chapter we have compared two visions (with a nod to a third) of the goal of history. In many respects, Islam and the USA are incomparable, as we said at the outset. On the other hand, because of the enduring history and global reach of Islam and because of the worldwide "empire" and ambitions of the USA, the differing visions carried by the two portend likely conflict in the decades ahead as globalization continues to develop. For Islam's vision of the end of

history to be realised, the fundamental separation of the sacred and
the secular, which is fundamental to the USA, would have to be overcome. For the USA's vision of the end of history to be realised, the
Dar al-Islam as an all-encompassing global community would have
to fail.

One of the important questions before us today is whether radical Islamism is truly a movement of, or from within, Islam. Or is it
a parasitic fringe movement influenced in a major way by Western
secular ideologies of radical revolution, as some claim.[14] If radical
Islamist movements fail, will that represent a failure of Islam, leading to the further sidelining of Islam with respect to the shaping of
cultures and societies around the world? Or, to the contrary, would the
demise of radical Islamist movements help to cleanse Islam of a cor-
rupting parasite and thereby encourage the survival and perhaps even
the revival of authentic Islam? If the latter scenario played out, could
Islam then find itself at home in more and more parts of the world as
one of the major religions among others coexisting within religiously
pluralistic societies? Or would authentic Islam be able to grow only by
continuing to expand the *Dar al-Islam* until the latter became the very
definition and constitution of globalization?

And what shall we make of the USA's mission of leading the
world to its true goal of freedom and democracy for all people? Would
it be possible for the USA to lose its global leadership role and accept
a new place as one among many states in a world that might become
even less democratic than it is today? Would the USA be able to give
up its vision of the end of history and its claim to be the exceptional,
god-chosen nation and find its place in a world moving to a different
goal altogether? Or is America's civil-religious nationalism so central
to its identity that the republic could not survive the loss of its global
preeminence and the demise of the hope of progress toward freedom
and democracy as the goal of history?

These questions spark others. Will globalization take the form of
ever increasing conflict and diversity even while various characteristics of flattening and shrinking come to define the contours of life
for all peoples? Could globalization move in the direction of some
kind of transnational governance not shaped by democracy, nationalism, Islam, Christianity, communism, or any other known religion
or ideology? Will people throughout the world eventually give up all
expectations of, and driving ambitions toward, any particular goal or
end of history?

These questions may be unanswerable today, but they should not
be ignored as irrelevant for our understanding of history, politics,
economics, and globalization. Judaism, Christianity, and Islam have
generated ways of life oriented toward an ultimate purpose and end
of history. Those religions are all very much alive today. And they

continue to suffer or to thrive in the midst of many "secular" religions, such as communism, nationalism, and destructive radicalisms of various kinds. For several centuries, Enlightenment-derived ideologies prophesied the end of religion and the eventual realisation of a universal, enlightened end of history. What is now becoming apparent is that religions never did die but have been challenged and partially displaced by new secular, ideological religions, many of which are themselves now in decline. That is why we should keep a close eye on the most vibrant, history-shaping movements in the world today, such as American civil-religious nationalism and Islam (both traditional and radical), to see how they contribute to the shape of global history. And that is why Christians—in community—should become more and more engaged in thorough, self-critical, all-of-life reformation. True discipleship of Jesus Christ, by the power of the Holy Spirit, allows for no accommodation to the civil religions and false ideologies of this age. Finding ourselves and the whole of history in the biblical story entails a different way of life than those lived in the stories propagated by Islam and the American civil religion.

JAMES W. SKILLEN (Ph.D., Duke University) is president of the Center for Public Justice. His most recent books are *With or Against the World: America's Role Among the Nations* (Rowman and Littlefield, 2005) and editor (and contributing author) of *Prospects and Ambiguities of Globalization: A Critical Assessment at a Time of Growing Turmoil* (Lexington Books, 2009).

NOTES

[1] See Efraim Karsh, *Islamic Imperialism: A History* (New Haven, CT.: Yale University Press, 2006), 1-8, 62-83; James Turner Johnson, *The Holy War Idea in Western and Islamic Traditions* (University Park, PA: Pennsylvania State University Press, 1987), 29-42, 60-75; and Hugh Kennedy, *The Great Arab Conquests: How the Spread of Islam Changed the World We Live In* (New York: Da Capo Press, 2007).

[2] Karsh, *Islamic Imperialism*, 2-4, 22-23, 26-27, 63. On Christianity and the Roman Empire, see Walter Ullmann, *A History of Political Thought: the Middle Ages* (New York: Penguin Books, 1965), 38-129.

[3] Karsh, *Islamic Imperialism*, 4-5.

[4] On the early history of the relation between Christianity and Islam see Richard Fletcher, *The Cross and the Crescent: Christianity and Islam From Muhammad to the Reformation* (New York: Viking Press, 2005).

[5] See Barnaby Rogerson, *The Heirs of Muhammad: Islam's First Century and the Origins of the Sunni-Shia Split* (New York: Overlook Press, 2000, 2004).

6   See Karsh, *Islamic Imperialism*, 21-103, and Fletcher, *The Cross and the Crescent*, passim.

7   See Vali Nasr, *The Shia Revival: How Conflicts Within Islam Will Shape the Future* (New York: W.W. Norton, 2006); and Paul Berman, *Terror and Liberalism* (New York: W.W. Norton, 2003), esp. 52-102.

8   Johnson identifies at least three different historical Muslim conceptions of state-craft and the justifiable use of force. See his *The Holy War Idea*, 136-65.

9   For more on this see Robert A. Markus, *Christianity and the Secular* (Notre Dame, IN: University of Notre Dame Press, 2006).

10 I have developed this argument in greater detail in James W. Skillen, *With or Against the World? America's Role Among the Nations* (Lanham, MD: Rowman and Littlefield, 2005), 67-110.

11 See Lloyd E. Ambrosius, *Wilsonianism: Woodrow Wilson and His Legacy in American Foreign Relations* (New York: Palgrave McMillan, 2002), 1-64.

12 See Richard M. Gamble, *The War for Righteousness: Progressive Christianity, the Great War, and the Rise of the Messianic Nation* (Wilmington, DE: ISI Books, 2003).

13 Niall Ferguson, *Colossus: The Price of America's Empire* (New York: The Penguin Press, 2004), 78. See also Benjamin Barber, *Fear's Empire: War, Terrorism, and Democracy* (New York: W.W. Norton, 2003), 67-101.

14 See, for example, Berman, *Terror and Liberalism*, 121-210.

Climate Change and the Rapid Dynamic of Globalization

by Bob Goudzwaard

The Gospel, Globalization, and Global Warming

Many years ago, I made a visit to St Paul's Cathedral in London where you will find a remarkable painting on one of its pillars. Someone is walking on a path in almost complete darkness, but he carries a lantern with him. The subscript says: *Jesus, the light of the world.* It is not only a beautiful and unusual painting of the Lord Jesus, the Lamb of God, but is a message to all those who are passing by. It is as if this painting says: it is on the concrete ways of this world, which are often dark, that you may meet your Lord and Saviour carrying his own burning Light. This light may be not so very far away, but instead very near to us, and in the very places where we no longer see any hope to continue, to walk on.

I refer to this image because it has particular pertinence to our topic of globalization. Is not a light also available here for our path, perhaps even this unique Light? It might appear at first that the likelihood of this Light illuminating our path through globalization is not great. After all, globalization is a process which mainly evolves outside of our will and intentions. Moreover, is it not too complex to deal with in a truly spiritual way?

Or to come at this from another angle: we hear much about climate change and global warming—a theme which since the impressive movie by Al Gore is accompanied by a great deal of hype in the United States, Canada and Europe. The movie and the hype increase our awareness of the problem of global warming and may even move us to think with others about possible solutions. But these solutions are usually of a technical or fiscal nature, like the improvement of energy efficiency, or reductions in CO_2 emissions in our production and consumption. Is that not too far away from the world of our Christian faith? Of course, we have to find and implement those solutions, but there seems to be no reason in this specific and separate case to refer explicitly to the Gospel or to the need to follow Christ.

I can share this feeling, but only as a first impression. Is climate change indeed an isolated phenomenon requiring technical solutions? Is climate change, for instance, fully isolated from the entire process of globalization and our appraisal of it? Modern people—and we are all in some sense modern people in our way of thinking and acting— have a tendency to see each problem primarily as an isolated problem, as a case in itself, because that seems to make it easier to come to effective solutions. But, in reality, problems are often connected. And if we persist in treating them as isolated cases, then often we have to conclude later on, and not without pain, that our solutions are not working at all.

Globalization and global warming are deeply interconnected. Just look to the simple fact that globalization, which in its most simple definition stands for the opening and widening of all our economies to the international or global arena, also implies strong and continuous growth of industrial production in most countries. And in that way, globalization also directly contributes to the growth in fossil fuel and energy usage. All experts see this worldwide increase as the main reason for the increase in the emission of greenhouse gases, which leads to further increase in global warming. If globalization and climate change are indeed closely intertwined, then there is at least some reason to also deal with them as interconnected realities. Perhaps their interconnectedness has further ramifications, perhaps even of a spiritual or religious nature.

I begin by taking a careful look at the character of globalization. After that I join what we have learned about globalization to the burning issues of accelerated climate change, which are connected to the rising sea levels and with the melting of ice caps in such places as the Northern parts of Canada. It could be that, after seeing the deeper connections between these problems, the Light of the Gospel unavoidably enters into our discussion. For neither globalization nor accelerated climate change are value-neutral problems. There is surely more at hand!

Characterising Globalization

There are many definitions and descriptions of globalization. It would take too much space to name them all. But one thing is clear: all of these descriptions indicate the many *dimensions* of globalization. It is not only an economic phenomenon, namely that national economies are increasingly opening themselves to each other and to the international arena; nor is it only or mainly, a technical phenomenon that modern technologies, especially in the field of transport and electronic communications like the Internet, are now spreading over the entire earth; nor is it even that citizens of various nations and cultures are linking much more easily than before. Globalization also has a cultural dimension that is related to a growing worldwide exchange of cultural products like movies and fashions and that has already led to worldwide hit parades and huge global music festivities.

Moreover, it is important to recognise that globalization changes over time, so that new dimensions are regularly popping up. I would particularly mention at this point the rapid expansion of worldwide financial markets. They have not only grown remarkably in size, but they have also begun to dominate, to a considerable extent, the future of many business firms and even entire economies. In other words, globalization is a highly dynamic process of mutual international interaction on several levels, but even more than that, it is a multi-level form of global *interference*. The aspect of interference is not usually mentioned in the many definitions of globalization that are put forward.

Global interference is not a matter of what happens when we, with our economies and societies, enter the world scene, but just the opposite: it is what the world—the world-markets, the world-economy, the world of global finance—is doing with our economies and ourselves. It is a dynamic reality that is interfering with our daily affairs. Indeed, it sometimes looks as if a completely new layer of existence has been added to our human lives. Globalization occurs on a level of which we have become a part without giving our permission and sometimes even without our immediate awareness. *Time* magazine stated some years ago in a special issue that globalization was leading to a "global awakening" of humankind, and I see this as an accurate description.

My home country, the Netherlands, provides an example. In the last year the number of take-overs of classical major Dutch firms like Stork, the Dutch State Mills, and the biggest Dutch Bank, ABN Amro, has multiplied. What interests me is not that these firms or banks are being bought by other solid banks or companies, but rather that they are financially attacked and later on dissolved by so called global venture-capitalists, global hedge funds or international private equity funds. That is the infringing movement, the *interference* that is coming from the global level itself. Financial speculative globalization begins now to overwhelm concrete national economies, subjecting them to the will of mainly speculative global investors and to the laws of short-run profitability. That is also a part of globalization, and most of us may feel it is a very undesirable part of this dynamic reality. For now our economies seem to stand on the threshold of becoming more dependent than ever before on the will and the whims of the worldwide financial markets.

What can we do? It seems as if globalization belongs to that piece of history that just envelops us, and for which there is no real alternative available—thus, the urgency for a deeper analysis of the non-neutral, perhaps even ideological, roots of this rapidly growing worldwide new reality.

Before I attempt such an analysis, I must prevent a possible misunderstanding. In our time we see the emergence of several anti-globalization movements that see and describe the entire process of globalization as intrinsically bad and even demonic. That is not what I have in mind. As Christians we should be more careful in our judgements; the process of globalization enables and has already brought about many life-giving situations. I mention the increasing communication between citizens of all nations, and access to better modern medicines for the sick and the handicapped. Globalization has also offered to some nations of the South the possibility for further economic growth and less poverty. It is neither all liberative nor all oppressive.

Perhaps, and this takes us a few steps further, we can say that we should distinguish between different *styles* of globalization, not only oppressive ones but also liberative ones. First, though, it is important to acknowledge that some of the major rich countries of the North, with the majority of large transnationals, view globalization as more than just an interesting process. They often also see it as a very desirable *project*, which has to be developed and promoted by all means and in all directions, especially towards and into the countries of the East and the South. Such a project does not sound innocent and indeed is not.

In our search for the deeper roots of the process of globalization, two possible avenues look promising, and we will follow both of them. The first avenue is to look more carefully at the intrinsically *modern* character of this whole process, which I do in the other chapter I have contributed to this book. You might benefit from reading its description of the religious roots of modernisation as background to this chapter. The second avenue is to question the incredible dynamic that is so much a part of the globalization process. *How do we explain that dynamic?*

The Rapid Dynamic of Globalization

How then do we understand the incredible *dynamic* of globalization, which mainly derives from its market-orientation? Let me briefly sketch a history: Since the time of the Renaissance a strong dynamic element has been present in Western cultures, related to a deep desire not only to know everything which can be known but also to conquer the world, to fill it with one's presence. That dynamic element was present in the invasion of Latin America by the Spanish conquistadores; it was present in the race between the European states to vest their colonial power all over the world; it was present in the American frontier with the opening of the West. And so it does not look like an overstatement if we were to say that globalization is also some kind of late, secularised missionary activity of the West, namely an attempt to fill the world with our presence, to bring the good news of our style of modernisation to even the most remote corners of the earth.

In my view, even this description does not explain fully the dominant dynamic element in globalization. If we, for instance, look at the way that the financial markets play a leading role in the global scene, then there is no doubt that this leading role has much to do with the extremely dynamic characteristic of those markets. They are the most dynamic global force, and thus they take the lead. Is there perhaps not some kind of over-emphasis in our time upon what is economically and technologically powerful; do we not search for a dynamism by which our societies can identify themselves to some extent, so that they can even try to enforce their progress with the highest possible speed?

We can illustrate this with an interesting metaphor. Imagine the latest and most modern train, which travels at a fantastic speed through the countryside. In relation to such a high-speed train there are two positions, two perspectives that are possible. The first possible perspective is viewing *from within*. Just imagine that you are travelling in such a high-speed train, and *en route* you are sitting in a comfortable chair. From that position everything looks quite stable and peaceful. No thought is given to any need for an emergency stop; the journey seems to be continuing uninterrupted. Of course, if you look outside through the windows, you will perceive great movement there, but it is a virtual movement of the landscape itself. It looks as if it is moving backwards, as if it is staying *behind*. This is, of course, an illusion created by the fact that your own speed seems to you to be a stable frame of reference; this illusion makes that which really stands still seem as if it is moving away behind you.

Imagine a second possible position in relation to the same high-speed train. Now you are standing in the open air outside the train, only metres away from the tracks where this vehicle will pass by. This is the *view from the outside*. What will be your impression then? What will dominate your view of the train? Of course, it will be that this train is travelling so very fast, with great momentum, passing by in just one or two moments, and with much noise. Perhaps you will be looking to some spot just ahead of the train to note if it is travelling safely and not threatening some children who are trying to cross over the tracks.

This metaphor demonstrates clearly that in relation to dynamic processes you can have at least two different perspectives, which are specifically related to the point of view from which you perceive the movement. If you stand *outside* the train, with your feet firmly rooted in real sand or clay, your view will be very different from the view *within* the train.

Let us now suppose, for a moment, that we as modern human beings are inclined to identify ourselves easily with our own dynamic economic and technological patterns, and so we tend to see ourselves as an intrinsic part of that dynamic world. Then our own personal outlook on reality also will presuppose such a dynamic standpoint. Thus we will be inclined to judge the entire outside world from that dynamic point of view. That implies at least two things. First, we will see and appreciate strong dynamic patterns in our societies as completely *normal*. But, secondly, we will also be inclined to see what is not moving as rapidly as we are as somehow staying behind and therefore as, to some extent, *abnormal*. If we begin to identify ourselves with all dynamic movements then these tendencies will of course increase. The equilibrium we experience within the train will have become our only point of orientation, and we will have decided to view what happens outside in terms of our momentum, rather than considering any possible alternative perspective.

This high-speed train metaphor has significance for our evaluation of the current accelerating dynamic patterns of globalization. Firstly, it is indeed striking how easily particularly modern people—modern politicians and modern economists—are inclined to see the dynamic pattern of ongoing globalization as simply a natural pattern. They are obviously inclined to prefer the view from the *inside*. But secondly, how easily they, and often we ourselves, tend to perceive poor countries which just stay where they are financially as *under-developed*, as lagging behind. Poor men and women in the midst of modern societies are also often seen by many of us as just *under-performing*. And if we take our relation to nature as a criterion, then we also can observe that the dominant view is usually not one of deep respect for our environment; it is a barrier to growth. Modern people often feel irritated if nature or the environment gets in the way by posing limits to what we wish or desire. Those of us who are modern will often look at those restraints as barriers to forward movement, barriers that need to be overcome by technological or scientific achievements.

What I am trying to communicate here is that modern Western people cannot assume that globalization is simply a process that overcomes us, a process that has nothing at all to do with our own world-and-life-view. We should be aware of the simple fact that as modern people we are brought up and educated in a rational world of mainly self-created and progress-related institutions, so that we have a natural tendency to prefer the view from the *inside*, and so to identify our own dynamic world with the real world. Thus we will be inclined to favour the project of rapid globalization, even if tensions arise from all the adaptation that is required around us. We live by making progress and prefer the rapid way, and that way of life fits fully with what modernity is deep down: an attitude and a perspective on life which lives in the hope of enduring growth and progress, made possible by the works of our own hands. That hope in growth and in progress trusts in the good and efficient working of the market mechanism as our final orientation point within a moving world.

But is it wise to live with this perspective? Is it wise to look at other more traditional countries, which often have older cultures than our own, as countries that are under-developed? Should we look at the disenfranchised primarily as those who are staying behind, as those who also have the smell of some kind of abnormality? Some of us will say: "No!", but perhaps others will concede: "Yes!" For we should not forget that this view, which I have already called the dominant Western *dynamistic* view, is deeply optimistic. In this view, dynamic progress, whether technological, economic or scientific, will always be with us, and that progress will always enable us to overcome possible limits as if they were just temporary restraints. We might say that whatever, or whoever, tends to lag behind, therefore, has a moral obligation of their own: to adapt as soon as possible to what is normal in the dynamic sense, joining our march towards a better future for all, which is now often called *globalization*.

Global Warming—Facing the Limits of Dynamic Globalization

It is at this point that the choice of our hearts and minds begins to matter, and here I want to reintroduce the problem of climate change and global warming. Why do I choose this problem, and not another problem like, for instance, world poverty? My reason is not only the strong linkage between globalization and global warming, but also, and even more so, the desire to expose an interesting but also embarrassing new situation. In global warming and with the accelerated climate change, we meet—probably for the first time in our civilisation—a problem for which the modern perspective, the outlook from within, no longer really helps. That is, the modern dynamistic model no longer leads to any satisfactory solution.

Trusting that most readers are somewhat familiar with the causes of global warming and the impressive movie by Al Gore *An Inconvenient Truth*, let me just make a few connections explicit. Global warming is closely related to the presence of so-called greenhouse gases, whose growth—I mention here specifically carbon dioxide—is inevitably related to the global use of fossil fuel energy—coal, oil and gas—which is needed to maintain the rising level of the world's industrial production. Greenhouse gases have always been present in the atmosphere, but only after 1750, the start of the industrial revolution in Europe, did they show a remarkable increase of their concentration. Sir John Houghton, the ex-chairman of the UN Panel on global climate change, states in his Faraday lecture[1] that since the beginning of that industrial expansion the amount of carbon dioxide in the atmosphere has increased by over thirty-five percent and is now at a higher concentration in the atmosphere than for many hundreds of thousands of years. He estimates that if no action is taken to curb the emissions of oil, gas and coal, the carbon dioxide concentration will rise to two or three times its pre-industrial level during the twenty-first century, which implies a potential rise of the global average temperature between two and six degrees Celsius.

In the appendix of the so-called Stern Review, an outstanding report to the British Government by the most qualified scientists of the country, you find a scheme in which some of the consequences are shown. A temperature increase of two degrees over the entire century is the lowest prediction. But already that rise of temperature will mean an increasing number of people at risk from hunger, especially in the Northern deserts of Africa; the disappearance worldwide of all small mountain glaciers; and a potential threat to the water supplies in several areas. Coral reef systems will be extensively and eventually irreversibly damaged. If, though, we come within the range of a three to four degrees Celsius increase, the hunger in Africa may increase from 25% to 60%, the water supply in Africa and the Mediterranean will decrease more than 30%, and many species, from 20% to possibly 50% of their present number, will face extinction. Hurricane intensity will double, a partial collapse of the Amazon rainforest is predicted, and the melting of the Greenland ice sheet will become irreversible. This also implies the end of the permafrost, which will bring enormous amounts of hydrocarbon (methane, CH_4) into the atmosphere, a greenhouse gas that is twenty-five times more effective than carbon dioxide. Pacific islands and low coastal areas are already threatened by the rising sea level, but with a 5% temperature increase the rising sea level will even threaten major world cities, like London, Shanghai, Tokyo and New York.

These are alarming predictions. And they are not the projections of people who live in the world of fantasy but are the result of careful interdisciplinary research by teams of scientists with substantial expertise, and their findings are also supported by a number of other international reports. The time has come to act decisively. Did not a shock occur for many people with the release of Al Gore's movie, when even President Bush declared that this problem had to be tackled somehow? We can take his statement as a sign that we live in the presence of a real peril (after all, he is surely not a president who is prone to doomsday thinking!). So international panels have been formed, and several proposals have been formulated in order to soften or to counter these possible developments.

The main line of these proposals is clear and can be laid out in three broad categories. The *first* is bringing down the already existing amount of greenhouse gas emissions into the atmosphere by, for instance, re-forestation. Forests absorb the carbon dioxide they need for growth directly from the air. The *second* category of measures tries to reduce the use of fossil energy—coal, oil, and gas—in favour of other, non fossil-based types of energy, such as an increased use of nuclear energy but also the promotion of less risky forms of energy-production like wind and water power, biomass energy, hydrogen energy, and a better use of the heat inside of the earth. That effort to promote carbon-efficiency can be directly effected by, for instance, subsidies but also indirectly by price controls or taxing measures. As an example, the Stern Report is much in favour of a high, so-called, carbon tax. Also in this context, new international, regional or global markets are proposed and already partially implemented, markets in which you can buy or sell "emission-rights", for instance the right to emit into the atmosphere so many tons of carbon-dioxide in a specific country. The hope is that if you have to pay for that right you will be more reluctant to use fossil energies.

The *third* category—you will note that I travel at high speed through some of these existing possibilities—is to diminish the use of energy in relation to all that is produced and consumed, so that the energy per product is brought down. This is the path of so called energy-efficiency. You can save energy in both the production and the consumption sphere. Here, as well, direct measures are possible (restrictions and prohibitions) next to indirect measures (using the price system and greening the tax system). For instance, more human energy can be employed. That is, labour instead of capital in the processes of production, transportation and distribution. I am strongly in favour of most of these proposals, for they indeed can make a huge difference.

Something remarkable remains, though, in our decision to respond to global warming in these three broad ways. Let me draw your attention back to the question of whether improving the carbon and energy efficiency of all that is and will be produced and consumed is enough—really enough—to do the job. Without diminishing in any way the need to take most of the measures I have just mentioned, I outline three considerations that sustain my doubt in their sufficiency as a response to global warming.

My *first* consideration is the enormous speed and volume of so many economic developments that occur now in the global arena, most of them in the context of what we refer to as the rapid process of globalization. We live in a time of an enormous expansion of several global markets. Here I mention not only the enormous growth of transnational companies all over the world, but also the fantastic growth and expansion of the so-called financial markets. The amount of financial derivatives has now reached a size which is more than ten times the size of the combined Gross National Product in the entire world; more international speculative capital continues to flow within a two day period, around the world, than the total amount of debt of all "less developed countries". We see how anxious most national governments have recently become about the dynamics of global capital, the capital flows, and what this financial dynamic might do with their societies and economies. They are often reducing their taxes on capital and capital-movements, simply out of fear for what this new Big Brother might do with them and their economies—as if it had and has a life of its own. Of course this kind of financial dynamic does not diminish the worldwide growth of industrial production. It actually enhances it strongly, with all the consequences for increasing CO_2 emissions. National economies are in a sense haunted by the financial markets and so they continually increase their levels of production and exports in an endless search for the highest possible profitability. Is not this a good reason for deep concern?

Let me state my first point in another way. In a special edition of *Future*, some global developments have been described which occurred in the forty years between 1950 and 1990. The world population doubled. Simultaneously, the use of energy rose by a factor of five, and world industrial production even grew by a factor of seven! Combined with the expected growth of the world population, an approximate six-fold increase could be calculated from the impact of all this human activity on nature and on the over-all carrying capacity of the environment.

Let us now suppose for a moment, that this process of multiplication goes on for the next forty years, given so many national and international, political, economic and also financial driving factors. With knowledge of these numbers, do you suppose the countervailing measures which I just summarised will be adequate even if they are implemented world wide? Or, in terms of the Kaya identity[2], will not the dynamic growth of the first two factors of the equation (i.e. population and industrial production per capita) more than absorb the total gain in the possible improvement of the carbon and energy efficiency? The calculations of *Future* were made for the period between 1950 and 1990, but we are now already halfway through another forty-year period, while the tendencies remain exactly the same! What about a third period of forty years, after the 2130? And keep in mind that the development of India and China (and Brazil?) will also have to be factored in!

There is a second consideration in my serious concern about the size and the limitations of our present reactions, not at the level of statistics but at the level of ideological commitments. I already referred to the important British Stern Report, which is focused on the negative consequences of the global rise in temperature. This report insists very clearly that there is an urgent need to cut back on the level of those emissions, which is certainly true. At the same time, it strikes me that in the entire report no questions are raised about the increasing volume of industrial production, especially in the richer countries.

> Tackling Climate Change is the pro-growth strategy for the longer term. And it can be done in a way that does not cap the aspirations for growth of rich or poor countries.[3]

Why does the report make this statement? Have political considerations entered into the scientific debate? I understand that especially less wealthy countries urgently need further economic growth, just to be able to cope with the poverty of the millions of their inhabitants. *But what makes the undisturbed continuation of industrial growth in rich countries so important, so essential, that those aspirations should never be discussed?* For it is beyond any doubt that industrial growth per capita in the rich countries is one of the main sources of the increases in greenhouse emissions!

It would be too easy, too cheap, to refer only to political pressures on the authors of this report. Perhaps this statement was for them an honest statement. Even so an important follow-up question will arise. Could it be that the authors of the report are merely putting their trust in new technological advances and new markets or taxing devices to such an extent that they honestly believe their own statement that rich countries can continue almost forever our material economic growth? To return to my illustration of the high-speed train, here we see an example of a view from inside the train. I would venture that no lasting solution is possible if our own modern societies go on identifying themselves with their own dynamic achievements and economic potentials. What makes the issue of global warming and climate change so extremely sensitive and even critical is that they are both directly connected with the use of energy, that kind of resource which alone forms the heart of our modern industrialised societies! For energy cannot be recycled like other natural resources, and that already makes energy unique. But energy can also make or break the dynamics of modern economic growth, and thus also the dynamics of globalization itself. Said otherwise: we, as modern people, are now indeed reaching the limits of our own modern dynamistic outlook on life and the future. Given the present combination of a limited availability of fossil fuel resources and of a growing deep vulnerability of the earth and the environment from the warming process, we seem compelled to give up our isolated outlook from the *inside*. A new, deeper and broader view on reality is needed.

Getting Off the Train for a New View

My third consideration is a desire to listen to those who are standing *outside* the train. Thoroughly modern people can find hope in another possible view, the perspective from *outside*, which is open to the possibility that a train travels too fast. Or, said otherwise, it is a view that admits that some forms of our present economic dynamics are too extreme to be fully sustainable, given the risks of accidents for nature, for the poor, and also for our own children. But where do we find the foundation for that other outlook, that perspective from the *outside*? And if we find it, can this view also be made truly effective for our contemporary social life?

Here I would like to call on some unexpected testimony: voices from the churches of South Asia. The letter I will quote from is a testimony to what they see around them as the consequences of modern culture's deep attachment to its own self-made high-speed train. Let me quote a section of the letter that was written in Bangkok in 1999 during the heat of the Asian Crisis by the delegates of churches from the South. Southern churches are speaking here in response to a crisis directly related to the unexpected movements of global capital. Several capitalists were speculating on the sudden fall of the currencies of Thailand and other South Asian countries, and their plan succeeded: the value of these currencies dropped, indeed dramatically. A deepened poverty in Thailand and Indonesia was the result. There is thus a cry in this letter addressed to the churches of the North to give due attention to what has happened to them, the poor. The impoverishment of the South is at least partially caused by the enrichment of the North. Forced economic adaptation and modernisation of the South is threatening to demolish their way of life. They write:

> Next to the pain and suffering in the South, there are the threats in the North. We heard about poverty, coming back in even your richest societies; we received reports about environmental destruction also in your midst, and about alienation, loneliness and the abuse of women and children. And all that, while most of your churches are losing members. And we asked ourselves: is most of that not also related to being rich and desiring to become richer than most of you already are? Is there not in the Western view of human beings and society a delusion, which always looks to the future and wants to improve it, even when it implies an increase of suffering in your own societies and in the South? Have you not forgotten the richness that is related to sufficiency? If, according

to Ephesians 1, God is preparing in human history to bring everyone and everything under the lordship of Jesus Christ, his shepherd-king—God's own globalization!—shouldn't caring (for nature) and sharing with each other be the main characteristic of our lifestyle, instead of giving fully in to the secular trend of a growing consumerism?[4]

Do you see how remarkably and naturally the faith perspective enters our discussion of globalization and global warming?

The letter not only calls the North to look to the South, it calls the North to try standing on "the outside" with them and to hear a deeply spiritual word spoken to the heart of a restless modern society. I read this text saying something like this: *"If you know all this and see this growing misery for us as just a natural fate, then is there not something really wrong in your whole outlook on life? Are you not, within your own modern societies, caught by an illusion, an illusion which brings you repeatedly to hasten towards an always better future for yourself, but at the same time forgetting reality as it really is, filled with the continued suffering of so many?"* The need for repentance and a renewed understanding of the concept of sufficiency enters into our consideration of consumption, and we see that, in the view of the churches of the South, sufficiency is not related to pain and misery, but to richness and the joy of saturation.

Here we can point to the necessity for a spiritual component to any solution in which we put our hope. It is not by accident that the alternative perspective, the view from outside, starts with what is given to human beings and with what needs to be preserved, rather than starting with something we have produced with our own hands. The distinctive view from the outside is intrinsically creational. By beginning with what is given to us by our Creator and by giving priority to what needs to be preserved in respect and care, we make relative the work of our own hands, our own material progress, which is still seen by so many, also by millions of Christians, as the holy shrine of our entire existence and civilisation.

Which Way Forward?

What then is the way forward? Two concluding remarks I wish to make about this extremely serious question. What first impresses me is the need to openly and even forcefully challenge the still-powerful illusion in Western societies that our own technological progress can fully save us. A kind of spiritual war has to be fought against all world-and-life-views that do not start from respect for what is given us by the good Lord to care for and to preserve. The order of our political and economic thinking—first we need growth, and *only on that basis* can we give more care—is thoroughly irresponsible. Christians and Christian churches, particularly, have a task here. For they, God willing (and they themselves willing), can not only lay bare the deep secular roots of our present illusions, but they can also, with the support of a growing number of experts, build up the potential to break through the public lie that more material consumption in our already rich countries will lead us to more happiness. Just the opposite is true—which turns a mainly negative message into an announcement that is mainly positive! The shadow side of the message is indeed that the more we continue on our present path of unlimited material expansion, then the more we need to rob the earth, the more we will overburden our vulnerable ecosystems, and the more we will have to engage in a rat-race to obtain the final dregs of the depleted supplies of the energy-reserves in this world, even if the price is making war and fighting in remote areas. But the positive side is that we can earn more real peace, more *shalom* for all, in avoiding all these pains. And by the timely acceptance of levels of economic saturation, in private material consumption as well as in disposable income, the more realistic horizons for the economies of our societies will come into view. It sounds extremely strange, but working and consuming less will in the end do more good for us, for our kids and for nature than trying to work always harder and producing and consuming always more. "Enough" and "saturation" are underdeveloped concepts in economics and politics, but these can truly open a door where other efforts fail.

My second concluding remark is that there is indeed real hope for the future, in very practical terms. But that hope cannot be formulated in terms of the outcome of detailed blueprints for a relatively far future. Real hope comes, so to speak, not primarily *from* us but may come *to* us, perhaps already here and now. There is only one precondition, namely that our societies and our communities are willing to follow consistently a way guided by principles of good care for what and who is weak, but also mixed from the very start with elements of joy and relaxation. For some forms of stepping forward by stepping back (the Hebrew word is *bechinon*, giving up) have indeed to accompany us from the very start in the necessary transformation of our own rich economies.

Let me become more specific. Just imagine for a moment the radical scenario that, in concern for this beautiful but vulnerable creation and for the future of our own children, the public willingness grows in modern rich societies like Canada, Holland, and perhaps even the United States, to refrain jointly from further annual percentage increases in material consumption and personal income, especially when and where these lead to a higher emission of greenhouse gases.

That could form the basis, as a kind of first step, of a national covenant in these already rich societies; a covenant between the organisations of employers and employees, chambers of commerce, the government, churches, and several civil groups and movements to accept together a kind of zero-ceiling for the general growth of the material consumption per capita.

This choice could be the economic starting point for a gradual conversion of our national economies to more sustainable economies, somewhat similar to the way in which in 1940 until 1945 the British economy was turned into a war-economy. For less growth in material consumption sets labour and resources free, which then can also be used in another way: to come to a number of new investments or re-investments. Here we should think not only of investments to push back all levels of further natural and ecological damage in each sector of production, but also to make space for more public and common care for the weak (our social capital). This also makes capital transfer possible to diminish the debt-burdens for poor countries that drive them now to always-higher export, and energy, levels. And last but not least this additional economic room can be used to stop deforestation, to plant new forests in Canada, for instance, and to introduce everywhere, also on the roofs of our houses, new forms of clean energy.

As this begins to work and proves to be successful, also in terms of the creation of new forms of employment here and less burdens on the shoulders of the poor countries, another step may follow: namely the gradual bringing down of the material and energy activity levels of the modern rich society—the forgotten second term of the Kaya identity! This will also have the hidden blessing that the current over-loaded burdens of working hard (i.e. stress, burnout) will be significantly diminished or perhaps can be almost entirely taken away. *Shalom* in line with joint self-restraint is economically possible, feasible and even highly desirable, as soon as it is accompanied with an open eye for the needs of others and for coming to help our presently so deeply suffering natural world.

The number of special holy-days in medieval times was once estimated to amount to one sixth of the total amount of working days, far more than in our over-productive modern societies. Is that not an almost entirely forgotten wisdom? Our economic horizon, said in other words, should not be on expansion, but upon the blossoming of our economic life. Or, given the differences between cultures and nations, an *orchard* of blossoming economies. The metaphor of the tree comes here to the fore. In the internal economy of a living tree all cells are fully involved in the promotion of a process of a healthy, blossoming growth. But that inclusive type of growth is only possible because no tree ever has set its mind on expanding to the greatest height and growing to the clouds, (as we ourselves in the rich countries are still inclined to do) and so cause unnecessary damage to other living cells, and perhaps even suffering and pain in God's entire creation.

"Suffering and pain in God's entire creation": those words remind me of what St. Paul wrote centuries ago to the Christians in Rome. In Romans 8 he wrote about the groaning of the whole created universe, obviously not only people but also animals—like coral reefs and polar bears. The groaning is not without hope, for it is a groaning as if in the pangs of childbirth. A new world is coming. "The creation waits in eager expectation for the children of God to be revealed" (Romans 8:19, TNIV). Deep words! Remarkable words! For here it even seems as if our present suffering nature is also looking to us. Waiting for us, in the hope that we will begin to live up to and uphold the standards that make us recognisable to the groaning creation as God's true daughters and sons.

....

Bob Goudzwaard (Ph.D., Erasmus University) is professor emeritus of economics and cultural philosophy at the Free University of Amsterdam, and advisor to the Department of Justice, Peace, and Creation of the World Council of Churches. A few of his more recent publications are *Hope in Troubled Times: A New Vision for Confronting Global Crises* (with Mark Vander Vennen and David Van Heemst) (Grand Rapids, MI: Baker, 2007) and *Globalization and the Kingdom of God* (Grand Rapids, MI: Eerdmans, 2001).

NOTES

[1] http://www.st-edmunds.cam.ac.uk/faraday/CIS/houghton/index.html (accessed 4 April 2009).

[2] The Kaya identity is a formula that projects the level of human impact on the climate, specifically in the form of emissions of the greenhouse gas carbon dioxide, based on four factors: population, GDP per capita, energy use per unit of GDP, emissions per unit of energy consumed.

[3] http://www.hm-treasury.gov.uk/d/CLOSED_SHORT_executive_summary.pdf (accessed 4 April 2009). The full report can be found at http://www.hm-treasury.gov.uk/stern_review_report.htm

[4] *Letter to the Churches of the North*, Symposium of South Asian Christian churches on the Consequences of Economic Globalization (November 12-15, 1999, Bangkok, Thailand), http://www.kairoseuropa.de/english/bangkok-letter.doc (accessed 4 April 2009).

Globalization and Religious Fundamentalism

by Robert Joustra

Introduction

In this essay I am concerned with the question of the relationship
of two of the most controversial and woolly buzz words in contemporary international politics: globalization and fundamentalism. Asking this question assumes a few things. First, that both terms have
practical and substantive cognitive value such that they can usefully
organise our understanding and practice of global politics; and second,
that using them in a comparative fashion may yield further explanations which can help us better explain and understand international
relations (IR).

I begin straight away by confessing my suspicion that these assumptions are in error. While I would retain globalization as an important category for analysis, I am not at all convinced that fundamentalism—at least the way it is characterised in the present literature of
global politics—is a useful concept. It is a concept which tends—like
the broad majority of political science—to misunderstand what religion actually is. It suffers from historical and cultural amnesia, and
results in misleading, naive and ultimately damaging foreign and domestic policies.

This caveat given, the thrust of my argument will therefore be
to relate existing ideas on globalization to a redeveloped concept of
religion and fundamentalism in global politics. I remain unconvinced
that fundamentalism is the *best* term for this effort, but it has popular-
ity and utility in both theological and political circuits whereas other
concepts have none. My reasons for its adoption are more pragmatic
than they are intellectual; it may well be that the new wine will burst
the old skins, but at the very least in the process we may chart new
territory for students of religion and politics.

First, it is my overall argument that religion, as it is often understood in North America, was invented as part of the political mythology of the Enlightenment, and especially liberalism—a concept which
has emerged as being understood as universal to other cultures and

civilisations.[1] This mythology evolved religion into a private body of beliefs or doctrines, rather than as social loyalty, a public truth expressed in a community of believers. After the religious wars on Europe's continent in the seventeenth century, religion as a *public* social matter was carefully curtailed, and religion as a private series of personal convictions was cultivated. The secular was public, the sacred was private—carefully locked away where it could do no harm.

Political constellations which challenge these sacred/secular boundaries are easily (mis)labelled fundamentalist, a charge which is becoming easier to fix upon not merely those outside, but also those within Western political communities. If we are to properly explain and understand the phenomenon of fundamentalism in globalization we must first attend to these mythologies and to the gods and stories that animate its structures.

Second, I suggest that fundamentalism as a concept has an Enlightenment conception of religion built into it. As such, its use for understanding non-Western or non-liberal societies is limited. However, by recasting what we mean by religion, we might refashion fundamentalism to retain some use. It will be up to the reader to judge how successful this effort is.

Third, we will test this new definition of fundamentalism by applying it to what is labelled Islamic fundamentalism. This framework suggests that radical militarism in Islam has at its root an alternative theo-political vision, one which challenges the assumptions of Westphalian Christendom. Islam, like the new faces of Christianity in the global south, vexes secularist IR. However, Islam's history and political theology, while imparting important similarities, also carries its own unique and troubled history. We must not jump to the conclusion that since Islam and worldviewish Christianity both fundamentally challenge secularist IR they represent compatible visions of global affairs. On the contrary, this new lens for fundamentalism and globalization tells us that such alternative visions represent conflicting metanarratives, a clash which can take hideously violent forms. It is in the final section that I wish to ask how to properly *read* the rise of Islam and "Islamic fundamentalism", and what may be done to live wisely in this tumultuous era.

The globalization of fundamentalism does not signal the end to a belief in reason, but it does indicate an end to a belief in secular reason. Only in Western polities, where the political theologies of Enlightenment liberalism linger on, could the global resurgence of religion be mistaken for anything else but the malaise of secularism, and a call to engage and explore the emergent geography of religion in a post-secular world.

Globalization and Religion

Debates about what does and does not constitute globalization are wide ranging, but for our purposes I intend to be brief and simple by defining it merely as the compression of time and space.[2] It is a centuries long process, which has progressed rapidly in recent history. It is further a multi-dimensional phenomenon. It is neither the exclusive domain of economists, nor of scholars of international relations. Globalization represents the kind of intellectual puzzle that belies the careful dissection of one or another academic discipline, the compartmentalisation of government bureaucracies or even the well meaning intentions of philosophers and theologians. It is a foil to the modern tendency for expertise in minutia, and instead calls for the kind of capable and wide angled analysis so often demonstrated by public intellectuals and journalists.

At the heart of the debate on globalization is the dispute between homogenisation and heterogenisation—between things becoming more the same, or more different. The predominant economic view of globalization—that commoditisation is sweeping the globe in what has been called McDonaldization[3]—takes the homogenisation theme for granted. This overlooks important factors of global life, and its reduction of human interactions to the economic sphere cannot, I believe, be sustained in the final analysis. Instead I suggest globalization is "both and": it globalizes, but also localises—an idea that has been captured in the Japanese word *dochakuka* meaning something like global localisation, or the more succinct term *glocalization*.[4]

This means that while globalization does bring ideas, people, materials and—importantly—religions more and more into contact, the effect is not a simple one-sided accommodation. It is the case that as religious peoples and ideas rub shoulders they become more relative, but it is also the case that as this happens peoples and religions become *more* traditional, more localised, and more internally entrenched. Roland Robertson calls this one of the key factors behind the growth of religious fundamentalism, naming numerous religious movements which have become *globaphobic*.[5] The question of what theologies or sociologies are operative within a religious community to push it in the direction of either relativisation or globaphobia is one well worth further reflection.

Globalization has certainly influenced the practice of religion—but it is also true that religion—specifically the Enlightenment myth of religion—has profoundly influenced the trajectory of globalization and global politics. Leonard Thompson defines a political myth as "a tale told about the past to legitimise or discredit a regime".[6] In international relations such myths form an important purpose to help explain and understand global politics. Probably the most formative mythic event is the foundation of the modern state system and the Peace of Westphalia. This is one of the first dates any student of globalization will learn about how and why global politics work. And while it would be historically naive to imagine that political liberalism and the modern separation between religion and politics stretched no further back than this, it is not without reason that scholars focus on this historical moment as the birth of a new constitution of international order.[7]

The Peace of Westphalia was implemented only after a frightening period of continental devastation wrought by the Wars of Religion (1550-1650), and specifically the Thirty Years War (1618-1648). According to IR orthodoxy the Wars of Religion demonstrated unequivocally that when religion becomes involved in international public life it results in violence, war, revolution and the collapse of global order. The story goes that the rebirth of Christendom in the Renaissance and Reformation took European public life by storm, and with religion and its absolutist claims now activated by growing swaths of Europe's population, instability promptly ensued. It was only out of the devastation wrought by religious wars that Europeans were able to finally rise above the primitive impulses of conflicting theologies to embrace a system of liberalism and religious toleration. The modern state, with its privatisation of religion and increasing secularisation of politics, rose to limit religion's domestic role, minimising the damage which religious disagreement might cause, and finally ending the destructive role which religion had played in medieval European life. It is not without coincidence that our historical periodisations label the political constitution of the *Respublica Christiana* the Dark Ages, liberated only after a long, bloody struggle to embrace a more cosmopolitan and tolerant politics.

In this sense the first strand of Westphalia is a secularising one. Westphalia was the culmination of a centuries long metamorphosis, gradually supplanting one political order with another. The *Respublica Christiana* had no sovereignty, no supreme authority within a territory. From pope to Holy Roman Emperor all the way down authority was united in the church as the Body of Christ. With only the exception of small patches none of these authorities enjoyed the qualities of sovereignty prior to this point. Hence there was an intimate mingling of politics and religion, with the church exercising a variety of offices, including those that are traditionally considered civil. The pope exercised legislative, executive and judicial powers.[8] The emergence of sovereignty in international society is therefore connected to the marginalisation of the religion. In order for the modern state to be born, religion needed to be reconceived.

This is what scholars refer to as the Westphalian presumption in IR—that religious and cultural pluralism cannot be accommodated in international public life. The Westphalian settlement was understood as providing a way that religious and cultural pluralism could be taken seriously in international society, but within the safer confines of domestic politics. The Peace of Augsburg (1555) and the Congress of Westphalia (1648) adopted the principle of *cujus regio, ejus religio*—a ruler determines the religion of the realm—making religious toleration and non-interference (on religious grounds) in the domestic affairs of other states paramount. Pluralism was one of the main principles of the Westphalian international order.[9] Through the principles of the Westphalian settlement, state sovereignty, *cujus regio, ejus religio*, and the balance of power, the ability to accommodate religious pluralism in international society was built into its frame.

One of the chief problems with this traditional myth is its account of the Wars of Religion. The myth of Westphalia is predicated firmly on a modern concept of religion. Reading religion with our peculiar modernist lenses it is difficult to get a correct sense of what the Wars of Religion were actually about and, ultimately, to explain and understand religious fundamentalism around the globe today. The error is in retrospectively applying our modernist conceptions of religion onto non-modern political cultures.

In medieval Christendom Christians did use the term *religio* though not particularly often and then in reference only to the communal life of monastics.[10] Thomas Aquinas, for example, used *religio* as referring to the activity of giving proper reverence to God in worship. From this we could suggest that religion in early modern Europe was foremost a community bonded by common worship. By contrast when we speak of religion we mean a set of propositional doctrines or beliefs we hold to be true, or a set of interior impulses directed toward the transcendent. The distinction is germane to properly reading religion in global affairs. What was at stake in the Wars of Religion was a sacred notion of community defined by religion, as each community fought to define, redefine or defend the boundaries between the sacred and profane as a whole.[11]

The result has been that the modern concept of religion came to separate the virtues and practises of the Christian tradition from the communities in which they were embedded. Scott Thomas writes,

> The modern concept of religion began to emerge in the late fifteenth century, and first appeared as a universal, inward impulse or feeling toward the divine common to all people. The varieties of pieties and rituals were increasingly called "religions", as representations of the one true *religio* common to all, apart from any ecclesial community.[12]

An important early sixteenth century change came when *religio* began to shift from being representative of virtues, supported by practices of an ecclesial community, to becoming a system of doctrines or beliefs, which might exist quite apart from an ecclesial community. Thinkers such as Hugo Grotius and William Chillingworth began to defend what Christianity teaches, rather than what Christianity simply is: the true worship of God.[13] It was this very move in the definition of religion which prompted the twentieth century philosopher Paul Tillich to comment that in these high middle ages the priest exchanged his ecclesial garb for a university frock, an intellectual move which has long since defined both the matrix of Christendom and the political theology of the West.

This mythology of religion's inherent instability in modern polities combined with an emerging secularism, which questioned the future of religion generally. If religion was merely a set of foundational beliefs or propositional truths on which activity in the world was predicated, would not other beliefs or truths suffice? Might they not serve us better than the weary track record of medieval Christendom; might not a material foundation for culture and society, or a cosmopolitan categorical imperative serve humanity better? Political ideologies—Marxism, liberalism, socialism, nationalism—do precisely this, channelling loyalties toward an object rather than God. International law, institutions and organisations advance their purposes with little thought of religion. So it is also with parties, unions, lobbies and forces through which people urge, advocate and rebel. Despite their myriad of differences these ideologies bear within them the birthmark of this common theo-political ancestry: the temporal as distinguished from the spiritual, politics from religion.

How does modern politics conceive of religion given this history? Daniel Philpott provides an illuminating definition of religion based upon the history of international politics. He writes that, "religion is a set of beliefs about the ultimate ground of existence, that which is unconditioned, not itself created or caused, and the communities and practices that form around these beliefs".[14] What we may conclude from this is that liberalism's political theology is itself religious in nature. As Elizabeth Shakman Hurd writes, "to define the boundaries of the secular and the religious is a political decision"[15]—and as Jacques Derrida has argued, the separation of religion from politics is also a theological one. The Westphalian settlement constitutes religious as well as political elements by its own terms—a primordial secularism which, contrary to popular belief, does not provide for neutrality, but premises political and religious activity according to its own design.

The real problem with trying to apply the Westphalian concept of religion to the study of many of the societies of Eastern Europe, central Asia and the non-Western world generally is that they have often not reached this same theo-political consensus—or are struggling not to make it. The conception of religion as privatised and marginalised is generally incompatible with the political cultures of these regions. This is why strong religions and weak states still characterise so much of the developing world. These states and their religious communities are in the midst of a fight to define, redefine and defend the social boundaries between the sacred and the profane in the midst of modernisation and globalization.[16]

As we begin to unravel the modern concept of religion, we begin to understand how contemporary thought maps fundamentalism and religious extremism. Recall that the Wars of Religion are a founding moment of barbarism and intolerance, an alternative political order which, according to the mythology of Westphalia and of modern religion, results in chaos, violence, intolerance and destruction. This can be avoided only by allocating religion to the realm of domestic politics, and globalizing the machinations of the secular state. Nevertheless we have just unveiled that the secular (read neutral) nature of modern state is suspect. If we take this observation seriously we find that not only is religion back in international relations—it never really left.[17] Moving forward to define *fundamentalism* we must be careful to dissect exactly how these concepts prefigure our explanations and understandings of fundamentalist religion around the globe.

What is Fundamentalism? Toward a Post-Enlightenment Cartography

Who or what is a fundamentalist? If the animating political order of the international system already has a carefully prescribed relationship between the secular and the sacred, anything which challenges this prevailing nostrum could be fundamentalist. The intrusion of religion into public life generally is highly suspect. Philip Jenkins argues that the picture can be even more complex. Often adherents of the same faith label each other fundamentalist by virtue of their stance on moral or hermeneutical issues. By North American standards the ideas expressed by many African churches in debates on sexuality might seem fundamentalist.

It is ironic given the origins of the term in a 1920 edition of the Northern Baptist (U.S.A.) periodical, T*he Watchman-Examiner*, whose editor was a self-described conservative evangelical Protestant doing "royal battle" to preserve the fundamentals of the Christian faith, that it is now used most frequently to describe Islam.[18] The path from Baptist conservatism to radical Islamic militarism is not an obvious, or—at times—a coherent one.

In North America the term gradually grew to become a kind of catchall description for ultraconservative intolerance. Used in this fashion the term was almost always detracting, and certainly subjective. Once we expand the term fundamentalism to cover the intrusion of religion and religious ideas into the public realm—anyone who treats religion as something that should shape all of one's daily life—its application and utility becomes even more woolly. Popular representations can also be selective. Jenkins writes that "if your reading of the Bible inspires you to help the poor, that is passionate religious commitment. If it leads you to denounce homosexuality, you are a fundamentalist."[19] In the United States and Canada terms such as "evangelical" are developing into synonyms, commensurable labels for intolerant social conservatives.

Since the term has its origins in Christianity it is difficult to apply it to other religious contexts. Islam has its own form of fundamentalism—*usuliya*—though this means something not altogether similar. If we read fundamentalism as a literal or conservative reading of sacred scriptures then by definition all Muslims be fundamentalists—no orthodox Muslim would suggest Muhammad himself had anything to do with the composition of the Quran, but rather had the role of receiving dictation. This would amount to Christian fundamentalism, though in neither case does this reveal anything particularly germane about the adherent's subsequent politics. Therefore if all fundamentalism is not created equal, how are we to intelligently discern a way forward?

Clearly fundamentalism rests on both a Christian and modern basis. The term is born out of the same political mythology that I have already suggested is problematic to apply to other regions and cultures of the world. Yet fundamentalism is not merely a term of secularist abuse; it retains some cognitive content. There are common themes that arise from traditions around the globe that seem to be captured in the term. These shared characteristics tell us much about the movements themselves, but also a great deal about the secular world which interprets and reacts to them. One should not adopt the term fundamentalism merely to make facile generalisations, or ignore the detail of individual movements and their contexts, but instead to try and gain an understanding and comparative analysis of the similar characteristics and organizing logic that emerges from these groups. The label can be misleading—as can terms such as capitalist, socialist, conservative, liberal—but such general umbrella categories do indeed form useful categories for organising analysis. Thus understood we might agree that a useful way to define fundamentalism would be referring to *a discernible pattern of religious militancy by which self-styled true believers attempt to arrest the erosion of religious identity, fortify the borders of the religious community, and create viable alternatives to secular institutions and behaviours*.[20] From this I wish to suggest three brief ways in which fundamentalism is popularly, if problematically, applied.

Types of Fundamentalism

First, it serves originally as an internal referent for a religion concerning some aspect of religious purism or interpretation. It suggests a hermeneutic orthodoxy. Fundamentalists, while often celebrating their own emphasis on religious purism, can be pejoratively cast as ignorant and regressive within a faith. This usage has a potential global North/ South divide. Where as in the global north the ideologies of secularism and liberalism thrive within domestic religious discourse, the global south grows increasingly suspicious of this duality. The twin charges of liberalism and fundamentalism in global religious dialogue are a brewing recipe for religious schism.

Second, fundamentalism may refer to any religion or religious idea which attempts to intrude upon the public square, whether in national or international politics, for the attempts of reform or debate. Traditionally in Western Christendom this has taken the form of social and moral issues, but it need not necessarily take such a role. Again it is the political consequences of the religious ideas themselves that subjectively apply. Tommy Douglas impelled by his Christian faith to introduce universal health care to Canada would hardly fit such a label. Yet moral and sexual conservatives in the contemporary evangelical mainstream could hardly be discussed in the same breath without the sting of fundamentalism. Religion in the public square may only be accepted insofar as it reinforces the established political theology handed down from Enlightenment liberalism—and its particular vision of the good life. As van der Veer and Lehmann note, "when religion manifests itself politically it is conceptualised as fundamentalism. It is almost always interpreted as a negative social force directed against science, rationality, secularism—in short, against modernity."[21]

Third, and finally, we can understand fundamentalism as being not merely an emphasis on religious purism or orthodoxy, but also the violent means by which this purism attempts to establish itself. This violent fundamentalist chafes against religious liberalisation, but also the secularist separation of politics and religion. It is not merely the unbelievers within its own ranks, but also the infidels outside its established theo-political order which merit challenge. At its heart is a far more fundamental mission than mere theological purity, though this is primary—just as its mission is also more but not less than the reordering of the dominant abominations of Western political theology.

On the first kind of fundamentalism I have very little to add. Each religious tradition weighs its respective claims regarding orthodoxy and purism differently, and it seems unnecessary to speculate on the normative elements by which this might properly be done. This is a debate for theologians, missiologists and biblical scholars. Nonetheless it is difficult to imagine how fundamentalism as a concept could be consistently and usefully applied in this context.

The second kind should by this point strike us as ironic, since by its own claims it is self-refuting. The interjection of religious ideas into international public life can hardly be seen as aberrant—such ideas already animate its fundamental structures. What secularist defenders fear is not merely the introduction of religious elements, but the collapse of the established theo-political consensus. Calling this kind of exchange fundamentalist is the great political trump card of secularists and liberals—it is "out of bounds". However, if Daniel Philpott is correct and global politics is undergoing once more a "revolution in sovereignty", this theo-political order is likely to become only more and more hotly contested, as the global resurgence of religion wakes up the slumbering secularist West. One could call this *postmodern fundamentalism*, an attempt to recover theo-political traditions and concepts which challenge the prevailing structures of modernity. However, since this is almost certainly misleading it may be helpful to think of this in its more particular manifestations as, for example, *political Islam*[22] or *worldviewish Christianity*.

It is the third kind of fundamentalism that will form my final section, the same topic of analysis which launched the Fundamentalism Project.[23] The flashpoint of 9/11 for what I will call *radical fundamentalism* has become an icon for secularism's religious phobia. Nearly three thousand civilians died on September 11, 2001, an attack that was motivated both by a fanatical religious purism and a political theology which regards the Westphalian synthesis as despicably secularised. Radical fundamentalism is not confined to Islam, but for reasons of history Islam's particular political theologies never adapted to the liberal international order. What began in the early twentieth century as an internal moral critique of Islamic civilisation, over decades became radical Islamic fundamentalism identifying the sources of Islam's decline both within and without, advocating a singular violent antidote.

Nevertheless it is useful to consider the characteristics of radical fundamentalism broadly, before attempting to trace the origins and nature of radical Islamic fundamentalism specifically. The Fundamentalism Project outlines nine characteristics of radical fundamentalism—five ideological, and four organisational.[24]

Ideological Characteristics of Radical Fundamentalism

1. Radical fundamentalism is *reactive*. The source of this reaction is the same: the erosion and displacement of religion. It

may include other consequences of secularisation and relativism, but radical fundamentalism is always first and foremost concerned with the erosion of religion and its proper role within society. Therefore there is always the protection of some religious content, some traditional beliefs or associated norms. These reactions both oppose and exploit secularism—thus we see fundamentalists adopting mediums of mass communication and modern technologies.

2. Fundamentalism is *selective* in three ways. First, it is not merely defensive of tradition but also serves to reshape that tradition, especially to distinguish itself from the mainstream. Second, fundamentalists select some aspects of modernity which they embrace—including modern organisational and technological structures. Third, fundamentalists select certain consequences of modernity and secular society for special opposition. The target of this opposition may change over time, as global events and organisational capacity unfold.

3. A black and white, or *dualistic worldview* is common. The world of the spirit or of light is juxtaposed against the world of matter, and of evil. Reality is divided into two realms—those outside and contaminated in sinful ignorance and doom; and those inside, pure and redeemed.

4. *Absolutism and inerrancy* often revolves around a combination of both sacred scriptures and traditional interpretation, though absolutism implies that such interpretation is without the contingency we might assign to the act. Therefore hermeneutical methods developed by secular philosophy are vehemently opposed.

5. Finally *millennialism and messianism* characterise radical fundamentalist ideology. The good will ultimately triumph over the evil, a triumph which is preceded by the emergence of a saviour or messiah figure. Millennialism offers an end to suffering and waiting and messianism a powerful redeemer through which to affect this.

Organisational Characteristics of Radical Fundamentalism

1. *Membership* in fundamentalist movements is usually divinely elected, a remnant or last outpost of faithful followers. This is a powerful means by which to achieve group solidarity. This solidarity usually translates into a strong belief in particular divine rewards for those within, not available to those without.

2. A dualistic worldview evolves into *sharp organisational boundaries* between the saved, and the sinner. Dividing walls

or other spatial metaphors are common characteristics. This separation will also be displayed through dress, vocabulary and media consumption.

3. Fundamentalist movements have an *authoritarian structure*. While membership is voluntary, and those within are considered equal, nonetheless the typical fundamentalist organisation is led by a charismatic icon, in which the follower places extraordinary or divine qualities. This tension between voluntarism and charismatic authority makes fundamentalist movements extremely fragile. Since there can be no loyal opposition there is a tendency toward fragmentation.

4. *Behavioural requirements* have great detail and are strictly enforced. This includes grooming, dress, speech—rules about drinking, sexuality, childhood discipline and more. There is censorship of certain reading materials and close supervision of listening and viewing practices.

These characteristics should make it clear that to conflate the three popular uses of fundamentalism I sketched out is extremely unhelpful. Increasingly struggling Islamic and Christian societies in the developing world do not merit our scorn for adapting their theologies and beliefs to particular cultural and political contexts. To expect these political communities to adopt, en masse, the political theology of the Westphalian consensus is not merely impractical, but itself smells of a kind of liberal fundamentalism, which can tolerate no deviance from its ordered international constitution. Political Islam, which advocates public prayer and progressive *sharia* law, cannot reasonably or helpfully be lumped together with the radical fundamentalists of 9/11. Militancy may be expressed without recourse to violence.[25] If we conflate these two then we make fundamentalist and terrorist synonymous terms. It should be clear from the above characteristics that while both may have superficially similar religious elements, their animating theologies and organisational logic are quite different.

I do not mean to suggest that all political theologies are equally true and authentic paths to sustaining human community. To argue that first principles motivate our political constellations, and that those principles therefore merit study, is not to morally and politically equate those constellations. Oliver O'Donovan aptly notes that "only theorists could be so foolish as to think that it did not matter *which* concepts one grasped—apart, that is, from the morally immature". He goes on to say that,

> a class of sixteen-year-olds, told for the first time that what one calls a 'terrorist' another calls a 'freedom fighter', may miss the point so badly as to conclude

there is no difference between the two; but that is the
privilege of being sixteen. The mature adult knows it
is because one and the same thing can *look different*
that we need the two concepts of 'freedom fighter'
and 'terrorist' to differentiate. Those two concepts are
not interchangeable.[26]

And neither, of course, are our political theologies. Some cultivate
and sustain human flourishing and others repress, degrade and destroy.
Radical fundamentalism, among these, is no mere romantic alternative
political order.

Islam and Radical Fundamentalism

Sohail Hashmi generalises three strands in Islamic political theology.[27] In the first place "statists" generally accept the territorial state,
and see Islam as being an important source of national identity, while
viewing it otherwise as an impediment to modernisation. Think of this
political theology as *secularist Islam*. Second, Islamic international-
ists, while accepting separate Islamic states, assert pan-Islamic obligations which transcend the interests of individual member states—a
variety of *political Islam*. Thirdly, Hashmi identifies what he calls
Islamic cosmopolitans, those for whom the territorially delimited sovereign state is a relic of European imperialism, weakening Islam and
violating core Islamic tenets. Ayatollah Khomeini would be emblem-
atic of this, someone who supported Islamic revolution far beyond the
borders of Iran. This third strand of political Islam could be labelled
radical Islamic fundamentalism, though it is widely agreed that this
represents only a small niche in the spectrum of Islamic views of
political theology.[28] The beliefs and actions of radical Islamic fundamentalism run counter to much of the mainstream Islamic tradition;
a tradition which prohibits direct, intentional killings of innocents,
the global enlistment of Muslim civilians in warfare and one which
requires a justly constituted authority.[29]
     As we might expect, radical Islam's confrontation is as much with
the unbelievers within as with the non-believers without. This is why
radical Islam's struggle cannot be naively reduced to a universalised
war between Islam and Christianity. It is not just Christianity or even
the historic traditions of Western Christendom that radical Islam rejects, though with these it certainly has friction. The central issue is
the secularised political theology which challenges its own matrices
of authority, along with the particular instances of offence between
Islam and the United States.[30] Radical Islamic fundamentalism utterly
rejects the Westphalian synthesis, its conception of religion, sover-

eignty and statehood—and it finds other Islamic societies with these
elements equally contemptible.

Sovereignty in international politics is monopolised by the state.
This monopolisation is considered a religious abomination by radical
fundamentalists. Osama bin Laden's fatwa of February 1998 says,

> In compliance with God's order, we issue the follow-
> ing fatwa to all Muslims: the ruling to kill the Ameri-
> cans and their allies—civilians and military—is an
> individual duty for every Muslim who can do it in
> any country in which it is possible to do it, in order
> to liberate the Al-Aqsa Mosque [Jerusalem] and the
> holy mosque [Mecca] from their grip, and in order
> for their armies to move out of the lands of Islam .
> . . This is in accordance with the words of Almighty
> God, "and fight the pagans all together as they fight
> you all together", and "fight them until there is no
> more tumult or oppression, and there prevail justice
> and faith in God".

These radical fundamentalists are not a state, but religious actors, bound together by their political theology which claims to act on
behalf of the *umma*—the Muslim community, wherever it might be.
Their authority dramatically supersedes traditional state boundaries,
undermining a core Westphalian tenet of non-intervention in another
state's religion—*cujus regio, ejus religio*. Radical fundamentalism is
dedicated to exactly the opposite; influencing states and regions to
religious purism and orthodoxy, and instituting Islamic societies under
the common authority of *sharia* law.

The modern state system provides for spheres of religious freedom, where confessional norms are not admitted, at times even leading to the suppression of such norms. By contrast radical Islamic fundamentalism imagines a unified political community under the divine
law of *sharia* in every sphere of society. While Western political theology uses a variety of mechanisms to mediate authority in politics and
society,[31] radical Islam imagines a direct revealed structure for the nature of politics. Nevertheless even radical Islam cannot imagine such
a relationship between religion and politics to be so uncomplicated, as
beyond a common rejection of the detestable Westphalian consensus,
very little actual consensus exists in the Islamic world about precisely
what political Islam should look like.[32]

The roots of radical Islam can help clarify its goals. The first ar-
ticulators of this tradition were Sunni, writing in the front half of the
twentieth century. Writing primarily against the fall of governments
and international order into secularism, these writers advocated an

intensive jihad, or holy struggle, against the evils of confining religion wrongly to the private sphere. This perspective is known generally as *Salafiyya*, derived from *al-Salaf al-Salih*, meaning "venerable forefathers".[33] With the abolition of the caliphate in 1924 they exercised little systematic influence until the late 1970s.

Aby Ala Al-Mawdudi was one of the earliest radicals, and the founder of the Jama'at-i Islami Party in Pakistan. He argued that states themselves are a Westernised corruption, and actively campaigned against the creation of Pakistan, though he later participated in Pakistani politics for three decades. Despite this he was never a nationalist or a strong supporter of the state. He called for a universal jihad, though not a violent one, against the imperialism of both the West and the Soviet Union during the cold war.[34]

A third important figure, Hasan Al-Banna, founded the Muslim Brotherhood in 1982. Secularism for Al-Banna, just as for Al-Mawdudi, was aberrant. Islam was a total world and life view, one which could not be confined to the private sphere. He organised night schools, hospitals, clinics and factories, while teaching specifically Muslim labour laws. The Brotherhood was meanwhile organising violent operations against declared enemies of Islam, though Al-Banna formally denounced these actions. The present day party continues its life in politics as well as its radical fringe.[35]

The Egyptian Sayyid Qutb is probably the most prominent Sunni radical after World War II. Karen Armstrong writes that "every significant Sunni fundamentalist movement had been influenced by Qutb".[36] When Qutb first joined the Muslim Brotherhood his ambitions were to accommodate Western democracy to Islam. It was only after his imprisonment by Nasser in 1956 that he began to suggest military action. Here he decided that religious and secular people could never coexist peacefully. In his final publication, *Milestones*, he declared that the existing order in all countries, including so called 'Muslim' ones, was anti-Islamic, and called on Islamic activists to prepare themselves to replace the present *Jahili* (that is, barbaric ignorant) order.[37] This extension of jihad to the struggle against secularist-Islamic syncretism made other Muslims like Nasser also apostate. This jihad was to be even more fierce than that within the Prophet's own time because in this case the corrupters were not ignorant, but deliberate violators of God's laws. Thus a campaign akin to the original expansion of Islam was to be organised, repeating the establishment of Islam through migration, expansion and conquest. Unsurprisingly, Nasser had Qutb executed in 1966.

It was the second generation of radical Islamic fundamentalists that began to translate religious resistance into violent acts. In recent years, with the fall of the Soviet Union, these fundamentalists have targeted the United States as an instrument of Satan, oppressing

Muslims and threatening Islamic civilisation with secular culture and power. Such a critique of the modern world, a call for violence against the modern international order, the focus of which is the United States, came together in the al-Qaeda movement. Following September 11, 2001 bin Ladin said,

> This war is fundamentally religious . . . Those who try
> to cover this crystal clear fact, which the entire world
> has admitted, are deceiving the Islamic nation. This
> war is fundamentally religious . . . This fact is proved
> in the book of God Almighty and in the teachings of
> our messenger, may God's peace and blessings be
> upon him. This war is fundamentally religious. Un-
> der no circumstances should we forget this enmity
> between us and the infidels. For, the enmity is based
> on creed . . . The unequivocal truth is that Bush has
> carried the cross and raised its banner high.[38]

Radical Islamic fundamentalism of this type represents a power-ful ideological challenge to the Westphalian synthesis, and to inter-national order generally. In many ways Christians, Jews (especially Israel) and the Western world remain a target because it produces and reinforces this very apostate international order, often within Islam's own regions of influence. Bin Ladin even attacks the United Nations for its attempt to

> divide the largest country in the Islamic world . . .
> This criminal, Kofi Annan, was . . . putting pressure
> on the Indonesian government, telling it: You have 24
> hours to divide and separate East Timor from Indone-
> sia by force. The crusader Australian forces were on
> Indonesian shores, and in fact they landed to separate
> East Timor, which is part of the Islamic world.[39]

Bin Ladin repeats consistently that this is a "religious war", yet almost as if to deny him his prize, popular globalization scholars have turned to material, social or historical answers to explain fundamen-talism in Islam, and other major world religions. The West cannot see it as a religious war because it does not comprehend that its interna-tional order is predicated on theological principles, not merely politi-cal ones. And while these theo-political principles of secularism and political liberalism may indeed stand in need of challenge, we must also recall that the challenge of violence, terrorism and barbarism may never serve as a *just* means by which to ameliorate the tensions and conflicts of global public life. Such radicalism has in apathy and cynicism abandoned the call toward the common good, and in so doing has abandoned those very principles—faith, hope and love—which make any *jihad*, any struggle, worth fighting.

Conclusion: What is to be done?

On February 17, 2008, the *New York Times* ran a headline article, "Stifled, Egypt's Young Turn to Islamic Fervor". The article argues that broken economic models precede broken social models, which produce radical Islamic fundamentalism. We find out that Egypt has always fought a long and hard battle with extremism and as economic instability produces broken social institutions, especially marriage, increasing numbers of young people turn to radical religion as solace. Got religious fundamentalism? Move in a Dell or Nike factory.

We *must* do better than this. Globalization theory cannot afford to retain its religious illiteracy. When foreign policy analysts look at radical fundamentalism they see everything except religion, as though we have bought the secularist idea that material prosperity produces happy, content non-religious people. I have argued that religion and the political theologies which animate our international order are no historical blip on the progressive path of humanity; that the political theologies of other civilisations, particularly Islam, provide sharp relief to the contemporary international constitution. The suggestion that bin Ladin, the son of a Saudi billionaire, invests in weapons and terrorism because of his material shortfalls is nonsense; radical Islamic fundamentalism does not war for concessions at the WTO, stronger global labour agreements or an end to American agricultural subsidies. It wars to reconstitute international order according to its own particular political theology, to end the apostate occupation of its holy places, impose its own variant of *sharia* law and convert America and its allies to Islam. Dell factories and Nike plants won't cut it.

Further, this deep challenge is being echoed not merely by radical Islamic fundamentalism, but also by political Islam generally and an increasingly political Christendom, emerging from the corners of the developing world. These conflicts are not insignificant, and both political leaders and cultural elites must begin to explain and understand these new challenges with far more sophistication. In the academy at least one new sub-discipline is on the rise based on this inference. The growth of international political theology (IPT)[40] has been timed with the decline of the secularist consensus. The emergence of alternative theo-political voices has been most marked within Islam and Christianity—religions commanding more than half the globe's loyalty. To coherently organise such conversations we must also be attentive to our own political theologies. The development of IPT seems to be a promising first step in this direction.

Second, at the same time we must do *no worse* than the secularist hermeneutic we see in contemporary globalization studies. Global conflict cannot be neatly dissected into the clash of political theologies, as though such fundamental disagreements were the only causes of conflict. Genuine material disparities do indeed contribute to a growing instability in international relations, and while a dismissive genuflection from popular media toward religion is problematic, the domination and degrading exploitation of developing world economies through the matrices of global capitalism is equally disturbing. It may prove short-sighted to ignore religious conviction and its animating political theologies, but it may prove equally damning to ignore the political and economic culpability which animates and reinforces extremism's rise. In this chapter I have tried to balance what I perceive as the over-emphasis of traditional international relations scholarship on material and power politics. I do not, however, intend to banish such explanations. On the contrary, ideologies of consumerism, absolute security and identity interlock to mutually reinforce a corrupted international order. Combating radical fundamentalism will take a good deal more than intelligent identification and military resistance—it will take recognising our own destructive radicalism of consumption and security. Such forms of resistance can take the battle against radical fundamentalism right to our doorstep.

Finally, by intelligently discerning critical differences between political theologies, and especially between political Islam generally and radical fundamentalism, we begin to see *what* must be resisted, and what might be accommodated. Citizens do indeed have an obligation to support government resistance to terrorism. While we must challenge the wisdom at times of government strategies of resistance, we owe our governments both intelligent criticisms and support.[41] The task of government is the pursuit of justice, not merely the protection of its citizens. Global governance would be much aided by this revelation, calling the great states of the globe forth into more than mere statist posturing, but forth into service of our neighbour, forth into service of the common good and forth into the pursuit of justice.

Hope, commented Martin Wight, "is not a political virtue: it is a theological virtue".[42] Wight may be right. I have argued in this chapter that theological virtues have a way of cropping up in all kinds of political ways. Politics may be too narrow to confine the virtue of hope—it is—as Wight argues, an overflow of first principles, of theology and of faith. Ideologies of fundamentalist religion, identity, consumerism and security bear their own marks of hope, a shifting, often violent misdirection of the deep yearning of human hearts for something better. The solution political scholars suggest is a new "big idea" to organise our theory and practice of politics and economics. Global politics needs more than bigger ideas; it needs a prophetic voice to call human communities to hope that does not disappoint. This voice renews, restores and prefigures a better coming order, giving us—and all creation—a final ground on which to have "hope in troubled times".[43]

···

ROBERT JOUSTRA (Ph.D. cand., University of Bath) is a researcher with Cardus and a part-time lecturer in political science at Redeemer University College in Ancaster, Ontario. He is assistant editor with Jonathan Chaplin on the forthcoming book *God and Global Order: Religion and American Foreign Policy* (Baylor University Press, 2009).

NOTES

[1] This suggestion owes its substance to both conversations and readings with my doctoral supervisor Scott Thomas, who himself writes on this topic in *The Global Resurgence of Religion and the Transformation of International Relations: The Struggle for the Soul of the Twenty-First Century* (New York: Palgrave Macmillan, 2005).

[2] I adapt this definition from Roland Robertson in the first chapter of Max Stackhouse's series on "God and Globalization". Stackhouse and Paris, *God and Globalization. Volume 1: Religion and the Powers of the Common Life* (Harrisburg, PA: Trinity Press International, 2000), 53-68.

[3] Benjamin Barber, *Jihad vs. McWorld* (New York: Times Books, 1995).

[4] Stackhouse and Paris, *God and Globalization I*, 64.

[5] Roland Robertson, "Globalization and the Future of Traditional Religion", in Stackhouse *God and Globalization*, 60. Robertson himself borrows this from Gary T. Burtless et al., *Globaphobia: Confronting Fears about Open Trade* (Washington: Brookings Institution, Progressive Policy Institute and Twentieth Century Fund, 1998).

[6] Leonard Thompson, *The Political Mythology of Apartheid* (New Haven, CT: Yale University Press, 1985), 1.

[7] Daniel Philpott does some of the best work in this regard, calling such momentous occasions as Westphalia "revolutions in sovereignty", which he predicates are subsequent developments of revolutions in ideas, especially religious ones—or what we may call here political theology. His excellent book on this topic is well worth reading: Daniel Philpott, *Revolutions in Sovereignty: How Ideas Shaped Modern International Relations* (Princeton: Princeton University Press, 2001).

[8] Daniel Philpott, "The Challenge of September 11 to Secularism in International Relations", *World Politics*, 55 (October 2002), 72.

[9] Scott Thomas, "Taking Religious and Cultural Pluralism Seriously" in Fabio Petito and Pavlos Hatzopoulos (eds.), *Religion in International Relations: The Return*

from Exile (New York: Palgrave Macmillan, 2003), 24.

[10] Philpott, "The Challenge of September 11 to Secularism in International Relations", 67.

[11] Thomas, "Taking Religious and Cultural Pluralism Seriously", 25.

[12] Ibid, 26.

[13] Ibid, 26.

[14] Philpott, "The Challenge of September 11 to Secularism in International Relations", 68.

[15] Elizabeth Shakman Hurd, *The Politics of Secularism in International Relations* (Princeton: Princeton University Press, 2008), 16.

[16] This is a point made particularly well by Thomas in his opening chapter, "The Revenge of God" in *The Global Resurgence*, 26.

[17] An observation which carries a great deal of weight if you concede that variations of secularism are themselves a religious kind of phenomenon. Elizabeth Shakman Hurd makes this case impressively in her second chapter, "Varieties of Secularism", *The Politics of Secularism*.

[18] Gabriel A. Almond, R. Scott Appleby and Emmanuel Sivan, *Strong Religion: The Rise of Fundamentalism around the World* (Chicago: University of Chicago Press, 2003), 1-2.

[19] Philip Jenkins, *The New Faces of Christianity: Believing the Bible in the Global South* (Oxford: Oxford University Press, 2006), 11.

[20] I borrow this definition verbatim from the Fundamentalism Project, and specifically Almond, et al., *Strong Religion*, 17.

[21] Peter van der Veer and Hartmut Lehmann (eds.), *National and Religion: Perspectives on Europe and Asia* (Princeton: Princeton University Press, 1999), 3. As quoted in Shakman Hurd, *The Politics of Secularism*, 119.

[22] Abdullahi A. An-Na'im defines political Islam as "the mobilization of Islamic identity in pursuit of particular objectives of public policy, both within Islamic society and in its relations with other societies" (An-Na'im, "Political Islam in National Politics and International Relations", Peter Berger (ed.), *The Desecularization of the World*, (Grand Rapids, MI: Eerdmans, 1999), 103. I agree with him here that political Islam is neither new, transient or entirely negative, which is why it is important to separate political Islam from radical Islamic fundamentalism.

[23] From 1987 to 1995, the American Academy of Arts and Sciences undertook a major comparative study of anti-modernist, anti-secular militant religious movements on five continents and within seven world religious traditions called the Fundamentalism Project. The network spanned hundreds of scholars around the world, convened ten conferences with extensive field work analysing fundamentalist movements, their institutions and relationships to government policy. A companion of articles and books were also published under the leadership of Martin E. Marty (University of Chicago) and R. Scott Appleby (University of Notre Dame). These include a variety of texts which the reader may find useful to pursue the topic, among them the latest volume which I used extensively in preparing this chapter, Almond, et al., *Strong Religion*.

[24] This is a brief summary of a much broader discussion in the second chapter, "Fun-

damentalism: Genus and Species" of Almond, et al., *Strong Religion*.

[25] A helpful summary of the problems with "fundamentalism" can be found in Almond, et al., *Strong Religion*, 14-17. This includes the difference between militancy and violence, which I borrow from this source.

[26] Olivor O'Donovan, *The Desire of the Nations: Rediscovering the Roots of Political Theology* (Cambridge: Cambridge University Press, 1996), 15.

[27] I draw the following distinctions from Sohail Hashmi, "Interpreting the Islamic Ethics of War and Peace", in Terry Nardin (ed.), *The Ethics of War and Peace* (Princeton: Princeton University Press, 1996); a discussion I first found summarised by Daniel Philpott in "The Challenge of September 11 to Secularism in International Relations", 86.

[28] Philpott, "The Challenge of September 11", 84.

[29] James Turner Johnson, "Jihad and Just War", *First Things* (June-July 2002).

[30] Philpott, "The Challenge of September 11", 84.

[31] Examples here could include the Catholic concept of subsidiarity, or the neocalvinist perception of sphere sovereignty (or differentiated authority). Each of these models provides for unique and distinct norms governing the different spheres of life.

[32] Bassam Tibi, after an extensive review of the literature of contemporary radicals, further concludes that the restoration of the caliphate, the unity of Islam under a single head, can no longer even be considered a widely shared goal. Radical Islamic fundamentalists no longer speak of the restoration of traditional Islamic order, but rather of a new order, with clearly modern aspirations (Bassam Tibi, *The Challenge of Fundamentalism: Political Islam and the New World Order* [Berkeley: University of California Press], 138, 152).

[33] Philpott, "The Challenge of September 11", 87.

[34] Karen Armstrong, *The Battle for God: A History of Fundamentalism* (New York: Ballantine Books, 2000), 236-238.

[35] Tibi, *Challenges of Fundamentalism*, 58.

[36] Karen Armstrong, *Islam: A Short History* (New York: Modern Library, 2000), 170.

[37] William E. Shepherd, *Sayyid Qutb and Islamic Activism: A Translation and Critical Analysis of Social Justice in Islam* (New York: Brill, 1996), as quoted in Philpott, "The Challenge of September 11", 88.

[38] As quoted in Paul Marshall, "Living with Islamism", *Comment* Magazine (September 29, 2008).

[39] As quoted in Paul Marshall, "Living with Islamism".

[40] Vendulka Kubalkova has written the most extensively on this topic in "International Political Theology", in Petito and Hatzopoulos. However, her framework for IPT is animated by the Constructivist school and retains much of its "unbearable lightness", as Scott Thomas puts it (*The Global Resurgence of Religion*, 93-96). A more promising departure might be the work of Olivor O'Donovan's *Ways of Judgement* or Herman Dooyeweerd's concept of the *cosmonomic idea*.

[41] Such intelligent criticism could be greatly aided by the further application of Just War theory, a doctrine with a long and measured history. One such resource could be Jean Bethke Elshtain's measured volume, *Just War Against Terror: The Burden*

of American Power in a Violent World (New York: Basic Books, 2003).

[42] Cited in Jim George, "Realist 'Ethics', International Relations, and Post-Modernism: Thinking Beyond the Egoism-Anarchy Thematic", *Millennium* 24, 2 (Summer 1995), 206.

[43] Bob Goudzwaard, Mark Vander Vennen, and David Van Heemst's recent book, *Hope in Troubled Times: A New Vision for Confronting Global Crises* (Grand Rapids, MI: Baker Academic, 2007) provides a good overview of the pressing ideologies and political theologies of global order.

Creatures in a Small Place: Postcolonial Literature, Globalization, and Stories of Refugees

by Erin G. Glanville

Tourists and Natives

A few months ago my Facebook news feed was overwhelmed with a spate of pictures of friends on vacation in Cuba, Jamaica, and the Dominican Republic. Deals on all-inclusive, beachfront vacations in the Caribbean must have been spreading through their Internet networks because my news feed was quickly flooded with squares featuring smooth white beaches separated from a bright blue sky by a clean line of ocean water. Clicking on the virtual square beaches, I found that the albums were almost indistinguishable from each other beyond the faces of the vacationers; albums featured the usual "legs stretched out on the beach towards the ocean" self-portrait followed by shots of the towel sculptures maids had left on their beds, of the pool bar where they took advantage of the all-inclusive booze, and of "us and our friendly waiter [insert name]" for the week. It would be dishonest not to admit that the pictures tugged at very deep desires in me: to escape the stress and busyness of my work, to be pampered by people to whom I owe nothing, and to indulge in unusual sensuous experiences. For a moment I considered planning my honeymoon "there", thinking only broadly of the Caribbean.

But I could not erase the memory of the stinging words I had read a few years ago in Jamaica Kincaid's acerbic essay on tourism in the West Indies, and in Antigua particularly. "If you go to Antigua as a tourist, this is what you will see", Kincaid's piece "A Small Place" begins, going on to creatively describe the experience of North American tourists at Caribbean resorts.[1] "That water—have you seen anything like it? Far out, to the horizon, the colour of the water is navy-blue; nearer, the water is the colour of the North American sky . . . Oh what beauty! . . . you have never seen anything like this. You are so excited. You breathe shallow. You breathe deep."[2] But her insider (or outsider, as your perspective may be) description of tourism is posited as a form of deliberate and self-centred forgetfulness: "since you are on your holiday, since you are a tourist, the thought of what it might be like for someone who had to live day in, day out in a place that suffers constantly from drought, and so has to watch carefully every drop of fresh water used . . . must never cross your mind".[3]

Kincaid's angry words further unmask the illusion that waiters, bartenders, maids, and tour guides are happy to introduce my friends to West Indian cultures and subsequently point to the absolute difference between tourists and their native servants:

> That the native does not like the tourist is not hard to
> explain. For every native of every place is a potential
> tourist, and every tourist is a native of somewhere. . .
> Every native would like to find a way out, every native
> would like a rest, every native would like a tour. But
> some natives—most natives in the world—cannot go
> anywhere. They are too poor. They are too poor to go
> anywhere. They are too poor to escape the reality of
> their lives; and they are too poor to live properly in the
> place where they live, which is the very place you, the
> tourist, want to go—so when the natives see you, the
> tourist, they envy you, they envy your ability to leave
> your own banality and boredom, they envy your ability
> to turn their own banality and boredom into a source of
> pleasure for yourself.[4]

Here Kincaid simultaneously distinguishes and integrates the identities of North American tourists and West Indian natives so as to demonstrate the inequalities of access to the "global experience" that exist in a globalized world. In a small place, as the book is titled, one's culture, infrastructure, and economy is dependent on bigger places.

Kincaid tells the story of a library that is not rebuilt because of neocolonial politics. In a small place one's necessarily stationary life can produce insular communities with little knowledge of how they are influenced by or could influence global networks. The cultures of "small places" are frozen in time and place so that they can continue to be bought by people from "big places", their own bodies, made exotic by Facebook albums, and their culture, made simple and happy, are their major exports. Without enough money to leave the country, they *become* exportable commodities. Kincaid's book is balanced by a strong internal critique of Antiguan society, but for young Christians in the West, her blistering critique of privileged tourism as an integral part of globalization presents an opportunity to become sensitive and open to voices from small places. As contested as the words "margin" and "centre" are in postcolonial theory, I want to argue that postcolonial studies offers a critique of globalization from the margins of global power, making postcolonial studies a key contributor to discussions of globalization.

Two Postcolonial Relationships to Globalization

> The academic tribunes of globalization do not usu-
> ally include the end of formal empires or the wars of
> decolonization in their accounts of our planet's com-
> mercial and political integration. They are mostly a
> complacent bunch, more content with pondering the
> enigmas of weightless economic development than the
> violence that seems to be proliferating around it.[5]

Rebecca Todd Peter's excellent article on a Christian ethics of globalization presents 'postcolonialism' alongside 'earthism' as two models of globalization that resist two dominant models of globaliza-tion, which she labels 'neoliberalism' and 'developmentalism'.[6] She sees postcolonialism's focus on democratised power and global social justice as useful for Christians who struggle to be ethically active in a globalized world and who want to move towards reworking neocolo-nial networks of power. I agree with her thesis; I choose to participate in postcolonial conversations because their pursuit of justice in a glo-balized world is more overt than in most other disciplines. To borrow a metaphor Bob Goudzwaard uses in his article in this same volume[7], reading postcolonial literature allows readers to hop off the fast-moving train of first world globalization for a while and inhabit a perspective from the ground. This is precisely what Jamaica Kincaid's "A Small Place" allows me to do as a potential jet-setting tourist. Once off the train, so to speak, I can see the damage that my consumption of this exotic experience might do to others without the resources to buy a ticket for the train. To use the words of Gilroy in the opening epigraph, postcolonial studies does not let us ignore the violence surrounding both historical and contemporary globalizing processes, forcing us to face globalization's shadow side.

Before discussing the relationship of postcolonialism to globaliza-tion in detail, allow me a very brief description of postcolonial stud-ies for those not familiar with the discipline. Susan VanZanten offers a straightforward definition of postcolonial literature as "writing that emerges from peoples who once were colonized by European powers, now have some form of political independence, but continue to live with the negative economic and cultural legacy of colonialism".[8] The two amendments I would make are, first, the inclusion of literature birthed in settler colonies during (or dealing with) the colonial period and the movement toward independence (Canada and Australia are two examples of settler colonies—where the colonialists never left); and second, the concession that the cultural legacies of colonialism are not always only negative. On the whole, postcolonial fiction effects untell-ings, retellings, or overwritings of official Western versions of history,

cultures, and the interactions of cultures and so provides alternative
sources of knowledge about the world. Postcolonial theory makes use
of these alternative epistemologies to address a wide variety of interdisciplinary issues.

In the case of globalization, one of the greatest insights that
postcolonial studies offers us is that globalization is rooted in the
material history of imperial conquest, cross-cultural travel, and
economic exploitation and, thus, that studies of it cannot merely
describe it as a universal and neutral phenomenon. The assumption
that the negative effects of globalization cannot be "blamed" on
anyone or anything because they are a natural outworking of global
exchange, this assumption is part of what our epigraph would deny
in its insistence that the violences of integration be remembered and
studied by globalization scholars. To make such a statement is not
to deny the positive effects globalization has created for many, but
it is to keep us from theorising utopic futures from within our privileged academic positions. Similar to neo-Kuyperian scholarship,
which strives to understand the religious or philosophical orientations of social phenomena, postcolonial scholarship's collection of
concepts and keywords has been gathered from global literature for
the purpose of uncovering the cultural assumptions underlying global phenomena and with the aim of democratising cultural power.
Though postcolonial studies and globalization studies have been
distinguished in the contemporary academy, a situation Gilroy rails
against in the epigraph to this section, it could be argued that the
histories of globalization and of colonisation are one and the same.
The European projects of colonial conquest in the seventeenth,
eighteenth, and nineteenth centuries are what laid the groundwork
for our world's interconnectedness today.

The colonial history of globalization is clearly exemplified in the om-
nipresence of the English language and in its role as the world's vehicular
language for global business, politics, education, etc. The spread of the
English language took place through British colonial education, was ne-
cessitated by European power in world trade, and continues to dominate
literary studies despite postcolonial attempts to globalize the discipline.
That is, few international bestsellers are not written in English. Though
some English-speakers might thank their lucky stars that English turned
out to be the global language despite the messy and unpredictable process
of globalization, human beings and not lucky stars are responsible for
producing the current situation. Globalization is not a neutral progression
of human culture. The networking of continents, cultures, and cities has
its roots in the deliberate power-grabbing and colonial conquest of European nations in the past 300 years. The reason many people in Kenya can
speak English and Kikuyu and Swahili has to do with the colonial control
Britain had over that territory from 1890 to 1963.

Knowing this about globalization's material history, Kincaid and other authors from around the world take their work in a direction that has its roots in anti-colonial theory, starting in the 1950s with Frantz Fanon (i.e. postcolonial theory before it was known by that name). Frantz Fanon argued that, in order for Africa to be properly decolonised, African national cultures must be cultivated. Thus the work of authors like Ngugi wa Thiong'o, who wrote the children's series about a child named Njamba Nene as a way of re-educating African children about anti-colonial groups such as the Mau Mau. Contemporary anti-colonial scholars, then, are highly critical of globalization—both because it results in a degree of cultural homogenisation and because economic and political control are maintained by first world nations. The assumption that global underdogs desire progressive modernisation and the fact of nations' unequal power are built into the current dynamics of our globalized world. We can conclude two things about globalization as a historical process then: first, that it has never lived up to the utopic vision of moving beyond borders and working towards equal access to world-wide power and is instead driven by the self-interest of nation-states, and second, that its narrative of inevitable and desired progressive modernisation means third world countries will always be seen to trail just behind countries that are on the cutting edge of modernisation. Thus the neocolonial character of globalization that anti-colonialism tries to uncover.

Key Concepts in Post-Colonial Studies explains that anti-colonial scholars often theorise globalization by focusing on the failure of post-colonial[9] African states and then putting partial blame on the neocolonial nature of globalization. They then illustrate neocolonialism by studying the United States and its global power within the economic system of capitalism.[10] In fact some would argue that this kind of resistant, or oppositional, critique is what makes postcolonialism useful as a discipline. Linda Hutcheon, Canada's best known literary scholar on postmodernity values postcolonial art's "strong political motivation that is intrinsic to its oppositionality" because that keeps it in "the realms of social and political action".[11]

Some, however, are unsure that anti-colonial critiques are as radical as they appear. Simon Gikandi, in his thorough article on the relationship between globalization and postcoloniality, suggests that postcolonial critiques of globalization as neocolonialism are "premised on the belief that decolonization had failed in one of its crucial mandates—the fulfilment of the dream of modernity and modernization without the tutelage of colonialism".[12] Far from being radically oppositional, he is saying, anti-colonial critiques of globalization actually can *support* the end goals of Enlightenment-influenced models of globalization: they demonstrate that formerly colonised nations will always lag behind in the story of modernisation but do not necessarily challenge the legiti-

274 ERIN G. GLANVILLE

macy of the story to begin with. They may bring to light global inequalities without questioning the assumption that becoming a modern nation is the first step to success for former colonies.

Here is where we find another set of postcolonial scholars who take globalization's colonial history and, eschewing simple oppositionality, try to rejig the world by focusing on cultural exchange. Gikandi's article goes on to describe, what he calls, *truly* postcolonial (by this he means, not anti-colonial) theorisations of globalization, or what I will call, postcolonial diasporism.[13] Most basically, diaspora studies coincides with a stream of writing within postcolonial theory that examines contemporary migrations of people groups and the resultant intercultural exchange that takes place. As a new collection of essays on diaspora theory explains, the countless migrations taking place in the twentieth and twenty-first centuries can be compared with one another and theorised as a whole because of the new field of diaspora theory.[14] That is, rather than producing only individual sociological studies of specific migrations, diaspora studies allows scholars to theorise more broadly about migrations and movements, about those migrations' relationships to nation-states and to global networks, and therefore about the relationships between nation-states and globalization.

Diaspora theory has become an interdisciplinary field focused on intercultural exchange and has tended toward celebrating the possibilities of globalization as a result. Again, a history might be helpful here. Postcolonial diasporism is a more popular form of postcolonialism than is anti-colonialism and finds its roots in the work of Homi Bhabha, Edward Said, and Gayrati Spivak during the early 1980s. These authors posited a comparative rather than purely evaluative study of intercultural mixing. So instead of painting a stark picture of the world as split between oppressors and the oppressed, they turned to softer terms like "hybrid" and "syncretic" to positively describe the mutations of culture that happen in the world of global exchange. In these analyses colonial history can be subverted by its very own prodigy—globalization.

Major figures in contemporary diasporism then produce analyses of globalization that have a decidedly optimistic tone, most notably anthropologist Arjun Appadurai's recent work. Appadurai's 1996 book *Modernity at Large: Cultural Dimensions of Globalization* focuses on the two social phenomena of mass media and global migration. Since mass media and human migration exist outside of (or across) national borders, Appadurai envisions such post-national phenomena as a potentially positive way forward beyond, what many diaspora scholars see as, the repressiveness of modern states. In the first chapter of the collection of essays that he edited on globalization, Appadurai demonstrates a two-fold focus in his analysis: while globalization is "characterized by disjunctive flows that generate acute problems of social well-being", he sees the cultural aspects of globalization as providing a strong counter to the economic unevenness of globalization.[15] Celebrations of global *culture* as a way of imagining a globalized world beyond the *economic* power of nation-states typify the postcolonial diasporic response to globalization. Thus postcolonial diasporism points us to the global flows of people, rather than money, and examines the way those flows are subordinated to but also challenge global power relations. The reason for postcolonial celebration of global culture and not global economies is clarified in Kincaid's answer to the question "Do you know why people like me are shy of being capitalists? Well, it's because we, for as long as we have known you, were capital."[16] Paying attention to third world cultures by "reading" their stories, poetry, oral traditions, and music can give us insights into alternative epistemologies and narratives of the world, narratives that can be powerful in challenging the story of progressive and inevitable modernisation. Now having some anti-colonial and postcolonial diasporan insights in hand, our discussion can turn to the subject of their study: literature as a cultural object in a global context.

Literature of Migration and Globalization

I have been asked the question, and just as often ask myself the question, "why do literary scholars study topics like globalization?" Part of the aim of this book is to explore not only the economic and political aspects of globalization but to recognise the place of culture in globalization. Postcolonial diaspora studies is vitally involved in understanding the relationship between culture and globalization. It claims to locate culture in art, images, and text rather than in nations, or to put it differently, since cultures do not stay within national borders in a world of constant migration and since cultures move with people and are transformed in new contexts, we cannot only refer to nations nor only to economics when we talk about culture. Postcolonial diasporism wants to study the culture that has been drawn outside the lines and is therefore at the centre of the discussion over culture and globalization. It reads the stories of people in migration to understand how their culture has weathered travel and to glean wisdom from persons who have had to face the limitations of their own culture in a new place.

While Kincaid uses the terms tourist and native to separate the haves from the have-nots in globalization, Zygmunt Bauman uses a different set of terms to get at another reality for people. Instead of drawing a picture of dynamic first world movers and stagnant third world subjects, he focuses on two types of people who migrate: he labels them "tourists" and "vagabonds". Bauman begins his analysis of globalization by acknowledging that in the current milieu mobility is "the uppermost among the coveted values—and the freedom to move, perpetually a

scarcity and unequally distributed commodity, fast becomes the strati-
fying factor of our late-modern or postmodern times".[17] The freedom
and ability to move is a basic benefit of globalization that is highly inac-
cessible to most of the world. For those who are global "vagabonds"
(i.e. "unwanted migrants", as an opinion article in my local newspaper
called refugees), globalization produces not just Kincaid's distinction
between those who tour and those who stay put, but it also intensifies
the split between those who choose to move and those who are forcibly
moved. If Appadurai is right and globalization is characterised by disjunctive flows, an accurate account of globalization needs to recognise
that some of those flows are chosen and some of those flows are forced.

For insights into the nature of globalization, insights that account
for its unevenly distributed boons, I turn now to the stories that Mary
Jo Leddy has recorded in her book *At the Border Called Hope: Where
Refugees are Neighbours.* As I have shown above, postcolonialism is
helpful for bringing us to the point where displaced people—and I am
especially interested in refugee-ed peoples' perspectives—are acknowledged as legitimate and important voices to listen to when assessing
globalization. Listening to refugee-ed peoples on globalization makes
sense in the context of this essay. For one, they are from a place of
global powerlessness, that is, from no place in particular—from the
realm of citizenshiplessness. But also, their complicated relationship to
nation-states coincides with postcolonial debates over the usefulness of
modern states to the pursuit of global justice, highlighting tensions between national and global orders. In the next section I discuss two main
insights that arise from listening to the stories of refugee-ed people.
First, the difficulty refugee-ed people face when trying to seek refuge
in Canada brings into relief the religiously held commitment nations
have to self-interested economic growth. Second, we are challenged to
understand our own vulnerability and the deeply interdependent state of
the world in the context of globalization by reading about the responses
of refugee-ed Christians to the injustices that faced them in their home
country and that now face them in their new host country.

Refugee Flows and (what's the matter with) Globalization

The world becomes not a limitless globe, but a small,
fragile, and finite place . . . with strictly limited resources that are allocated unequally. This [perspec-
tive] is not the globalized mindset of the fortunate,
unrestricted traveler or some other unexpected fruit
of heavily insulated postscarcity and indifferent over-
development. It is a critical orientation and an oppositional mood triggered by comprehension of the simple

fact that environmental and medical crises do not stop
at national boundaries. . . .[18]

Taken as a whole, the stories that Leddy has recorded can feel
heavy—the numerous stories of unjust global processes, of bludgeon-
ing national structures and of the horrific results for refugee-ed people
in Canada begin to compound. Reading long chunks of the book in one
sitting, I would find my hands in fists, my forehead stretched tight, and
my eyes dry with intensity. Clearly people who are looking for refuge
in Canada have had a difficult, and often impossible, time communicating their experiences to civil servants at all levels of government let
alone ensuring their claims are considered thoroughly and with timeli-
ness. Though they reside in a relatively powerful nation, their voice still
comes from the "small place" of their citizenshiplessness. They may
be able to find expensive fruit in the supermarket that comes from their
home countries, but their own value as civic participants has not been
acknowledged yet.

Published as an appendix to the book, "A Call to Conscience: A
Statement on Refugees from Faith Communities of Canada" was written
in June of 1995 and signed by representatives of groups from all major
religions.[19] The statement's main concern resides at the national level
(i.e. the immoral policies of Immigration Canada), but hidden away in
a later paragraph I find a key global critique of the way globalization
functions unevenly when it comes to national borders. This paragraph
points to the obvious and disturbing reality of how carefully capital
flows are considered and accommodated versus how consistently human flows have been dammed through carelessness, indifference, and
selfishness:

> It is tragic that while we are opening our borders for
> business, we are closing them to desperate people.
> We are profoundly disturbed by rumours of our gov-
> ernment's plan to shut out refugees who arrive at our
> border via the United States. Our estimation is that any
> such policy would drastically reduce the number of
> refugees who could find safety in Canada.[20]

Furthermore, while Canadians may claim that Canada is already
going above and beyond the call of duty in assisting people refugee-ed
by third world conflicts, the statement reminds its readers that "the vast
majority of refugees are welcomed and sustained by countries in the 'the
two thirds world'" and that "it is almost impossible for refugees who are
in danger of their lives to get a visa from a Canadian immigration officer
overseas".[21] Refugee stories force us to ask what basic commitments
shape a global system in which money is allowed to flow freely across

state borders, often causing the displacement of people, but in which people fleeing persecution have an increasingly difficult time getting across those same borders.[22] Speaking to the issue of national security rather than economic growth, Luke Bretherton gives this balanced perspective in his helpful article on the duty of care to refugees:

> Liberal democracies are helpful insofar as they provide a limited peace. However, as the treatment of asylum seekers makes clear, they have made an end in and of themselves and their common lives are based on objects of love—notably, individual and collective self-fulfillment and autonomy—that inherently tend toward hostility to needy strangers. They tend toward hostility to needy strangers because the pursuit of such goods directs us away from the just and generous consideration of the needs of others.[23]

Pursuit of good living in a nation need not be put over against opening ourselves to those on the outside, he goes on to explain, calling on the Christian tradition of cosmopolitanism as his proof.

An anti-colonial critique of globalization might argue that the existence of power differentials amongst nation-states is what is wrong with globalization. Less powerful nations need to be given the opportunity to catch up to the developed world politically, financially, technologically, etc. A postcolonial diasporan critique of globalization might argue that the nation-state sovereignty paradigm is what creates these inequalities and that, alternatively, global movements, transnational solidarities, and interethnic loyalties will reduce our selfish, isolationist tendencies. To their credit, both critiques refuse to take the inequalities produced by globalization as a natural state of affairs. These inequalities are a result of, among other things, a colonial history and an ongoing nation-state sovereignty paradigm that pits national self-interest over against the global duty to care for human beings. Both areas of scholarship articulate alternatives that might lead to a democratisation of voice and of access at an international level.[24] But both overtly base their alternatives in humanist convictions. One assumes human power relations as the only absolute reality, and the other trusts the humanity of good people, without national allegiances, in solidarity against national exclusions. So, to simplify these varied and complex groups of scholars, in response to global inequality we can move in the direction of anti-imperial anger or move towards a celebration of transnational cultures.

Neither response is what we find in the stories that Mary Jo Leddy recounts of refugee-ed people in Canada. Tellingly, the heaviness of Leddy's refugee stories does not stick in our throats when the stories are savoured, rather than consumed, gulped in one sitting.[25] What struck me as most surprising and most hopeful in the stories Leddy tells is the way in which her faith perspective results in a quality of hope that might not seem a natural outcome of the circumstances. While her readers are called to anger and celebration, they are more importantly called, in response to unjust political structures, to sit at the border of hope, listening, bearing witness to what they hear, and advocating for those who come from small places. This, more than any other response, requires significant selflessness and/or an acknowledgement of the interdependent world we live in.

As someone who has spent most of her life living at that border, Leddy has had the opportunity to experience microcosms of global politics and history. One of the places the microcosms appears is in her stories about Romero House, a home for refugee claimants in Toronto, Canada. One year, Leddy writes, "I wondered whether our house would soon become a little Mogadishu, a place of beauty and harmony torn apart by seething tribal conflicts".[26] A doctor was arriving from the Hawiye tribe, and one couple already in residence was from the Darood tribe. Asha, the Hawiye woman, had grown up in a family whose hotels were patronised by Italians and then, because of shifting global politics, by Soviets. A simple postcolonial critique of power could not account for the intricacies of her life and its overlaps with varying levels of political power; she had been implicated with both the powerful and the powerless *and* those temporarily privileged by the powerful. Surprisingly Omar and Fadumo, the Darood couple, became quite close with her very quickly. In a moment of deep connection Omar said to her "I am sorry about all the fighting . . . It is not good for any of us. Your children gone. Our children gone. The people at the top play their little games and we get thrown away."[27] Asha responded, "We have all been thrown to the other side of the world . . . and I am sorry for what has happened to your family, Omar". Rather than carry the conflicts over power into their new home, these people found themselves on the same side of global power structures and realised quickly their dependence on one another for friendship and solidarity in a new place.

Being displaced has a way of making us dependent on or even aware of our dependency on others. Leddy's book tells story after story of refugee-ed people who realised their own vulnerability and were then moved to act on behalf of others. This, I think, is one of the insights refugee stories gives us into globalization: that the world is a small place, deeply interconnected in a way that makes all people vulnerable. To put it in terms that have been repeated in various ways in many texts on refugees: we are all potential refugees. Taking on this view requires an about-face for jet-setters like me who think we can consume anything for a price, and it may also call us to live out of that vulnerability rather than try to consolidate power at any number of levels—personally, ecclesiastically, nationally, globally.

Globalization produces the "small world" of Jamaica Kincaid who is virulently angry at the neo-colonial forces that interfere in Antigua, the island where foreigners splash about in the water and natives carefully conserve their drinking water. And alongside this exists the "small world" that tourists inhabit, where I can speak with someone in church one Sunday and the next week see them in the Caribbean on Facebook. But globalization, understood rightly, has the potential to create a third "small world", which Leddy's stories point us to. Gilroy's epigraph gets at this world in humanist terms, but I would like to express it in terms of Christian faith. I see recognising God's role as creator and sustainer of the world to be key for understanding our roles as creatures in the world, while humanism maintains human beings as the arbiters of ethical choices—a centre that leads as easily to self-centredness as it does to love for the neighbour. Being part of a globalized world can foster in us a sense of the interconnections in God's one, small world; it can give us a sense of both our dependency on others and also our status as creatures and creation. What we learn from refugee stories is that the world is a small place, but not because it is so easy to get from one place to the next and not because we often meet people who know people we know halfway across the world. Rather, the world is a small place because it is one broken, fragile creation, dependent on God's daily provision and interdependent in the way he created it to be.

Gilroy uses the term "small place" in our opening quote to describe how a "planetary consciousness" might help first world dwellers to recognise their dependence on the rest of creation.[28] His thesis has much to recommend it, but I suggest that a recognition of God's continuing presence in the world is what is needed if we are to sustain the tiring task of re-visioning ourselves as part of a globalized small place—only satisfied when we can resist the communal selfishness of our individual cultures. A good place to start nurturing growth in that direction is with the basic belief of the many faith groups who signed "A Call to Conscience", i.e. that human beings have a responsibility for the lives of other human beings regardless of citizenship and that our commitments to trust, hope, and love trump our desires for wealth, our self-interest, and our addiction to ease. Recognition not only of our interdependence on each other but also of our dependence on God, the creator, means we are all in the same boat, not jostling for position. For us to get to the point where we do not see the primacy of national self-interest in global politics as self-evident, and thus to a point where "small places" are heard and acknowledged more often, we must already have a sense of our own vulnerability despite the veneer of global power and we must recognise the value in listening to the stories of "small places". Semira, a woman from Eritrea who traveled to Canada with five small children, recognised her own dependency despite her apparent strength and had it right when she recalled, "God look[ed] after my children".[29]

Imagine the generative potential for globalization if Christians in first world countries were to begin thinking of themselves as creatures again, as creatures and not only consumers, as creatures and not only tourists, not primarily as people with the ability to visit "small places" for pleasure but as people *from* the small place which is God's one, good creation.

....

ERIN G. GLANVILLE (Ph.D. cand., McMaster) is in her final year of doctoral work in the department of English and Cultural Studies at McMaster University. She has been a part-time lecturer at Redeemer University College and a research assistant at McMaster University until recently, moving to Sydney, Australia to finish up her dissertation on refugee narratives and church-based activism. She has authored encyclopedia articles on Canadian writers Neil Bissoondath and M.G. Vassanji, has a chapter forthcoming in *Rerouting the Postcolonial: Directions for the New Millennium* (Routledge, 2009), and is co-editor of a forthcoming volume on creativity, agency, and displacement.

NOTES

[1] Jamaica Kincaid, *A Small Place* (New York: Farrar, Straus and Giroux, 1988), 1.

[2] Ibid, 13.

[3] Ibid, 4.

[4] Ibid, 19.

[5] Paul Gilroy, *Postcolonial Melancholia* (New York: Columbia University Press, 2005), 55.

[6] Rebecca Todd Peters, "The Future of Globalization: Seeking Pathways of Transformation," *Journal of the Society of Christian Ethics*, 24, 1 (2004), 105-133.

[7] See page 235-237 in this volume.

[8] Susan VanZanten Gallagher, "New Conversations on Postcolonial Literature", in *Postcolonial Literature and the Biblical Call for Justice* (Jackson: University Press of Mississippi, 1994), 5.

[9] Post-colonial (with a dash) refers to the historical reality of a new era beyond direct political colonisation, in contrast to postcolonial (without a dash), which refers to the discipline.

[10] In their introduction to a special edition of *The South Atlantic Quarterly*, Susie O'Brien and Imre Szeman criticise this perspective as being too simplistic, since it relies on only a national sovereignty model to help us understand political power in a globalized world where various "sites and modalities of power" exist ("Introduction: The Globalization of Fiction/the Fiction of Globalization", *The South Atlantic Quarterly* 100, 3 [Summer 2001], 608). However the United States fits uneasily, if at all, into postcolonial discussions. Because of its colonial history, Canada is considered a postcolonial settler nation, but because of the United States' current global power, it does not readily share that label.

[11] Linda Hutcheon, "Circling the Downspout of Empire", in Ian Adam and Helen Tiffin (eds.), *Past the Last Post: Theorizing Post Colonialism and Post-Modernism* (Calgary:

University of Calgary Press, 1990), 168.

[12] Simon Gikandi's analysis of globalization and postcoloniality aptly focuses on their shared tension with nation-states. ("Globalization and the Claims of Postcoloniality", in *South Atlantic Quarterly* 100, 3 [Summer 2001], 636).

[13] I resist calling those contemporary postcolonial studies focused on hybridity and cultural exchange "authentic" in distinction to the anti-colonial roots of postcolonial studies since those roots still largely shape the discipline today. Instead, I see the two streams operating side-by-side in the discipline with two different strategies.

[14] Jana Evans Braziel and Anita Mannur, *Theorizing Diaspora: A Reader* (Malden, MA: Blackwell Publishing, 2003), 3-4.

[15] Arjun Appadurai, *Modernity at Large: Cultural Dimensions of Globalization* (Minneapolis: University of Minnesota Press, 1996), 6.

[16] Kincaid, *A Small Place*, 37.

[17] Zygmunt Bauman, *Globalization: The Human Consequences* (New York: Columbia University Press, 2000), 2.

[18] Paul Gilroy, *Postcolonial Melancholia*, 75.

[19] Mary Jo Leddy, *At the Border Called Hope: Where Refugees are Neighbours* (Toronto: Harper Collins, 1997), 275.

[20] Ibid, 277.

[21] Ibid.

[22] For further reading on this topic, see Anne McNevin's article "Irregular Migrants and Neoliberal Geographies", which does an excellent job of unpacking the relationship between the freedom of financial flows as enabled by Special Economic Zones and offshore financial markets and the border policing that is triggered by migrant labourers. ("Irregular Migrants, Neoliberal Geographies, and Spatial Frontiers of 'the Political'", *Review of International Studies* 33 [2007], 655-674).

[23] Luke Bretherton, "The Duty of Care to Refugees, Christian Cosmopolitanism, and the Hallowing of Bare Life", in James K.A. Smith (ed.), *After Modernity? Secularity, Globalization, and the Re-enchantment of the World* (Waco, TX: Baylor University Press, 2008), 151.

[24] To further explore the active maintenance of unequal access to international exchange see the fourth chapter in Bob Goudzwaard's *Beyond Poverty and Affluence: Towards a Canadian Economy of Care* (tr. Mark R. Vander Vennen; Toronto: University of Toronto Press, 1995) which shows the very practical ways in which wealthy nations are privileged in the processes of the International Monetary Fund and of international trade organisations.

[25] In his 2009 book, *In Bed with the Word: Reading, Spirituality, and Cultural Politics*, Daniel Coleman refers to spiritual reading as the kind that "chews on difficult, even painful passages; it doesn't push them to the side of the plate nor does it swallow them whole". (*In Bed with the Word: Reading, Spirituality, and Cultural Politics* [Edmonton, AB: University of Alberta Press, 2009], 100).

[26] Leddy, *At the Border Called Hope*, 58.

[27] Ibid, 65.

[28] Paul Gilroy, *Postcolonial Melancholia*, 75.

[29] Leddy, *At the Border Called Hope*, 57.

Convergence or Clash?
The Coming Global Future[1]

by David T. Koyzis

Progress and its Discontents

As the Cold War was coming to an end in 1989, Francis Fukuyama, then an official with the US State Department, published a
ground-breaking article, "The End of History",[2] which he eventually
expanded into a book.[3] In it he argued that the sorts of ideological
conflicts characterising much of the modern era were drawing to a
close. A global consensus was developing in favour of liberal democracy and the free market, while other "ideologies", such as hereditary
monarchy, fascism and communism were falling out of favour, having
been conquered by an obvious superior. Widely discussed in academia
and the popular media, the visibility of Fukuyama's argument was
enhanced by the stunning spectacle of the fall of the Berlin Wall and
the dramatic collapse of the east European communist régimes over
the course of a few weeks that autumn.

Fukuyama's thesis is a recent example of the general belief that
history not only has a purposeful character, but at some point will
reach its final consummation, a notion owing much to Christian eschatology, albeit in secularised form. G. W. F. Hegel and Karl Marx
are Fukuyama's predecessors in this respect. All three are progressive
thinkers, assuming that, as history moves, it is propelled forward towards a society in some sense superior to that in which we currently
find ourselves—this superiority being measured by the expansion of
human freedom over against its impediments.[4] But unlike either Hegel, who sees the bureaucratic state at the end of this process, or Marx,
who foresees the advent of the classless and stateless society, Fukuyama sees liberal democracy and capitalism as the ultimate achievements of this historical movement.

A related school sees history moving as inexorably as do Hegel,
Marx and Fukuyama, but its adherents are far less optimistic over
the goodness of the changes effected by the process. The old cliché,
"You can't fight progress", sums up this view succinctly and resonates
with many who are less than enthusiastic about, say, a new road being

built through a previously forested area. Jacques Ellul (1912-1994) is perhaps the best-known proponent of this view. For him technique— or rather Technique, with a capital T—takes on the character of an autonomous force, moving small-scale economies towards corporate capitalism, which in turn calls forth statist policies leading inevitably to totalitarianism.[5]

George Parkin Grant (1918-1988) follows Ellul's argument, applying it to the plight of his own country, Canada, torn between its older traditions of virtue—tied as they are to local communities and their undergirding religious commitments—and the relentless pull of liberalism and technology coming from south of the border. Is Canada destined to become assimilated into a US-dominated North America? In his classic *Lament for a Nation*[6], this is precisely what Grant argues. Even if Canada somehow manages to retain its formal political independence, its deep economic and cultural ties to a dynamic and more powerful neighbour will effectively empty this independence of any practical significance. Canadians and Americans alike will be shopping at the same stores, watching the same television programmes, eating the same food and, ultimately, worshipping the same gods.

Remarkably, both the positive and negative variants of the belief in homogenisation share a central conviction: that historical forces acting autonomously are the principal motive behind this grand movement through time. Though we may appear to be making multiple decisions on a day-to-day basis, in reality we are captive to impersonal forces conditioning, if not determining, the content of those decisions. Court judges may sincerely believe they are upholding impartial justice in applying the law to particular cases, but in reality they are acting merely as agents of the dominant economic class, whose interests are embodied in their decisions. Revolutionaries may think they are taking matters into their own hands by rising up to throw off the shackles of oppression. In reality, they are merely conforming to an age-old pattern of class antagonism, whose twists and turns are subject to the ongoing development of productive forces.

Similarly, the invention of the automobile just over a century ago apparently offered us an alternative mode of transportation to the bicycle, the horse, the railways and, most basically, our own feet. However, once the automobile had effectively shaped the landscape of our cities and the surrounding countryside, the option of using these other means of transport was no longer readily available to most of us. We deluded ourselves into believing that each technical innovation would make us freer than before, yet we eventually found ourselves enslaved to that technique, fashioning our cultures and living spaces around it. The possibility of doing otherwise had in the meantime evaporated, with governments now subsidising the dominant technique at the expense of the others. Whereas the US and Canada had subsidised the railways in the nineteenth century, by the middle of the twentieth both were ploughing funds into a network of expressways predicated on the assumption of near universal automobile ownership.[7] It did not take long for rail passenger service to decline, effectively depriving those preferring it of this mode of travel.

Late in life Ellul admitted to the early influence of Marx on his intellectual development, and, even after his conversion to Christianity in 1932, his reading of theologian Karl Barth confirmed for him the value of the dialectical thinking he had admired in Marx.[8] Consequently it is not surprising that something akin to Marx's historical materialism can be seen to function in *The Technological Society*, wherein productive forces, i.e. the development of discrete technical innovations, drive the larger movement towards, not freedom as in Marx, but slavery to a statist totalitarianism. All of us are inexorably caught up in this process, and the task at hand for the Christian is not to try to change or redirect this, which is impossible, but to live as best one can in the midst of it. For Hegel, Marx, Fukuyama, Ellul and Grant "progress"—whether spoken of in reverent tones or with a touch of bitter irony—is inevitable. We may continue to live under ostensibly democratic constitutions, but because all political problems are ultimately matters to be addressed by the technically competent, there will be nothing left to talk about in any meaningful way. Friedrich Engels believed that in the classless society the state will wither away. For those of a more pessimistic bent, the state will instead expand beyond any reasonable limits, while political deliberation in the context of policy-making will become pointless.[9] If it is not stifled altogether, interest in it will gradually fade.

For some observers technology's progress goes hand-in-hand with Westernisation. The ubiquity of McDonald's golden arches is one of the more obvious manifestations of this phenomenon. It is usually thought to imply the gradual and eventual acceptance of typical Western economic and political institutions, such as stock exchanges and a democratic form of government. Here Fukuyama's Hegelianism is tempered with a Nietzschean element. His "Last Man" is a middle class suburbanite, working a forty-hour week, shopping at the local mall and watching television in his off hours. His life is plagued by a vague *ennui* with no higher purpose; it is a life shorn of struggle, risk or danger, preoccupied only with comfortable self-preservation. With the end of the ideological struggle of the Cold War, this Last Man is spreading his existence into the far corners of the globe, with no genuine alternative way of life standing in its way.

There is something to be said for this interpretation, as indicated by some striking evidence. In much of the world, especially the West itself, traditional folk dress, with all its colourful variety, has all but vanished, to be trotted out at the occasional ethnic festival and then put away again for another year. In its place we have something called *fashion*, a global phenomenon with designers in London, Paris, Rome and New York setting the agenda for much of the world. Folk music has been supplanted by commercial *popular* music, with radio, television, CD players and now iPods disseminating the same marketable songs to a huge international audience.[10] Of course the Internet has radically democratised the communication of information, enabling anyone with a computer to post his or her own website and to broadcast ideas instantaneously across the globe.

Us and Them

However, not everyone buys into this vision of the inevitable homogenisation of the globe. Writing in 1993 in *Foreign Affairs* and three years later in a widely-acclaimed book, Harvard University's Samuel P. Huntington coined the term "Clash of Civilizations" to characterise the post-Cold War world.[11] While the world had apparently been characterised by an ideological bipolarity between 1945 and 1989, after the latter year it had become evident that the world could more accurately be seen as multipolar, with cultural boundaries separating several ancient civilisations. For Huntington these civilisations are best understood with reference to their religious roots. The largest civilisations are the post-Christian Western, the Islamic and the Chinese. But also of significance are the Latin American, Eastern Orthodox, sub-Saharan African, Hindu, Buddhist and Japanese civilisations.

One could, of course, quibble with his categories,[12] but his central point remains: the world is *not* becoming Westernised. In fact, as technology makes its way from the West into these other civilisations, the latter, far from becoming carbon copies of the West, find themselves physically empowered to reassert their own distinctive characteristics. The Internet itself, far from being an homogenising force, allows not only the CBC, the BBC and the large American news networks to have their say, but it permits Al Jazeera, Serbian nationalists, Confederate sympathisers and American monarchists to have theirs as well. The medium may be the same, but the messages being disseminated are quite divergent.

With such civilisational differences comes a certain amount of strife. In the new century wars are occurring along the boundaries separating these civilisations. In fact, even now the borders surrounding Islam are especially bloody, as Huntington provocatively put it, with recent conflicts raging in Nigeria, Sudan, Israel/Palestine, Afghanistan, India/Pakistan, Chechnya, Bosnia and Kosovo.[13]

The 9/11 terrorist attacks in the US, along with similar attacks in

London, Madrid and Beslan, Russia, appeared to bolster Huntington's thesis, although President Bush and others sought to play it down for obvious political reasons: after all, if the ensuing conflict had been framed as one between two rival civilisations, there would apparently be no alternative to total war, with domestic Muslims viewed as potential fifth columnists for the enemy, namely, Islam itself. More significantly, there could be no victory for either side in such a war, given the numbers of adherents involved and the tenacity of particular religions and the cultures growing out of them. Loyalty to communism proved to be an inch deep among those who finally threw off its yoke between 1989 and 1991. Because of this the seemingly endless (at the time) Cold War lasted barely four decades, an exceedingly brief moment in the larger flow of history. By contrast, Christianity and Islam alike have their roots in deep, centuries-old traditions claiming that God has revealed himself in specific and exclusive ways to his people. Such beliefs are not easily shaken or displaced. A feasible foreign or defence policy must necessarily pursue what lies within the realm of the possible, and invoking civilisational conflict is hardly in accord with this necessity, much less with the principles of the just war or, better, justified warfare.

Nevertheless, a spate of new books has appeared since then devoted to understanding why "they hate us" so much. Ironically, their authors appear to be recovering something of the bipolar conception of the world that Huntington had so recently laid to rest. Yes, multiple civilisations still exist, but the West now stands out as especially modern and corrosive, with "the rest" lashing out to avoid falling victim to its contamination. After all, the West is not merely one civilisation among all the others; even in its prolonged state of decline it exerts tremendous power—power that at once attracts and repels those on the outside. Three observers exemplify this approach.

First, English philosopher Roger Scruton argues that, while non-Western societies stand on traditional religious foundations in which consent plays little if any role, their Western counterparts are based on the social contract, with its associated voluntaristic conception of community and obligation.[14] Westerners have expanded the range of their choices and have built an entire political system out of this. The Western achievement has been to hold together communities through loyalty to a political process defining the rights and duties of citizens. Since this process does not require a religious basis, Westerners have been able to separate church and state, religion and politics.

Scruton is definitely a partisan of the Enlightenment, with its faith in human reason and technical progress. Insofar as non-Westerners have the temerity to resist the inexorable historical movement towards individualism, voluntarism and proceduralism, they are apparently being atavistic and reactionary. Worse, they are doing so in the name of religion—something we Westerners long ago learned to domesticate and keep in its place. The West has no choice but to defend itself in the face of such fanaticism.

It is not difficult to see the spiritual connections between Scruton and the progressive thinkers mentioned above. Scruton implicitly follows much earlier Western opinion in seeing civilisation as a unidirectional process. There are no multiple civilisations; there are only civilised and uncivilised. Much as the European colonists in the Americas and elsewhere saw themselves as the vanguard of civilisation in savage lands, so Scruton views the West as a force for advancing freedom and progress in a world stubbornly clinging to backward manners and mores. It can ill afford to hold to a live-and-let-live policy. It must actively defend itself in the face of anti-progressive forces that threaten its way of life.

Paul Berman advances a thesis similar to Scruton's.[15] The war against terrorism is simply the latest round in a protracted struggle between the proponents of liberty and their totalitarian enemies. While this struggle was an intramural Western one for much of the twentieth century, with fascists and communists carrying the antiliberal banner, the twenty-first century sees this banner being taken up by Islamists, such as the followers of the late Sayyid Qutb (1906-1966).

Qutb was born in Egypt and had the opportunity to visit the US shortly after the end of the Second World War. While there he visited a Christian worship service and later a church dance in Greeley, Colorado. What he took to be the blatant eroticism of the dance offended him, and he was at a loss to know how these Christians could offer worship to God one moment and then engage in such an obviously "immoral" recreational pastime the next.[16] After returning to Egypt, he was co-founder of the Muslim Brotherhood. Qutb's critique of Christianity is that it is intrinsically dualistic, separating religion from the rest of life—especially public life. In this respect, he believed Islam to be superior to Christianity and secularism alike, due to its apparently more integral worldview. Qutb was a seminal figure in the development of what is now variously known as radical Islam or Islamism, which constitutes a potent challenge to the post-Christian West.

Of course, neither Scruton nor Berman would buy into Qutb's analysis. After all, the genius of the West is in successfully keeping religion and politics apart and thus avoiding the fanaticism of so much of the Islamic world. Accordingly, neither believes the West has anything of substance to repent of, except perhaps not being vigilant enough in the defence of its own liberal principles. That liberalism itself might be fundamentally flawed is a possibility that neither is prepared to entertain. Yet Qutb's critique of Western dualisms does manage to pinpoint a weakness in contemporary post-Christian liberalism—a failed or failing political illusion that is incapable of accounting for, and thus doing justice to, both the genuine pluriformity of a healthy society and the universal disposition of human beings to embrace a vision of ultimate meaning for life.[17]

Unlike Scruton and Berman, Meic Pearse does not approach the issue as even a critical partisan of the Enlightenment project.[18] Pearse is a Christian, and as such he can see things that the other two cannot. Yes, the post-Christian West is built on the enhancement of personal freedom of choice, and this intensified some four decades ago as the liberalism dominating North American life moved into its most recent stage, which I have elsewhere labelled the "choice-enhancement state".[19]

In the choice-enhancement state, government adopts ostensibly benevolent neutrality towards a variety of lifestyle choices. Whether two people decide to marry, to live together in an unofficial and impermanent sexual relationship, or to move promiscuously from one brief sexual encounter to another, the law plays no favourites and refrains from dictating how consenting partners should behave towards each other in the privacy of their own quarters. Similarly, whereas a previous generation expected as a matter of course that legal divorce would be difficult, if not impossible, to attain; that abortion would be restricted if not entirely prohibited; and that reproductive sex would be officially preferred to non-reproductive sex; contemporary liberals look on such policies as unfair and discriminatory insofar as they infringe on freedom of choice. All choices should be treated equally; no choice should be officially favoured over others.

The difficulty with the choice-enhancement state is that, while government can make pretence of neutrality in these areas, it cannot credibly deny the unequal consequences following upon the exercise of these choices. If easier divorce helps people to escape from bad marriages, it also contributes to an increased number of shattered families, with all of their attendant dislocations and dysfunctions, including psychological trauma in children and the increased poverty that inevitably accompanies the financial division of a household. Government may decline to "stigmatise" divorcees or to place legal obstacles in their way, but it cannot proclaim that divorce will have no harmful effects on everyone involved and on the larger society. It may similarly abstain from adversely judging non-marital intercourse, but it cannot issue an edict against the proliferation of unwanted pregnancies or sexually transmitted diseases. Government may legally affirm that single-parent families are "just as valid"[20] as two-parent families, but it cannot declare that there will be no damaging fallout from the choice to end a marriage or that fatherlessness will not negatively impact the offspring.

When these undesirable consequences do indeed occur, rather than acknowledge that the quest to validate all lifestyle choices equally cannot be sustained over the long term, partisans of the choice-enhancement state increasingly call on government to act to nullify these consequences so they can continue unhindered in the pursuit of this smorgasbord of choices. Although the modern welfare state was originally created to cushion the harsh edges of capitalism and to provide a social safety net for those caught up in the vicissitudes of the marketplace, after about 1960 it increasingly undertook to protect people from the negative outcomes of their own choices.

Of course, all this has come at a steep price. It is a price that the West as a whole has thus far been able and willing to pay, mostly due to its enhanced technical capacities and continually expanding economies. Yet even within the West the changing attitudes associated with the choice-enhancement state have effectively exacerbated local poverty, as some have pointed out.[21] But the largest impact has been on the non-Western world, which has necessarily had to bear more of the cost, with far greater danger to its very survival. Here is where Pearse's argument comes in again.

Although there are several sides to this Western exceptionalism, Pearse focuses on the sexual revolution of the past forty years.[22] In a wealthy society, the short term effects of sexual indiscretions are cushioned in part by the market economy's enhanced productive capacity and the welfare state. An out-of-wedlock pregnancy does not generally threaten starvation—although it may increase the likelihood of continued poverty in certain sectors of society. By contrast, in a premodern society, which includes virtually every non-Western civilisation, any breach of the norm of sexual fidelity will have immediate serious consequences, not only for the individual involved, but potentially for the entire community, which is more dependent than we are on the cycles of nature.

Who is Right?

So which interpretation is correct? Is the West inexorably homogenising the rest of the world, such that its mores and ways of life will come eventually to characterise every society from Dakar to Dacca, from Tokyo to Tehran, from Bangalore to Brasilia? Or might the West in reality be dying, with current birth-rates below replacement levels and rival civilisations waiting in the wings to take its place, even in the heart of Europe itself?[23] Depending on which is right, one might assess the rage of radical Islamists differently. On the first interpretation, Islam, like other non-Western civilisations, is on the defensive, sensing its values being undermined by the pervasiveness of rock music, materialism and loosened sexual mores. Terrorists are thus lashing out from a position of weakness, fearing that their societies' ways are under threat from a more resilient culture.

On the second interpretation, however, the seemingly all-powerful West is really in terminal decline and, through the dissemination of its secularising ideas throughout the world, threatens to pull everyone else down with it. Islamists sense weakness and are taking advantage of it to put forward *sharia* law and submission to God through the prophet Muhammad. Perhaps then the terrorists are asserting their claims from a position of strength, believing that the West will be too weak to withstand their assaults.

At this point it is not clear which interpretation is correct, and no consensus has developed either to offer guidance or to invite refutation. It is something of a cliché to argue that the truth is somewhere in between, although some might be inclined in this direction. By the middle of this century we and our descendants will almost certainly have a clearer picture concerning the trajectory of the West in its relationship to other civilisations. In the meantime we are at least compelled to acknowledge that, even after the ideological struggle characterising the Cold War era came to an end, we never really reached the end of ideology itself as Fukuyama assumed and as sociologist Daniel Bell had predicted.

Nevertheless, despite the lack of consensus on the position of the West vis-à-vis the rest of the world, whichever stance we take on this issue does matter. Indeed it has grave implications for the future success of even a modest effort at facilitating international co-operation. Three factors that have hampered the success of the United Nations in creating a global zone of collective security are that (1) membership has so few conditions attached to it, in contrast, e.g. to NATO and the European Union; (2) its membership includes nations with vastly different political cultures and, along with this, what Walter Lippmann calls traditions of civility; and (3) its members are in the grip of differing, and sometimes outright conflicting, political ideologies, most of which, I would argue, lead to a distorted view of the world.

If the world is gradually homogenising, along Hegelian lines, then it may be only a matter of the West exercising a certain patience with the UN as it waits for the remainder of the world to catch up with its principles of democracy, human rights and the free market. If civilisation is a straight line leading in a single direction, and if our own societies lie at the end, then we can be confident that the rest will eventually end up like us, even if they are not now. The current defects in the UN and other international instruments will sooner or later be rectified.

On the other hand, if Huntington is correct that the world's civilisations are ancient and more-or-less permanent features of the global landscape for the indefinite future, then our view of the efficacy of the UN and other international instruments must be adjusted accordingly. Perhaps we will put less confidence in the UN's most visible institutions, especially the General Assembly and the Security Council, and invest the bulk of our efforts in other avenues of foreign policy, expecting more from those like us and less from those unlike us.

At present the single most successful effort at supranational integration, *viz.*, the European Union, is encountering this dilemma as it weighs in the balance whether its priority should be *broadening* or *deepening*—broadening to take in more members beyond the current twenty-seven or deepening its own internal unity enabling it to become something close to a single actor on the world's stage. Already the EU is straddling one of Huntington's civilisational boundaries, insofar as the traditionally Orthodox Christian states of Greece, Cyprus, Romania and Bulgaria are now members. With Turkey's longstanding application for membership, the EU is considering extension beyond another cultural boundary, *viz.*, that separating the West from the Islamic world. As it does so, it will inevitably hamper efforts towards articulating and maintaining support for a common foreign policy issuing from Brussels.

Yet most efforts at international co-operation fall well short of expectations for supranational unity. In 1999 even NATO's unity with respect to Serbia and Kosovo was put under severe strain as the vast majority of Greece's citizens sided with Serbia, with whom they share strong religious and cultural ties. If co-operation across civilisational boundaries is not altogether impossible, it is nevertheless more difficult than co-operation within such boundaries.

If the dilemma between convergence and clash has implications for international politics, it is also relevant to the domestic politics especially of those countries straddling Huntington's civilisational boundaries, but also of Western nations accepting non-Western immigrants.[24] Countries such as Canada, the United States and Australia have long experience taking in and assimilating immigrants from the far corners of the world. To be sure, the hyphenated Canadian or American is a perpetual feature of the cultural landscapes of these countries, and old world traditions may be retained in some measure by, e.g. Italian-Canadians or Greek-Americans. Yet subsequent generations come to see themselves as citizens of their current homeland first, with only a residual sentimental loyalty to the land of their forebears. The latter may manifest itself in cuisine, folk customs and the observance of religious or ethnic holidays.

Yet what of those immigrants whose religious loyalties might put them in a more or less permanent adversarial position vis-à-vis the host country's culture and political institutions? What if these cannot or decline to be assimilated? Such fears have been aired in the past, of course. Many nineteenth-century American Protestants repeatedly expressed fears over an influx of Catholic and Jewish immigrants into their country.[25] More than a century later, most Americans agree that such newcomers and their descendants enriched the nation's culture. Yet there can be no doubt that, even by the 1920s, after two generations of mass immigration had effectively ended, America was a different place than it had been half a century earlier. Some have sought to deal with the dilemmas of immigration by embracing an official multicultural policy based on a liberal version of tolerance.[26] Others are less sanguine about this approach and its efficacy in preventing potential intercommunal conflict.[27]

Delving into the larger immigration issue obviously goes beyond the scope of this chapter. However, two things are worth noting. First, the reality of diverse ethnic or religious communities living within a single polity can complicate the ordinary political task of peacefully conciliating diversity, as Sir Bernard Crick puts it.[28] Second, if political institutions and processes are themselves dependent on particular religiously-based worldviews, then an enduring shift in a country's undergirding cultural assumptions, e.g. from Christianity to secularism, or from secularism to Islam, will inevitably have an impact on the continued functioning of these institutions. If Huntington is correct in his analysis, then some might see cause for concern. If Fukuyama is right, then perhaps such worries are overstated. Once more the jury is still out.

Conclusion: Grappling with Globalization

If the truth does not exactly lie between the two interpretations discussed above, it may be that both have correctly grasped the same interconnected phenomena, though from different angles: (1) the continued secularisation of the West, albeit accompanied by preliminary evidence that this process may finally have run its course[29]; (2) the continued de-secularisation of the rest of the world outside the West, as exemplified by the increased militancy of radical Islam and the explosive growth of Christianity in Africa and Asia[30]; (3) the steady advance of information technology, which has had the paradoxical effect both of facilitating communication among different communities and of enabling them to air—and potentially harden—their differences in less than constructive ways; (4) the uprooting of previously settled peoples and their consequent migration across political and cultural borders; and finally (5) the failure of the old gods and their replacement by newer, but no less deadly, ones.

These are not discrete phenomena that just happen to coincide in our lifetime. They are in fact interconnected in such a way that they form a larger pattern many have recently labelled *globalization*. Globalization implies that the world's peoples—nations, provinces, cities, neighbourhoods; political, ideological, economic and spiritual communities—are becoming increasingly interdependent on a global scale. This development is generally thought to be unprecedented due to the huge leap in technical means over the past one hundred years or so.[31] The "Global Village" has been with us for close to half a century, if not longer.[32] Yet this increasing interconnectedness has by no means extinguished the human need for more proximate communities and the traditions they engender. Despite cosmopolitan hopes to the contrary, humanity as a whole is too abstract an entity to command the allegiance of ordinary finite persons. Thus globalization will always be greeted with ambivalence in many quarters.

There is, of course, more than one way to answer the question of how we should go about living our lives in a globalizing world. To begin with, I believe that, as Christians who know that our world belongs, not to ourselves, but to God, we have a responsibility to unmask the religious roots of the conflicting ideological visions of our time. Simply defending the West, as some argue we must do, will hardly be sufficient if we are not aware of the peculiar idolatries to which Westerners are especially prone. Yet neither should we debunk the West *tout court*. Due to God's faithfulness to his creation and to the historic and positive influence of biblical religion, there is much in the West that is worth celebrating and defending. Yet, ironically, it is precisely where the West makes its greatest contributions that it is most likely to go astray.

For example, there is nothing intrinsically amiss in the shaping of technology, contrary to the views of Ellul and Grant. In fact, I would argue that part of our calling as those made in God's image is to develop human culture and to bring out the latent potentialities in his creation. This includes pencils and pens, clothing and shoes, books and book-binding, indoor plumbing, electrical power, as well as the more sophisticated technical innovations enhancing communication and transportation, such as the telephone, the personal computer and, at least in principle, the automobile.[33]

However, the dark side to all this is that, as we increasingly gain control over the forces of nature, we are more and more tempted to view ourselves as gods for whom nothing is ultimately impossible. In so far as we do so, we, like the builders of the Tower of Babel (Genesis 11:1-9), come to claim self-sufficiency and to imagine that we can get along without God. We dare to believe that we can save ourselves through our own efforts. Therapy replaces repentance. Indifference supplants forgiveness. The expansive will supersedes community and the obligations flowing therefrom. Rights talk replaces ordinary political discourse. In such a context it is hardly surprising that observant Christians, Jews and Muslims alike should find this hubristic spirit of modernity offensive.

Some commentators will urge that the "rest" needs more economic development to catch up with the West. More foreign aid will help to ease the bitterness fuelling terrorism. In other words, the rest of the world needs to become more like us, especially materially. That there is something to this cannot be denied. Constitutional government, the relative lack of corruption, the rule of law, societal differentiation and even the much maligned market economy are worthy achievements that ought not to be disparaged. These might be called the *structural* components of modernity and for these we rightly give thanks to God. We can only hope that these may catch on throughout the globe, though perhaps not precisely in our peculiarly Western form.

Nevertheless, as Christians we should always maintain a healthy scepticism towards what the larger society terms progressive. Globalization, insofar as it represents increasing interdependence amongst peoples on a worldwide scale, is itself neither good nor bad. At its worst, it may affect the accelerated spread of the idolatrous ideologies outwards from the post-Christian West. At its best, it could bring the benefits of clean water and better health care to remote corners of the world racked by chronic disease and hunger. In the former case, one might wish that the world were a little less interconnected to prevent the outflow of destructive worldviews, while in the latter case one could wish for a more thorough globalization in the interest of relieving poverty. Neither proponents nor opponents of globalization are self-evidently progressive, despite their respective conflicting claims. This is, of course, due to the impact of sin on all human enterprises, including the building of empire and liberating from empire, appropriating and rejecting technology, adopting and opposing legal or political reform.

This makes any and every effort to bring healing to our own communities and to others a precarious endeavour indeed, which is ample reason for maintaining a resolute attitude of humility as we live our lives in God's world. Our best efforts in behalf of God and our neighbours will inevitably be fraught with the difficulties attendant upon our status as *simul iustus et peccator*—at once righteous and sinner, as Martin Luther famously put it. This status affects us, not only as individuals, but also as members of the pluriform communities in which we are embedded. This should not be grounds for doing nothing or for throwing up our hands in despair. Yet it is cause for expecting at most modest gains from our feeble attempts at transforming the world for the sake of Christ's coming kingdom. If our world belongs to God, as we properly confess, then it is ultimately he himself who will bring about its final redemption in his own good time. We can take comfort in the knowledge that God can use our achievements for his purposes, however tainted our motives for undertaking them. But we can also rest in the awareness that even our failures will not ultimately delay the coming of his kingdom—a kingdom in which the redeemed serve God and neighbour, displaying the richness of their respective cultures—*restored and fulfilled* cultures—while recognising their ultimate unity as members of that one body, bound together eternally in the love of Christ.

··

DAVID T. KOYZIS (Ph.D., Notre Dame) is Professor of Political Science at Redeemer University College, Ancaster, Ontario, Canada. He is the author of the award-winning *Political Visions and Illusions* (InterVarsity Press, 2003).

NOTES

[1] This chapter began its life as the LambLight Lecture delivered at Trinity Western University, Langley, British Columbia, on 6 December 2006.

[2] Francis Fukuyama, "The End of History", *The National Interest* (Summer 1989).

[3] Fukuyama, *The End of History and the Last Man* (New York: The Free Press/Simon & Schuster, 1992).

[4] See Robert Nisbet, *History of the Idea of Progress* (New York: Basic Books, 1980), for a comprehensive treatment of the subject.

[5] Though few have read the voluminous corpus of Ellul's writings in its entirety, among his best-known books are *The Technological Society* (New York: Alfred A. Knopf, 1964), *The Political Illusion* (New York: Alfred A. Knopf, 1967), and *The Technological System* (New York: Continuum, 1980).

[6] George Parkin Grant, *Lament for a Nation: The Defeat of Canadian Nationalism* (Toronto: House of Anansi Press, 1965).

[7] For a positive assessment of this development in the US, see Dan McNichol, *The Roads that Built America: The Incredible Story of the U.S. Interstate System* (New York: Sterling Publishing Company, 2005). For an analysis of the interaction between highway planners and citizens negatively affected by this development, see Raymond A. Mohl, "The Interstates and the Cities: The U.S. Department of Transportation and the Freeway Revolt, 1966–1973", *Journal of Policy History*, (April 2008), 20, 2, 193-226.

[8] Ellul, *Perspectives on Our Age: Jacques Ellul Speaks on His Life and Work* (New York: The Seabury Press, 1981), 4-5, 17-18.

[9] For some observers this triumph of technocracy is accompanied by an end to ideology. See Daniel Bell, *The End of Ideology: On the Exhaustion of Political Ideas in the Fifties* (New York: Free Press, 1960), esp. 393-407.

[10] See my own "Commercialization and the Death of Singing", *Comment* Magazine, June 2004, http://www.cardus.ca/comment/article/227 (accessed 11 November 2008).

[11] Samuel P. Huntington, "The Clash of Civilizations?", *Foreign Affairs* (summer 1993), 72, 3, 22-49; and *The Clash of Civilization and the Remaking of World*

Order (New York: Simon & Schuster, 1996).

[12] For example, one might view Latin America, not as a civilisation of its own, but as an extension of the West. Certainly Argentina, with its history of substantial European immigration, sees itself as Western and even European. See Alberto Conil Paz and Gustavo Ferrari, *Argentina's Foreign Policy*, 1930-1962 (tr. John J. Kennedy; Notre Dame, IN: University of Notre Dame Press, 1966), 24-49. On the other hand, one might treat the English-speaking democracies as constituting a civilisation in their own right. Something of this approach can be seen in Sir Winston Churchill, *A History of the English-Speaking Peoples*, 4 volumes (New York: Dodd & Mead, 1956-58).

[13] Huntington, *Clash of Civilizations*, 256-258.

[14] Roger Scruton, *The West and the Rest: Globalization and the Terrorist Threat* (Wilmington, DE: ISI Books, 2002).

[15] Paul Berman, *Terror and Liberalism* (New York: W. W. Norton & Co., 2003).

[16] Mike Peters, "Roots of terrorism reach to 1949 Greeley", *The Greeley Tribune*, 24 February 2002, quoting Qutb's own account in *Ma'alim fi-l-Tariq (Milestones)*, 1965.

[17] For a more in depth analysis of liberalism, see my own *Political Visions and Illusions: A Survey and Critique of Contemporary Ideologies* (Downers Grove, IL: InterVarsity Press, 2003), especially 42-71; and "Free to Choose", in Simon Smart (ed.), *A spectator's guide to worldviews: Ten ways of understanding life* (Sydney, NSW, Australia: Blue Bottle Books, 2007), 127-142.

[18] See Meic Pearse, *Why the Rest Hates the West: Understanding the Roots of Global Rage* (Downers Grove, IL: InterVarsity Press, 2004).

[19] Koyzis, *Political Visions*, 60-65. The discussion in the following paragraphs republishes in a slightly different form material appearing in those pages.

[20] "Valid? With reference to what?" asks Pearse (46).

[21] See for example the argument of Myron Magnet, *The Dream and the Nightmare: The Sixties' Legacy to the Underclass* (New York: William Morrow, 1993).

[22] Pearse, *Why the Rest Hates the West*, 43-47.

[23] See for example Walter Laqueur, *The Last Days of Europe: Epitaph for an Old Continent* (New York: Thomas Dunne Books/St. Martin's Press, 2007). Although Laqueur's focus is Europe, much of his analysis has broader applicability.

[24] Huntington himself takes up this issue in his controversial article, "The Hispanic Challenge", *Foreign Policy* (March/April 2004) 141, 30-45. Those disputing Huntington's thesis include Jorge Capetillo-Ponce, "From 'A Clash of Civilizations' to 'Internal Colonialism': Reactions to the Theoretical Bases of Samuel Huntington's 'The Hispanic Challenge'", *Ethnicities* (2007) 7, 116-134.

[25] E.g. Bruce Levine, "Conservatism, Nativism, and Slavery: Thomas R. Whitney and the Origins of the Know-Nothing Party", *The Journal of American History* (September 2001) 88, 2, 455-488, for an account of the influence of the nativist Know-Nothing Party in the United States in the 1850s.

[26] E.g. Shalom Lappin, "Multiculturalism and Democracy", *Dissent* (Summer 2007), 54, 3, 14-18.

[27] E.g. Bernard Lewis, "The Third Wave: Muslim Migration to Europe", *New Perspectives Quarterly* (Summer 2007), 24, 3, 30-35.

[28] Bernard Crick, *In Defence of Politics*, 5th ed. (London: Continuum, 2000), pp. 15-33. On the other hand, if ethnic or religious cleavages co-exist with other crosscutting cleavages, with individuals identifying with different groupings depending on the issue at stake, then this conciliatory activity is likely to be more successful than if individuals identify with a single group for *all* purposes.

[29] E.g. Joshua Livestro, "Holland's Post-Secular Future", *The Weekly Standard*, 1 January 2007, Volume 012, Issue 16, http://www.weeklystandard.com/Content/Public/Articles/000/000/013/110vxfxj.asp (accessed 28 October 2008).

[30] E.g. Philip Jenkins, *The Next Christendom: The Coming of Global Christianity* (Oxford: Oxford University Press, 2002).

[31] That said, it may be that the church, from the outset some two millennia ago, has been viewed as a potentially global community, a consciousness that is probably more vivid to Roman Catholics than to other Christians, primarily due to their church's supranational organisational structure. Moreover, Dante Alighieri's imperial political theory was based on the assumption of two universal rulers over humanity: the Pope and the Emperor (*De Monarchia*, c. 1315). The notion of a global community of humankind has further roots in Stoicism, suggesting that the theoretical basis of globalization may find its roots in both that school and Christianity.

[32] The term is generally thought to have originated with Marshall McLuhan in 1962, but was first used by Wyndham Lewis in 1948. See Lewis, *America and Cosmic Man* (London: Nicholson & Watson, 1948); and McLuhan, *The Gutenberg Galaxy: The Making of Typographic Man* (Toronto: University of Toronto Press, 1962).

[33] I must immediately qualify this statement by noting that, due to human sin, every cultural innovation inevitably has a negative side. The automobile, while allowing tremendous personal mobility in those societies it has shaped, also pollutes the air and encourages the individualistic patterns of settlement exacerbated by liberalism. Yet this can in no way discredit ingenuity as such. See my own "Jacques Ellul: Creation, Fall and Cultural Engagement", *Comment* Magazine, August 2006, http://www.cardus.ca/comment/article/337 (accessed 11 November 2008), republished as "Getting Engaged (or not)", in dialogue with Brian Janaszek, in print edition, December 2006, 30-39.

Cities As a Place for Public Artwork:
A Glocal Approach

by Calvin Seerveld

A city is not an artwork, I dare say, but a meeting place of people, an organised, dated/located social complexity where artistry has an integral role to play; this is my thesis. And, I believe, no city worth its salt today in our technocratically geared culture can ignore the fact that local city inhabitants carry on their lives in a Good Samaritan proximity with happenings around the globe. So, to introduce the theme that cities are a place for public artwork—and what that means—I propose, in adumbrated fashion, a *glocal* (a global-local, bifocal graduated consciousness) focus for understanding city life and artwork good for a city.

First I give a few orienting thoughts about *city*: the importance of "place" for human life and a thumbnail reference to the history of cities. Then I make clear the meaning of *glocal* as a Christian conception for approaching daily life and cities in a normative historical way amid GlobalIZATION. Finally, this chapter deals with the problems and blessings open to *glocal (neighbour-minded) city public art*.

Place and City

Every creature always is somewhere. Placement is as fundamental to creaturehood as being inescapably dated. Place is not the same as "space". I take "space" (*espace, Raum*) to be an abstract quantitative amount of extension. "Spaces" are the measurable distances between markers, or "space" is the indefinite, practically measureless expanse of the heavens above us earthlings. A "place", you could say, is "concrete space", a location (*Ort, lieu*), a locale, a geographic site one can inhabit. Place has an entitary identity beyond its longitudinal-latitudinal coordinates.[1]

You have a birthplace, which usually stamps the paper of your subsequent pilgrimage with its watermark. If you have ever belonged some place—grew up there, lived there so many years—that spot of earth or territory where you put down roots served as a home base from where you now come. Being no place in particular can get you down after a while, as if you are *en passant*—the struggle of many an immigrant family and certainly the plight of dislocated refugees.

The wandering Jews of Older Testament renown, after exiting from Egypt, were at least travelling to a "promised land", because the LORD God of the biblical psalms promised to be the true believers' "at-home" (*ma`on, Zuflucht*, safe refuge, Psalm 90:1). Lapsed Catholic Heidegger struggled philosophically with the incontrovertible "there-ness" (*dasein*) of humans, and the human dilemma of *dwelling* unsettled as a heavenward, earthbound, intermediary creature under an unknowable Divinity, *building* things though we be mortal.[2] Crusty New England American poet Robert Frost was less agonised about our earthy placement, since "One could do worse than be a swinger of birches". But Frost knew also the sad displacement of the vagabond hireling: "Home is the place where when you have to go there, / They have to take you in". Even "the homeless" in Toronto and other metropolitan cities, who walk the daytime streets carrying sodden blankets and plastic bags on their backs like the portable houses of snails, pitch their night time digs, take up their *pied à terre* under sheltering bridges around empty metal drums burning refuse for the centring warmth of a hearth.

A *sheltering place*, (where you are inside rather than outside, to be able to rest somewhere—"Gimme shelter!") *is an existential requisite of being human*. A person needs a place, a habitat for one's humanity to stay intact rather than unravel.

This ontic reality of *place* is the phenomenological grounding for my homespun understanding of *city*. My provisional working definition of city is this: *a city is an inhabited sheltering place of great population density whose fractal unity provides the clearing for an immense interdependent diversity of cultures, languages, commercial activities, beliefs and commitments strange to one another to become functionally structured toward societal exercise of our native human neighbourhoodedness*. A city is best grasped, is my thought, as a God-given institutional opening variously humanly embodied somewhere to highlight good, full-bodied, neighbourly sociality.

Naturally all kinds of activities go on in the settlement of a city, because we corporeal humans are constituted to act in a variety of ways: buying and selling takes place in a city; municipal governance and policing of sorts is necessary; families are raised, children are schooled, newspapers, libraries, sports fields, hospitals and cemeteries are operational. But a city is not first of all a business. A city is not primarily a political state or nation. A city is not merely a collection of families, partners and singles. A city is a city is a city whose streets, houses, stores, offices and buildings that contain people are *integrated by the common civic task of socialising neighbours and strangers coming and going facilitated by its geographic placement*.

Much more needs to be said to fill out this skeletal philosophical suggestion on the primal socialising nature of city. Different cities at different times have exhibited different characters in constituting and caring for their civil cohesion. Ancient cities, before Christ walked the earth, like Ninevah, Babylon and Alexandria, as walled citadels with ziggurats, germinated agricultural hinterlands around their city limits, furthering markets and becoming trade centres; record-keeping and writing fostered city archives and libraries. When the republican city of Rome went imperial during the Caesars (c. 50 BC - 100 AD), Roman citizenry had more clout than MasterCard (cf. Acts 16:35-40; 22:22-24): war, booty, the baths, *vomitoria*, dozens of holidays per year for the spectacles of chariot horse racing in the Circus Maximus (seating more than 100,000) and gladiatorial "games" that showed the brutal, cruel underbelly of Roman "justice" for the few in the city.

When Benedict of Nursia (c. 480 - c. 543 AD) founded a monastic order, its cloisters showed a truly "anti-city" position since Benedictines were dedicated to relinquishing property, prestige and power for a community of prayer, Scripture study, and manual labour. But the regular Church itself, which assumed temporal as well as eternal authority over human lives, in concert with the feudal setup of noble lords and serfs, developed episcopal cities whose informal layout of streets for foot-walkers followed irregular topography and whose city landscape was usually dominated by a towering cathedral. As guilds of artisans grouped in privileged trade "quarters"—neighbourhoods, you could say—comparable to the parishes of the ruling bishop's subalterns, Paris (and Cairo!) began universities (Paris, 1150 AD, Al Gazel in Cairo, 988 AD) that kept cultural storage firmly in the hands of clerics (and imams). But after the discovery of gunpowder and cannonballs altered city fortifications and layouts in Europe and Asia, a mercantilist regime of oligarchic despots gradually formed in nation-state cities like Venice (and even Amsterdam), where moneyed capital, banking, bureaucratic licensing and commercial taxation came to be a more valuable societal control than owning (medieval) real estate.

As Western cities became capitalist strongholds laid out on a straightforward grid, private gain trumped public care for the poor. London, Manchester, New York, Pittsburgh, and Bethlehem, Pennsylvania, split the city populace into sybaritic patrician estates on the one side of the railroad tracks and overcrowded slum ghettoes on the other, choked by factory pollution. The Romantic Idealism, which impelled middle class denizens to go reside in suburbs, trying to reinstate rural features into urban living, has foundered on the unreality of believing that the drive for survival and success at the expense of one's neighbours can ensure lively well being.[3] The boring conformity of hedonistic materialism is a blight on both the suburb and many a post-industrial city today because corporate franchises, cybernetic fluidity of capital and high speed techno-communication tend to get people to tread habitat water and not feel at home anywhere in particular— every man and woman and our belongings seem to be in flight, and the city of endless desires is virtually consumptive.

Global and GlobalIZATION

The Christian faith charters a global outlook and action because the Bible says God created the whole world. And non-human creatures on earth and in "space" like the sun, winds, mountains, water, trees and animals, are not just a brute "environment" for humans to master and waste, but are actually God's theatre of operation,[4] in which we humans, who make our historical entrances and exits every 80 years or so, are to be caretakers (Psalm 104, Genesis 1:1-2:3). Humans who disbelieve that Jesus Christ was the Son of God in history are still in charge of caring for and cultivating the whole world and have often been more proactive than narrow-minded followers of the Christ.

The Newer Testament teaches clearly that once you accept the cosmic reach of God's injunction to humans to institute the Lord's *shalom* of fruition and reconciliation everywhere,[5] then every child in need anywhere becomes my neighbour (Luke 10:25-37). And any place within reach is an opening for us to share wisely in making it a winsome spot, safe to inhabit, with a spirit of peace.[6] No human should think he or she has to save the world; that's God's affair. But the biblical perspective, I believe, is markedly global: it is our inescapable human vocation to be responsible for building wherever we are, with whatever gifts have been entrusted to us, build concrete places and relationships that embody God's deep compassion for doing justice for God's creatures (John 3:17; 1 John 3:11-24).

"GlobalIZATION", however, is "*global*" on a power trip: you, locally, are not in control because something *global* has already decided the matter.[7] For example:

- Expect your severance pay package as dye-maker in 90 days, since General Motors is closing its auto parts plant in Oshawa or Windsor, Ontario, and building a new one in Mexico.
- You have lived all your life in Seattle? Get ready to move to Chicago since Boeing Corporation, enticed by a $60 million public money subsidy, is moving its corporate headquarters there (2001).
- There is *nothing* you can do as Japanese and German government representatives sitting on the World

Bank council to stop Wolfowitz from being appointed president (2006).

- In 1997 Thailand, Indonesia and South Korea faced bankruptcy as countries because of powerful currency speculators following the ideological policy of capital market "liberalisation". When the International Monetary Fund (IMF) bailed out the G7 dollar banks who held the bad debt, they blamed the East Asian countries and crippled them with high interest rates, penalty taxes, and dictated trade terms which stifled those countries from being able to make any local economic policies as "sovereign" nations.

"GlobalIZATION" emphasises the fairly recent intensification of worldwide interconnectedness of good and evil deeds because of the incredibly fast transportation now available, lightning-like telecommunication, increasing interdependence of production and consumption of goods, the massive migration of exploding populations and climate-changing pollution, and a nervous concern in powerful circles about the proliferation of weapons of mass destruction in different hands. But there is more to it than the time-and-place compression that forces us humans in the whole wide world to act as if we exist in a *"global high rise"*.[8]

The hidden "more" to our being *"globalized"* is that a deadly drive to be the surviving fittest seems to be the overpowering dynamic inside the Capitalistic economic order which dominates world cultures. Laissez-faire, Darwinian uneconomical wheeling-and-dealing—call it "Neo-Liberal", if you will, or "Casino Capital*ism*"[9]—has assumed a covert almighty power in the world; no one person personifies it. It is systemic almighty power like what the Bible calls invisible "principalities, powers, and dominions".[10] Amnesty International and *Medecins sans frontières* will show up in person at any country open to receiving their services, but a truly "global" organisation is more than inter-national and has a curious impersonal anonymity. The World Bank, IMF, and World Trade Organization are supra/trans-national bodies more like the Internet, which is not so much here or there so much as nowhere in particular, but can touch down everywhere there is a Bill Gates terminal. These organisations wield precisely the kind of inscrutable distanced covert centralisation of pre-emptive, decisive power Saint Augustine feared would happen if the *civitates terrenae*, instead of fighting amongst themselves, would consolidate against the *civitas Dei*, the community of people rooted in God-obedient service.[11]

I am not suggesting a "conspiracy theory" in the globalization of our cities. The fact that every one of my sold-in-Canada Dell computer

CALVIN SEERVELD

parts is marked made-in-China, and that the software specialist walking me in Toronto through the steps to install my high-speed upgrade is talking English on the phone from India, is not the result of a malicious mafia conspiring to kill local manufacturing and servicing jobs. It is just that outsourcing is in the grip of an all-embracing policy gut to maximise profits with cheaper labour. "Time means money; place is unimportant": so goes the unfettered Capitalist creed. The (American) Idol of competitive moneyed Success runs roughshod over any other consideration—let the devil take the hindmost!

Think of it like a drug, alcohol or gambling addiction: how can an individual overcome its hold alone? If our ruling corporate culture respectfully serves an undercover Idol of Greed—always More!—no wonder the few rich get richer and the many poor get poorer, increasing the gap between them globally, inexorably. The USA did not join the international Kyoto Protocol (1997/2005) on combating climate change, it was said, because the measures required would affect adversely the unrivalled American standard of living. To live in subjection to the no-god of "We First *Überalles*!" is to be blinded to the presence of neighbours, a deeply unbiblical, dehumanising *pou sto*, the place-where-you-finally-stand, that cannot help but be resented albeit envied by the weaker peoples of the world. But the fact that the hidden bankrupt status of the United States of America has become exposed in the September/October 2008 global financial collapse shows that GlobalIZATION induces the vanity (i.e. a bubble of stinking hot air) of pseudo-reliability. Money is no longer a token of exchange for resourceful goods, but has become an idolised commodity itself—a false no-god, sinking sand on which to build your earthly city.

However, instead of thinking GlobalIZATION is inevitable and acquiescing to its wresting responsibility away from local authorities for shaping one's city, and instead of promoting the idea that Chicago or Toronto wants to become a globalized actor too with the Big City Boys, even at the "Second City" level, I propose for consideration the alternate tack of thinking and acting *glocally*. Even if "GlobalIZATION", which is an utterly complex historical phenomenon, a human construction, has assumed the juggernaut dimensions of a principality, I believe it can be exorcised from our culture, God willing, so that a redemptive dynamic can bestir a city and remake it, step by step, historically "new".

A Glocal Corrective to the Power of GlobalIZATION

By "glocal" I mean *a committed world-and-life vision that is "globally" (i.e. cosmic historically) aware but acts* first-of-all *locally from the place you call home*. The conception of "glocal" as a norm for reflecting, willing and doing, is as biblically simple as the imperative "Love God

above all, and love your neighbour as you respect yourself."[12] Awareness that the Creator God has posited worldwide ordinances for humans
to follow (for instance, practise justice, thrifty generosity, undeceptive
speech, faithful partnering, reliable commitments, efficient instruments)
which hold for everybody—awareness that Christ-follower you *and* your
agnostic believing neighbour *both* can default historically in discovering
and doing God's cosmic will for creaturely daily life—these should keep
neighbour love and self-respect in tandem.

The biblical vision of an interconnected world of places with a
peaceable kingdom of *flora*, *fauna*, and humans is sharply different
from the skewed Darwinian vision of constant struggle of "bared tooth
and bloody claw" where winner takes all. But the biblical vision is not
projecting an Idealistic Utopia, because Christians know about that
dirty three-letter word people usually only use to describe others: *sin*.
Sin is not just a private matter, but also a public global reality in a
Christian reading of the world. That's again where "glocal" comes
in, humbling one's efforts: the biblical Scriptures enjoin humans to
bear fruit in God's world beginning in your own locality—one needs
to put one's own house in order first before offering to correct others—branching out as, through faithful seasoning, you receive broader
openings and tougher assignments (Matthew 25:14-30, 20-23). It is a
biblical Christian mission to redeem whatever is placed in your path
and to show particularly a repentant, saintly hospitality to strangers—
that is, to be cosmopolitanly receptive, even vulnerable, to what is
not your particular cup of tea, and to let your service be educated and
modified by anything worthwhile that comes from a foreign neighbour
to invigorate your Way.

It is critical for a glocal approach to act historically, not like revolutionaries who assume they can start with a clean slate to make something "new", and also not "pragmatistically". A pragmatist has goals,
and will use practically any necessary means to achieve the goals. A
Christian approach, I think, affirms a norm for getting things changed
which one steadily follows, even if the goal is modified during the
process and even if the attempt fails. I would formulate the principle
for those who wish to implement a glocal approach with historical
sanity as follows: 1. regenerate, 2. speciate, and 3. diaconate the state
of affairs you face in your generation.[13]

1. To *regenerate* the economic service that the IMF and World
Bank were originally intended to perform, that is, to re-attach its provision of capital to local needs, money policy should focus on creating
jobs and improving vocational training and land reform rather than aim
at profits for financiers to take out of the country. That is, rich transnational organisations can best help a poor country by reining in the prof-
iteering dynamic and uneconomical economics of quick fix, by slowly
building up the civic social domain of public institutions (its roads to

local markets, literacy and health services, uncorrupted courts, labour unions), and funding the "unprofitable" time-consuming work. You regenerate an over-bearing Growth-economy import by trimming its sails to adjust to the local social fabric; you forge a *glocal* economics.

To regenerate a city milieu of 3 million inhabitants to the joy of different bustling neighbourhoods, like the Danforth Greektown district of Toronto or the Asian international Devon Avenue community in Chicago, the municipal powers who set budgetary priorities and zoning should focus on transforming public housing, as Larry Bennett proposes; this will incorporate poorer and more ethnically diverse families into a neighbourhood of affordable dwellings (both high-rises and town houses) that is not a market-based solution which favours moneyed interests.[14] Chicago mayoral authorities need to listen to and help local community leaders upgrade their schools with imaginative "Blackboard Jungle" teachers—not turn them into military-style academies—and fund improvement of public transit to connect suburban regions with the downtown loop to regenerate pride in the place where one lives, and avoid the "gentrification" fix which, as Charles Suchar says, commits "cultural genocide",[15] displaces the marginalised folk yet again, and composes a block of yuppie sameness that is deadening to city life. *To regenerate city life entails providing local rootage of the human activity, which is integral to the setting of the whole large city complex of neighbours.*

2. To *speciate* political responsibilities in the present uncertain climate of global quasi-supreme transnational bodies like the United Nations (1945), the International Court of Justice in the Hague (1946), the International [War Crimes] Court (July 2002)—often bullied or unaccredited by the present faltering USA government—would be to have various legal nation-state authorities, regional alliances like NATO (1949) and APEC (1989), and NGOs like Amnesty International, act as a kind of confederated check to hold accountable in their own jurisdictions actions by the global organisations as warranted or not. The historical principle of speciating political responsibilities complements the policy of subsidiarity: the less inclusive organ to rule normally has priority for decision-making and judgement. (You don't use the Supreme Court to settle a minor neighbourhood fracas.)

Trouble comes when there is a jurisdictional dispute or a quarrel on whether justice has been served. For example, a nation-state must protect its citizens against global powerhouses who exercise single-issue concerns when the transnational organisation manipulates interest rates and ruins a national economy. Nation-states should tax the unjust inflow and outflow of such transnational speculative capital. But Amnesty International rightly calls a nation-state to task when a legal government violates the rights of groups of individuals within its national borders; and the WTO Board (1994) correctly challenges those who talk free trade but make it unfair trade by setting up one-sided protectionist tariffs that undercut legal agreements. So sometimes the nation-state must regulate the unjust global organisation, and sometimes the international body must challenge the nation-state's "legal" actions—"legal" is not always "moral"—as unjust. *The glocal norm of speciation rests with the clumsy normativity of confederated political regulative powers*, rejecting the Godfather Boss institution, which overrides all other dispensers of justice throughout the world.

To speciate responsibilities of city life leaders could start by recognising that money is not the only or the final horizon looming above developmental decisions on city life. There must be wise political regulation of economic transactions: just-doing trumps profit-making. Historically-sound movement toward a more normative city life gives specific dimensions of the city their relative interactive worth. Indeed, a police force needs to be converted from untrained blue collar enforcement officers into salaried, educated professionals who are promoted on the basis of merit, not on the basis of being politically correct; but the media need to keep police honest by reporting critically on "community policing", keeping in public discussion the balancing of crime solving and crime prevention, since safe streets *everywhere* in the city is a priority. City leaders need to think "retail" as well as "wholesale", so to speak, but special business and labour union interests, political factions' aims, basic medical health concerns also for the poor, synagogue-church-mosque-temple needs, and other special project—all must be honoured and adjudicated so that they sub-serve the informal civic social institutional nature of the city.

As David Moburg put it, citing the "iron rule" of Alinsky's Industrial Areas Foundation: "Never do for others what they can do for themselves"[16]; the social commonweal must be the orienting horizon. *To speciate city life means to interrelate the specific, distinct decentred voices* (a city is not just buildings; it is the people inhabiting the buildings[17])—*so they can each contribute their special gifts to a connected deepening of civil life.*[18]

3. The *diaconate* step in the glocal mandate anchors how we humans may try to retrace our wrong turns and somehow undo cumulative misdeeds with a new start: *the Christian world-and-life visionary diaconate move anchors opportunities to take up "global" matters in looking at them from the local starting point.* For example: wise proponents of human rights in an Inuit settlement or African tribal locality should tune such a basic question toward a communitarian rather than towards a democratic practice, because the communities in question live out of consensus rather than settle injustice by majority vote. Rather than introduce the animosity of litigation, "human rights" would be melted into the rigours of reconciling victims and oppressors in the presence of the whole community. Or again: since the health of

people is such a public matter, why should health services in a land be organised for private profit? Not-for-profit hospitals must cover their expenses, pay nurses and doctors good salaries, maintain the equipment and premises, but its patients are not to be treated like customers! The spirit in not-for-profit elderly rest homes is amazingly cheerful in distinction from the tight mercenary keep in many commercial ventures, because there has been diaconate knowledge at work in the institution that does not treat health care as a business.

A corrective international move, suggested by Joseph E. Stiglitz' newest book, *Making Globalization Work* (2006), would be to give votes on key policy matters also to the un-powerful, two-thirds world, agriculturally struggling nations, so that decisions on reciprocal tariffs are made, for example, by more than "free-floating" financial pluto-technocrats. Alternative proposals by NGOs for transparency, accountability, enforcement of conflict-of-interest protocols need to be given due weight so that "global" organisations tackle truly global problems like peace, HIV-AIDS and malaria epidemics, and environmental degradation, instead of fussing only with debits and credits.[19]

Diaconate work in the city would reclaim city streets for living. A city street with sidewalks is a public people place and not merely a vehicular corridor or thruway. A neighbourhood city street with sidewalks is for pedestrians and not just parked cars. A city street is lively when it is walked by different persons at different times for a variety of reasons—to go to the library, to buy milk, to walk the dog, to stroll and look at people, to visit a restaurant with friends, or maybe even—miracle!—to walk to work. A well-used street is safe because the residents, shop-keepers, and other walkers provide unofficial, casual surveillance over what goes on, like self-government. It is rather difficult to change the long avenues, wide boulevards, and monotonous gridiron layout of city streets once it is all in "place", but if instead of "slum clearance" there is an in-fill development opportunity to revamp a district, don't push the people out, says Jane Jacobs; go for short blocks, cross-streets, keeping some old buildings mixed in—not just high profit new construction; situate family homes and elevator apartments for childless couples near work places; hide little parks and bikeways so they can be discovered.[20] Diaconate action in a city does not mean simply to dilute its cement with rural green spots, but entails *building up a rich diversity of districts whose places brim over with a kind of distinct cheerful hospitality*.[21] Greenwich village in New York City, Chinatown in Toronto, and Old Town in Chicago are vibrant sections of their cities which invite strangers—"cities are, by definition, full of strangers"[22]— into their home territory, and so reach out to give away their special treasury of talents as part of the whole city. In my glocal judgement, even more than its architecture (which can be dictated by globalized fashion), a spirit of *placed hospitality* is the mark of a normative city.

A Glocal Correction for Cities and their Artistic Responsibilities

If "glocal" means *a biblically Christian outlook and approach to change matters of fact to be more in line with God's cosmic norm for a responsible human love of self and neighbour*, what does that entail for artistry in a city like Chicago and Toronto (cities in which our family has lived—13 years in Chicago, 36 years in Toronto)? Be concrete. If I reject the GlobalIZED art world of Mammon for setting standards and art policy (the renowned Getty Museum in California paying many millions of dollars for a single Van Gogh painting of *Irises* (1889); Southeby's, in the spring of 2008, knocking down a little old Tom Thompson landscape painting for 1.7 million; and the abnormal, virtual, tourist-centred cities like Las Vegas—as Jean Baudrillard says in *Amérique* (1986), "Las Vegas is impossible! But there in the desert it is!"[23]), then what in the world is God's will for human artistry? In a city? Could (and *how* can) local city artists respect themselves and share their gifts with neighbours and help the city openly receive strangers as guests (hospitality) so that the home art territory flourishes with its own city identity?

Chicago is not New York City or Florence but is mid-Western America with the Old 1893 Columbian World Exposition behind it; then the Chicago Art Institute's (begun 1891) unusual exhibition of the 1913 New York Armory Show; then the 1933 Century of Progress Exposition. Chicago is home base to the early skyscrapers along with the stinking stockyards and meatpacking plants Carl Sandburg's poetry made famous.

And Toronto is not Montréal or Tokyo, but is a former very British settlement in Central Canada which slowly became a city of annexed suburbs around the time of "The Great War" (1914-1918), where landmarks like Massey Hall with the Toronto Symphony and Mendelssohn Choir (1894), the Grange brick home bequeathed to be the kernel of the Art Gallery of Ontario (1910), and the Royal Ontario Museum (1914) quietly continued their tasks next to Maple Leaf Gardens with its hockey (1931) and its Eaton's and Simpson's shops renowned for their mail order catalogue business. Toronto gradually became a prosperous, good city of immigrant multi-ethnic neighbourhoods—Jewish, Italian, Portuguese, Chinese, and Caribbean peoples—by the 1970s, home to Jane Jacobs and visionary Marshall McLuhan. Toronto city artistic life, one might say, seems today to be more events than repositories—active commercial art galleries, the Harbour front Authors' reading series, New Music concerts, parades and Caribana festival—while taking on the burden of being a financial centre, sprawling with one-tenth of the total population of the whole country.

Glocal Regeneration: Bringing Fresh Aesthetic Air into the City

Underneath artistic practice is the resident imaginative trait of humans, which we call "aesthetic". All people, by nature, normally feel, speak, think, believe, and imagine things among the various ways one acts, even if they don't become therapeutic counsellors, orators, scientists, evangelists, or artists by profession. It is this pre-artistic *aesthetic* feature of humans and God's world whose integral importance is sometimes overlooked in society.

To fool around, tell jokes, and play games is *aesthetic activity*: it takes imagination to make believe you have knights and bishops attacking the opponent's king in chess, and that certain squares in hop-scotch are taboo. To grow flowers in a garden, or to swing on a rope in a tire is aesthetic activity that is good for nothing except day-dreamy wonderment at bodily movement in fresh air and loveliness. To blow bubbles is simply fun, and stirs a child or adult's imagination pleasantly. To watch fountains, especially if illuminated at night, helps one *aesthetically* wile away time. From a Christian standpoint, not all time is money: aesthetic time spells leisure, and it is a gift God saw was good ("leisure" is not the same as "luxury"); leisure like sleep is taking a deep breath in daily work time. All kinds of time can be valuable and redemptive.

Parks are *aesthetic places* in a cityscape, geared to encourage people to take and give aesthetic time to one another: you sit on a park bench to chew the fat, walk around arm-in-arm, throw Frisbees, or, in the city of Geneva, Switzerland, have a friendly game of chess; that is, you *congregate* to interact with newcomers and old acquaintances and exercise kibitzing neighbourliness. This is why if a park becomes unsafe gang turf, it is a deep wound in a city's life. A park is by nature to be *public*—that is, accessible and free to anybody willing to accept the common good on offer. "Public" is best if it is intergenerational, interracial, for poor as well as rich, and handicap-friendly.

In contrast to a park one needs to note that a mall is a privately owned environs pretending to be park-like, a safe place for seniors to sit around idly in between coffees, but is totally geared to sell merchandise and continually turn everybody onsite into a consumer— "FOR SALE, from 30% - 50% off!" There are fairytale bridges and an artificial lake with little harmless waves for the kids in West Edmonton Mall, cluttered kitsch among the shops stoking a carnival-esque mood in Minneapolis' Mall of the Americas to loosen your inhibitions and purse strings. The malls I've visited have pseudo-aesthetic touches, quite different from genuine aesthetic attention like a rainbow of paint

Outdoor chess game in Geneva, Switzerland

around a bicycle path (formerly cattle-crossing) culvert off the Don Valley Parkway in Toronto, put there, not to sell anything, just to brighten your commute as you pass by. So a city does well if it consecrates resources for *aesthetic places*, not just as relief from constant hard-sell advertising, but also as an integral positive feature of the main sociable quality that defines a good city.

Glocal Speciation: Ethnic Neighbourhood Street Mural Art

Rainbow culvert at the side of the
Don Valley Parkway, Toronto

Aesthetic activity assumes full-blown artistic nature when its imaginative background character crystallises, you might say, into the
determined crafting of surprising objects and events which take on an
independent entitary imaginative life of their own. A lovely blue mural in
the Mission district of San Francisco encourages you to think porpoises
and cool water amid the sweltering heat. Such street art, like taking a
whole wall of a building near a postage-stamp park in London, England,
where office workers eat their bag lunch, or painting a humongous, hu-
morous ungainly dinosaur on a back alley wall in a tough section near
Kings Cross railroad station, tell you this neighbourhood cares about
you, whether onlooker or inhabitant—"Have a good day, if you can!"

From a glocal perspective, the famed *Wall of Respect* mural (1967-
1969) at 43rd and Langley, Chicago epitomises city street art at its best,
saying "This place is our home, and we are proud of it. The rich may
drive out the poor, but we are staying!"—I took this photo in February
1970, about a year before it was destroyed by fire. The hooded Ku Klux
Klan exist in their upper red panel, but so do portraits of Muhammad Ali,
arms raised in victory, and Martin Luther King (murdered in 1969). And
this Wall of self-respect—conceived by an African-American community,
painted and re-painted in public with a community of people watching and
cheering them on—this wall reaches out with its "Black is beautiful" open
hand—not a fist with a knife—to clasp with a white hand and a brown hand
together holding up a symbol of angry confronting faces circumscribed
with the word PEACE! William Walker who lived in this neighbourhood
also did a 1977 viaduct at 56th Street and Stony Island (restored 1993):
Childhood is without prejudice—overlapping faces of different races—to
affirm the multiracial diversity of the city as a welcome strength.

Since I left my teaching position in Chicago in 1972, 200,000
Mexican immigrants have made their homes in Chicago and have followed up the amazing precedent of their native country where Diego

The Wall of Respect, 43rd & Langley,
Chicago, 1967-71

Rivera and David Alfaro Siqueiros (1896-1974) received government aid in the 1920s to cover whole buildings in Mexico City with historical scenes and symbols encouraging everybody to get education, training with tools, to honour culture "Made in Mexico!" To make Chicago home, neighbours and students followed the direction of Aurelio Diaz to decorate the railroad embankment on 16th Street in the Pilsen area with a confident variety of Chicano profiles. There are miles of murals below the railroad tracks, not all in mint condition. Current murals I saw in the spring of 2008 have gotten more aggressive to try to stop ruining this Mexican Chicago neighbourhood, depleting its affordable housing being ravaged by the high financed clutches of so-called "developers". Artwork can elicit smiles or induce troubled sighs, protesting injustice. Public mural art can tend toward a simplified poster-like point because viewers normally read it as they pass by. The Roman Catholic school there needs a barbed wire fence to protect vehicles in its parking lot, but on the parking space wall shows a mural presenting the happiness of being baptised into the church communion connected to the school.

The Puerto Rican community in Chicago significantly placed a forty-six-foot cement mural on the National Guard Armory in their neighbourhood with conga drummers drumming for *Paz Pan Libertad*, a glocal reminder that worldwide issues of peace, poverty, and the deep wish to be free from fear are present right there at North and Kedzie Avenue in the city.

Our family was cheered when we first moved to Toronto to read in *The Globe and Mail* about a local scrap metal dump operator, Leon Kaminsky, who braved the catcalls of his colleagues to hire a few Ontario College of Art students to paint the illustrious history of collecting and disposing of refuse on his walls at Eastern Avenue (now destroyed). To us it showed respect for honest labour with imaginative flair.

Leon Kaminsky scrap metal dump, Eastern
Avenue, Toronto, 1970s (now destroyed)

The well-known Canadian Oji-Cree artist, Jackson Beardy, was asked by the predominantly white Christian Reformed Church community to design murals for both the inside and the outside of their Family Centre that ministers to First Nation needs at Selkirk Avenue and Powers in the city of Winnipeg, Manitoba. Beardy designed the mural; First Nations youngsters did the painting under supervision; it was one of the few buildings not defaced in a rumble in the area a few years afterward.

Jackson Beardy, Indian Family Centre, Selkirk &
Powers, Winnipeg, 1985 (restored 2006)

Lining the corridors of the city of Toronto's international airport, through which all entering passengers must walk, were murals welcoming visitors from various continents and cultures, extending a knowledgeable light artistic handshake (now destroyed).[24]

Pearson International Airport, Toronto,
formerly Terminal One, 1973
(now destroyed in rebuilt facility)

There are fine murals at Regent Park apartments currently under-going renovation in Toronto, bringing a bright spot to the drab streets, honouring world diversity located right there, pointing an upward-bound poster-like moral, showing the unity in wanting safe living quarters. Will the housing-in-progress complement the mural art? *Artistic activity from the bottom-up can serve a city well*, culturally reaching and enriching neighbours who have never seen the inside of an art museum.

Regent neighbourhood, Toronto, 2008

Glocal Diaconate: Public Artwork Good for City Life

Art has the task in God's world, I believe, to open up one's neigh-bours to notice nuances of meaning we casually overlook. Artwork is to be done to help those who are imaginatively handicapped to experi-ence enriching, perhaps troubling, subtleties and ambiguities in God's world of which it is worth becoming wary and aware.

Painterly art and sculpture in art galleries, like symphonies in con-cert halls, like novels or poetry read (aloud) from books, are God-giv-en opportunities to explore and share the surprising hidden riches of created creatures *coram Deo*. Those who are custodians of art, such as museum curators, symphony conductors, performers, and literary crit-ics, need to mediate artistry to the public who may only hear sounds at a concert instead of sonata-formed tones, or read words rather than a plotted narrative, or see only strange shapes and a jumble of colours instead of art. So, when you bring the public into the art gallery, there should be docents to teach the children the language of pictorial art, and also informal instruction and free entrance one evening a week for adults who are too bashful or poor to investigate this strange world of artistry on their own.

And when you take art out of its curated *art place* and deposit it in the general public area you need to be wise in the selection. There is a difference between art in public places and public art. Public art does not put Rodin's *Thinker* (1880-81) up on a pedestal in the city of Detroit to see what the local tough guys make of it. Public art exemplifies what I call "double-duty" artistic engagement. Double-duty artistic activity encapsulates art-making within non-artistic activity so that the artist must fulfil two norms, do double duty. The product needs to honour well-crafted artistic ambiguity *and* serve the non-artistic purpose for which it was drafted. Advertising art needs to heed the aesthetic norm of metaphorical allusiveness *and* the economic norm of supplying good resources for people's needs, if it would be good advertising artistry. If a given ad is engaging art but pushes wasteful luxury, the piece has failed its double duty. If an ad extols a thrifty project but the art is weak, it has failed its double duty. *Public city art, from a glocal perspective, is artistry conceived and executed to further neighbourly interactive sociability,* and sometimes to commemorate outdoors the city's history and city life itself.

The Tilted Arc of Richard Serra (1981) thumbed its nose[25] at the people who walked across a bland New York City plaza between the *Beaux Arts* courthouses and the International-style Federal Building around it. The art piece was 120 feet long, 12 feet high and one inch thick of industrial Cor-Ten steel, which deliberately held the place hostage to its implacable, unfriendly presence. When it was finally removed amid lawsuits in 1985, the place came to look rather empty.

By contrast, when a Henry Moore (1898-1986) reclining figure is put in a park near flowers, it seems to invite any sheep nearby to nudge against it. Moore's huge marble *Reclining Figure* (1957-58) beside the UNESCO building in Paris supplements that organisation's

Henry Moore, *Two Large Forms*, outside
Art Gallery of Ontario, 1966-69

caring for the children of the world by having the vulnerable mother figure's periscope of a neck and head stay on the lookout for trouble. And the huge Moore bronze sculpture of vertebrae outside the Art Gallery of Ontario is a people-friendly child-climbable artwork that says, "Welcome! Touch me!" and brings a roly-poly quieting life to the street corner.

I was sceptical when I was told of Chicago's Millennium Park, since it was part of Mayor Richard M. Daley Jr.'s attempt to make Chicago attractive to tourists, and it was well-funded by mega-corporations. But an unhurried visit dispelled my qualms. British Anish Kapoor's (b. 1954) elliptical *Cloud Gate* (2004) is an incredible steel-plated bauble shaped like a drop of liquid mercury that reflects the cityscape, sky and clouds, and every spectator within sight. You can walk under and through it and see your crazy-mirror-type elongated reflections. Its 110 tonnes look like a warped bubble, fascinating, playing back whoever/whatever is in the neighbourhood.

Anish Kapoor, *Cloud Gate*, Millenium Park,
Chicago, 2005

And then nearby there is the inch-deep pool of water between Jaune Plensa's (b. 1956) two facing fifty-foot high fountains on which videos of 1000 different Chicagoan inhabitants' faces are projected every thirteen minutes, smiling, slowly pursing their lips, until a stream of water gushes out of their mouths; and when that stops, splashes of water cascade down from the top of the facing fountains on all sides for children to get wet and scream in delightedly. Millennium Park in Chicago, as I see it, has gone beyond putting art in public places, and has now produced *public city art promoting neighbourly interactive sociability*. (The corporate sponsors are discretely noted in the cement underfoot.)

Jaune Plensa, The Crown Fountains, Millenium
Park, Chicago, 2004

Certain public art can speak for the city as a whole. Zadkine's (1890-1967) aching commemoration of the 14th of May in 1940 (on which date, without warning, Nazi Germany bombed the inhabited heart out of the city of Rotterdam) shows the city's contorted body rising up again, arms raised to heaven still pleading for relief—a moving symbol of an historic city event that forced the defenceless country of the Netherlands as a whole to capitulate and become enemy occupied territory. May Lin's well-known *Vietnam Veterans Memorial* (1981-1982) graces the city of Washington, D.C. as testimony to the utterly evil banality of ideological war—58,939 humans killed on just one side for what? The polished black granite unites all who attend its reflecting sombre witness in a quieting common sorrow; this is good glocal public art, close to home and crying out to curb a nation's penchant for ambitious global control.

Ossip Zadkine, *The Destroyed City*,
Rotterdam harbour, 1946-1953

I am still looking for a city—even a corporate sponsor—with
the vision to find a place inside city limits for *Cathedral of Suffering* (1994) by Wikstrom. This installation won a prize in an
Amnesty International art competition but has not yet been cast.
Five poles and three figures wait for you to walk toward it in a
field: the woman figure is bent to shield herself helplessly from
the unstopping attack; the little child, arms raised to protect its
face, has its own solitary grown-up pole; the spread-eagled man
is crucified in the torture of hanging between two poles; and the
empty pole stands waiting for another victim. Evil and sin are
insatiable in our global and local society. As you walk away from
this poignant sculptural testimony to our own horrendous permit-
ting of such terror happening, even as you read this—too cruel for
earth to bear, and chillingly unacceptable to the heavens, *place-
less*—it occurs to you: maybe the empty pole is meant for me.

Britt Wikstrom, *Cathedral of Suffering*, maquette
awaiting a commission,1994

Public artwork is not itself urban renewal and does not necessarily reform an elected government plagued by militaristic advisors. But glocal public art, by its Christian regenerating, speciated, diaconate nature can appeal to all who experience its nuanced power to act differently, locally, if we keep conscious the cosmic overview of God's will for neighbourhooded human lives.

Glocal mission

What can a city with a committed glocal Christian vision do about art?

1. *Upgrade the aesthetic life of its inhabitants* with projects like *Shooting Back*, in which a band of professional photographers spent time with homeless youngsters in a New York city ghetto teaching them the art of themselves, photographing the nuances of their own backyard lives: playing near the railroad tracks, bathing your younger brother in the sink, helping a wounded bird, finally getting a shot of your brother doing the back flip just right! Without developing people's underground aesthetic life awareness, taking up art can be a rootless put-on.

2. *Put in the city budget money for street art, school and library murals, site-specific artwork for hospitals and public buildings and especially playgrounds.* Public artwork like the benches in a playground can unite different ethnic neighbourhoods, getting the children and watchful parents to sit down together rather than allowing diverse groups to build up imaginary walls between "us and them".

3. *Resist the temptation to go Disneyland global with gondolas in the Chicago River or a Wonderland permanently at Toronto's waterfront.* A city is to become a meeting place, home, first of all for its inhabiting citizens in neighbourhoods, not a brief stopping/shopping

site for tourists. And if our major cities cannot handle the *Cathedral of Suffering* because our nations are complicit in militarist expeditions in Iraq or Afghanistan or who knows where, maybe municipal leaders could find it possible to commission artwork meant to be a public invitation to friendliness: go ahead, sit down on a bench outside the Glenn Gould studio on Front Street, Toronto, for a little chat with Glenn, and thank him for playing Bach's Goldberg Variations.

Ruth Abernethy, *The Glen Gould Gathering*,
Front Street, Toronto, 1999

A thoughtful, light-hearted public artwork which deserves to be a landmark, rests in the heart of Toronto's financial district downtown: there is carved out a minute park where seven large bronze cows by Saskatchewan artist Joe Fafard (b. 1941) graze peacefully on the spot of grass. It is as if Torontonians know God spared the wicked repentant city of Ninevah years ago because God cherished its cows (it says so in the last verse of the Jonah book of the Bible)! So maybe God will accept Toronto's public artwork of cows as an offering to spare us in the coming world crises.

Jane Jacobs encourages a city not to come out with a "master plan" from on high to make a Utopia, because a city is not a "scientific design problem", she says, to be solved at the drawing board: *a city is a place of neighbours who need to build fruitful social relationships from the grass roots meeting places up*. To become a "city of refuge", if not "a city of God", will be a blessing upon generations of people faithfully "loving just-doing, being merciful, and walking humbly with God" (Micah 6:8), and probably will need to be fused with "prayer and fasting" (Matthew 17:14-21). Glocally conscious artistry, I believe, can be a little step in planning to redeem city living from the power of GloballZATION and in helping to make our cities "new".

322 CALVIN SEERVELD

Joe Fafard, *The Pasture*, Wellington Street,
downtown Toronto, 1985

CALVIN SEERVELD (Ph.D., Free University of Amsterdam) is Senior Member
emeritus in Philosophical Aesthetics at the Institute for Christian Studies,
Toronto, Ontario, Canada. Some of his books include *Bearing Fresh Olive
Leaves: Alternative Steps in Understanding Art* (2000), *A Christian Critique
of Art and Literature* (1995/1963), *On Being Human: Imaging God in the
Modern World* (1988), and *Rainbows for the Fallen World* (1980).

NOTES

1   K.J. Popma examines how it is possible to conceive of the simultaneity of spatial reality as an aspect of creatural temporality, in *Inleiding in de Wijsbegeerte*, 3rd edition (Kampen: H. Snijder, 1951), 62-65; "Successie en Gelijktijdigheid", in *Philosophia Reformata*, 19, 1 (1954): 1-31. His analysis prompts me to understand spatiality as a modal aspect of creatures, and "place" as an entitary spatial reality (like a point, a location).

2   Heidegger, "Bauen Wohnen Denken" (1951) and ". . . dichterisch wohnet der Mensch" (1951) in *Vorträge und Aufsätze* (Pfullingen: Neske, 1954), 145-162, 187-204.

3   "In the suburb . . . home domesticity could flourish, forgetful of the exploitation on which so much of it was based." Lewis Mumford, *The City in History. Its Origins, its Transformations, and its Prospects* (New York: Harcourt, Brace & World, Inc., 1961), 494.

4   *Theatrum Dei* is a phrase prompted by John Calvin, *Institutio Christianae Religionis*, I.VI.2.

5   Cf. *basileia tou theou* in Acts 1:1-8, and *diakonia tes katallages* in II Corinthians 5:16-21.

6   Cf. Psalm 34:11-14, Matthew 5:9, Romans 12:9-21, James 3:13-28.

7   "Like Chicago, suburban towns are affected by globalization, immigration, and economic restructuring—converging forces that are largely beyond local control". Kenneth Fidel, "The Emergent Suburban Landscape", in John P. Koval, Larry Bennett, Michael I. J. Bennett, Fassil Nemissie, Roberta Garner, Kiljoong Kim (eds.), *The New Chicago: A Social and Cultural Analysis* (Philadelphia: Temple University Press, 2006), 77.

8   "Global village" is a wistful, dated metaphor, I think; in a "global high rise" we exist spatially on top of one another, and time-wise, in each other's hair, compelled to respond, or be unresponsive, to the deeds of virtual strangers in one's face (like junk mail on your personal computer).

9   The way "financial managers" deal with the virtuality of "volatile global capital", (as described in Bob Goudzwaard, Mark Vander Vennen, David Van Heemst, *Hope in Troubled Times: A New Vision for Confronting Global Crises* [Grand Rapids, MI: Baker Books, 2007], 140-141), seems much like players gambling at a casino baccarat table.

10   *archai exousia kostmokratoria* (cf. Ephesians 6:12, Colossians 1:15-16).

11   This thought is hinted at in *De civitate dei*, XIV.28 and XV.4.

12   Cf. Deuteronomy 6:4-9, Leviticus 19:18, Matthew 22:34-40, Romans 13:8-10.

13   My early exploration into the problem of understanding "tradition" and "normative historical change" ("Footprints in the snow", *Philosophia Reformata*, 56, 1 [1991]: 1-34) led to an attempt to reform Herman Dooyeweerd's threefold conception of "historical development" as "differentiate, integrate, individualise". I first enunciated the formulation of "regenerate, speciate, diaconate" in the Festschrift for Robert Knudsen, *Westminster Theological Journal*, 58, 1 (Spring 1996): 41-61, 56-59. Then I related the idea of "historical obedience" to the matter of "glocal culture" in my contribution to the volume honouring George Vandervelde: Michael W. Goheen & Margaret O'Gara (eds.), *That the World May Believe: Essays on Mission and*

Unity (Lanham: University Press of America, 2006), 45-66.

[14] Larry Bennett, "Transforming Public Housing", in Koval et. al., *The New Chicago*, 276.

[15] Charles Suchar, "The Physical Transformation of Metropolitan Chicago: Chicago's Central Area", in Koval et. al., *The New Chicago*, 65, 76.

[16] David Moberg, "Back to Its Roots: The Industrial Areas Foundation and United Power for Action and Justice" in Koval et. al., *The New Chicago*, 239.

[17] "The city is not so much a mass of structures as a complex of interrelated and constantly interacting functions—not along a concentration of power, but a polarization of culture." (Mumford, *City in History*, 85).

[18] I understand Ed Chamber's guideline that Moburg formulates—"Help the powerless in society organize to gain power to get what they *need*' [my emphasis] (Moberg, "Back to Its Roots", 240)—within this "social commonweal" orientation: city-wide *need*, not special interest *wants* is the speciated criterion.

[19] Joseph E. Stiglitz, *Making Globalization Work* (New York: Norton, 2006), 281-285. How about an international convent, like the land mind treaty initiated by Canada's Lord Axworthy (1997), signed to place a heavy tax on all inter-nation military arms sales to be paid by the sellers and buyers to the WHO or charitable foundations for salvaging women and children in war zones.

[20] Jane Jacobs, *The Death and Life of Great American Cities* (New York: Random House, 1961), 150-151, 175, 181, 187-192, 380-381, 393-396, 409-410, 416.

[21] "Each ethnic group [around Devon Avenue] caters mainly to its own population but keeps its doors open to all." (Padma Rangaswamy, "Devon Avenue: A World Market", in Koval et. al., *The New Chicago*, 225).

[22] "Great cities are not like towns, only larger. They are not like suburbs, only denser. They differ from towns and suburbs in basic ways, and one of these is that cities are, by definition, full of strangers." (Jacobs, *Death and Life of Great American Cities*, 30).

[23] *Amérique* (Paris: Grasset, 1986): "*L'Amérique est un gigantesque hologramme . . .*", 33. "*Il est vain d'opposer Death Valley comme phénomème naturel sublime et Las Vegas comme phénomène culturel abject. Car l'un est la face cachée de l'autre, et ils se répondent de part et d'autre du désert. comme le comble de la prostitution et du spectacle au comble du secret et du silence*", 67. "*Les États-Unis, c'est l'utopie réalisée*", 76.

[24] These murals were designed by Ministry of Transport architect Malcolm Bett, and were painted by the non-artist Ministry of Transport painters during slow periods in the winters of 1972-1973. (This information was researched and provided by Lee Kathryn Petrie, Manager of Cultural Programs, Corporate Affairs and Communications, Greater Toronto Airport Authority.)

[25] "I am not interested in art as affirmation or complicity", writes Richard Serra in his 'Introduction by Richard Serra', Clara Weyergraf-Serra and Martha Buskirk (eds.), *The Destruction of Tilted Arc: Documents* (Cambridge: MIT Press, 1991), 13.

Imagining Globalization as a Christian Literary Critic

by Susan VanZanten

Globalization, as both theoretical construct and historical movement, has become increasingly significant in recent literary study. In
2001, the Modern Language Association devoted an entire special issue of their flagship publication, *PMLA*, to the topic of "Globalizing
Literary Studies". Since then, *Cultural Critique* (2004), *American Literature* (2006), and *Modern Language Quarterly* (2007), among other
major literary journals, have published theme issues on globalization.
Giles Gunn comments, "The challenge for students of the humanities .
. . is not to decide whether globalization deserves to be taken seriously
but how best to engage it critically."[1] Literary scholars' struggles to
understand the impact of globalization on their work are complicated
by the fundamental ambiguities of globalization: is it a recent or long-
existent occurrence, is the term descriptive or prescriptive, is globalization the path to world peace or to the regime of Big Brother?

Globalization involves connections across the planet, connections
created and analysed in a variety of ways. A key trope that frames
many of these analyses is that of "flow". For example, one standard
sociology textbook states that globalization involves complex patterns
of "economic, military, technological, ecological, migratory, political
and cultural flows".[2] The absence of religion from this list demonstrates a common blind spot in many discussions of globalization, although the authors may assume that religion is a subset of culture. The
way we imagine and engage with globalization and literature depends
on how we see the world. For those of us who read, study, and delight in literature while dwelling within the Christian metanarrative,[3]
globalization provides new opportunities and poses crucial questions.
I will argue that Christian analysis and assessment should draw primarily on our anthropology—the unique Christian response to the question, "Who are we?" Beginning with the premise that we have been
created by God as physical, social, religious, and imaginative beings,
I will discuss some of the implications of globalization for literary
studies, noting some constructive insights that have emerged. Among
many pertinent issues for the Christian literary critic, I will examine

three aspects of globalization with major implications: globalization's economic impulse, its challenge to the nation-state, and its religious component. The essay will then conclude with a critical analysis of three standard world literature anthologies in one attempt to imagine global literature as a Christian.

The Economic Impulse within the Cultural Flow

Two common approaches to globalization emphasise its economic basis and political effects. While social scientists tend to privilege the economic and political as foundational generators of movement, literary critics have usefully highlighted the role of the textual and symbolic streams of the "global cultural flow".[4] As Gunn explains, "cultural interactions, negotiations, and transformations have often proved at least as fateful as economic or political ones if only because the former have frequently determined the way the latter could be understood and actualized".[5] Similarly, Paul Jay notes, "We can no longer make a clear distinction between exchanges that are purely material and [those that] take place in a cultural economy. Indeed, that these two forms of exchange have always overlapped (and that they are becoming increasingly indistinguishable) is a singular feature of globalization."[6] From Franz Fanon's consideration of the role of narrative in both colonial control and liberation movements,[7] to Appadurai's recent argument for the centrality of the imagination in the global cultural economy, scholars have demonstrated the formative power of metaphor, symbols, and narrative. Yet globalization's insistence on the power of the economic has also contributed to a renewed, post-Marxist awareness that literature is a commodity, rather than exclusively an aesthetic object, and has prompted provocative new explorations of the way in which commoditisation affects literary production and reception. Texts carry "cultural capital",[8] and the material conditions of publishing and distribution play significant, although often unacknowledged, roles in our textual encounters and judgements. Examining the impact of the global economy on the production, study, and enjoyment of literature directly challenges Romantic and modern theories of literature as a purely aesthetic form, free from the taint of capitalism, economics, and the material.

Take the existence of "African literature" as a body of work read across the world. Although oral African literature has been sung and recited for thousands of years in local contexts, the African novel is a relatively recent phenomenon that emerged in the twentieth century with the spread of education, literacy, and independence. The grand African canon manufacturer was William Heinemann Ltd, which inaugurated the Heinemann African Writers Series (AWS) in 1962 with

Chinua Achebe's *Things Fall Apart* (originally published in 1958). The AWS initially planned to produce an affordable paperback series featuring writing by black African authors directed toward a general African readership. But as independent African nations emerged (with the support of nationalistic literature as Fanon predicted), African schools needed inexpensive editions of African texts to replace the European texts of the colonial syllabi. The AWS thus evolved into a major textbook series, publishing work by major contemporary African writers, along with classic earlier works, transcriptions of oral literature, traditional African folk material, and non-fiction accounts of African culture and history. Yet Heinemann was also a global company with an extensive international distribution system in the United States, Britain, and the Commonwealth nations and thus was pivotal in introducing Western readers to Africa literature. Writing in 1992, Kwame Anthony Appiah explains, "One cannot too strongly stress the importance of the fact that what we discuss under the rubric of modern African writing [in the West] is largely what is taught in high schools around the [African] continent."[9] The commercial aspects of publishing had potent effects on what Western readers could even conceive of being "African literature", much less judge aesthetically and critically.

The recent history of the AWS reveals the further changes taking place in the publishing industry with the continuing globalizing reach of technology. An orally chanted praise poem first moves from its original village auditors to a larger audience through transcription and publication, but the advent of digital technology provides an even broader audience as well as an unparalleled speed of dissemination and flow. Although some of the AWS titles remain available in hard copy, many are out of print. Chadwyck-Healey is now publishing the complete series of 359 volumes digitally, with the full run scheduled to be completed in 2008. For a substantial fee, the series will be available on CD-ROM or in perpetual online access. It will also be included as part of Literature Online, the world's largest cross-searchable database of Literature in English, providing even more opportunities for connections and flow.[10] This move from physical to digital text raises substantial questions about accessibility. The unfettering from paper and ink may give more people a chance to read these works, but costs, technological infrastructure, educational opportunities, and readers' preferences will also affect distribution. While providing a rich resource for scholars, the digital collection will probably be less accessible for students and general readers, both in Africa and internationally. What this might do to the canon of African literature remains to be seen, although Chadwyck-Healey has stated that in the spirit of the original publication mission of AWS, it is committed to making the series available for free or at a reduced cost for African readers.[11]

Due to economic and educational scarcities, Africa has only a miniscule market of readers for physical texts, much less electronic ones. Many African writers are published overseas initially and only later find a national or regional African publisher.[12] Writing in English and, to a lesser degree, in French is a decided advantage, making it far more likely that a global publisher will acquire the text. Works that materially exist only in local journals and periodicals, issued by small indigenous publishers, and even on websites and blogs, have far less chance of making their way into either the Western pedagogical or the "world" literature canon. Harald Weinrich laments that those "writers who lack the good fortune of having grown up in a genuinely anglophone or a postcolonially anglophone land" will find it difficult to become internationally recognised.[13] The majority of authors who have achieved critical and public acclaim as global writers—such as Salmon Rushdie, J.M. Coetzee, Michael Ondaatje, Zadie Smith, and Jhumpa Lahiri—write and publish in English.

These swirling eddies of economic and symbolic exchanges make sense to Christian critics, who embrace the material world in their rejection of Gnosticism and Manichaeism, but also acknowledge how texts embody worldviews and are able to affect material life by informing responses, impacting political activity, and inspiring action. Reductive views of texts as economic tokens of exchange (Marxism), transcendent aesthetic expressions (Romanticism), or determinative systems of power (Poststructuralism) all oversimplify the multifaceted nature of the created world. Christians believe that they live in a material world in which physical and economic realities play a role, yet they also acknowledge that humanity has been gifted with abilities to and responsibilities for entering history and acting in meaningful ways, including writing and reading creative texts. Christian readers in an increasingly global world thus should remain alert to the complex interactions between economic and symbolic exchanges, between commodity and creativity.

The Contested Nation-State: Centre and Margins

Economic analyses of globalization often predict the triumph of transnational capitalism and an accompanying decline in the political sovereignty of the nation-state. The economic downturn of 2008 may belie the triumphalism, but the international nature of both the crisis and its potential solutions continues to challenge nineteenth-century political divisions. The world is allegedly entering "a new epoch of human history" in which traditional nation-states will become irrelevant.[14] The ubiquity of transnational corporations, the worldwide culture promulgated by mass media, the spread of democracy and capitalism, and shifts of populations through exile and immigration all contribute to this state of affairs. Neo-liberals optimistically view globalization as a further stage of the spread of Enlightenment values, such as democracy, freedom, and universal appreciation for Shakespeare. Although neo-Marxists agree that globalization promotes similarity, they fear that this flattening unanimity will consist of the crass "Americanization" of the world or "the triumph of an oppressive global capitalism".[15] Other theorists do not foresee the complete destruction of the nation state, arguing that the binary identifications established by nationalism (in/out; them/us; citizens/aliens) are becoming more rigid as the regional blocs of Europe, the Asia-Pacific, and North America dominate the international economy. Such sceptics believe that "deeply rooted patterns of inequality and hierarchy in the world economy . . . contribute[s] to the advance of both fundamentalism and aggressive nationalism such that rather than the emergence of a global civilization . . . the world is fragmenting into civilizational blocs and cultural and ethnic enclaves".[16] When "things fall apart", as William Butler Yeats wrote presciently in 1921 and was echoed by Chinua Achebe in 1948, "mere anarchy is loosed upon the world". Tribalism trumps cosmopolitanism, perhaps increasingly so as the economic picture darkens.

Such disputes over the history, status, and future of the nation-state have profound repercussions for the way in which we conceive of and organise the study of literature.

The strength and identity of diasporic communities; the emerging global genres of graphic novels, YouTube videos, and other "Webspace" productions; and the anthropological theory of "traveling cultures",[17] all work against the traditional division of literature on national or even regional grounds. "If globalization is characterized by the growing deterritorialization of culture", Jay states, "by the fluidity of its movement across nation-state boundaries, and by its tendency to survive and mutate in diasporic pockets thriving within the borders of multiple countries . . . then the disruption of traditional connections among territory, culture, nation, and literary expression will increase".[18] However, the relationship of national and global remains contested and fluid. Cultural flows move from East to West as well as West to East, South to North as well as North to South. The globalization of texts is chaotic, syncretic, code-mixing, polyvalent, and, for some, epitomises true postmodernity.[19] Postcolonial theory's concepts of ambivalence and hybridisation help us grasp the multi-directional flow of globalization. Texts are thereby no longer seen solely as productions of national identity, but now are also studied as participants in a global culture. The modern idea of the self, formed by individual and national identity, is being replaced by a textually constructed postmodern global self. *The Autobiography of Benjamin Franklin* at

one time formed a united vision of American identity, but today's cosmopolitan citizen inhabits multitudinous strands of being—cultural,
ethnic, religious—in works such as Jhumpa Lahiri's *The Namesake*.

Globalization's growing challenges to the centrality of the nation-
state provokes us to re-think literary studies' customary nationalist
paradigm. Does it make sense in today's world to study "Contemporary
Canadian Literature"? How legitimate is it to organise our study of
literature by national units of American, Australian, British, Canadian
or South African literature? Why should we confine our analysis of
globalization to modern industrialisation, nationalism, and capitalism
when globalization, it can be argued, stretches back to the fifteenth century, if not earlier? Such presentism ignores the age of world empires,
the initial spread of Christianity and Islam, the development of maps
and maritime travel, global exploration, the hunt for silk and spices, and
colonial expansion.[20] If one understands globalization as part of a long
historical process rather than solely a post-modern phenomenon, should
we even study "Seventeenth-Century British Literature"? Perhaps we
should return to the masterpieces of national literature and consider
them in new contexts, examining their global as well as European or
North American context. I am not arguing that we should completely
give up the nationalist paradigm in literary studies but rather that we
abandon that paradigm at strategic points. Recent work in Shakespeare
studies, for example, has examined texts such as *The Tempest* in light
of sixteenth-century global expansion, as well as the ways in which
Shakespearean plays have, or have not, been easily translated today into
other languages and cultures. If Renaissance definitions of race support
the lust for world exploration and the definition of European identity,
how do these ideas inform *Othello* or *The Merchant of Venice*? Why
is *King Lear* so popular in East Asia? And why do African audiences
enjoy *Macbeth* but have such difficulty with *Hamlet*, finding it entirely
reasonable that a dead chief's younger brother would marry his elder
brother's widow?[21] Frederick Buell distinguishes the approach in which
a First World academic provides an "ethnoperspective" on Shakespeare,
from "postcolonial Shakespeare", which "has left the bush, has been
conducting its work in both Western and postcolonial academies, and
has been dedicated from the start to criticizing and refiguring the discourses of those academies. It seeks, in short, to transform and pluralize
common discourses, not inhabit separate universes."[22]

The temptation to continue inhabiting separate universes is highlighted by Shu-Mei Shih, who lambasts the discipline's attempts to
globalize literary studies through "technologies of recognition" that
produce "the West" as the agent and "the rest" as the object of recognition. While Shih acknowledges that the "sheer negligence or
feigned ignorance" of others that precedes recognition is the greater
evil, she tartly identifies the Western-centric nature of many analyses

of global literature, which quickly slip into binary oppositions of "us" and "them".[23] Shih advocates an "intersubjective" approach, in which texts exist in a complex field of relations to multiple subjects and objects: "Dialogic intersubjectivity is . . . always among more than two. Although the West contributes to the non-West's sense of self . . . there is always room for other relational identifications and identities and even for disidentifications."[24] This approach calls for interactions from multiple viewpoints, for multiple-voiced conversations rather than simple one-to-one dialogues. Furthermore, Shi argues that national identifications should be suspended in favour of linguistic locations to avoid labelling works or authors as "the exceptional particular"; for example, the 2000 Nobel Prize winner in Literature, Gao Zingjian, is better read and understood as a Sinophone rather than Chinese author, given his residency in France and fluency in French. By moving from national groupings to linguistic groupings, we could define the local in non-territorial ways.

While nationalist paradigms are important aspects of conversations about texts produced as part of a drive to establish national identity, even these local concerns have global components. For example, the "Young America" movement, exemplified by Irving's "Rip Van Winkle" or Emerson's "The American Scholar", should be viewed within the context of the worldwide development of nationalism in the nineteenth century. And even Emerson's much-vaunted "Americanism", Lawrence Buell demonstrates in his Phi Beta Kappa award-winning *Emerson*, was thoroughly permeated by Emerson's extensive reading in East Asian sources. The great transcendentalist father's local act of constructing a uniquely "American" identity is, in fact, intrinsically interrelated with global currents. The existence of the global produces the local: "globalization . . . covertly produce[s] cultural differences rather than efface[s] them".[25]

Similarly, many twentieth-century works, such as Ngugi wa Thiong'o's *A Grain of Wheat* or Nelson Mandela's *Long Walk to Freedom*, are part of a postcolonial revolutionary nationalism, in which narratives serve to create national identity. In Fanon's analysis, such narratives—as opposed to the earlier demeaning colonial narratives and initial impulses toward nostalgic national narratives—create a true national culture. Interpretation from a nationalist perspective is thus crucial. But Fanon continues by insisting that a fully developed nationalism is tolerant and syncretic, "will make such a culture open to other cultures and . . . will enable it to influence and permeate other cultures".[26] Many efforts to create community by asserting national identity through textual production and symbolic representation speak in two directions: the local and the global. For example, Achebe writes *Things Fall Apart* to show his African readers "that we in Africa did not hear of culture for the first time from Europeans" as well as to suggest to his European readers some of the complexity and humanity of indigenous Igbo culture.[27]

From within the Christian worldview, the decline or demise of the nation-state may pose troubling issues with respect to peace and order, but in terms of allegiance and identity, the nation-state makes many demands antithetical to Christian commitment. The idolisation of one's national identity often comes at the cost of authentic Christian commitment to love of the neighbour, care for the earth, and worship of the one true God. Reading, analysing and enjoying global literary texts may prompt us to question and redefine our ultimate allegiances and identities. Taking a global approach to literature allows us to balance our local identity—given to us through particular embodiment in a physical, social world—with a cosmopolitan identity endowed by humanity's common formation in the image of God and responsibility for the created world.

A Post-Secular World: The Spread of Christianity

The third aspect of globalization that I wish to discuss has had less impact on literary studies to date than the economic impulse and the future of the nation-state. One major flow consistently overlooked in discussions about the globalization of literary studies is the spread of Christianity. Modernisation and globalization have led not to secularisation, as Western scholars once expected, but rather to an unprecedented expansion of religious faith. We live in a post-secular age. Peter Berger, one of the most prominent proponents of the secularisation thesis in the 1950s and 1960s, now admits, "the assumption that we live in a secularised world is false. The world today, with some exceptions . . . is as furiously religious as it ever was, and in some places more so than ever."[28] One central characteristic of this post-secular world is the fact that Christianity is no longer the religion of the West. A huge demographic shift is underway. While Christian faith ebbs in the North and West, it continues to rise in the South and East.[29] As Philip Jenkins says, "the center of gravity in the Christian world has shifted inexorably southward" during the last century.[30] Much to the surprise of secularisation theorists, the postcolonial world did not become a secular world: "With the dismantling of colonial empires after World War II, there was a widespread assumption that Christianity would dwindle and die in Africa, India, and Southeast Asia. It has been assumed . . . that Christianity's presence and prestige were integrally related to its perceived association with the colonial enterprise."[31] Instead, more people have converted to Christianity since the end of colonial rule than in the entire period of the colonial empires.[32] Some globalization theorists view the spread of Christianity as another instance of Western imperialism,[33] but Lamin Sanneh's work suggests the Eurocentric bias of such claims. In reference to indigenous societies' "discovery" of Christianity, Sannah states, "Christianity was received and expressed through the cultures, customs, and traditions of the people affected" rather than replicating "Christian forms and patterns developed in Europe".[34] Many African scholars, such as Kwame Bediako, claim that Christianity is an African religion, not an import; it is "the renewal of a non-Western religion".[35] Rather than a unidirectional current of European Christianity flooding Africa, we find a more complex multidirectional flow underway.

Theological transformations occur as African, Asian, and Latin American Christians read the scriptures in differing cultural contexts. This struggle to understand the gospel within a new culture has existed ever since Peter received the stunning news that the kingdom of God also included the Gentiles. Because humans are creationally formed as social and cultural beings, they can only apprehend the Christian *kerygma* within a social and material context. In different cultural contexts, language, narratives, images, and metaphors—the bread and butter of the literary trade—help form new understandings of Christianity, because one crucial way in which human beings explore ideas and images is through the creation of stories, poems, legends, songs, and tales. Missiologist Andrew Walls predicts that the massive relocations of Christianity will produce another cultural transformation like that which took place in the early Christian church's interaction with Greek culture. When Christianity is received and expressed through new cultures, customs, and traditions, both the Christian tradition and cultural productions are transformed as indigenous peoples struggle with the degree to which they need to reject their own history and culture to become Christian, as well as the degree to which they can accommodate Christianity to indigenous practices. Although we may think about such hybridisation as a one-way process—that is, Christian images and ideas taking on a new life by entering into a local culture—the reverse also occurs, as indigenous cultural expressions facilitate new understandings of Christianity. In *Jesus of Africa*, Diane Stinton examines the ways in which African Christians have "understood and responded to Jesus in light of received biblical teaching and their own cultural heritage".[36] She identifies four overlapping models of African Christologies: Jesus as Healer, Ancestor, Family or Friend, and Chief or King. As African Christianity increasingly touches Western society, these new models may begin to inform Western theology and art. Just as Dante in medieval Italy or Melville in Jacksonian America wrestled with Christianity in the images and stories that were part of their culture, so today we find rural African women hearing a sermon in a city and then composing songs on their way back to their villages, producing oral literature that both translates the Christian message and transforms it, producing new artistic understandings.

If "cultural interpenetration and intermingling have become the global norm",[37] both Christianity and literature will undergo massive changes as the demographic shift to the South and East continues. Consequently, we need to make a concentrated effort to study the new literatures coming out of the Christian South and East. As Christianity continues to become a non-Western religion, the production of literature in global population centres will emerge from predominantly Christian cultures and societies. If, as Gunn says, symbolic interactions, negotiations, and transformations determine the way in which economic and political interactions are understood and actualised, they play an even more significant role in religious interactions. The North's and West's understanding of Christianity will be transformed as Southern and Eastern Christianity affects us. These multi-directional flows of meaning, power, and effect will need much study.

The failure of the secularisation thesis also suggests the need for critical re-examination of literature emerging from twentieth-century world encounters. If Christianity was not ebbing during this period, it might have played a more prominent role in literature than we have acknowledged. Jenkins points out that in a recent survey of *100 Christian Books That Changed the Century*, the only work by a Southern writer was *Cry, the Beloved Country*, by white South African Alan Paton.[38] But what was happening in the world of literature during the twentieth century in Africa, Latin America, and Asia? And how did that reflect and inform the massive religious transformations underway? Surely Shusako Endo's *Silence*, Ngugi wa Thiong'o's *A River Between*, and *I, Rigoberto Menchu* represent and reflect on momentous aspects of the twentieth century. Most secular literary critics have ignored the complex role of Christianity in the development of postcolonial cultures and literature, preferring to associate it simplistically with imperialism and oppression.[39]

Another crucial facet of post-secularism is the global spread and rising profile of Islam, accompanied by a profusion of misunderstandings, negative stereotyping, and internal hermeneutic contestations. The *World Christian Database* estimates that Muslims will make up 21.5 percent of the world's population by 2010, up from 12.6 percent in 1910. During the same period, Christian religious affiliation is projected to hold steady at around 34 percent.[40] The complexities contained within the rise of Islam in the contemporary world are represented in literary criticism by the breadth of perspectives extending from Edward Said's *Orientalism* to Salmon Rushdie's *The Satanic Verses*. With rising numbers of both Muslims and Christians, the impact of fundamentalism in both traditions, and the lessening of national power, the post-secular age may lead to tragic conflict. When Jenkins speaks of the "next Christendom", he alludes to the first

Christendom—the shared religious worldview of the Middle Ages that controlled politics and society. Jenkins posits that as nation-states are weakened by globalization, a similar unified global Christianity could emerge. He warns that the first Christendom included the horrors of the Crusades, the Inquisition, witch hunts, and religious pogroms, as Christendom defined itself in terms of what it was not. Pointing to some of the most violent instances, Jenkins sombrely concludes that "[the] Christian-Muslim conflict may in fact prove one of the closest analogies between the Christian world that was, and the one coming into being".[41] As Christianity continues its global spread, we have a responsibility to use the resources of our discipline to try to avoid the terrible errors evident in the history of the first Christendom. As Guillory demonstrates, in the construction of cultural capital, *who* reads and *why* people read are as important as *what* is read. We don't want a new Christendom that repeats the appalling past of the first Christendom. We need to insist publicly on the value of contributions from local points of view. We need to read and dialogue with a variety of texts arising from the Islamic world. We need to recognise and call attention to our all-too-human tendency to define ourselves or our community by positing binary Others.

World Literature Anthologies: An Embarrassment of Riches

Globalization's greatest impact on literary studies has been in the expansion of the canon, with the goal of making our reading and view of the world less Eurocentric and more cognisant of other non-Western cultural traditions. This change is clearly evident in the recent publication history of North American textbooks of world literature, which reveals a spiralling vortex of economic and symbolic exchanges in definitions of world literature, but also demonstrates markedly different concepts of the nature of the global. For the Christian scholar committed to dialogue and cosmopolitanism, the leading texts offer conspicuously different choices for globalizing literary studies.

The concept of world literature began in 1827 when Goethe coined the term *Weltliteratur*, operating within a then-prevalent European assumption that literature uniquely captured the national spirit, or the expression of a people and their culture. Goethe envisioned world literature as moving beyond texts of European national identity to include Chinese novels and Serbian poems, but until fairly recently, most textbooks in "world" literature were decidedly Eurocentric. The globalization of literary studies in the Anglo-American academy did not begin until the 1970s, when the discipline's conception of the "world" began to move beyond the West. Initially, publishers complemented an established collection by issuing a supplementary volume of non-Western texts. This process began in 1977 when Norton published a "companion volume", *Masterpieces of the Orient*, to the standard anthology it had been publishing since 1956, the *Norton Anthology of World Masterpieces*. Subsequently, in 1995, Norton produced a two-volume "expanded edition" of World Masterpieces by adding texts from Asia, Africa, the Caribbean, and native America. That same year St. Martin's two-volume *Western Literature in a World Context* put the "world" back into world literature, although even its title continued to privilege the Western tradition. In 1999 Prentice Hall issued *Literatures of Asia, Africa, and Latin America*, designed to complement the fifth edition of its two-volume *Literature of the Western World*. The scope of world literature was expanding, but the cohering principle, for the most part, remained the centrality of the Western tradition.

The first truly "global" anthology, *The World of Literature*, was also published in 1999 by Prentice Hall. This huge volume emphasised cross-cultural relationships and was arranged into three chronological periods (Ancient, Middle, and Modern) without a distinctive European centre. The ironic fact that this text competed against Prentice Hall's own simultaneously published three-volume anthology can be traced to the turbulent history of publishing mergers and acquisitions. *The World of Literature* project originally began in 1994 with Macmillan, but when Prentice-Hall bought out Macmillan's American branch, it acquired the project, and the text went through three editors before finally coming into and rapidly going out of print. A similar fate overtook *Modern Literatures of the Non-Western World*, published by HarperCollins Educational, which was acquired by Addison Wesley Longman in 1996. The global market for literary texts, competing commercial interests, and the growth in international conglomerates substantially affected the possibilities of symbolic exchange.

In the current transnational circulation of cultural capital, world literature instructors can choose from three standard anthologies: *The Norton Anthology of World Literature* (2002), which expands the still available *Norton Anthology of World Masterpieces*; *The Bedford Anthology of World Literature* (2003), which replaced St. Martin's *Western Literature in a World Context*; and *The Longman Anthology of World Literature* (2004), the newest entry in the world literature course-adoption sweepstakes.[42] In these anthologies, world literature's scope continues to expand, but each conceives of and presents globalization differently. All three take the currently popular anthology format of six individual volumes. With 4 million words crammed into 6,000 pages, each is an impressive collection, providing, as the editors of two out of the three put it, "an embarrassment of riches". All have complementary websites with supporting material, including helpful audio pronunciation guides. All use similar chronological divisions for the six volumes, although other strategies of organisation differ, as we shall see. And all include the complete texts of *Gilgamesh, The Odyssey, Agamemnon, Oedipus the King, Medea, Lysistrata, Sakuntala and the Ring of Recollection, Beowulf, Inferno, Candide, Notes from the Underground, The Metamorphosis*, and *Things Fall Apart*. Instructors face difficult choices, based upon their own definition of world literature, favourite works, and pedagogical objectives. Each anthology has a distinct character, which I will illustrate by discussing its treatment of the Hebrew and Christian Scriptures.

The *Norton*, despite significant geographical expansion, is the least global in its approach. It overtly embraces its great-books heritage, arguing that masterpieces "repay close study", based upon their artistry and complexity.[43] World literature is made up of such masterpieces, which are both culturally rooted and universally applicable, but the *Norton* does little to demonstrate the ways in which these masterpieces interact across cultures. Texts are presented primarily as aesthetic objects within certain cultural parameters, and global connections are made only on the supporting website that technology has made *de rigueur* today. Except for the opening of Volume 1, the first five volumes are organised solely by region: i.e. "Poetry and Thought in Early China", or "The Renaissance in Europe". In the sixth volume, *The Twentieth Century*, geographic divisions are jettisoned for one sweeping category of "The Modern World: Self and Others in Global Context". Here entries are arranged by order of the author's birth date, because "separation in the modern world is no longer possible".[44] This volume takes literary modernism as its thematic centre, examining the ways in which Anglo-European authors struggle with language and how that struggle is refracted in twentieth-century non-Western literature. The structure of the *Norton* implies that globalization is a twentieth-century phenomenon, and even then, the Western tradition lies at the heart of the *Norton*'s universe.

This Eurocentric focus is apparent in the *Norton*'s treatment of biblical pericopes, all of which appear in the King James Version—significant for its literary influences, but not notable for linguistic accuracy or historical sensitivity. The Hebrew Scriptures are termed "The Bible: The Old Testament" and are grouped with *Gilgamesh* and a few Egyptian poems in Volume 1. New Testament passages are placed at the opening of Volume 2 in a section oddly titled, "From Roman Empire to Christian Europe", which consists solely of these biblical passages and some excerpts from St. Augustine. There's nothing from either Rome or Christian Europe. The Bible is thus presented as solely a Christian text, with no attention to its Jewish identity, and of primary interest for the imagery and language the King James Version provides for the development of Western literature.

If the Norton represents a traditional approach, *The Bedford Anthology of World Literature* is the exuberant Old Navy of anthologies. With a large font, two-colour design, and three hundred illustrations, the *Bedford* has a visual liveliness that matches its expansive editorial drive. Each of its six volumes contains both regional divisions and two types of cross-cultural clusters. Clusters called "In the World" trace themes such as love, religion, women's rights, travel, freedom, and imperialism. "In the Tradition" clusters highlight a specific literary tradition, such as courtly love lyrics or war literature. Introductions end with a list of suggested connections to texts in other volumes. The *Bedford*'s supporting website includes discussions of the ways in which themes of world literature continue to apply to the twenty-first century (relating *Things Fall Apart*, for example, with the events of 9/11).

There's no question but that the *Bedford*'s scope is expansive. What is lacking, however, is a sense of coherence. What led its editors to choose one author over another, one work over another, one tradition over another? What *isn't* world literature? The Preface gives no clear editorial philosophy. "We have", the editors vaguely say, "tried to open new perspectives and possibilities".[45] The canon of world literature, they comment, is now broader; we no longer use formalistic or generic principles of organisation; there is greater interest in literature's historical and cultural contexts. But while the contextualising material is impressive, we are nonetheless left with an impression of an immense grab bag of possibilities. The hodgepodge of approaches is apparent in the *Bedford*'s treatment of the Scriptures. Book 1's selections of Hebrew Scriptures are given in the New English translation, because it is "unusually clear and readable".[46] Material from Genesis, Exodus, Job, the Psalms, and the Song of Songs appears in a regional section, "The Ancient Hebrews"; a passage from Deuteronomy is found in an excellent cross-cultural cluster called "Creating Cosmogony". While the *Norton* associates the New Testament with the fate of the Roman Empire, the *Bedford*'s passages from Luke, Matthew, and Corinthians occur in a regional section linking Christianity and Islam, acknowledging the crucial nature of these religious interactions.

The third major collection, the *Longman Anthology of World Literature*, has clearly benefited from the superb guidance of its general editor, David Damrosch. His philosophy is concisely presented in the introduction and visibly governs the editorial choices: works of world literature are those texts that gain in translation, whether cultural, historical, or linguistic. They can circulate profitably, in an intellectual sense. Some great works are so closely tied to their local origin that they don't generate much meaning outside that context. Other great works may be read one way in a national context and a different way in a global context. Damrosch's pithy yet rich Preface describes the "double conversation" in which works of world literature participate: "with their culture of origin and with the varied contexts into which they travel away from home".[47] Selections, then, are made of "compelling texts" that "foster connections across time and space", but these texts are initially introduced and located within their particular cultural contexts.[48] "Our introductions don't seek to 'cover' the material", Damrosch writes, "but instead try to uncover it, to provide ways in and connections outward".[49]

The contextualising and connecting material provided by the *Longman* occurs in the printed text, rather than being exiled to the website. Regional divisions predominate in the first three volumes, given the more geographically discrete development of regional traditions before the mobility of the early modern era of exploration. The global organisation of the last three volumes reflects the increasing circulation of world literature. All six open with a section called "Crosscurrents", highlighting a period-specific issue faced by many cultures, often in conversation with each other. For example, *The Medieval Era* opens with "Contact, Conflict, and Conversion", bringing together tales of travel from a variety of intrepid people who ventured beyond their own borders. Besides the connections facilitated in Crosscurrents, the *Longman* also supplies a grouping called "Resonances", brief selections that illuminate a particular work through source readings or responses from other centuries or regions. Following the *Odyssey* in Volume A, for example, are responses to Homer by Kafka, Derek Walcott, and the Greek poet George Seferis. The conditions of textual production and exchange are thus addressed.

The Scripture selections demonstrate the way in which the *Longman* orchestrates the double conversation between culture of origin and differing contexts of reading. A wide variety of translations and organisational sites are employed for biblical pericopes. Genesis 1-11, in an energetic translation by Robert Alter, appears in the Crosscurrents section on "Creation Myths" that opens Volume A. The Song of Songs (Jerusalem Bible translation) and Job (Revised Standard Version) are in a regional grouping, "The Ancient Near East". The Joseph story and Ruth (New International Version) are presented in a thematic unit called "Strangers in a Strange Land". Unlike the *Bedford* and the *Norton*, the New Testament selections are found in the anthology's first volume, presented in the context of "The Culture of Rome and the Beginnings of Christianity". Selections from Luke and Romans (New Revised Standard Version) thus appear together with those from Catullus, Petronius, Tacitus, and Juvenal. Scripture selections again appear in Volume C as part of a cross-cultural focus on the rise of the vernacular, with comparative early modern translations of Psalm 23 (the Vulgate and the Bay Psalm book) and the Gospel of Luke. The broad variety of translations and contexts provided by the Longman for the Scriptural pericopes simultaneously captures their diverse historical locations, enduring literary and spiritual legacies, and complex global interrelationships.

As the evolving nature and current contents of these three standard anthologies demonstrate, globalization affects the study of literature today in multiple ways. These repercussions stem both from the material and economic realities of literature, and from globalization's challenges to the dominant cultural model of the nation-state—two developments with special resonances within a Christian understanding of the world. Furthermore, as the Christian church grows in the global south and east, and the number of Muslims expands across the globe, producing, reading, and interpreting texts will constitute a crucial flow in the tides of world history. Christian literary critics must pay close and careful attention to these developments so that the reading of literature will affirm a Christian anthropology and thereby cultivate Neighbours rather than produce Others.

SUSAN VANZANTEN (Ph.D., Emory University) is Professor of English and Director of the Center for Scholarship and Faculty Development at Seattle Pacific University. She is the author of *A Story of South Africa: J.M. Coetzee's Fiction in Context* (Harvard, 1991) and *Truth and Reconciliation: The Confessional Mode in South African Literature* (Heinemann, 2002), is coauthor, with Roger Lundin, of *Literature Through the Eyes of Faith* (Harper, 1989), and is the editor of *Postcolonial Literature and the Biblical Call for Justice* (University Press of Mississippi, 1994).

NOTES

[1] Giles Gunn, "Introduction: Globalizing Literary Studies", *PMLA* 116 (2001), 21.

[2] David Held, et al, *Global Transformations: Politics, Economics, and Culture* (Stanford: Stanford University Press, 1999), 7.

[3] My analysis will rely on an understanding of worldview, including the Christian worldview, as being narrative rather than propositional, dynamic rather than absolute, and dialogical rather than monologic. In other words, I agree more with N.T. Wright than with Dockery and Thornbury. See N.T. Wright, *The New Testament and the People of God* (Minneapolis: Fortress Press, 1992), 122-126; David S. Dockery and Gregory Alan Thornbury (eds.), *Shaping a Christian Worldview: The Foundations of Christian Higher Education* (Nashville: Broadman & Holman, 2002). On worldview, see David K. Naugle, *Worldview: The History of a Concept* (Grand Rapids, MI: Eerdmans, 2002).

[4] Arjun Appadurai, *Modernity at Large: Cultural Dimensions of Globalization* (Minneapolis: University of Minnesota Press, 1996), 37.

[5] Gunn, "Globalizing", 21.

[6] Paul Jay, "Beyond Discipline? Globalization and the Future of English", *PMLA* 116 (2001): 37.

[7] Franz Fanon, *The Wretched of the Earth* (tr. Constance Farrington; New York: Grove Press, 1963).

[8] Pierre Bourdieu's theory of cultural capital has been most usefully elaborated with respect to literary studies by John Guillory, *Cultural Capital: The Problem of Literary Canon Formation* (Chicago: University of Chicago Press, 1993).

[9] Kwame Anthony Appiah, *In My Father's House: Africa in the Philosophy of Culture* (New York: Oxford University Press, 1992), 55.

[10] Chadwyck-Healey Literature Collections, http://collections.chadwyck.com/marketing/products/about_ilc.jsp?collection=aws (accessed 25 June 2008).

[11] Proquest Company, *Proquest to Support African Libraries, Universities with Access to New Online "African Writers Series"*, Cambridge, UK, 10 August 2005.

[12] For a case study of the canonical rise of Zimbabwean novelist Tsitsi Dangarembga, see Susan VanZanten Gallagher, "Contingencies and Intersections: The Formation of Pedagogical Canons", *Pedagogy* 1 (2001), 57-66.

[13] Harald Weinrich, "Chamisso, Chamisso Authors, and Globalization", *PMLA* 119 (2004), 1345.

[14] Held, et al, *Global Transformations*, 4.

[15] Ibid, 4.

[16] Ibid, 6.

[17] Reinaldo Laddaga, "From Work to Conversation: Writing and Citizenship in a Global Age", *PMLA* 122 (2007), 451. James Clifford proposes that contemporary anthropologists pay new attention to the mobility of cultures as well as the dis-locations of culture, *Routes: Travel and Translation in the Late Twentieth Century* (Cambridge: Harvard University Press, 1997).

[18] Jay, "Beyond Discipline?" 38.

[19] Frederick Buell, *National Culture and the New Global System* (Baltimore: Johns Hopkins University Press, 1994), 327.

[20] On globalization as a recent phenomenon, see Anthony Giddens, *The Consequences of Modernity* (London: Polity, 1990); and David Harvey, *The Condition of Postmodernity: An Enquiry into the Origins of Cultural Change* (New York: Blackwell, 1989). On the long history of globalization, see Roland Robertson, *Globalization: Social Theory and Global Culture* (London: Sage, 1992).

[21] Imtiaz Habib, *Shakespeare and Race: Postcolonial Praxis in the Early Modern Period* (Lanham, MD: University Press of America, 1999); Laura Bohannan, "Shakespeare in the Bush", *Natural History* (Aug/Sept. 1966), 28-33. Rpt. in *Language: Readings in Language and Culture*, Virginia P. Clark, Paul A. Eschholz, and Alfred F. Rosa (eds.) (New York: St. Martin's, 1998), 27-36.

[22] Buell, *National Culture*, 230.

[23] Shu-Mei Shih, "Global Literature and the Technologies of Recognition", *PMLA* 119 (2004), 17.

[24] Ibid, 18.

[25] Lawrence Buell, *Emerson* (Cambridge: Harvard University Press, 2004), 9.

[26] Fanon, *Wretched*, 245.

[27] Cosmo Pieterse and Dennis Duerden (eds.), *African Writers Talking* (New York: Africana, 1972), 7.

[28] Peter Berger, ed., *The Desecularization of the World: Resurgent Religion and World Politics* (Grand Rapids, MI: Eerdmans, 1999), 2.

[29] In 1900, eighty percent of the world's Christians lived in Europe and North America, but in 2000, sixty percent of the world's Christians were living in Africa, Asia, and Latin America. David J. Barrett and Todd M. Johnson, "Annual Statistical Tables on Global Mission: 2004", *International Bulletin of Missionary Research* 28, 1 (2004), 25.

[30] Philip Jenkins, *The Next Christendom: The Coming of Global Christianity* (Oxford: Oxford University Press, 2002), 2.

[31] Donald M. Lewis (ed.), *Christianity Reborn: The Global Expansion of Evangelicalism in the Twentieth-Century* (Grand Rapids, MI: Eerdmans, 2004), 2.

[32] Lamin Sanneh, *Whose Religion is Christianity? The Gospel beyond the West* (Grand Rapids, MI: Eerdmans, 2003), 41.

[33] Steve Brouwer, Paul Gifford, and Susan D. Rose, *Exporting the American Gospel: Global Christian Fundamentalism* (New York: Routledge, 1996).

[34] Sanneh, *Whose Religion*, 22.

[35] Kwame Bediako, *Christianity in Africa: The Renewal of a Non-Western Religion* (Edinburgh: Edinburgh University Press, 1995).

[36] Diane B. Stinton, *Jesus of Africa: Voices of Contemporary African Christology* (Marynoll: Orbis, 2004), 6.

[37] Frederick Buell, *National Culture*, 312.

[38] Jenkins, *The Next Christendom*, 4.

[39] See Susan VanZanten Gallagher, "New Conversations on Postcolonial Literature", *Postcolonial Literature and the Biblical Call for Justice* (Jackson: University Press of Mississippi, 1994), 3-33.

[40] http://www.gordonconwell.edu/ockenga/globalchristianity/resources.php (accessed 15 March 2009). Despite the percentages holding steady, with the steady increase in the world's population, the total number of Christians has increased.

[41] Jenkins, *The Next Christendom*, 12.

[42] Prentice Hall appears to have given up on a global approach: *The World of Literature* is out of print, as is *Literatures of Asia, Africa, and Latin America*, although some of the latter's content now appears in three individual, regional texts: *Literature of Latin America*, *Literature of the Middle East*, and *Literature of Asia* (all 2003). (A volume of African literature has never appeared.)

[43] Sarah Lawall et al. (eds.), *The Norton Anthology of World Literature*, 2nd ed., Vol. 6 (New York: Norton, 2002), xvii.

[44] Lawall et al., *Norton Anthology*, xviii.

[45] Paul Davis et al (eds.), *The Bedford Anthology of World Literature*, Vol. 1 (New York: Pearson Longman, 2004), vi.

[46] Davis et al, *Bedford Anthology*, 138.

[47] David Damrosch et al. (eds.), *The Longman Anthology of World Literature*, vol. 1 (New York: Pearson Longman, 2004), xix.

[48] Damrosch et al., *Longman Anthology*, xxi, xx.

[49] Ibid, xxii.

Education, Globalization, and Discipleship

by Harro Van Brummelen

My university degrees happen to be from the three Canadian universities ranked in the top fifty in the World University Rankings published annually in the *Times Higher Education* [THE].[1] The alleged legitimacy of these rankings is underscored by the fact that THE bases them on a carefully weighted average of six scores based on "120,000 data points" related to teaching, research, globalization, and employability.[2]

THE is proud that its rankings are its most widely read feature and that they provoke strong global reactions. The publication points out that as a result of its rankings, Germany gives increased funding to some smaller research institutions in efforts to improve their rankings. Similarly, many Asian institutions implement strategies to gain standing in the top 100. Its rankings, THE adds, are particularly useful "for ambitious staff operating in an increasingly globalized university world" since they reveal an institution's place in "the world market".[3]

McGill University's principal Heather Munroe-Blum has certainly boasted about the fact that her university is the top ranked Canadian one (20th in the world in 2008). She holds that Canadian universities must engage in a race to attract global financial and intellectual resources and build global networks to "spark innovation and generate prosperity".[4] In order to win in the world market and advance economically and socially, universities need to be like McGill with large numbers of international and globally-engaged faculty and alumni who purposefully collaborate in global knowledge networks.[5] Munroe-Blum uses both the reality of globalization and the need to retain a high ranking in the World University Rankings to urge the Canadian and Quebec governments to provide more funding for higher education.

Rankings of universities, including THE ones, have been criticised, of course. Should the number of citations of its faculty outweigh what an institution contributes to the welfare of its community? Should scores that employers give universities, indicators of the perceived economic contributions of its graduates, play such a foremost role? Should universities be compared as a whole or, rather, on the basis of their mission and vision that indicates specific functions and

orientations? Does a university with an overall score of 69.9 deserve a
rank that is 20 higher than one with a score of 67.9?

The World University Rankings reflect the worldview biases of
those who construct the statistical process.[6] One such worldview assumption is that the contribution of universities to global economic well
being is one of their key aims. Another is that globalization is inevitably
positive. And since the internationalisation of faculty and students helps
globalization, it counts heavily in the rankings. Finally, the rankings
give statistical scores to a fraction of a percentage point. They are therefore presumed to be scientific—and consequently granted authority by
most academic, political, and business leaders around the world.

An extensive survey of students in Canadian universities published by *Maclean's* magazine asked the question, "Does your campus
foster student success?" Paradoxically but not unexpectedly, students
ranked the three universities that I attended second, third, and seventh
last out of fifty-two Canadian universities. The top ten were all small
universities where teaching and interpersonal relationships are held
to be important.[7] The views of students about quality education bear
little resemblance to the views of university rankers—or to those who
champion academic globalization.

The Nature and Scope of Globalization

With major universities striving for high world rankings and wanting to compete in the process of globalization, we need to consider the
nature and scope of such globalization. In one sense globalization can
be traced back to the Roman Empire and the spread of Christianity. In
more recent human history, however, globalization is rooted "in the
modernist impulse to 'conquer' the world and nature".[8]

The past two centuries have seen a shrinking concept of space, increased worldwide connections and interdependencies, and the emergence of influential supranational organisations and corporations. What
affects each nation and what also affects all levels of education are new
global technologies of communication that shape our identity, our way
of life, and what we hold to be important in life. Ever since the Dutch
East India Company ruled the oceans as arguably the first multinational
corporation, the foremost force behind globalization has been the goal
of economic growth and economic power. Market capitalism has led to
an unprecedented integration of technologies and markets. The rules of
capitalism dominate the world-wide economy. An Americanisation of
habits of consumption is shaping cultures around the world, accompanied with a faith in continued economic growth and prosperity.

At the same time, this capitalistic globalization has been characterised by "its lack of sense of obligation to others, poor sense of the

public, and private relativism".[9] Moreover, both within nations and between nations, the economic gap between rich and poor has amplified. The poor, whether persons or nations, have become increasingly marginalised. Both the debt policies of international financial agencies and the brain drain from poorer to richer nations are creating wide-reaching inequalities. A resulting backlash again market-driven globalization has created a ready context for increased conflict, warfare, and terrorism. Such conflicts often involve local or regional voices that want to withstand globalization and its effects.

Let me give four examples of how globalization impacts education. First, higher education is no longer viewed as a public trust that enhances the *whole* of human welfare: not only the economic but also the spiritual, moral, social, aesthetic, and scientific spheres of life. It is increasingly seen less as something that examines and exchanges ideas and insights. Rather, it is held to be a commodity to be provided, bought, and traded. The General Agreement on Trade in Services (GATS), for instance, includes education as a commodity, an article of trade, which must be regulated internationally.[10] Te Velde of the Overseas Development Institute writes that "Good quality schooling determines trade and inward investment" and is "important for participating in knowledge intensive exports". Why must students be taught knowledge and skills? So that education helps trade and economic growth and so that firms can expand.[11] Thus the most popular programmes taken by international students are business degrees.

Second, governments and non-government international organisations as well as multinational corporations have become deeply involved in shaping education. They sponsor standardised tests and publicise resulting rankings of educational institutions. They fund carefully chosen educational ventures and subsidise students to take specified certificates or degrees. They develop and support curricula that prepare graduates for internationally recognised professional qualifications. They are involved in global marketing of educational programmes. Corporations also maximise profits in poorer regions of the world in ways that may undermine educational infrastructures. While the pervasive influence of international agencies and corporations has been a source of both benefit and harm, more and more they are setting the basic agenda for higher education throughout the world, mainly through funding and other pressures that are difficult to resist.

Third, a world-wide mobility of students and academic staff as well as the development of ICT (Information and Communication Technology) has led to increased global networking and internationalisation of teaching and research. While English has become the standard language used for cross-cultural communication, foreign language programmes and cross-cultural understanding have also advanced. Student mobility has, however, also led to a brain drain in poorer countries and a brain gain in richer ones. Graduates who are nationals of poor nations tend to seek employment in wealthier ones, often the ones where they have studied.

Fourth, education, and especially higher education, is being seen worldwide as the key to economic success. Mark Malloch Brown, Administrator of the United Nations Development Program, typically told the World Education Forum in 2002 that education is a prerequisite for a developing country's competitive success. Without an effective education programme, he added, other investments will fail to bring economic benefit.[12]

Globalization in education is not likely to be reversed: the world has become too interdependent. And globalization *has* led to certain benefits. It has enabled collaboration on scholarship and research projects. Information and research results have become readily available throughout the world. Globalization has also made lifelong learning easier to promote and achieve. It has enabled nations such as India and China to boost the education of millions who have been able to take on more responsible positions and have lifted themselves out of poverty. Moreover, links with diverse cultures have enriched many.

Yet market-driven globalization has also inexorably brought about an emphasis in education on precise, measurable outcomes. This has meant that education has focused much more on individual achievement than on developing community and promoting compassion, justice, and equity.[13] Basic educational questions are often no longer asked. What are the purposes of education? Is it mainly to promote economic growth and trade? Or are there deeper, more meaningful aims? Should education, for instance, help students understand their cultural and religious heritage? To explore their role in building a healthy, sustainable community and culture and nation? To critique the values that undergird market globalization? To become committed to a responsible and responsive way of life? Should education be controlled by international agencies or should local communities develop educational priorities? How can we prevent emerging nations from not losing their brightest future leaders? And shouldn't schools and universities try to resist the ills brought about by capitalist globalization even as they laud its positive outcomes? But before considering what education should be about, I want to give some specific examples of the effects of globalization on education.

Examples of the Effects of Globalization on Education

Economics Nobel Prize winner Joseph Stiglitz has argued that the policies of the International Monetary Fund, the World Bank, and the World Trade Organization have reduced income and living conditions in many countries. They often provide loans and funds only if countries adopt policies of increased taxes and interest rates or of freer trade policies that cause the economy to shrink, making it more difficult to provide funds for education.[14] The World Bank, for instance has mapped out educational priorities based on analyses of national education systems, and extends loans for educational initiatives in emerging nations on the basis of its priorities:

> Ignoring the quality of education limits economic growth. All primary, secondary, and general education projects approved by the World Bank's Board of Executive Directors in 2007 address education quality and cover student learning assessments. . . . A key study on Education Quality and Economic Growth demonstrates empirically the causal relationship between cognitive learning outcomes and economic growth. A five-volume tool kit on designing educational assessment systems is being published to help countries with the implementation of sustainable national assessments of student achievement. . . . Students will need higher levels of knowledge and skills—particularly in the areas of mathematics and science—if they are to participate meaningfully in the world of work.[15]

Regrettably, however, in developing countries such policies "often encourage an emphasis on inappropriate skills and reproduce existing social and economic inequalities", and may well erode educational quality because schools no longer meet the needs of the local community.[16]

The Organization for Economic Co-operation and Development (OECD) shares the World Bank's view that education is essentially an economic commodity. The OECD may well have the most effect on the globalization of education in the world today. Its well-known Programme for International Student Assessment (PISA) assesses reading, mathematical and scientific literacy knowledge and skills of 15 year olds—knowledge and skills that are deemed essential for full participation in the economic life of any society. Sixty-two countries participated in the 2006 tests. Governments paid close attention to the results. In 2008 the OECD also published a report to "ensure that post-secondary education contributes to economic and social objectives: foster links to employers, communities and labour markets; [and] promote effective university-industry links for research and education".[17] One of its objectives is to provide a precise and quantitative measure of learning outcomes so that educational institutions can be held accountable and so that families have information on their relative performance.[18] The OECD is exploring possibilities for assessing and comparing post-secondary learning outcomes internationally. It has criticised Canada for a lack of standard post-secondary education quality control. As a result, a pan-Canadian document has been developed that outlines standards for degree programmes. To different extents, provincial governments and agencies are also assessing the quality of post-secondary education and are discussing the possibility of assessing learning outcomes for certain programmes.

Working in concert with the OECD and UNESCO, the European Community has worked hardest to standardise and integrate post-secondary education through its European Commission. In the late 1980s it launched a system of transnational post-secondary credits. The 1999 Bologna declaration and subsequent process led to the comparability of diplomas and the assessment of programme quality. The lengths of baccalaureate, master's, and doctoral programmes were standardised to three, two, and three years respectively. While participation is voluntary, Forty-five countries had signed on by 2003. In 2004 the Commission published its *European Benchmarks in Education and Training*. Its major aim was to improve the competiveness of European education in the world economy. Countries that do not sign on will be excluded from the European Higher Education Area. Then both the country and its graduates will be at a competitive disadvantage.

The OECD and UNESCO have encouraged non-European countries to consider the Bologna-based model for their own post-secondary institutions.[19] In response, Latin America has begun to work on joint programmes with Europe. Australia has spearheaded the Brisbane Initiative to try integrating Asian higher education.[20] The Canadian Council on Learning has recommended that Bologna must lead to a pan-Canadian system of higher education. The University of Victoria in British Columbia has already added the Bologna-inspired credit system to its summer course lists.[21] Some senior higher education analysts in the United States are suggesting that Bologna is a bandwagon that will become the dominant model of higher education in the world.

However, little discussion has taken place about the ultimate goals of education. What drives the agenda is the desire to become or remain competitive with other regions in the world. This raises a number of questions about the implications of the Bologna initiatives. Will post-secondary institutions be able to maintain a unique mission and vision when guidelines for quality assurance include required feedback from employers and data about employability of graduates?[22] When national accreditation bodies must comply with these and other extensive standards, what will happen in the long run, for instance, to a discipline such as philosophy? Or to innovative course content and pedagogical strategies without direct marketplace relevance?

Specific countries have felt compelled to respond to globalization pressures. One of the strategic objectives of South Africa's Higher Education Plan is to produce graduates with the skills and competencies to meet human resource needs. Its higher education curriculum is therefore now aligned with assessment practices that ensure goal-driven teaching and learning. However, at the same time, its focus on Western-style human resource needs has led to concern about a loss of indigenous African cultures and an imposition of Western values on local communities.[23] In other African countries such as Ethiopia, Ghana, and Swaziland, the Structural Adjustment Programs of the International Monetary Fund and the World Bank have led to higher fees for even basic primary schooling, higher dropout rates in secondary education, and post-secondary education that stresses vocational training rather than liberal studies.[24] In Taiwan, a Ministry of Education 2003 assessment of institutions of higher education led to protests, especially by humanities and social science scholars. They claimed the Ministry was imposing Western or Americanised "global" standards based on technocratic, quantitative scientific methods. Nevertheless the government used the evaluations to rank institutions on the basis of productivity. These, in turn, determined levels of funding.[25] More generally, globalization agendas have led East Asian governments to force higher education institutions to become more efficient and more responsive to marketplace requirements.[26] They must fall into place with quality that is defined in terms of homogeneous, globally-defined outcomes related to economic growth.

Globalization of education has also led to the establishment of corporate and for-profit post-secondary institutions. More than 2,000 corporate "universities" established by companies ranging from McDonald's to Lufthansa provide professional development for their employees. Very few are accredited or engage in research. Many other for-profit institutions offer professional degrees. Two of the most prominent for-profit universities are the University of Phoenix and Kaplan Higher Education Corporation (a division of the *Washington Post*). Phoenix has 350,000 students at 200 campuses in the United States and four other countries, as well as offering courses online. It focuses on professional programmes in business, nursing, teacher education, and counselling. Kaplan has 70,000 students at seventy campuses in the United States, the United Kingdom, Ireland, and Singapore. It boasts that it is purely market-driven, preparing persons for employment in fast-growing occupations. Institutions like these are teaching institutions in a limited number of professional fields. Usually they do not engage in research.

A parallel but not unrelated development to the establishment of a huge number of such universities worldwide is that many public colleges and institutes have sought and acquired university designations. One result is that the concept of university has undergone a change. In particular, research no longer has to be an integral role of universities. A second upshot is that many professional programmes are developed and taught solely on the basis of the needs of business and industry. A third consequence is that competition for students has led many universities to restructure courses and programmes so that they can be marketed effectively, often world wide. And a broader effect is that general education in the liberal arts is often no longer considered a desirable grounding of university education. All of these developments are closely linked to the globalization of higher education.

Modernity, Postmodernism, and Globalization in Education

What should be clear from the foregoing is that the global higher education agenda today is driven by what Jacques Ellul called *la technique*, that is, the application of efficient methods not only to technology and its applications, but also to the economic, social, political, educational, and even athletic spheres of life. The result of modernity as embodied by Enlightenment ideals has resulted in rational and efficient methods being applied to all areas of education: curriculum development[27], methods of teaching[28], and assessment of student achievement. As Ellul concluded, technique presupposes rationality and efficiency as the dominant values.[29] And the exercise of those values in prescribed ways has become a demand for the recognition and approval to carry out functions in our society, including in education.

Technological progress has enabled globalization to occur. But it is also repeatedly forcing education into a technological straitjacket. The faith commitment behind this is that the world needs efficient educational strategies. Such methods will lead to competencies for the workplace that, in turn, will enable the world's gross economic product to continue to grow. The economy must continue to be profitable for large corporations. Therefore education must teach the competencies needed to contribute to a prosperous and sustainable economy.[30] This is accompanied by the mass media shaping children and adolescents into individualistic, self-centred consumers. All this has led to narrowing the meaning of education as well as how human beings are viewed.

La technique of modernity has led to the growing demand for measurable performance standards assessed through extensive testing. In British Columbia, for instance, the Ministry of Education has developed three sets of performance indicators: first, in literacy; second, in numeracy; and third, in social responsibility. I appreciate that social responsibility was included, even if its "performances" focus somewhat narrowly on values that help sustain a healthy society and economy. But the Ministry chose to assess achievement solely on literacy and numeracy. Most teachers, even if aware of the existence of social responsibility performance indicators, neglect them. What becomes important is to judge the "success" of education on the basis of prescribed reading, writing, and mathematical skills. The implied metaphor for the Foundation Skills Tests is judgement: judgement of individual students, judgement of teachers, and judgement of schools.

The best-selling issue of the largest newspaper in British Columbia is the one that reports the rankings of all schools based on the results of such tests. Yet studies consistently show that such tests constrict the curriculum, with many schools spending a great deal of time "teaching to the tests". The North American (and increasingly global) emphasis on supposedly objective, measurable results through standardised, "high stakes" tests has meant less emphasis, for example, on teaching history, foreign languages, and the fine arts—and on fostering creativity. The metaphor for student assessment becomes judgement; for classrooms, efficient production; for curriculum, product quality control.

At the post-secondary level there are, as yet, few standardised tests except for entry into programmes. But a friend of mine who teaches statistics to 400 students each semester at a large Canadian university measures student success solely on multiple choice test questions. It is not because he likes to do so, but because it is an "efficiency" forced on him. Students become dehumanised objects to be processed and ranked. It was in part my misgivings that prevented a standardised test for Bachelor of Business Administration degrees to become compulsory for programmes in British Columbia that did not have accreditation from American business programme agencies. A two-hour test that is already used by high ranking institutions to boost enrolment would have determined programme quality. Assessment is used to validate or reject, whether it be individuals or programmes. Few consider how assessment ought to be a blessing for students and programmes, or how it ought to extend grace as well as justice. Regrettably, we are so embedded in modern educational culture that we accept such practices without much thought.

Postmodernism has often objected to modernist globalization. However, it too creates problems. In the educational branch of postmodernism called constructivism, which is popular with educational theorists in the West, knowledge is a personally constructed product. Therefore a constructivist science text says, "Right answers are not possible in a constructivist textbook. It goes against the philosophy."[31] Teachers are there to help children construct knowledge on the basis of students' own perceptions and reasoning. Teachers may ask questions to help students probe further or to help them resolve discrepancies. However, students must create orderliness out of the chaos of their personal experience and then impose it on their created world.

   David Jardine tells how a constructivist teacher scolded him for complimenting a boy that his writing reminded him of Dylan Thomas. That was, according to the teacher, an illegitimate imposition of his views. He was only allowed to say, "Tell everything about your writing". Jardine rightly concludes that if this approach is used consistently, students become individual little "gods" of their own constructed but limited story.[32] They become the focus and agent of the world *they* have created. They can only talk about the object or issue in light of their own personal constructs. There is no universal knowledge. There are no absolutes. There is no metanarrative that grounds and guides them. They produce things in their own image. Constructing the world in light of our own experiences leads to loneliness, a lack of community, a lack of shared values, and a lack of common purpose.

   Chet Bowers has argued that such constructivist self-determination contributes to an individualistic consumerism.[33] Seeing the rational individual as the supreme source of authority and progress undermines moral commitments, a common memory, and a vision based on a balance between personal and the public good. When students make themselves the epicentre of their social world, "the prospects of a healthy civic life become increasingly problematic".[34] They tend to become rootless individuals who serve the interests of hyperconsumerism. Ultimately constructivism fails to see that some intergenerational knowledge transfer is necessary for sustaining culture—and for critiquing our taken-for-granted cultural patterns of thinking and acting. It turns out that modernism and postmodern constructivism in education share Enlightenment notions about individualism and progress.

   How does this relate to globalization? Bowers shows how, in the world beyond the West, constructivist pedagogies have become another mode of pro-Western colonisation that contributes to the decline of earth's life-supporting ecosystems.[35] Constructivism ignores "the diversity of cultural-knowledge systems, as well as the wisdom that many of these knowledge systems achieved about sustainable living within the limits of local bioregions".[36] Bowers argues that in parts of Albania, Turkey, Pakistan and Mexico the implementation of constructivist practices is intensifying social stress. The reason is that constructivism ignores cultural diversity and how cultural traditions provide moral and social frameworks that can sustain mutually supportive and sustainable communities. The Western export of constructivist educational strategies, in other words, undermines the intergenerational non-Western cultural knowledge that sustains indigenous societies.

   In short, both market-driven globalization and post-modern constructivism result in the imposition of Western capitalist and consumerist values on large parts of the world. The question then becomes, is there a "third way" to educate children in a more responsible manner? That I will consider in the next section.

How Then Should We Educate?

God's world is a mystery to be explored and unfolded. It is to be interpreted and understood. It is to be valued and cherished. It is to be delighted in and savoured. It is to be shaped creatively and played with imaginatively. It is to be lived with and taken care of responsibly. It is to be valued for what it is and it can become. And all this is to be done on the basis of faith in God as our Creator, Sustainer, and Redeemer. Enabling students to do so as unique image bearers is what education should be all about. Education is not just a preparation for students functioning as unquestioning producers and consumers in a market-driven economy. Nor is it just a way for students to construct their own personal reality. Rather, education ought to prepare students to be and become responsive and responsible disciples of Jesus Christ.

Some years ago I wrote a paper on education for discipleship that later became the basis of one of the core values of my institution, Trinity Western University.[37] I used the example of Dietrich Bonhoeffer as my starting point. Despite his incarceration in a Nazi concentration camp, Bonhoeffer continued to rejoice in God's good gifts of life: mountains, flowers and animals; family members and friends; and the fine arts, literature, and theology. He boldly persevered in promoting truth, justice, responsibility, and goodness, always pointing to the God of the Bible as the one on whom we must depend as their source. He put aside personal ambition in order to openly oppose the Nazi regime. Courageous, unselfish and humble, he understood that God called him to be a player in God's Story of redemption and hope. Bonhoeffer was executed a few days before the end of World War II. However, his life of discipleship was a victory of faith, hope, love, and freedom in Jesus Christ.[38] His book, *The Cost of Discipleship*, today still influences thousands of people around the world.[39]

Educating students in the way Bonhoeffer described and lived discipleship is obviously difficult to do in a secular or public educational setting. To do so entirely requires faith-based institutions. After all, such education means that teachers encourage students to place their faith in the Triune God, submit to Jesus as their Redeemer and Teacher, and to love others as He loved us. It means that they champion the truth of Scripture and the truth that is Jesus Christ. It means that they model and show how one's faith shapes one's thought, actions, and dispositions. It means they care for their students' spiritual, moral, emotional, social, aesthetic, and physical as well as their intellectual growth. It means they show particular care for the needy both within and outside the school: the marginalised, the vulnerable, the academically weak, the abused, the emotionally unstable, the frail in faith, and the poor. It means that they foster a learning community that will hunger and thirst after both personal and social righteousness and justice.

Schools that nurture discipleship develop programmes that help students understand how God calls them to be part of His Story: creation, the human fall into sin, the redemption of the world through Jesus Christ, and hope of complete restoration when Christ returns. To explore with their students the significance of this metanarrarive, schools must regularly explore four questions with their students. What is God's intention for the particular area of creation or culture that is being investigated? How has this purpose been distorted by the effects of human disobedience and sin? How does God want us to respond so that we restore, at least in part, the love, righteousness, and justice God intended for the world? And how can we help our students develop a deeper understanding of, experience in, and commitment to a Christian way of life?[40] Using these questions we enable students to experience and explore the marvel and mystery of God's grace in creation, the destructive power of sin in their lives and in the world, and the potential of restoration through the saving grace of Jesus Christ. I will very briefly describe some implications of each question for classroom teaching and learning.

First, what is God's intention for the particular area of creation or culture that we will investigate? God requires us to obey His creation or cultural mandate to develop and unfold the earth's possibilities, to be His co-regents as we develop culture (Genesis 1:28; 2:15). We therefore provide a wide range of learning opportunities related to both God's provision for us in our physical reality and in His provision for human life. We develop competence in language arts, insights in life-related issues, discernment in what the Bible says about faith and life, creativity as well as proficiency in the fine arts, know-how in the mathematical and physical sciences—and throughout foster appropriate social and critical thinking skills. We encourage students to deepen their commitment and enrich the meaning of their lives, to appropriate the biblical vision as their own, and to act on the basis of what they profess. We help students unfold the possibilities latent in God's creation while being stewardly cultivators of the God-given gifts within and around us. During such exploration we no doubt include learning some of the skills assessed on standardised tests. However, we go much beyond that, pointing students to the diversity and complexity of gifts and resources that make life full of wonder and promise.

Second, how has God's purpose been distorted by the effects of human disobedience and sin? Students need to know what is happening in society. They need to unmask the idols of our times such as materialism, hedonism, economic growth at all costs, and violence. They need to explore why God gave us the Great Commandment to love Him above all and our neighbour as ourselves. They need to understand not only personal sin but also the systemic sin of societal structures and practices that cause injustice, poverty, and conflict. How could the Holocaust or the Rwandan massacres happen in countries that are at least nominally Christian? Why are children forced into industrial slavery or, worse, into becoming child soldiers? Why do we face huge ecological problems? Why do we have a homeless problem? Only by understanding the roots of personal and social problems can we guide students to have, practice, and apply a thoroughly Christian mind as they live in a secular culture.

Third, how does God want us to respond so that we restore, at least in part, the love, righteousness, and justice God intended for the world? We help students see that God calls disciples to obey everything that Jesus commanded us (Psalm 19, 78; Matthew 28:20). Learning is basic to the concept of discipleship. Students must learn to ask and consider questions that enable them, as part of the Christian community, to be salt and light in our society. Responsive disciples will attempt to re-create small corners of culture into more God-glorifying ones, even as they recognise that until Christ returns, sin will continue to affect and even undermine such efforts.[41] Students need to discuss human rights (including rights for Christians and other minorities), legal and economic justice (especially for the disadvantaged that Jesus talked about), and integrity in politics and business dealings. They need to be asked to respond personally to issues and commit themselves to certain values and courses of action. What personal meaning did they glean from their learning? We need to give them opportunities for personal response. Learning opportunities inside and outside the classroom must provide not only academic insight and spiritual discernment, but also hands-on projects and service practica that aim to promote what is right and good. We help students to apply what they learn in their personal contexts. Hearing must lead to doing; reflection must lead to action. Knowledge in the biblical sense is never just intellectual. Rather, it involves obedient response, also in academic settings.

Fourth, how can we help our students develop a deeper understanding of, experience in, and commitment to a Christian way of life? God calls disciples of Jesus to persist in their hunger and thirst for righteousness and justice. Whether teachers or students, they will aim to serve each other and society in obedience and with integrity so that their Father in heaven will be glorified. For them, discipleship is a life-long response of putting into action God's saving work in their lives and obeying God with deep reverence (Philippians 2:12). And even students who have not yet made a decision to serve Jesus Christ can be involved in activities that will help them understand some of the richness of discipleship. We provide students with guided on- and off-campus opportunities for confirming and reinforcing their calling as apprentice members of the Kingdom of God.

One final point that relates to all four questions: The apostle Paul already emphasised the importance of being part of a community: "We are all parts of his one body; and each of us has different work to do. And since we are all one body in Christ, we belong to each other, and each of us needs all the others" (Romans 12:5). Community is essential for growing as disciples. Lesslie Newbigin describes how a community true to its Christian calling will understand and display a gospel framework for life. It is a community of praise, thanksgiving and boundless love. It is a community of truth that is modest and realistic but also sceptical of modern propaganda. It is a community that has deep concern for its surroundings. It is a community that offers sacrifices of love and obedience as it exercises its diverse gifts in the public life of our society. It is a community of hope, one that rejects the false technological optimism of Western culture but also the nihilism and despair of modern Western literature. In short, it is a community that provides a foretaste of a social order where God's peace and justice are evident.[42] It is within such a Christian community context that teachers and students can help one another grow in faith, love and discernment, experiencing together what being a disciple means. Here they can learn to support each other in leading lives worthy of their calling (Ephesians 4:1). Here they can also become excited about a vision of the Kingdom of God, working to change beliefs and practices that are contrary to the way of Jesus. Also in the way we structure learning we need to break away from North American individualism that undermines the biblical concept of community.

No school or university will reach these ideals. Sadly, some non-religious institutions structure teaching and learning in ways that are closer to the ideal than do many Christian institutions. For instance, Quest University in Squamish, British Columbia, is a small non-religious undergraduate liberal arts college that has a compulsory two-year foundations programme. It provides a breadth of knowledge about the world and our place in it. It offers an integrated approach to learning that helps students become aware of present-day issues and future possibilities. All this occurs within a small, supportive community setting. Courses include ones such as *Democracy and Justice, Fate and Virtue, Reason and Freedom,* and *Modeling Our World with Mathematics.* The *Sense of Self* course deals with the foundations for and the problems with our modern sense of our unique individuality using authors such as Augustine, Freud, Virginia Woolf, and Charles Taylor. A *Global Perspectives* course orients incoming students to contemporary problems in the world such as intercultural communications, globalization and development, international relations, and global social issues such as AIDS, poverty, and environmental degradation.[43] What is clear here is that students investigate issues on the basis of questions similar to the four I posed above, although not from a Christian point of view. Quest fosters global citizenship by focusing on issues and events with international consequences, but does so in ways that critically analyse and assess the prevailing view that globalization must lead to a Western conception of economic growth.

Conclusion

The globalization of education rooted in the idol of predestined economic growth will not disappear. The forces to create homogeneous educational experiences that promote a Western conception of quality education are powerful and pervasive. While the globalization of education enables people to connect and collaborate, it has also tended to export Western individualism and materialism, creating mounting disparities between the rich and the poor as well as an unsustainable use of resources. That makes it all the more important that Christians maintain educational institutions that promote *shalom*, the biblical peace and justice that heals brokenness and restores relationships (Luke 1:51-53). Such institutions must define educational quality and excellence not just in terms of knowledge and skills that help students prepare for the marketplace, but in terms of enriching personal lives as well as the life and soul of our communities and culture. They need to identify and deal with the broad swath of critical issues that we must address as we live between Christ's ascension and His return. They must show how the gospel can bring freedom from the self-centred excesses of North American society. Then their graduates may be prepared to serve as humans who are not only globally aware, but who also are willing and able to join hands across the globe to build a more compassionate, a more just, a more responsible, and a more equitable world.

....

HARRO VAN BRUMMELEN (Ed.D., University of British Columbia) is Professor and former Dean of Education at Trinity Western University in Langley, BC. His best known books are *Walking with God in the Classroom: Christian Approaches to Teaching and Learning* (Purposeful Design Publications 3rd Edition, 2009; available in ten languages) and *Steppingstones to Curriculum: A Biblical Path* (Purposeful Design Publications 2nd Edition, 2002; published in four languages).

NOTES

[1] *Times Higher Education*, "The Top 200 World Universities" http://www.timeshighereducation.co.uk (accessed 24 February 2009).

[2] *Times Higher Education*, "Leader: A Measure Much Needed", October 9, 2008. http://www.timeshighereducation.co.uk/story.asp?sectioncode=26&storycode=403845 (accessed 24 February 2009).

[3] *Times Higher Education*, "Leader: A Measure Much Needed", October 9, 2008.

[4] Heather Munroe-Blum, "The Amazing Race", Speech to the Calgary Chamber of Commerce April 30, 2008. www.mcgill.ca/principal/speeches/lectures/amazingrace (accessed 25 February 2009).

[5] Heather Munroe-Blum, "Universities: Key Players in the Global Economy", Speech to the Conseil des Relations Internationales de Montréal, March 10, 2008. www.mcgill.ca/principal/speeches/lectures/universities (accessed on 25 February 2009).

[6] In the other well recognised world ranking of universities prepared by the Shangai Jiao Tong University, McGill placed only 63rd in 2007. The reason is that this ranking puts more emphasis on alumni winning Nobel prizes, being quoted in scientific journals, and on academic performance in relation to size—and less on internationalisation.

[7] *Maclean's*, 2009 Student Surveys, February 4, 2009. http://oncampus.macleans.ca/education/2009/02/04/2009-student-surveys/5/ (accessed 27 February 2009).

[8] Hans Smit, "Is Canadian Curriculum Studies Possible?" *Journal of the Canadian Association for Curriculum Studies* 6, 2 (2008), 108.

[9] Romulo F. Magsino, "Globalization and Education in the 21st Century", *Encounters on Education* 8 (Fall 2007), 55.

[10] Alan Ruby, "Reshaping the University in an Era of Globalization", *Phi Delta Kappan* 87, 3 (November 2005), 233.

[11] Dirk Willem te Velde, "Globalisation and Education: What Do the Trade, Investment, and Migration Literatures Tell Us?" Working Paper #254 (London: Overseas Development Institute, 2005), 7, 9, 61.

[12] Quoted in Sharon Jacobson, Hein Knobloch, Charles Koplinski, and Kathy Warren in "No More Time: Education Policy in Senegal", 2007, unpublished paper, http://globalizationandeducation.ed.uiuc.edu (accessed on 24 February 2009).

[13] Mark K. Smith, "Globalization and the Incorporation of Education", *The Encyclopedia of Informal Education* (2002). www.infed.org/biblio/globalization.htm (accessed on 24 February 2009).

[14] Joseph Stiglitz, *Globalization and its Discontents* (New York: W.W. Norton, 2002).

[15] The World Bank Education website, http://web.worldbank.org/WBSITE/EXTERNAL/TOPICS/EXTEDUCATION/ (accessed on 26 February 2009).

[16] State University.com, *"Globalization of Education—Globalization Theory, The Role of Education"*, in *Education Encyclopedia*. http://education.stateuniversity.com/pages/2010/Globalization-Education.html (accessed on 24 February 2009).

[17] OECD Directorate for Education, "Be More Purposeful in Guiding Tertiary Education, OECD Tells Governments", September 16, 2008. www.oecd.org/document/12/0,3343,en_2649_39263238_41313740_1_1_1_1,00.html (accessed on 24 February 2009).

[18] Organization for Economic Co-operation and Development, *Measuring Improvements in Learning Outcomes: Best Practices to Assess the Value-Added of Schools* (OECD, 2008).

[19] How closely organisations work together to specify standards in higher education throughout the world is illustrated by the fact that the International Network for Quality Assurance in Higher Education states in its policies that it will continue to promulgate the UNESCO/OECD Guidelines for quality provision. Its strategic plan asserts that it will liaise and collaborate with UNESCO, OECD, the World Bank, and the World Trade Organization. With headquarters in The Hague, the INQAAHE has grown from eight to more than 200 agency members between 1992 and 2008. Its aim is to establish international benchmarks for higher education and global recognition of qualifications. See www.inqaahe.org.

[20] The information up to this point in this paragraph is found in Jean-Emile Charlier and Sarah Croché, "How European Integration Is Eroding National Control over Education Planning and Policy", *European Education* 37, 4 (Winter 2005-6), 7-21.

[21] Léo Charbonneau, "The Bologna Conundrum", *University Affairs* 50, 3 (March 2009), 28-29.

[22] European Association for Quality Assurance in Higher Education, *Standards and Guidelines for Quality Assurance in the European Higher Education Area* (Helsinki: European Commission, 2005).

[23] Ria McDonald and Helen van der Horst, "Curriculum Alignment, Globalization, and Quality Assurance in South African Higher Education", *Journal of Curriculum Studies* 39, 1 (2007), 4-5.

[24] Ali Abdi, Korbla Puplampu, and George Sefa Dei (eds.), *African Education and Globalization: Critical Perspectives* (Lanham, MD: Lexington Books, 2006).

[25] Wang Huilan, "Education and the Discussions on Globalization: Between 'Winning the Competition' and 'Social Justice'", *Chinese Education and Society* 40, 1 (January/February 2007), 30-33.

[26] Ka Ho Mok, "Globalisation, New Education Governance and State Capacity in East Asia", *Globalisation, Societies, and Education* 5, 1 (March 2007), 13.

[27] See, for instance, the curriculum guides or *Instructional Resource Packages* that have been developed by the British Columbia Ministry of Education since 1995.

[28] See, for instance, Robert J. Marzano, Debra J. Pickering & Jane E. Pollock, *Classroom Instruction That Works: Research-Based Strategies for Increasing Student Achievement* (Alexandria, VA: Association for Supervision and Curriculum Development, 2001).

[29] Jacques Ellul, *Perspectives on Our Age* (Toronto: Canadian Broadcasting Corporation, 1981), 41-42.

[30] See, for instance, the mission statement of the British Columbia school system at http://www.bced.gov.bc.ca/resourcedocs/k12educationplan/mission.htm.

[31] Dale Baker and Michael Piburn, *Constructing Science in Middle and Secondary School Classrooms* (Boston: Allyn and Bacon, 1997), xv.

[32] David W. Jardine, Sharon Friesen, and Patricia Clifford, *Curriculum in Abundance* (Mahwah, NJ: Lawrence Erlbaum, 2006), 141-142, 147.

[33] The next two paragraphs are a summary of my description of Bowers' views in Harro Van Brummelen, "Reconciliation, Constructivism, and Ecological Sustainability", *Journal of Education & Christian Belief* 11, 1 (Spring 2007), 63-70. This is based on Chet Bowers, *The False Promise of Constructivist Theories of Learning: A Global and Ecological Critique* (New York: Peter Lang, 2005).

[34] Bowers, *False Promises of Constructivist Theories of Learning*, 32.

[35] Ibid, 5.

[36] Ibid, 9.

[37] Guy Saffold and Harro Van Brummelen (eds.), "Growing as Disciples in Community", in *Developing Leaders Together* (Langley, BC: Trinity Western University, 2001), 17-23.

[38] This paragraph is based mainly on the description of Bonhoeffer's life found in G. Leibholz, "Memoir", in Dietrich Bonhoeffer, *The Cost of Discipleship* (New York: Simon & Schuster, 1995), 13-33.

[39] Dietrich Bonhoeffer, *The Cost of Discipleship*.

[40] Harro Van Brummelen, *Steppingstones to Curriculum: A Biblical Path*, 2nd ed. (Colorado Springs: Purposeful Design Publications, 2002). In public settings teachers are much more limited in what they can do. However, they can still explore similar questions: How do we want the area of reality or culture that we will study to have developed or develop in the future? How has this purpose fallen short? How can we restore, at least in part, human and social dignity, respect, and justice as well as stewardship of resources? How can we instill our students with a sense of hope, strength, and courage despite the problems we/they face?

[41] Gloria Stronks and Doug Blomberg, *A Vision with a Task: Christian Schooling for Responsive Discipleship* (Grand Rapids, MI: Baker, 1993), 22-23.

[42] Lesslie Newbigin, *The Gospel in a Pluralist Society* (Grand Rapids, MI: Eerdmans, 1989), 227-233.

[42] Cf. http://www.questu.ca/ (accessed 2 March 2009).

The World is Your Playground: Competing Stories of Gospel and Globalized Adventure

by Rod Thompson with Athalia Bond

we are fractured people
living lives of many strands
pick a path, pick a story
the life you want is "on demand"

the world's your playground
your shopping mall, your stage
pick your setting, pick your character
pick your line and pick your page

adventurer, cool traveller,
businessman, entrepreneur,
hippy or hindu,
vegan or, like, "totally commercial"

we are fractured people
identities shift like sand
culture's a commodity
bought and sold on demand

we are broken people
set forth upon shifting seas
clutching at the driftwood-flotsam
drowning in our fantasies . . .

Stories that Collide

This is Athalia's poem. Glimpses of her story are woven through this chapter, giving personal voice to wider issues. Born and raised in New Zealand, Athalia lived with her family in Nepal between the ages of seven and twelve. The family then returned to New Zealand for her schooling. As a third culture kid she had to again find her place in Western society. At age seventeen Athalia travelled again—to Thailand, Nepal and England. Back in Auckland she returned to University, then during her first years of employment, sunk into deep depression. Athalia travelled to Los Angeles to work in the movie industry. Six months later, she came back to Auckland. Athalia spent nine months in an internship programme and over the past few years has been rediscovering her identity as a woman in Christ. She is about to travel again to Thailand and Nepal.

Athalia is a living testimony to the allure, the promise and the profound disappointment of the globalized story—or at least one dominant version of it—as well as the coherence, the grace and the deep hope of the biblical story of the gospel of Christ. She has wrestled in the tension of these two stories and tried to make sense of her life. She is representative of thousands, indeed millions of young people, who are faced with the same struggle.

It is a matter of urgency that churches are alert to this collision of stories. The global era of which we are part is about economics and ecology, business and politics, entertainment and travel. It is also about issues of identity and meaning in life. It is about Athalia. It is about me. It is about all of us finding our home in the story of the gospel in times of unparalleled global promises, opportunities, disappointments and challenges.

Athalia: "Going to the edge of a cliff . . ."

"Just like being one of the 'Famous Five'", I thought, "except that there are only three of us. Maybe we could be the 'Terrific Three' or the 'Talented Three' or even the 'Three Bonds', just like James except that we are children . . ."

My mind drifted in a reverie as we hustled through the airport. Mum and Dad had spent ages saying goodbye to everyone, crying and hugging a million times, and now we were running late. It didn't help matters that we were loaded down like pack animals, all the heavy items stowed in our hand luggage to avoid paying overweight penalties.

"Try not to make the packs look heavy. Try and stand up straight!" Mum whispered directions as we scooted past security guards and other luggage-laden travellers. We were finally off on our great adventure, the big move to Nepal. The weight of this was lost on my seven-year-old mind but the excitement of it wasn't. I was already transforming my brother, my sister and myself from ordinary children to worldwide adventurer extraordinaires. No more average daily life for us. We were moving to a village on a cliff (yes, that is what a seven-year-old imagines when they are told that a place is 800 metres above sea level!), and we would explore new lands, take down baddies, rescue hostages, and generally take on the world.

Mum reached for my pack to pull me up straight. "I can do it", I hissed, ducking out of her way, legs and arms flying as I struggled to maintain both my balance and my independence. Once I was finally upright, I bent my legs slightly and fixed my eyes on our gate, making a beeline for the gulfing chasm behind the smiling hostess, the bridge that marked the movement from everyday life to a life less ordinary. And, as I ran, I wondered whether it was dangerous living that close to the edge of a cliff . . .

The World's Your Playground I

The billboard announced: "The World's Your Playground". It struck me that this was a line from an increasingly intrusive story told and retold by advertisers, a story about the purpose of living in a globalized world. "The World's Your Playground"—and one tagline reads: ". . . and this is where you'll find *anything* you want to do, *anywhere* you want to do it!"[1]

There are many obvious incarnations of this story—*Disneyland* for example, which trumpets itself as the happiest place on earth, the place where dreams come true, and which features the song "It's a Small World After All", possibly the most played, heard, translated and annoying song ever, running on a continuous loop in Disney theme parks around the world with its own promise of universal peace.

The city of Las Vegas markets itself as "the largest adult playground in the world",[2] with its replicas of an Egyptian pyramid flanked by the Sphinx, a scaled-down New York skyline including the Brooklyn Bridge and Statue of Liberty, a near full sized replica of Venice's Piazza San Marco, a large volcano that erupts flames every thirty minutes, an Eiffel Tower and so much more.

Dubai, the "pearl of the Persian Gulf", is a more recent contender for playground of the world. The Arab city is building the world's largest theme park—no gambling (banned by Islamic law), but just about everything else. By 2012 Universal Studios, Dreamworks, Marvel and Legoland will all open *Dubailand* outlets. The "Tiger Woods", a golf course designed by Woods himself, will be lined with luxury homes and a boutique hotel. *Dubailand*'s Falcon City will have life-size replicas of the Eiffel Tower, the Pyramids and the Taj Mahal. Beauty Land will offer luxurious spas, while the Palmarosa development will feature a "wellness resort and health farm". Massive stadiums and a Formula One racetrack will be the focus of Sports City. The Bawadi strip, inspired by the Las Vegas strip, will have hotels and shopping. As currently envisaged, Dubailand will sustain

2.4 million residents and workers, nearly twice Dubai's population today.[3]

But the invitation to explore the global playground is more pervasive than any of these specific manifestations. Globalization has been described in the following terms:

> At the heart of globalization lie the new possibilities of commerce, travel and communication opened up by the technologies of our time. Commerce delivers more products than ever on a global scale; travel carries individuals to diverse and far-flung destinations; and communication brings the cultures of the world onto screens, speakers and telephone receivers in the intimacy of our own homes. The fuel that has enabled us to exploit these possibilities at such an alarming speed is the fuel of consumerism—the drive to deliver more goods to more people in more places than ever before.[4]

The language of opportunity is dominant—"possibilities", "products", "new", "diverse", "far-flung", "exploit", "speed", "more", "more" and "more". Such language is frequently married up with images of "play" and "adventure", "fantasies" and "dreams", becoming the storied promise of a new way to be human in this era of possibilities. These promises are urgent because of the demandingness of hypermodern life and the widespread awareness that we live in troubled times. Perhaps the globalized era won't last too long. So become an adventurer, determine the "100 Things to Try Before You Die"[5]—and go and play. Australian born recording artist Sam Sparro expresses something of this anxiety in the lyrics of his song "Living in the 21st Century":

> 21st century life—I got swept away
> I got 21,000 things that I got to do today.
> 21st century life—Well what can I say?
> The new world got me feeling so dirty
> Think I need to get down and *play*[6]

Life in 21st century Western nations is overwhelming. Each day there are 21,000 possibilities. In this new world of bewildering multiplicity, we need to get down and play.

This invitation is nowhere more evident than in the rising influence of Internet technology with an estimated 21.9% of the world's population now online.[7] Such technology brings new dimensions to the meaning of play. Games such as *Sims* and *Second Life* can be used to escape the mundane and re-image the world in terms of one's own pleasure and power.[8] Totally imagined worlds, never before seen, fantastic with dragons and magic, are created in *World of War Craft*[9] for example, attracting 7 million players worldwide.[10] Internet games are a global, storied phenomenon. Their inhabitants overcome barriers of both distance and language. Such games invite participation in multiple worlds. Play becomes escape. Escape can become life's meaning and goal.

Humanist author Paul Kurtz argues that humanness is defined by the adventures of autonomous individuals living in a world of possibilities.

> As I see it, creative achievement is the very heart of the human enterprise. It typifies the human species as it has evolved, particularly over the past forty to fifty thousand years: leaving the life of the hunter and the nomad, developing agriculture and rural society, inventing industry and technology, building urban societies and a world community, breaking out of the earth's gravitational field, exploring the solar system and beyond. The destiny of humankind, of all people and of each person, is that they are condemned to invent what they will be—condemned if they are fearful but blessed if they welcome the great adventure.[11]

For Kurtz, "sinners" are those who do not embrace the great adventure with its invitation to access, among other things, "the full range of pansexual pleasures".[12] Celibates, he argues, "have committed a sin against themselves, for they have repressed the most exquisite pleasure of all: the full and varied sexual life that is so essential to happiness".[13]

The World's Your Playground II

One is not surprised to find this story being told by radio-friendly pop stars and evangelists for humanism. It is more surprising perhaps to find a "sanctified" version of the same story on the lips of Christian preachers, lyricists and authors. In the popular 1992 song "The Great Adventure" performed by Christian artist Steven Curtis Chapman, the listener is invited to "get ready for the ride of your life" and to "discover all the new horizons just waiting to be explored" because "the love of God will take us far beyond our wildest dreams". The chorus goes like this:

> Saddle up your horses we've got a trail to blaze
> Through the wild blue yonder of God's amazing grace
> Let's follow our leader into the glorious unknown
> This is a life like no other—this is The Great Adventure.[14]

Images of adventure, exploration and playfulness abound. Life is exciting. There is a world to explore. Christ plays in ten thousand places![15] And becoming a Christian is stepping into the greatest adventure of all. Dreams will be realised and fantasies fulfilled. To be male, we are told, is to be wild, liberated for conquest, to undertake "a safari of the heart to recover a life of freedom, passion, and adventure".[16] Best-selling Christian authors write books exhorting us to become like David slaying the giant Goliath:

> Rush your giant with a God-saturated soul. *Giant of divorce, you aren't entering my home! Giant of depression? It may take a lifetime, but you won't conquer me. Giant of alcohol, bigotry, child abuse, insecurity . . . you're going down.* How long since you loaded your sling and took a swing at your giant?[17]

> David is envisaged as "a rough-edged walking wonder of God who neon-lights this truth: *Focus on giants—you stumble. Focus on God—your giants tumble.*" And because Goliaths (such as debt, disaster, deceit, disease and dialysis . . .) still roam our world, we must become adventurers of like calibre.[18]

I was recently at a youth church meeting during which the pastor spoke about an upcoming short term mission trip to Uganda. He and his team were to work with both the victims and perpetrators of the most vile atrocities. Their mission would target former boy soldiers of the rebel group known as Lord's Resistance Army. The team would only be away for a couple of weeks! It was deeply disturbing to me that the trip was described in terms of "excitement" and "adventure". There was no lament, certainly no tears, no awareness that engagement with the horror of excessive human evil is something other than an adventure.

In the same churches, new believers listen to and sing songs with lyrics such as:

> I'm gonna be a history maker in this land
> I'm gonna be a speaker of truth to all mankind
> I'm gonna stand, I'm gonna run
> Into your arms, into your arms again . . .[19]

and:

> . . . my heart is heavy
> Feels like it's time to dream again
> I see the clouds, and yes I'm ready
> To dance upon this barren land[20]

Rodney Clapp has asserted that consumerism is an ideology in which humans "are born, live, and die to consume material goods, experiences, an unending array of novel pleasures".[21] Is it not the case that Christian authors, songwriters and church leaders have bought into this consumer driven ideology? Are we not in peril of marketing a version of that story in which God's people are consumers of "spiritual" experiences and "mission" adventures? A story in which to be fully alive is to fulfil dreams and live out fantasies on a global scale? Is this not a radically different vision of the good life to that which is shaped by Calvary and the empty tomb of Messiah Jesus? Not a vision about the triune God of Scripture, not about sacrifice or redemption or the comprehensive renewal of the creation, rather the multiplication of "an unending array of novel pleasures". In buying into such a story, are God's people not faced with the prospect of devastating disappointment, of a fragmented and potentially self-destructive engagement with life?

Can we in fact proclaim that "the world is your playground" in ways that are true to the story of the gospel, rather than a misleading imitation of the story of global consumerism? *I believe we can.* However, if it is to be helpful it must arise from a more robust engagement with Scripture than is evident in the examples previously cited.

Athalia: "Encounters with a slightly wild God"

Life in Nepal was great . . . though my vision of a village on the edge of a cliff proved untrue! For the most part, life was ordinary and routine. Power cuts and cold showers soon become normal. So did catching rides to school on the back of tractors and chasing water buffalo off the school grounds in recess. There was, however, one adventure that never got old: encounters with a slightly wild, almost magical, quite magnificent God. I think it was easy to believe in God in Nepal. Life was surrounded, on both sides, with the presence of the supernatural. From the Hindu Pujas and the Buddhist morning call to prayer, from the mini-shrines on street corners, to the sacred mountain that towered over our town, the very air in Nepal was charged with it.

But most significantly, it was the presence of God in our strong, but broken, missionary community that made it impossible to disclaim the existence of God. There is a passage of scripture that says "God dwells with the broken hearted" and no place was this more evident than in the less-than-perfect lives of the missionaries we lived and worked with. Because of this I had, as a child, an unfailing faith in the love and mercy of a God who chooses to make his home and work his magic in the midst of weakness.

There is one encounter with this hidden but ever-present God that I have never forgotten. On a particularly stormy night, my parents' home group was meeting in our living room and being a bit older than my brother and sister, I was allowed to stay up in my parents' room reading. Ensconced in their bed, I sat listening to the home group singing and watched the wind play with the solitary candle on the nightstand. It became mesmerising, watching gusts of wind reduce the flame to a smouldering wick, only to be reignited again just before it died by another gust of wind.

As I watched I felt God's peace so strongly and I felt that I was seeing something significant about my life. At that moment, as a protected, playful ten-year-old, with no understanding of future struggles, I felt God say "Tali, your faith is going to be like that. There will be times when it will almost go out and there will be times when it will be in full flame. But I promise that I will never let it go out completely."

While Nepal had not fulfilled its promise of life on the edge of a cliff, I had no idea how significant this promise, and the understanding of God as the One who dwells with the broken hearted, would come to be in a time when I really did end up living on the dangerous edge of a cliff . . .

Playing in the Biblical Story I

How is the language of play "played out" in the biblical narrative?[22] What better place to start than with Proverbs 8 and its remarkable designation of wisdom. One commentator has suggested that the Hebrew term often translated "master workman" or "craftsman" in verse 30 might equally be rendered "little child" or "darling", enhancing the context in which "the emphasis is on the joyful play of creation rather than the hard work involved in it". If this is allowed, then 8:22-36 "may take Ms Wisdom from birth via the play of girlhood to the stature of adulthood".[23] Whichever is the case, there is no question that utter delight and playful joy properly accompanied the goodness of initial creation in its myriad diversity. This is fully in keeping with the sevenfold declaration "it was good . . . it was very good" as God surveyed his remarkable handiwork (Genesis 1:3, 10, 12, 18, 21, 25 and 31 ESV).

It is also consistent with the portrayal of God himself in Job 38-39. He has fashioned a marvellous, mysterious creation. Like a midwife he has birthed the seas gushing forth from creation's womb. He has taken the newborn waters, clothed them in clouds and wrapped them up in thick mists. He has spoken to them as to a child: "Thus far shall you come, and no farther!" The vast ocean depths, far from being untamed and frightening, are as an infant in his hands (Job 38:8-11). Who other than an imaginative, playful God would unleash wild donkeys to wander freely in desert places? (Job 39:5-6 ESV) And who would fashion such a creature as the ostrich, running hysterically, cruel and fearless, proud and yet foolish? For God has made her *forget* wisdom giving her *no share* in understanding (Job 39:13-18). The creator designs birds with tiny brains and powerful legs! "The lesson is that God can and does make creatures that appear odd and crazy to us if that pleases him. Imagine a bird that can't fly. Though it has wings it can run faster than a horse (v. 18 ESV)."[24] This is playful!

Made in the image of such a God, play is indeed one crucial element in a fully human life. And yet after the rebellion of Genesis 3, Adam and Eve are expelled from the delightful garden in which parading animals have been named. Play becomes a very mixed affair in the newly groaning reality. It is Jubal, son of the violent, boastful Lamech, who is remembered as father to those who play lyres and pipes (Genesis 4:21)—musicians and murderers, poets and polygamists in the line of the fugitive Cain.

Subsequently the Lord will frame Israel's individual, family and national life with festivals, on a daily, weekly, monthly and annual basis. Regarding the Feast of Tabernacles, the culminating event in Israel's calendar year, the Lord actually *commands* celebration: "You shall take . . . the fruit of splendid trees, branches of palm trees and boughs of leafy trees and willows of the brook, and you shall rejoice before the LORD your God seven days" (Leviticus 23:40). This is a commandment one might expect from the God who created a brilliant array of fruits and trees in the first place. They are to be enjoyed!

Yet, one of Israel's earliest exhibitions of play was anything but genuine celebration in accordance with God's covenantal purposes. At Sinai, "they rose up early . . . and offered burnt offerings and brought peace offerings. And the people sat down to eat and drink and rose up to play" (Exodus 32:6). What sort of play is this? Shouting and singing, food and dance, however not in the service of the Lord, rather a golden calf. The people had "broken loose" (Exodus 32:25 ESV); they were running wild. This is promiscuous "play", the word used in 32:6 suggesting a drunken, sexual orgy.[25]

"Play" can be thought of as directed more by imagination than regulation, more by creative freedom than restrictive boundaries. However, collective Israel's imaginings have here been enlivened by licence not liberty, lawlessness not love. Like children whose fun has become self-serving or cruel, the consequences are destructive. Relationships are ruptured. The game must end. It could all have been over for Israel in Exodus 32. Only intercession from Moses and mercy from God prevented that from being the case. Israel was playing in the wrong story.

Athalia: "Fractured, fragmented . . . and depressed"

"You're depressed." This was the third doctor to tell me this. It was the third opinion I had received. I still didn't want to believe it. People like me didn't get depressed. I had everything I could ask for in life, the identity I wanted, a great job, friends. I shook my head.

"You're wrong. It's not depression." I forced a smile, willing myself not to cry. As I pushed my chair back to exit the office, I smiled again, broadly, willing her to understand that I was not depressed, that I was happy, confident and capable, and inside, fiercely telling myself that the tears were just a symptom of my frustration.

It had been mild for a while. Life was just a bit of a grey haze, a bit dream-like. I had some problems sleeping at night and I didn't really sing any more. It wasn't major though, nothing to really worry about, I thought. Until it started to spiral out of control . . .

I started to feel more and more vulnerable. Like a city without walls, defenceless. Fractured and fragmented, I did not know who I was anymore. And I felt like I could never relax, that it was all up to me to hold the pieces together and up to me to keep my fists up. Very soon, even sleeping pills couldn't help me sleep, and every waking hour became plagued with anxiety. Sleep would eventually come on the nights I could cry myself to sleep, but I would wake again a few hours later. I lost weight. I lost hope. But I still managed to keep up the façade of togetherness in my daily life.

Rock bottom came as I was driving back up to Auckland after a weekend visit with my family. I had become painfully thin by this point and it was impossible to hide my mental state from my parents. While they managed to keep the depths of their concern hidden I found out later that it was at this point that they were almost ready to have me hospitalised. My own vision for my future was bleak. I had given up the hope of getting better or being able to hold down a job and hospitalisation seemed inevitable. As the power poles drifted past me the thought of just pressing my foot to the accelerator and closing my eyes became overwhelmingly appealing. At that point, with supreme effort and a will that was not my own, I pulled over to the side of the road, turned off the engine and prayed . . .

Playing in the Biblical Story II

Dimensions of play are evident throughout Israel's scriptures. Kings leap for joy (2 Samuel 6:14). Lovers sigh expectantly (Song of Songs 1:2ff.). There are songs and dances, riddles and proverbs, feasts, festivals, families and fun. At times these flourish.[26] However, more often they are sullied and prophets preach that Israel's play has become perverse. "I hate, I despise your feasts . . ." Amos cries on God's behalf. "Take away from me the noise of your songs", he commands (Amos 5:21-23). Judgement is pronounced:

> Woe to those who lie on beds of ivory
> and stretch themselves out on their couches,
> and eat lambs from the flock
> and calves from the midst of the stall,
> who sing idle songs to the sound of the harp
> and like David invent for themselves instruments of
> music
> (Amos 6:4-5).

These will be "the first of those who go into exile", declares the Lord (Amos 6:7). Indulgent, idolatrous play must cease. And yet prophets dream dreams of a future in which play will again be wholesome. In Isaiah's memorable words:

> The nursing child shall play
> over the hole of the cobra,
> and the weaned child
> shall put his hand on the adder's den.
> They shall not hurt or destroy
> in all my holy mountain;
> for the earth shall be full
> of the knowledge of the LORD
> as the waters cover the sea (Isaiah 11:8-9).

A shoot from the stump of Jesse, a son of David (Isaiah 11:1), will usher in such an era. Is it any wonder then that images of play abound in the accounts of Messiah Jesus. He comes "eating and drinking". And he is accused of being "a glutton and a drunkard, a friend of tax collectors and sinners!" (Matthew 11:16-19; cf. Luke 7:31-35). Israel still doesn't get it. In this "playful little parable"[27] Jesus describes two games commonly enjoyed by children in the marketplaces: "funeral" (a sad game) and "wedding" (a happy game). Israel is likened to unwilling playmates. No matter how God invites his people to respond, they pout and mutter, "I don't wanna play".[28] This generation has lost the plot. They do not understand John or Jesus. They respond neither to the prophet's stern call to repent nor the Messiah's joyful invitation to celebrate. They don't want to play "funeral" or "wedding"!

Celebratory joy is obviously not the only dimension in Jesus' life. However, it is a dominant one, particularly in Luke's account of the gospel events. So we have the remarkable words of Luke 10:21:

> In that same hour he rejoiced in the Holy Spirit and
> said, "I thank you, Father, Lord of heaven and earth,
> that you have hidden these things from the wise and
> understanding and revealed them to little children;
> yes, Father, for such was your gracious will".

Jesus is on the road to Jerusalem. He has "set his face" (Luke 9:51). Seventy-two others have just returned with joy from a gospel mission. At that same time Jesus "rejoiced in the Holy Spirit". This is unique in the gospel accounts. Jesus is not merely joyful. He is *exuberant*. He is overwhelmed with joy. One might say he has never been happier. Yet Jesus is on the way to Jerusalem. Luke uses the same word for overwhelming joy on one other occasion in Luke 1:47 on the lips of the pregnant Mary: "My spirit *rejoices* in God my saviour". Having conceived the Messiah, she exulted! These gospel events prompt heart-felt celebration. And notice the triune participation in Luke 10:21. Jesus rejoices in the Holy Spirit.[29] He voices thanks to the Father. This is a triune party! Yet Jesus is on his way to Jerusalem.

We ought not be surprised. Of course there are other dimensions to the gospel—great sadness, terrible pain, unimaginable suffering and the bewildering sacrifice of the Son of Man for the sins of the world. But for Luke, all of this is wrapped up in a narrative of hope, joy, homecoming and the kingdom of God. So it is that in Luke's account of the cross, Jesus speaks of paradise (Luke 23:43). So it is that Luke concludes his account with words of blessing, worship and great joy as Jesus ascends to the Father (Luke 24:50-53). Luke continues to tell the story in Acts, in which joy and generosity encompass sacrifice and suffering. He describes the work of the Holy Spirit through whom God renews life: the lame walk, leap and give praise to God (Acts 3:1-10). The gospel is going to the nations. Paul proclaims the kingdom from Rome boldly and without hindrance (Acts 28:30-31). In Isaiah's terms, the earth is being filled with the knowledge of the LORD.

As gospel truth and freedom are embraced throughout the world, God's grace brings renewal to humans and the entire created order. The words of Revelation convey this reality in song. John writes: "I heard every creature in heaven and on earth and under the earth and in the sea, and all that is in them, saying: 'To him who sits on the throne and to the Lamb be blessing and honour and glory and might forever and ever!'" (Revelation 5:13-14). Can we imagine the dimensions of play in the new cosmos? Can we imagine the playful triune God of creation and redemption joining with his people in untrammelled celebration in a world of *shalom*? This is something for which all who have played selfish, reckless games surely long. And this is after all the global story *par excellence*, a liberating alternative to that told by global consumerism.

Play, Problem-Posing and Purposeful Responding

Real play only makes sense in such a story because of gospel love, hope and redemptive grace. In such a story, play will not be "care-*less*"—destructive, selfish, without care. It will be truly "care-*free*"—the joyful response of those free to care, stewards and agents of God's kingdom, of those who understand life and play in the light of the cross and resurrection of Jesus. Such play generates wisdom. Blomberg writes:

> A rich encounter with God's world involves a joyful responsiveness to what God has made, rather than an overriding concern with control. Because God is in control, we are able to give ourselves up to him and his world without fear. We can play in his world and thus allow it to play on us. God's grace calls me to joy in abundance and richness of life, without pretending. . . . that its pain and suffering are an illusion: with C. S. Lewis, I am surprised by joy. . . . Because of the gospel, all of life is touched with a song.[30]

Blomberg suggests that, for those living out of the biblical story, such play opens up problems, prompting "players" to also become "problem-posers" asking questions such as "What ought I do, and how am I to accomplish it? How do I move in a normative direction?"[31] In a fallen world, things are not the way they ought to be. Those who play confront both goodness and distortion, wonder and waywardness. Problems are both posed *to* us and *by* us in the experience of play. Here is a catalyst for wisdom. In the words of Peskett and Ramachandra:

> Wisdom is generated and sustained by wonder. To wonder is to be intrigued, engaged, to behold and to be beholden to something. It is to be held in contemplation, to be provoked into thought. To wonder is to seek *to come to terms with* the unfamiliar. It is, then, the birthplace of language.[32]

And, for those living out of the biblical story, it will also give birth to "purposeful responding". Moving beyond detached reflection or passive questioning, character is formed through redemptive engagement with God's world. Blomberg writes: "A person of character is a person of integrity who responds faithfully to the norms for human living. Such a person knows the right thing to do and is disposed to do it. And such is a wise person."[33] Play/problem-posing/purposeful response is Blomberg's model for the rhythm of learning. We might argue that it is also a biblically informed model for the rhythm of life. The goal is to participate in God's transformational purposes as we make "*purposeful response* to *problems posed* in the *play* of experience". This is discerned in the context of "a fallen but redeemed-at-root creation".[34] Such is the pathway to wisdom and maturity.

Athalia: "I had a dream . . ."

"I am my Beloved's and he is mine and his banner over me is love." Those were the words of the first song I sung. I was singing again! "He brought me to his banqueting table and his banner over me is love." I had prayed and prayed for God to intervene. I had fallen to my knees and begged him to show me why this was happening to me, what was going on, why my life had so suddenly fallen apart, and slowly everything started to come together. I find it hard to put into words what God showed me . . .

Years of moving, from towns to cities, from country to country in pursuit of "the dream", my movement from one job to the next bigger, better, brighter job, and the bigger, better, brighter life, striving for the next big thing, and the great adventure, had left me worn, disillusioned and anxious.

My life had become conditioned towards striving and dissatisfaction. As I had moved from town to city it was easy to reinvent myself, to figure out what it would take to get the life I wanted and then perform, perform, perform. Moving meant no accountability. There was nobody who knew who I was or where I had come from. Dissatisfaction was easily fixed. Pick the identity, pick the clothes, pick the stage, the cast, the lines, all the essential ingredients for the perfect life, and then perform, perform, perform.

It was easy to have a disjuncture in my life between God and these actions. Church only served to reinforce the idea that the perfect life was mine for the taking. Songs like "Ask of me and I'll give you the nations", and the words of the preacher, "God's plans for you are beyond anything you can imagine; so dream big!" and "God wants to bless you! You just have to push through and reach for it!" fuelled this idea of performance as an end towards the perfect life.

In addition to creating the identity I wanted, I had a dream to produce Hollywood blockbusters. The theme song for my life became "I'm gonna be a history maker in this land, I'm going to be a speaker of truth to all mankind" and this mentally helped twist my own fantasies into "God's will" for my life. As I pursued God's "dream", my relationship with him slowly eroded from a living breathing vital relationship to a performance based system. Tick the boxes, pray the right prayers, it's a simple transaction, perform, perform, perform. As I performed, my already fractured identity quickly shifted from that of "Child of God" to "Servant of God", with acceptance grudgingly issued only if every "t" was crossed and every "i" was dotted. As I stepped onto the treadmill of constant striving, fuelled by grand visions of adventure and the nagging dissatisfaction of our consumer driven culture, I soon found out that this life is like living too close to the edge of a cliff. It's dangerous. It's easy to lose your balance . . .

Who Gets To Narrate The World?

What must church leaders and communities do to help God's people live faithfully, given the tension between these competing stories of gospel and globalized adventure and play? In posing these questions we join with Robert Webber in asking "Who gets to narrate the world"?[35] Which account of life will capture the imaginations, hopes and dreams of this generation and the next in our globalized era?

There is no question that it *won't* be the biblical story unless there is a renewed commitment to immersion in the complete library of biblical texts governed by our understanding of the gospel of Christ. David Steinmetz has helpfully compared the Bible to a mystery or detective story with two narratives.[36] It is, he suggests, like an enormous literary puzzle with two narratives. "The first is a sprawling, ramshackle narrative that does not seem to be leading any place in particular. It is filled with clues, false leads, imaginative hypotheses, and characters . . ."[37] However, he contends, in any good mystery story there is a *second* narrative, "one that is invariably recited by the principal investigator in the last or nearly last chapter. This narrative is crisp and clear and explains in considerable detail what was really occurring while the larger narrative was unfolding." Steinmetz continues: "It is important to understand that this second narrative is not a subplot, even though it is short. It is the *disclosure of the architectonic structure* of the whole story."[38]

A truly Christian reading attends to both narratives in scripture. It recognises that the second narrative—the disclosure of "the architectonic structure of the whole story"—is found on the lips of Christ and the apostles in texts such as Luke 24:44-47. The resurrected Jesus explains to those gathered:

> "These are my words that I spoke to you while I was still with you, that everything written about me in the Law of Moses and the Prophets and the Psalms must be fulfilled." Then he opened their minds to understand the Scriptures, and said to them, "Thus it is written, that the Christ should suffer and on the third day rise from the dead, and that repentance and forgiveness of sins should be proclaimed in his name to all nations, beginning from Jerusalem.

This explanation is but one of many examples in New Testament scripture of that crisp, clear second narrative. Both narratives must be thoroughly known. Biblical immersion is not an option for those who seek to live faithfully and play well. It will be both individual and communal. And it is more than Bible reading. It requires imaginative, varied engagement with God's word as we study, listen, memorise, sing, write poetry, draw, read, pray, sculpt, meditate, paint, chant, envision, chat . . . and play . . . in community with God's word and its triune author.

But this is not enough. Christian leaders and communities must more deliberately engage with, explore and expose the dominant story of globalized play and adventure, including "sanctified" Christian versions of it, that are untrue to the gospel story of Christ which insists that faithfulness is more important than unlimited choices, stewardship than multiple experiences, and sacrifice and compassion than self-interest and short term thrills. Humanness itself is being redefined in terms of multiplicity and change. Identity is up for grabs. All is flux and mobility. As Bouma-Prediger and Walsh conclude:

> Both postmodern tourists and global capitalists want to keep their options open, whether for the identities they will construct in cyberspace or the products they will buy at the mall. Both value choice over loyalty. And both remain deeply homeless because being at home requires an acknowledgement that we are not autonomous but interdependent and interrelated homemakers.[39]

And are not churches buying into this dominant narrative of global, postmodern homelessness when their meetings become fast-paced, slickly-produced performances? When preaching becomes anecdotal and formulaic? When streamlined, monocultural congregations are a primary strategy for church growth? When short term mission trips are spoken of as adventures?

With questions such as these in mind, even the well-established and very useful metaphor of the Bible as a "drama"[40] may be problematical, the idea that the church is caught up in a "theo-drama", that life is a "performance", that we are all "performers in the play".[41] Are we at risk of being heard to suggest that life is always dramatic?

And are there not dangers in Peterson's description of life as play at the commencement of *Christ Plays in Ten Thousand Places*? In responding to Hopkins' sonnet "As Kingfishers Catch Fire", he writes: "The central verb, 'play', catches the exuberance and freedom that mark life when it is lived beyond necessity, beyond mere survival".[42] The author continues, asserting that the purpose of life is to find "the vigour and spontaneity, the God-revealing Christ getting us and everything around us in on it, the playful freedom and exuberance, the total rendering of our lives as play, as worship before God".[43]

But there are times when life *is* mere survival and living beyond necessity not possible. Some days are *not* exuberant. They are exasperating or merely routine and dull. And surely worship is *more* than images of play or adventure can convey. Worship can also be helpfully characterised by images of waiting and lament, work and perseverance. In an era when the globalized consumer story brims with innovations, distractions, high expectations and adrenalin rushes, do we not need to temper the invitation to drama, exuberance, vigour and spontaneity with an equally important embrace of contentment, perseverance, silence and discipline?

Even as the musicians were taking us to new emotional heights, I have been deeply saddened watching gyrating, joy-filled teens in our churches, asking myself how they will cope sitting in a school Math class on Monday, mopping floors at the fast-food outlet after their next shift, or indeed embracing any tedious tasks in the week to come. Faithful living is not always fast-paced and dramatic, emotional and adventurous. We need a theology for the ordinary and mundane as well as the extraordinary and marvellous. A faithful rendering of the biblical story will give us both.

And a more perceptive engagement with the globalized, consumerist story will surely reveal its hollowness rather than inspiring imitation. It is not only fast-paced but finally exhausting. It is *all-consuming*. And it is producing a generation for whom entertainment is addictive and boredom a sickness in plague-like proportions.[44] One journalist, writing about high-tech millionaires in the late 1980s, remarks:

> They acquired vast houses in swanky neighbourhoods, Ferraris and Mercs, cute personal trainers, serious golf coaches, and copies of Luxury Hotels of the World. For me it was like watching a very ornate clock run down. Around 15 months later, with

> no more toys left to buy, they stared out over their
> manicured lawns and realized to their horror that they
> were bored out of their skulls.[45]

The fruits of such boredom include sexual addiction, aggressiveness, and high risk-taking adventures. Josef Pieper has argued that unless we "regain the art of silence and insight, the ability for non-activity, unless we substitute true leisure for our hectic amusements, we will destroy our culture and ourselves".[46] The globalized, consumer-driven story cannot inspire the wisdom whereby that is possible. It does not help us to make sense of play *or* seriousness, adventure or quietness. It encourages its adherents to be recklessly playful and careless in areas of life that require more care and responsibility—for example, issues of sexuality, decision-making, travel, or spending money—and to be far too serious in other areas of life that require greater playfulness—aligning our emotional well-being with sports results, parliamentary debates, snaring big business contracts, or completing research projects on time, for example!

Brueggemann claims that "those who have not cared enough to grieve will not know joy".[47] May we suggest that they will also play poorly, perhaps destructively. Real play and life-enhancing adventure will find their true meaning only as we understand life in accordance with the gospel of the crucified, risen and ruling Christ and the biblical story of which that gospel is the culmination. Playing out of the wrong story consigns us to foolishness not wisdom, immaturity not maturity, fragmentation not coherence, hyperactivity not contentment, chaos rather than a faithful rhythm of life and finally unbearable boredom rather than unrestrained gratitude and hope in God. May the Lord help us to play well as one aspect of living faithfully in response to the gospel.

Athalia: "I am truly able to play . . ."

Broken and weak, at the bottom of the cliff, the knowledge that God is the one who dwells with the broken-hearted, has been my lifeline and my hope. It is in this place that I have learnt what it means to truly call Jesus "Lord and Saviour" and, in my shortcomings, I have found that God's grace is truly amazing.

As I have started to understand how I fell so far I have been constantly helped by the words of Hebrews 13:5-6, the call to be content with what we have. I have discovered that I cannot pursue the "adventurous life" whether it is an adventurous career or the adventure of travel. Nor can I create my identity. My identity is given to me by God. I am learning to be content with whatever each day brings, to accept a bit of messiness and imperfection, and to find peace in the mundane.

I still forget what I have learned sometimes and I start to strive again. The vision I had of my faith like a flame, controlled and governed by the Holy Spirit, helps me rest in times like this and I know whether I am far from God or nearby, that my life is held in his hand and my faith governed by the security of his love and the wildness of his nature. I have rediscovered the "big adventure" of God, his wildness, his mystery and magic, but, most importantly, his goodness.

When I look back on my life, on my love of and need for adventure, on my search for identity, on my desire for fulfilment and purpose and fun, I see how much hard work it was. It is only now as I accept and find peace in the everyday and the mundane, and as my identity is made complete in weakness, that I am able to rest and, it is here, for the first time in a long while, that I am truly able to play.

....

Rod Thompson (Ph.D., Macquarie University), is Professor and Head of School of Theology, Laidlaw College, Auckland, New Zealand. He also teaches theology and worldview studies at the Maxim Institute. He is coauthor of *Shocked by Blessing* (National Institute for Christian Education, 2007).

Athalia Bond lives in Auckland, and is a student at Laidlaw College. She was an intern at Laidlaw College in 2008.

NOTES

[1] See http://www.yougodo.com/en/Home.aspx (accessed 27 November 2008).

[2] See http://www.usatourist.com/english/places/lasvegas/index.html (accessed 27 November 2008).

[3] See http://www.dubai.tv/blog/2008/06/13 (accessed 27 November 2008).

[4] Gerard Kelly, *Retrofuture: Rediscovering our Roots, Recharting our Routes* (Downers Grove, IL: Intervarsity Press, 1999), 140.

[5] See http://www.grantthorpe.com/100-things-to-do.htm (accessed 30 November 2008).

[6] Italics mine. See http://www.cduniverse.com/lyrics.asp?id=3999501 (accessed 30 November 2008).

[7] See http://www.internetworldstats.com/emarketing.htm (accessed 11 December 2008).

[8] Both these simulated communities boast millions of members which interact and

play in virtual world. See http://secondlife.com/whatis/economy_stats.php (accessed 11 December 2008).

9 See http://www.worldofwarcraft.com/info/wrath/index.xml (accessed 11 December 2008).

10 See http://www.researchandmarkets.com/reports/354478/massively_multiplayer_games_state_of_affairs.pdf. (accessed 11 December 2008).

11 Paul Kurtz, "Where is the Good Life: Making the Humanist Choice", http://www.secularhumanism.org/index.php?section=library&page=kurtz_18_3 (accessed 30 November 2008).

12 Throughout his article "Where is the Good Life: Making the Humanist Choice" Paul Kurtz uses religious language to emphasise his point.

13 Paul Kurtz, "Where is the Good Life: Making the Humanist Choice", http://www.secularhumanism.org/index.php?section=library&page=kurtz_18_3 (accessed 30 November 2008).

14 See http://www.lyricstime.com/steven-curtis-chapman-the-great-adventure-lyrics.html (accessed 30 November 2008).

15 The title of the best selling book by Eugene Peterson, in which we find much to recommend and to which we will refer again later in this chapter.

16 This is from the sales pitch for John Eldredge, *Wild At Heart: Discovering the Secret of a Man's Soul* (Nashville, TN: Thomas Nelson Publishers, 2001). As the book commences, the author appeals to a quotation from Teddy Roosevelt: "It is not the critic who counts, not the man who points out how the strong man stumbles, or where the doer of deeds could have done them better. The credit belongs to the man in the arena, whose face is marred by dust and sweat and blood, who strives valiantly . . ." (p. xiii). This sounds, to me, more like sentiments in line with German philosopher Friedrich Nietzsche than Jesus Christ.

17 Max Lucado, *Facing Your Giants* (Nashville, TN: Thomas Nelson Publishers, 2006), 6.

18 Ibid, 9.

19 From the lyrics of "History Maker". See http://www.christian-lyrics.net/artist/delirious/track/history-maker-lyrics.html (accessed 1 December 2008).

20 From the lyrics of "Rain Down". See http://www.christian-lyrics.net/artist/delirious/track/rain-down-lyrics.html (accessed 1 December 2008).

21 A description from author Rodney Clapp in an interview with Mark Van Steenwyk on 15 December 2005. See http://www.jesusmanifesto.com/2005/12/15/an-interview-with-rodney-clapp/ (accessed 1 December 2008).

22 The English word "play" is derived from Middle English "pleyen" (from Old English "plegian") meaning "to leap for joy, dance, rejoice, be glad". See http://dictionary.reference.com/browse/play. Throughout this chapter we will use it with such connotations. It is thus an appropriate word for what children do when they "play" but more widely for what is happening throughout all cultures when people enjoy life and celebrate in good things.

23 See the notes by Don Carson on Proverbs 8:1, in Donald Guthrie and J.A. Motyer (eds.), *New Bible Commentary: 21st Century Edition* (Revised edition; Downers Grove, IL: 1994).

[24] Elmer Smick, "Job" in Frank Gaebelein (gen. ed.), *The Expositor's Bible Commentary (Volume 4)*, (Grand Rapids, MI: Zondervan, 1988), 1039.

[25] See James Freeman and Harold Chadwick, *Manners and Customs of the Bible* (Revised edition; North Brunswick, NJ: Bridge-Logos Publishers, 1998), 128. The authors provide the following comment: "The Hebrew verb *sahaq*, translated 'play' in the KJV rendering of this verse, is highly suggestive of sexual activities. It is the same verb used in Genesis 26:8 that is translated 'caressing' in the NIV, and 'sporting' in the KJV. Considering the drinking that was taking place, and the nakedness, the worship of the calf may have turned into a drunken sex orgy, which was not uncommon among the pagans. More than likely some of the Israelites had picked up these ways of worshiping while slaves of the Egyptians, and had even worshiped with them or as they did."

[26] The Wisdom writings celebrate the play of the non-heroic everyday life of the typical Israelite. In contrast to our culture's obsession with celebrity-ism, these books give value to the glorious goodness of the play of the ordinary. See Ellen Davis, *Proverbs, Ecclesiastes and the Song of Songs*, (Louisville, KY: Westminster John Knox, 2000), 1-2.

[27] Don Carson on Matthew 11:1, in Guthrie and Motyer, *New Bible Commentary*.

[28] Lawrence O. Richards, *The Bible Readers Companion* (Wheaton, IL: Victor Books, 1991), 613. Published in electronic form by Logos Research Systens, 1996.

[29] There are a number of variant readings of the phrase "rejoiced in the Holy Spirit". These are discussed by I. Howard Marshall, *The Gospel of Luke : A Commentary on the Greek Text*. The New International Greek Testament Commentary (Exeter: Paternoster Press, 1978), 433.

[30] Doug Blomberg, *Wisdom and Curriculum: Christian Schooling After Postmodernity*, (Sioux Center, IA: Dordt College Press, 2007), 182-183.

[31] Blomberg, *Wisdom and Curriculum*, 180.

[32] Howard Peskett and Vinoth Ramachandra, *The Message of Mission* (Leicester, England: Intervarsity Press, 2003), 251.

[33] Blomberg, *Wisdom and Curriculum*, 203.

[34] Ibid, 204-205.

[35] Robert Webber, *Who Gets to Narrate the World? Contending for the Christian Story in an Age of Rivals* (Downers Grove, IL: Intervarsity Press, 2008).

[36] David Steinmetz, "Uncovering a Second Narrative: Detective Fiction and the Construction of Historical Method", in Ellen Davis and Richard Hays (eds.), *The Art of Reading Scripture* (Grand Rapids, MI: Eerdmans, 2003), 54-65.

[37] Steinmetz, "Uncovering a Second Narrative", 54-55.

[38] Steinmetz, "Uncovering a Second Narrative", 55.

[39] Steven Bouma-Prediger and Brian Walsh, *Beyond Homelessness: Christian Faith in a Culture of Displacement* (Grand Rapids, MI: Eerdmans, 2008), 263.

[40] See for example, Craig G. Bartholomew and Michael W. Goheen, *The Drama of Scripture: Finding Our Place in the Biblical Story*,(Grand Rapids, MI: Baker Academic, 2004). The metaphor of the Bible as a drama is of course widely used, by N. T. Wright, Brian Walsh and many others in their writings.

[41] See Kevin Vanhoozer, *The Drama of Doctrine: A Canonical Linguistic Approach*

to *Christian Theology* (Louisville, KY: Westminster John Knox, 2005), 17. I really like the metaphors being developed in Vanhoozer's work. However, I think there are still dangers to be recognised and avoided if possible. Such is surely the case with all metaphors. Metaphors reveal as well as conceal.

[42] Eugene Peterson, *Christ Plays in Ten Thousand Places: A Conversation in Spiritual Theology* (London, England: Hodder and Stoughton, 2005), 3.

[43] Peterson, *Christ Plays in Ten Thousand Places*, 3.

[44] See Richard Winter, *Still Bored in a Culture of Entertainment* (Downers Grove, IL: Intervarsity Press, 2002).

[45] Quoted in Winter, *Still Bored*, 96-97.

[46] Winter, *Still Bored*, 126.

[47] Walter Brueggemann, *The Prophetic Imagination* (Philadelphia, PA: Fortress Press, 1978), 112.

Printed in the United States
153746LV00003B/22/P

9 781573 834407